Developer's Guide to Delphi Troubleshooting

Clay Shannon

Wordware Publishing, Inc.

Library of Congress Cataloging-in-Publication Data

Shannon, Clay
   Developer's guide to Delphi troubleshooting / by Clay Shannon.
     p. cm.
   Includes index.
   ISBN 1-55622-647-0 (pbk.)
   1. Delphi (Computer file).   2. Computer software--Development.   I. Title.
   QA76.76.D47S483   1998
   005.265--dc21   98-43382
                                                 CIP

© 1999, Wordware Publishing, Inc.

All Rights Reserved

2320 Los Rios Boulevard
Plano, Texas 75074

No part of this book may be reproduced in any form or by any means
without permission in writing from Wordware Publishing, Inc.

Printed in the United States of America

ISBN 1-55622-647-0
10 9 8 7 6 5 4 3 2 1
9810

Product names mentioned are used for identification purposes only and may be trademarks of their respective companies.

All inquiries for volume purchases of this book should be addressed to Wordware Publishing, Inc., at the above address. Telephone inquiries may be made by calling:

(972) 423-0090

Dedication

For my wife, Cherri; my sons, Kelvin and "Sluggo" (Morgan); my parents, Ted and Rosalie; and Roger S.L. Hugi. Without them this book would have been delayed, unnecessary, impossible, and somewhat pointless.

Contents

Acknowledgements xxi
About the Author xxii
Introduction xxiii
   How This Book Differs xxiii
   Error Messages are Your Friends xxiii
   How to Find Specific Error Messages in This Book xxiv
   When There are Potentially Multiple Causes for the Same Error Message . . . xxvi
   When You Need More Information xxvi
   What's on the CD xxix

Error Messages 1
   "." Expected 1
   $DENYPACKAGEUNIT < > cannot be put into a package 2
   $DESIGNONLY AND $RUNONLY both specified 2
   $DESIGNONLY AND $RUNONLY only allowed in package unit 3
   $WEAKPACKAGEUNIT & $DENYPACKAGEUNIT both specified 3
   $WEAKPACKAGEUNIT < > cannot have initialization or finalization code 4
   $WEAKPACKAGEUNIT < > contains global data 4
   ';' not allowed before 'Else' 5
   < > already exists 5
   < > can't be added to this package because another file with the
      same base name (< >) is already in the directory of the package 6
   < > expected but < > found 6
   < > has no index for fields < > 7
   < > has the descendent < > in the Repository and therefore cannot
      be removed 8
   < > is a read-only file 8
   < > is a reserved word 9
   < > is already in the Repository. Replace it? 10
   < > is already in use by < > 11
   < > is an invalid filename 11
   < > is an invalid PageIndex value. PageIndex must be between 0 and < > . . . 12
   < > is not a type identifier 12
   < > is not a unique name 13
   < > is not a valid component name 13
   < > is not a valid date 15

Contents

< > is not a valid date and time. 16

< > is not a valid floating point value 17

< > is not a valid identifier 18

< > is not a valid integer value 18

< > is not a valid time. 19

< > is not a valid value for field < >. The allowed range is < > to < >. 20

< > must be saved before adding to Repository. Save now?. 21

< > or < > expected but < > found 21

{$R *.RES} missing or incorrect 22

16-Bit segment encountered in object file < >. 23

A CoClass must have at least one default interface 24

A CoClass must implement at least one interface 25

A component class named < > already exists 26

A component named < > already exists 26

A component named < > already exists in a descendent form 27

A device attached to the system is not functioning. 28

A dispinterface type cannot have an ancestor interface 28

A dispinterface type requires an interface identification 29

A field or method named < > already exists. 29

A module called < > is already installed 30

A page must be empty before it can be deleted 31

A reference to < > already exists in the Type Library 32

A required .DLL file, < >, was not found. 33

A user transaction is already in progress 33

A value must be specified for < > 34

A Win32 API function failed 39

Abstract Method Error 39

Abstract Methods must be virtual or dynamic 40

Access Violation (General Protection Fault) 41

Ambiguous Overloaded Call to < > 47

An error occurred while attempting to initialize the Borland
    Database Engine (error < >) 48

Another file named < > is already on the search path 48

Another file with the same base name (< >) is already on the search path 48

Application is not licensed to use this feature 50

Arithmetic Overflow Error 51

Array type required 52

Assertion failed 53

Assignment to FOR-Loop variable < >. 53

At End of Table 55

Bad global symbol definition: < > in object file < > 56

Bad packaged unit format: < >.< > 57

Bad unit format: < > 57
BDE Initialization Error $250I 58
Before you can deploy, you must complete the Web Deployment
    page of the Project | Web Deploy Options dialog 59
Bitmap image is not valid 60
Bits index out of range 60
BLOb has been modified 61
Break or continue outside of loop 63
Breakpoint is set on line that may have been removed by the
    optimizer or contains no debug information. Run anyway? 66
Call to Application.CreateForm is missing or incorrect 68
Call to RegisterClass is missing or incorrect 69
Can't change value while socket is active 70
Can't load [complib.dcl, cmplib32.dcl, vcl30.dpl, vcl40.dpl] 70
Can't load package < >.< > 73
Can't write .EXE file. Disk full? 73
Cannot add a session to the form or data-module while session < >
    has AutoSessionName enabled 74
Cannot assign to a read-only property 75
Cannot break, continue, or exit out of a finally clause 76
Cannot change the size of an icon 76
Cannot change Visible in OnShow or OnHide 77
Cannot connect, < > must contain a valid ServerName or ServerGUID 79
Cannot connect to database < > 80
Cannot copy a Repository Project to a directory underneath itself 81
Cannot create cursor handle 82
Cannot create file < > 82
Cannot create form. No MDI forms are currently active 84
Cannot debug project unless a host application is defined. Use the
    Run | Parameters... dialog box 85
Cannot enable AutoSessionName property with more than one
    session on a form or data module 86
Cannot find < > on the search path 87
Cannot find Engine configuration file 88
Cannot find implementation of method < > 89
Cannot focus a disabled or invisible window 90
Cannot hide an MDI Child Form 91
Cannot inherit from form < >. It contains a component with a blank
    name property 92
Cannot initialize local variables 92
Cannot initialize multiple variables 94
Cannot Load IDAPI Service Library 95

Cannot load IDAPI[32].DLL. 97
Cannot load language driver. 99
Cannot load package < >. It contains unit < > which is also
    contained in package < >. 100
Cannot locate IDAPI[01,32].DLL 100
Cannot make a visible window modal 103
Cannot modify a read-only dataset 104
Cannot modify SessionName while AutoSessionName is enabled 105
Cannot open component library <Path>\Complib.dcl 105
Cannot open file < > 106
Cannot open module because it is a dependent of < >,
    which is open as text 107
Cannot override a static method 107
Cannot perform this operation on a closed database 108
Cannot perform this operation on a closed dataset. 110
Cannot perform this operation on an active session 111
Cannot perform this operation on an empty dataset 111
Cannot perform this operation on an open database 112
Cannot perform this operation on an open dataset. 113
Cannot perform this operation with table open 114
Cannot perform utility while table is in use 115
Cannot read a write-only property 115
Cannot Run a Unit or DLL. 117
Cannot write EXE or DLL to disk 118
Cannot Write to Engine Configuration File 118
Capability Not Supported 119
Circular datalinks are not allowed 121
Circular Unit Reference [to < >] 121
Class, interface and object types only allowed in type section 123
Class < > not found. [Ignore the error and continue?] 124
Class already has a default property 126
Class does not have a default property 127
Class not registered 128
Class type required. 130
Clipboard does not support Icons 131
Code Insight(tm) features are disabled while debugging 132
Code Segment Too Large 132
COINITIALIZE has not been called 133
Column not a BLOb 133
Comma Expected 133
Compilation terminated; too many errors 134
Component already installed 134

Connection error—no server available 135
Connection in use by another statement 136
Constant expression expected. 138
Constant expression violates subrange bounds 138
Constant object cannot be passed as var parameter 139
Constant or type identifier expected 141
Constant out of range 142
Constants cannot be used as open array arguments 143
Constructing Instance of < > containing abstract methods. 144
Constructors and Destructors must have register calling convention 146
Constructors and Destructors not allowed in OLE automation section 146
CONTAINS clause is incorrect 147
Control < > has no parent window 148
Controls cannot be added to a data module 150
Corrupt table/index header 150
Could not create output file < > 153
Could not find IDataBroker in type library 154
Could not find interface < > in type library 155
Could not find object. Cannot load an IDAPI service library.
    File: ODBC32.DLL 156
Could not initialize IDAPI 157
Could not find interface IDataBroker in type library 158
Could not load < >. The OLE control may possibly require support
    libraries that are not on the current search path or are not present
    on your system 159
Could not load RLINK32.DLL 159
Could not load StdOle version 1.0 type library 159
Could not load Type Library 160
Could not load unit < > symbol information for < > Do you want
    to try to find this file yourself? 160
Data Base Error Database access resulted in error 161
Data Segment Too Large. 162
Data Structure Corruption. 165
Data Type too large: exceeds 2 GB 166
Database name missing 167
Dataset not configured for network access 168
Dataset not in edit or insert mode. 169
DAX Error: Class not registered 169
DAX Error: Name not unique in this context 170
DAX Error: Unexpected failure 171
DCOM not installed 171
Debug process is already running 171

Contents

Debug session in progress. Terminate? 172

Debugger kernel error. Error code: < > 173

Declaration expected but < > found 174

Declaration of < > differs from previous declaration. 175

Declaration of class < > is missing or incorrect. 176

DEFAULT clause not allowed in OLE automation section 176

Default property must be an array property 177

Default values must be of ordinal, pointer, or small set type 178

Destination must be indexed 180

Directory Is Busy. 181

Directory is controlled by other .NET file 183

Disk Error 187

Disk full. 188

Disk write error 189

Dispid < > already used by < >. 189

Dispid clause only allowed in OLE automation section 190

Division by zero 190

Duplicate case label 192

Duplicate database name < > 193

Duplicate field name < > 194

Duplicate implements clause for interface < > 195

Duplicate resource. 195

Duplicate session name < > 196

Dynamic method or message handler not allowed here 197

Dynamic method or message handlers not allowed in OLE
   automation sections. 198

EAccessViolation 199

EBitsError 199

EClassNotFound 199

EComponentError 199

EConvertError 200

EDivByZero 201

EFCreateError 201

EFilerError 201

EGPFault 202

EInOutError 202

EIntOverflow. 204

EInvalidCast 204

EInvalidGraphic. 204

EInvalidGraphicOperation 204

EInvalidOp 205

EInvalidOperation: Cannot create form. No MDI forms are
    currently active 205
EInvalidOperation: Cannot make a visible window modal 205
EInvalidPointer 205
Element 0 Inaccessible—use "Length" or "SetLength" 205
'END' expected but < > found 207
'End' expected but implementation found 208
END. missing at end of module 208
EOLEError 209
EOleSys—Class not Registered 209
EOleSys—Operation Unavailable 210
EOutOfMemory 210
EOutOfResources 211
ERangeError 212
EReadError 212
ERegistryException. 213
EResNotFound 213
Error 0—RLINK32 Error opening file < TypeLibrary >.tlb 214
Error 2—File not found 215
Error 4—Too many open files 215
Error 68—Circular Unit Reference 215
Error 76—Constant out of range 215
Error 94—"." Expected 215
Error 101—Disk write error 215
Error 102—File not assigned 215
Error 103—File not open 215
Error 104—File not open for input 215
Error 105—File not open for output 216
Error 200—Division by zero. 216
Error 201—Range check error 216
Error 202—Stack overflow error 216
Error 203—Heap overflow error 216
Error 204—Invalid pointer operation 216
Error 207—Invalid floating point operation 216
Error 210—Abstract Method Error 216
Error 215—Arithmetic overflow error 216
Error 216—Access Violation. 217
Error 219—Invalid Typecast 217
Error 220—Invalid Variant Typecast 217
Error 227—Assertion failed 217
Error Creating Cursor Handle. 217

Contents

Error Creating Form: Cannot inherit from form < >. It contains
   a component with a blank name property 218
Error Creating Form: Cannot inherit from form < >. Contains
   a component < > that does not support inheritance 219
Error creating form: Cannot open file < >.DFM 220
Error Creating Form: Duplicate resource [Type:,Name:]. 221
Error creating Process 222
Error Creating Variant Array. 223
Error Creating Window 223
Error in module < >: Call to Application.CreateForm is missing
   or incorrect 225
Error in module < >: CONTAINS clause is incorrect 225
Error in module < >: Declaration of class < > is missing or incorrect. 225
Error in module < >: 'END.' missing at end of module 225
Error in module < >: Implementation part USES clause incorrect. 226
Error in module < >: Incorrect field declaration: class < > 226
Error in module < >: Requires clause is incorrect 226
Error in module < >: USES clause is missing or incorrect 226
Error loading type library/dll 226
Error Opening Component Library 227
Error reading < >.< >: < >. 228
Error reading <Database>.SessionName. Duplicate database name '< >' . . . 229
Error reading <Session>.SessionName. Duplicate session name '< >' 229
Error reading symbol file. 230
Error saving I(Interface): The parameter is incorrect 231
Error setting debug exception hook. 231
EStackOverflow 232
EStringListError 232
EThread 232
EVariantError. 233
Except or Finally expected. 234
Expression expected but < > found. 235
External exception C0000008 236
Failed to get data for < > 237
Fatal Error: < >: Required Package '< >' not found 238
Field < > cannot be used in a filter expression 238
Field < >.< > does not have a corresponding component. Remove
   the declaration? 239
Field < > is not indexed and cannot be modified 241
Field < > is not of the expected type 242
Field < > must have a value 243
Field < > not found 244

Field <>.<> should be of type <> but is declared as <>. Correct
   the declaration? 246
Field definition not allowed after methods or properties 246
Field in group by must be in result set. 247
Field in order by must be in result set 248
Field index out of range 249
Field name already exists. Rename one of the fields 250
Field not found in table. 250
Field or method identifier expected 251
Field types do not match 252
Field value required 253
File <> not found 253
File access denied 254
File extension <> is not valid. Expecting <> 254
File is Locked. Table: <> User: <> 255
File not assigned 255
File not found <> 256
File not open 258
File not open for input 261
File not open for output 262
File or directory does not exist 263
File type not allowed here 264
Fixed column count must be less than column count 264
Fixed row count must be less than row count 265
For Loop control variable must have ordinal type 266
FOR-Loop variable <> cannot be passed as var parameter 267
Form <> links to form <> which cannot be found in the current
   project. Do you wish to remove/redirect the links to another form? 268
Form <> references another form and cannot be saved until <> is loaded . . 269
Function needs result type 269
General SQL Error—connection does not exist 270
General SQL Error—FROM keyword not found where expected 270
General SQL error. The [Commit,Rollback] Transaction request has
   no corresponding begin transaction 271
General SQL Error : SQL is too complex 272
GOTO <> leads into or out of TRY statement 272
Grid Index Out of Range 272
GROUP BY is required when both aggregate and non-aggregate
   fields are used in result set 273
High cannot be applied to a long string 274
Higher table level required 275
I/O Error 102 278

Contents

I/O Error 103. 278

I/O Error 104. 278

I/O Error 105. 278

Identifier expected but array found 278

Identifier expected but number found. 279

Identifier expected but <> found. 279

Identifier redeclared: <> 280

Illegal character in input file: <> (<>) 281

Illegal message method index 282

IMPLEMENTATION part is missing or incorrect 283

Implementation part USES clause incorrect. 283

Implements getter must be register calling convention 284

Incompatible types: <> and <> 285

Incompatible types: Parameter lists differ 290

Incorrect field declaration: class <> 291

Incorrect method declaration in class <> 291

Index already exists 292

INDEX clause not allowed in OLE automation section. 293

INDEX, READ, OR WRITE clause expected but ';' found 293

Index does not exist 294

Index is out of date. 295

Index is out of range 299

Index is read only. 300

Index not found 300

INSERT and UPDATE operations are not supported on
autoincrement field type 301

Insufficient memory for this operation 302

Insufficient SQL rights for operation. 303

Insufficient table rights for operation 303

Integer constant too large 304

Interface mismatch. Engine version different 305

Interface type required. 306

Internal error: <>. 307

Internal Error; Near: query shellmgr 308

Invalid argument to date encode. 309

Invalid argument to time encode 310

Invalid Batch Move Parameters 310

Invalid Bind Type 311

Invalid BLOb handle [in record buffer] 311

Invalid BLOb Size. 312

Invalid class string 312

Invalid class typecast 313

Invalid compiler directive: < > 313
Invalid field name. 314
Invalid field size. 315
Invalid field type 316
Invalid file name 316
Invalid floating point operation. 317
Invalid function result type 319
Invalid GUID format 320
Invalid index/tag name 320
Invalid index descriptor 321
Invalid index expression 322
Invalid message parameter list 322
Invalid package file < > 323
Invalid Parameter. 324
Invalid path 324
Invalid pointer operation. 324
Invalid property value 326
Invalid property value on line < > 326
Invalid resource format 327
Invalid type 328
Invalid Type Conversion 328
Invalid typecast 328
Invalid use of keyword 329
Invalid variant type conversion. 332
Key Violation 333
Label < > is not declared in current procedure. 334
Label already defined: < >. 335
Label declaration not allowed in interface part 335
Label declared and referenced, but not set 336
Label expected 337
Left side cannot be assigned to 337
Line number must be between 1 and < > 339
Line too long [more than 255 characters]. 339
List capacity out of bounds (< >) 340
List index out of bounds (< >). 340
Local class, interface or object types not allowed. 343
Local class or object types not allowed 343
Local procedure/function < > assigned to procedure variable 343
Lock file [has grown] too large 344
Lock time out 345
Lock Violation 346
Lookup information for field '< >' is incomplete 347

Low bound exceeds High bound 348
Master has detail records. Cannot delete or modify 348
Master has detail records. Cannot empty it. 350
Master record missing 350
Maximum Validity Check Failed 351
Memo too large 351
Metafile is not valid. 352
Method < > hides virtual method of base class < > 352
Method < > not found in base class. 354
Method < > with identical parameters exists already 354
Method identifier expected 355
Microsoft Transaction Server is not installed 356
Minimum Validity Check failed. 357
Mismatch in datapacket 357
Missing comma 358
Missing Data Provider or Data Packet. 359
Missing ENDIF directive 359
Missing operator or semicolon. 360
Missing or invalid conditional symbol in <$> directive. 362
Missing parameter type 362
Missing right quote. 363
Missing TableName property 363
Module < >s time/date changed. Reload?. 364
Module header is missing or incorrect. 365
Multiple Net Files found 366
Multiple Paradox Net files found/in use 369
Name conflicting 370
Name not unique in this context 370
Never-build package < > must be recompiled 370
No address specified 371
No argument for format '< >'. 372
No code was generated for the current line 372
No definition for abstract method < > allowed. 373
No MDI forms are currently active 374
No MDI Parent Active 374
No Provider Available 374
No SQL statement available 375
No user transaction is currently in progress 377
No Web browser could be located 377
NODEFAULT clause not allowed in OLE automation section 378
Not enough actual parameters 379
Not enough file handles 381

Not in cached update mode 381
Not initialized for accessing network files 382
Number is out of range 384
Number of elements differs from declaration 385
One or more lines were too long and have been truncated 386
Only register calling convention allowed in OLE automation section 386
Operation not allowed on sorted string list 387
Operation not applicable 387
Operation not supported 388
Operator not applicable to this operand type 389
Order of fields in record constant differs from declaration 392
Ordinal type required 392
Out of memory 394
Out of system resources 394
Overflow in conversion or arithmetic operation 395
Overloaded procedures must be marked with the 'overload' directive 396
Overriding automated virtual method <> cannot specify a dispid 396
Package <> already contains unit <> 397
Package <> can't be installed because another package with the
        same base name is already loaded (<>) 397
PACKED not allowed here 398
Page Fault in module <> at <> 398
Page name cannot be blank 399
Param <> not found 399
Parameter <> not allowed here due to default value 400
Passthrough SQL connection must be shared 401
Path not found. File <> 401
Path too long 402
Pointer type required 402
Printing in Progress 403
Procedure cannot have a result type 404
Procedure FAIL only allowed in constructor 405
Procedure or Function name expected 405
Program or unit <> recursively uses itself 406
Project <> raised exception class <> with message <>. Process
        stopped. Use Step or Run to continue.. 406
Property <> does not exist in base class 407
Provider name was not recognized by the server 409
Published field <> not a class nor interface type 409
Published property <> cannot be of type <> 410
Published real property <> must be Single, Double, or Extended 411
PutObject to undefined item 412

Contents

Query Is Too Complex 412
Query makes no sense 413
Range check error 414
Read failure. File: < >.val 414
Read or Write clause expected but identifier < > found 415
Record/Key Deleted 416
Record, object or class type required 416
Record Locked by another User 417
Redeclaration of < > hides a member in the base class 417
Redeclaration of property not allowed in OLE automation section 418
Required package < > not found 419
REQUIRES clause is incorrect 419
Selection contains a component introduced in an ancestor form
       which cannot be deleted 420
Server Execution Failed 422
Session name missing 422
Share not loaded. It is required to share local files 423
Slice standard function is only allowed as open array argument 424
SQL is too complex 425
Stack overflow 425
Statement expected, but expression of type < > found 427
STORED clause not allowed in OLE automation section 427
Stream Read Error 428
String constant truncated to fit STRING[ ] 428
String [literal]s may have at most 255 elements 429
Syntax error in query. Incomplete query clause 430
Table cannot be opened for exclusive use 430
Table corrupt—other than header 431
Table does not exist 432
Table does not support this operation 433
Table is busy 434
Table is full 435
Table is read only 437
Table is not indexed 437
Table or View does not exist 438
TActiveFormX declaration missing or incorrect 439
Text after final END 439
The < > method referenced by < >.< > does not exist. Remove
       the reference? 440
The < > method referenced by < >.< > has an incompatible
       parameter list. Remove the reference? 442
The Edit Buffer of < > is marked read-only 443

The Master Source property of < > must be linked to a DataSource 443

The OLE control may possibly require support libraries that are not
on the current search path or are not present on your system 444

The package already contains unit named < > 444

The package already requires a package named < > 445

The path entered does not exist. 445

The project already contains a form or module named < > 446

The search string cannot be blank. 447

The selected bitmap is larger than 24x24 447

The transaction isolation level must be dirty read for local databases 448

The type library has syntax errors. 449

This form of method call only allowed for class methods. 449

This package already contains unit named < > 451

This type cannot be initialized 451

Token not found 452

Token not found. Token :dbo. line number:1 452

Too many actual parameters. 453

Too many connections 454

Too many files open 454

Too many locks on table 455

Too many open cursors 456

Too many open files 457

Too many parameters 458

Translate error, value out of bounds 459

Tried to search marked block but it is invalid 459

Type < > has no type info 460

Type < > is not yet completely defined 460

Type < > must be a class to have a PUBLISHED section 461

Type < > must be a class to have OLE automation 461

Type < > needs finalization—not allowed in file type. 462

Type expected but < > found 463

Type expected but real constant found 464

Type of expression must be BOOLEAN. 465

Type of expression must be INTEGER 465

Type mismatch [in expression]. 466

TYPEINFO standard function expects a type identifier. 466

Types of actual and formal var parameters must be identical 467

Unable to load GDS[32].DLL 467

Unable to load RPTSMITH.EXE 468

Undeclared Identifier: < >. 468

Unexpected end of command 471

Unit < > was compiled with a different version of < > 472

Contents

Unit version mismatch: < > 472
Unknown Column 473
Unknown database 473
Unknown directive: < > 475
Unknown Identifier 477
Unknown picture file extension: < > 478
Unknown SQL Error 478
Unknown user name or password 479
Unsatisfied forward or external declaration: < > 480
Unsupported 16bit resource 481
Unterminated string 482
USES clause is missing or incorrect 482
Variable < > inaccessible here due to optimization 483
Variable required 483
Variant does not reference an OLE object 484
Variant is not an array 484
Vendor initialization failure: ORA[NT]7[1,2,3].DLL 485
Windows Socket Error: (10060), on API 'connect' 485
Write error on < > 486
You cannot add a < > to the current project because it is not
        an ActiveX library. Click OK to start a new ActiveX library project 486
You cannot specify a size for a field of this type 487
You must open a project before you can add an Automation Object 487
You must select a VCL class 488
Your application is not enabled for use with this driver 488

Index 491

Acknowledgements

No book is an island. Although most of the information herein was acquired through the direct approach ("just do(ing) it"), some of the information conveyed in this book was indirectly adapted from sources many and varied. Some of these sources included other Delphi books, magazines, Delphi newsgroups and mailing lists, the Delphi help documentation, examining OPC (other people's code), and conversations with workmates.

When I was a youngster, I often heard the expression "build a better mousetrap, and the world will beat a path to your door." I now know that this is not true. The world first must *know* about your mousetrap and usually have it offered to them before they will even consider it, no matter how good it is. An aid to me in making my "mousetrap" known has been the Internet, its newsgroups, and e-mail capabilities. Special thanks in this regard go to former coworkers Hugh "THue" Borst and Shankar "The Cobra" Kamath.

I appreciate the help I received from Inprise ("the company formerly known as Borland," as Delphi developer extraordinaire Dave Klein refers to them), most notably from Nan Borreson and Charlie Calvert.

A special thanks goes to Mark Johnson for putting me in touch with Wordware when I was looking for a publisher and they were looking for Delphi authors.

At Wordware, I would like to thank Pam Alba, John Ayres, Jim Hill, and Beth Kohler.

For their untiring efforts and skillful representation, I would like to convey a resounding "thank you" and "job well done" to my agents, David and Sherry Rogelberg at StudioB (visit www.studiob.com). In connection with this, I also thank a programmer's programmer, Ray Lischner, who encouraged me to engage an agent.

I want to thank the following individuals for contributing materials for the CD: Eric Engler, Ken Hale, Dave Klein, Walter Novacek, and Robert Vivrette.

For assisting me in refining my coding and technical writing skills over the past several years, I thank the gang at MLJT, Fred Petersen and Karen Rasmussen at Columbia, Dennis King, William Roetzheim, and Syed Alam.

Last but not least, I want to thank Rodney and Sharon Baldwin for their assistance, and "The Cartwrights," my mentors, fellow workers, friends, and "pards"—just because.

About the Author

Clay Shannon went from technophobe to "I need to learn how to use a computer in order to work as a German to English translator" to "I don't want to become a programmer or anything—maybe a power user" to "Programming is fascinating!"

Shannon attended Columbia Junior College in the beautiful gold rush community of Columbia, Calif., where he achieved a 3.73 GPA while earning a certificate in Applied Computer Studies. There he was introduced to Turbo Pascal, which made the transition to Delphi a natural one.

Shannon has worked intensely and extensively with Delphi since its release. A California native, he is currently residing in Brookfield, Wis. He specializes in Delphi database, utilities, and electronic sports memorabilia programming. Since that time, he has worked as a technical writer/Delphi and Access developer for Information Anywhere; Delphi developer for Marotz, Softgear, and John Deere; and is currently employed by Source Services as a technical consultant at Boeckh in New Berlin, Wis.

He has amassed thousands of downloads of his freeware and shareware software utilities, edutainment programs for children and adolescents, and electronic sports memorabilia, including but not limited to "Jersey Boy" (a Bruce Springsteen discography), "Time Zone," "Document Profiler," and a complete set of baseball programs. Many of these are included on the CD. Additionally, his suite of splash screen/About box components were featured in the "Notable Downloadables" section of the December 1997 *Delphi Informant*.

Shannon can be reached at **clayshannon@usa.net**.

Introduction

How This Book Differs

An array of excellent Delphi books are available. Few, however, contain much information on troubleshooting specific Delphi error messages. Ascertaining the causes of and solutions for error messages by reading the Delphi help files and scouring the indexes of traditional Delphi books can be a very time-consuming process.

This book fills that gap and serves as a quick reference for implementing quick solutions to 609 error messages you may receive while working with Delphi. Each error message is also elaborated on so you can understand how to prevent recurrences of the same problem in the future.

Error Messages are Your Friends

You may encounter error messages while working with Delphi at three distinct stages of development: design time, compile time, and run time. Design-time and compile-time errors are seen by the developer only. Run-time errors can be seen by both developer and end user. Run-time errors are not necessarily the fault of the developer—although the developer should account for the possibility of their occurrence and code "defensively" in anticipation of such possibility.

A separate category of error, which this book does not address, is logic errors. Logic errors do not directly generate error messages. In fact, they may not necessarily even produce error messages indirectly (although the results are not what is intended). Logic errors can go unnoticed indefinitely, and if discovered following deployment of the software, it is usually by end users.

This book will help you determine the cause of and solution for design-time, compile-time, and run-time errors.

When you receive *design-time errors* (message boxes telling you, sometimes a bit cryptically, what you did wrong), consult this book for more information.

Your first course of action when you receive a *compile-time error* message should be pressing the F1 key for context-sensitive help. Many times this will provide you with enough information to quickly solve the problem that led to the error message. In cases where the information is not specific or clear enough, though, consult this book. Delphi will help you determine the cause of the error by placing the cursor at or immediately following the line that failed (provided you have selected the "Break on Exception" option).

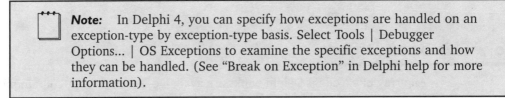

Note: In Delphi 4, you can specify how exceptions are handled on an exception-type by exception-type basis. Select Tools | Debugger Options... | OS Exceptions to examine the specific exceptions and how they can be handled. (See "Break on Exception" in Delphi help for more information).

If you are experiencing a *run-time error*, consult this book for explanatory information. Additionally, the F4, F7, and F8 keys come in handy. If you have "Break on Exception" turned on (select Tools | Environment Options..., and verify that the "Break on Exception" check box in the Debugging section of the Preferences page is checked), Delphi should dump you out at the piece of code causing the error. Place the cursor prior to this spot and hit the F4 key to "run to cursor." Your program will run until it reaches that spot and then pause. You can then "step through" the code a line at a time using the F7 (Trace Into) or F8 (Step) key, evaluating the state of things and the value of variables as you go. For more information, see "Debugger" in Delphi help.

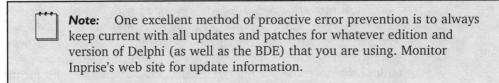

Note: One excellent method of proactive error prevention is to always keep current with all updates and patches for whatever edition and version of Delphi (as well as the BDE) that you are using. Monitor Inprise's web site for update information.

How to Find Specific Error Messages in This Book

For the most part, locating information in this book is very simple, as the error messages are presented in alphabetical order. For example, to find the discussion relative to the "**A CoClass must have at least one default interface**" error message, simply search for it near the front of the book (between "16-Bit segment encountered in object file < >" and "A CoClass must implement at least one interface," to be precise).

Error Messages that Contain Variables

Some error messages, however, are "dynamic," or "parameterized," in that the exact wording will differ according to the specific situation you are dealing with. As an example, the error message listed as "**Package < > already**

contains unit <>" in this book contains two "variables" which depend on the package to which you are attempting to add a unit and the name of the unit that already exists there. If the package to which you are attempting to add the unit is dclusr40.dpk, and the unit you are attempting to add is XProcs.PAS, but it has in fact already been added to that package, the error message would be "**Package dclusr40.dpk already contains unit XProcs.PAS**."

This should not be too much of a problem except perhaps where a "variable" occurs at the beginning of an error message. Even then, though, this is not a great obstacle if you realize that the beginning of the error message could be a "variable." For example, if you receive the error message " **';' expected but 'END' found**," you may be a bit confused about exactly where to find the discussion about this error message in this book. Even if you know where a semicolon is sorted in "alphabetical" order, you would not find this error message in that location, as the error message contains variables. If you realize, though, that this error message may display under various circumstances, you will know to search for it under "**<> expected but <> found**."

The moral of the story is: If you are not sure which part of an error message, if any, is a "variable," search first for the exact error message you got in alphabetical order; if you cannot locate it using that method, search through the section at the very beginning of the book where the error messages beginning with a "variable" ("**<>**") are located.

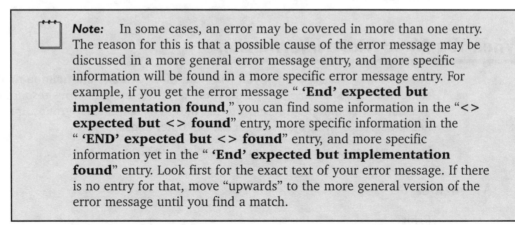

Note: In some cases, an error may be covered in more than one entry. The reason for this is that a possible cause of the error message may be discussed in a more general error message entry, and more specific information will be found in a more specific error message entry. For example, if you get the error message " **'End' expected but implementation found**," you can find some information in the "**<> expected but <> found**" entry, more specific information in the " **'END' expected but <> found**" entry, and more specific information yet in the " **'End' expected but implementation found**" entry. Look first for the exact text of your error message. If there is no entry for that, move "upwards" to the more general version of the error message until you find a match.

"Encapsulated" Error Messages

Sometimes Delphi will give you a long error message which "encapsulates" a more specific error message inside. For example, you may get an error like: "**Project <> raised exception class EClassNotFound with message 'Class <> not found'. Process stopped**." In cases like this, search for the error message within the error message (in this case **Class <> not found**).

Similarly, if error messages begin with "Fatal Error," "Run-time Error," "I/O Error," "Error in Module <>" or some such general category of error, search for the error message by the more specific message which follows that general categorization. For example, if you get the error message "**Fatal Error: <>: Required Package <> not found**," look under "**Required Package <> not found**."

When There are Potentially Multiple Causes for the Same Error Message

Some error messages can be generated by more than one clearly defined action. In many of these cases, the various potential causes of the error message are enumerated and discussed separately in the three sections which comprise each entry ("Possible Cause of Error," "Quick Fix," and "Additional Information").

In these instances, match the number in the "Possible Cause of Error" section with its corresponding discussion in the "Quick Fix" section (individual causes of errors are sometimes also discussed individually in the "Additional Information" section).

When You Need More Information

There will be occasions when you will want more detailed information than is contained in this volume. Fortunately for you, there are numerous resources available for Delphi programmers to tap into: magazines, user groups, Internet newsgroups, web sites, and, of course, other books.

Here are some of the best of what is available in each category:

Magazines

Print

Delphi Informant

Visit their web site at **www.informant.com** for sample articles, freeware components, information on subscribing, and more.

The Delphi Magazine

Visit their web site at **http://www.itecuk.com/dmag/** for sample articles in .PDF format, information on subscribing, and more.

Delphi Developer's Journal

Visit their web site at **http://www.cobb.com/ddj** for sample articles, information on subscribing, and more.

Electronic

UNDU (Unofficial Newsletter of Delphi Users)

All issues of UNDU (in Windows help format) are contained on the CD that accompanies this book. The web site below also contains new "standalone" articles that do not appear in these .hlp files.

```
http://www.undu.com
```

Delphi-centric Web Sites

A plethora of excellent Delphi web sites exist. Here are a few of them, from which you can link to others:

```
http://www.borland.com
http://www.delphiexchange.com
http://SunSITE.icm.edu.pl/delphi/
http://www.delphideli.com
http://www.delphi32.com
http://www.delumpa.com
http://www.torry.com
http://www.chami.com/tips/delphi/
http://www.mindspring.com/~cityzoo/cityzoo.html
http://www.advdelphisys.com
```

You can access the Inprise web site directly from Delphi 3 and 4 (if you have a web browser installed and an Internet account) by selecting Help | Inprise Home Page, Help | Delphi Home Page, or Help | Inprise Programs and Services.

Internet Newsgroups

Here are a few Internet newsgroups that deal with Delphi:

```
alt.lang.delphi
comp.lang.pascal.delphi.databases
comp.lang.pascal.delphi.misc
comp.lang.pascal.delphi.components.misc
comp.lang.pascal.delphi.components.usage
```

```
comp.lang.pascal.delphi.components.writing
```

Here are Inprise's Delphi newsgroups:

```
borland.public.delphi.objectpascal
borland.public.delphi.database.desktop
borland.public.delphi.database.sqlservers
borland.public.delphi.ide
borland.public.delphi.components.using
borland.public.delphi.multi-tier
borland.public.delphi.winapi
borland.public.delphi.internet
borland.public.delphi.oleautomation
borland.public.delphi.jobs
```

> **Note:** By the time this book is in print, the newsgroups may have changed from borland to inprise.

For a complete, up-to-date listing of Inprise's Delphi newsgroups, see

```
http://www.inprise.com/newsgroups/#Delphi
```

Newsgroup/Web Site

In a class by itself is Dejanews and its "My Deja News" service. Dejanews is a searchable archive of newsgroup postings. Point your browser at

```
http://www.dejanews.com
```

to access this web site. You can search for any information you want, for example "Delphi" and "Citrix" or—you name it.

Using "My Deja News," you can subscribe to newsgroups of your choice and access them via their web site. This can be much more convenient than the "legacy" method of configuring a newsreader and using it to access newsgroups.

Especially when you have a very specific and/or obscure question, or need information on something that post-dates this manuscript, Dejanews is an excellent source of information.

Delphi User Groups

Point your browser at **http://www.inprise.com/programs/user-groups/uglist.html#Delphi** for a list to find the one nearest to you.

Other Books

- *Delphi 3 Client/Server Guide* by Ken Henderson
- *Delphi A Developer's Guide* by Vince Todd and Bill Kellen
- *Delphi Component Design* by Danny Thorpe
- *Delphi Developer's Handbook* by Marco Cantú and Tim Gooch
- *Delphi In-Depth* by Cary Jensen, Loy Anderson, Joseph Fung, Ann Lynnworth
- *Delphi Programming Problem Solver* by Neal Rubenking
- *Delphi X Developer's Guide* by Steve Teixeira and Xavier Pacheco
- *Delphi X Unleashed* by Charles Calvert
- *Developing Custom Delphi 3 Components* by Ray Konopka
- *Hidden Paths of Delphi 3* by Ray Lischner
- *Mastering Delphi X* by Marco Cantú
- *Secrets of Delphi 2* by Ray Lischner
- *The Tomes of Delphi 3: Win32 Core API* by John Ayres, et al.

and don't forget Inprise's documentation (including the FAQs and TIs on the Delphi CD) and example programs (default location is C:\Program Files\Borland\Delphi X\Demos and C:\Program Files\ Delphi X\Help\Examples).

What's on the CD

The CD contains the text of the book in Microsoft Word and TXT formats, freeware components, freeware programs written in Delphi (many with source code included), Windows help (.hlp) files compiled by various individuals, and a Delphi database FAQ text file from Eric Engler.

Here is a table showing the CD directory structure:

Folder	Sub Folder	Description
AuthLink		Contains the source code for the "Author Linker," which can be used to compare two documents and reports words that are contained in both. When unusual words, or words misspelled the same way in both files, are found, it may indicate that the same person wrote both documents.
	Install	Contains the setup program and files for "Author Linker," described above.
Baseball	ALCentral	Contains the install program for "American League Central," a set of baseball "electronic memorabilia" programs.
	ALEast	Contains the install program for "American League East," a set of baseball "electronic memorabilia" programs.

Folder	Sub Folder	Description
Baseball (cont.)	ALWest	Contains the install program for "American League West," a set of baseball "electronic memorabilia" programs.
	BDS	Contains the install program for "Brave Dodging Stars," a set of baseball "electronic memorabilia" programs of the Boston Braves, Milwaukee Braves, Brooklyn Dodgers, and "Stars of the Negro Leagues."
	DiamondC	Contains "Diamond Cruncher," a utility for calculating batting average, win-loss percentages, ERAs, etc. The source code is here also.
	GBAS	Contains the install program for "Giant Brown Athletic Senators," a set of baseball "electronic memorabilia" programs of the New York Giants, St. Louis Browns, Kansas City Athletics, and Washington Senators.
	HallFame	Contains a "Hall of Fame Dream Team" program, where you can select a team of Baseball Hall of Famers and calculate their total "Total Player Rating."
	NLCentral	Contains the install program for "National League Central," a set of baseball "electronic memorabilia" programs.
	NLEast	Contains the install program for "National League East," a set of baseball "electronic memorabilia" programs.
	NLWest	Contains the install program for "National League West," a set of baseball "electronic memorabilia" programs.
	PoorHaus	Contains the program "Poor House," with which you can calculate the amount of money a player makes per hit, home run, etc., by plugging in his contract numbers and statistics. The source code is also provided.
Compnts	SameDiff	Contains components that allow you to compare two strings with each other for: • Commonality (words that both strings contain) using the TSameWords component —AND— • Divergence (words that appear in one string but not in the other) using the TDiffWords component.
	SplshAbt	Contains components that allow you to create distinctive splash screens and About boxes for your programs.
DayOWeek		Contains a program you can use to determine the day of the week for any date you enter. The source code is also provided.
dbfaq		Contains the del-db.txt Delphi Database FAQ text file from Eric Engler.
Dg2dt		Contains the text of the book in Microsoft Word and TXT formats for easy searching.
DocPrflr	Disk1	Contains the first diskette of the setup program for the "Document Profiler" program, which allows you to get an idea of the background and interests of the author of a document.
	Disk2	Contains the second diskette of the setup program for the "Document Profiler" program, which allows you to get an idea of the background and interests of the author of a document.

Folder	Sub Folder	Description
edutain	Animals	Contains the install program for the "Animals of the World" suite of programs.
	Edu	Contains the install program for the "Edutainment" suite of programs.
	Five25	Contains the install program for a suite of animal identification programs intended for young children.
	Nsk2dino	Contains the install program for a suite of programs about insects, animals of the rain forest, endangered animals, birds, and dinosaur identification programs intended for young children.
	Roknsol	Contains the install program for a suite of programs about rock and soul music.
	Transprt	Contains the install program for a suite of programs about various methods of transportation.
HlpFiles		Contains a compilation of Delphi TIs (Technical Information documents) provided by Ken Hale. The name of this file is Delphiti.hlp. There is also a compilation of Delphi 2 FAQs provided by Walter Novacek. The name of this file is Dfaqhlp2.hlp. It also contains two help files containing tips and tricks.
Jersyboy		Contains the program "Jboylite," which contains a listing of Bruce Springsteen albums and their contents. The source code is included.
NoTrace		Contains the "Shredder" program, which deletes a file so that it cannot be recovered. The source code is included.
Packers		Contains the "Packers" program, in which the user can select an "all-time" Green Bay Packers team.
SuperTrace		Contains a program by Dave Klein that can be used to debug .PAS files by creating a text file that records the order and time of the procedures and functions executed.
TimeZone		Contains the program "Time Zone," with which you can determine the current time throughout the world.
undu		Contains all the issues released in Windows help file (.hlp) format of UNDU (Unofficial Newsletter of Delphi Users) by Robert Vivrette.
W8snMsrs	Install	Contains the setup program for the "Weights & Measures" program, with which you can convert between various weights and measures.
	Source	Contains the source code for the "Weights & Measures" program.

Disclaimer

The Delphi 4-specific information in this book is based upon pre-release versions. For that reason, some of the information relative to Delphi 4's functionality may have been modified in the final release of Delphi 4.

Some information may refer to Borland which may need to be replaced with Inprise (system registry settings, directory paths, etc.). Rather than note this in each location where Borland is referred to, those to whom it applies can make a "mental" replacement where appropriate (Borland := Inprise).

Error Messages

"." Expected

Possible Cause of Error

You may have assigned a class or object to a variable. For example, if the name of your unit is "BigUnit," the following will generate this error:

```
procedure TForm1.WhateverClick(Sender: Tobject);
var
  AstroPitcher: String;
begin
  AstroPitcher := BigUnit;
end;
```

Quick Fix

Change the name of the variable. In the scenario shown above, a string should be assigned to the variable, like this:

```
procedure TForm1.WhateverClick(Sender: Tobject);
var
  AstroPitcher: String;
begin
  AstroPitcher := 'BigUnit';
end;
```

Additional Information

When you attempt to assign a class name to the variable, the compiler is expecting to find a class property of the proper type appended to the class name.

Use descriptive names for all identifiers—forms, units, components, variables, and constants.

$DENYPACKAGEUNIT < > cannot be put into a package

Possible Cause of Error

You may be attempting to place a unit compiled with the $DENYPACKAGEUNIT compiler switch into a package.

Quick Fix

Remove the {$DENYPACKAGEUNIT ON} compiler switch from the unit or change it to {$DENYPACKAGEUNIT OFF}.

Additional Information

This error message is unique to Delphi 3 and 4, as Delphi 1 and 2 do not use packages.

The {$DENYPACKAGEUNIT ON} compiler directive prevents the unit which contains it from being placed in a package.

{$DENYPACKAGEUNIT OFF} is the default setting.

$DESIGNONLY AND $RUNONLY both specified

Possible Cause of Error

You may have used both the $DESIGNONLY and the $RUNONLY compiler directives. These directives provide opposite functionality, so they cannot both be specified.

Quick Fix

Remove one or both of these compiler directives from the source file where both appear.

Additional Information

Both compiler directives are "off" by default. Their settings can be specified as either "on" or "off" in this way:

{$DESIGNONLY ON} or {$DESIGNONLY OFF}

{$RUNONLY ON} or {$RUNONLY OFF}

The default setting for both compiler directives is "off." In actuality, then, both compilers <u>can</u> be simultaneously specified, but if so, at least one of them must be "off," (which is the default setting anyway).

The {$DESIGNONLY ON} compiler directive causes the package (.DPK) file in which it appears to be compiled for installation into the Delphi IDE.

The {$RUNONLY ON} compiler directive causes the package (.DPK file) in which it appears to be compiled as a runtime-only package.

Use both the $DESIGNONLY and the $RUNONLY compiler directive only in .DPK files.

$DESIGNONLY AND $RUNONLY only allowed in package unit

Possible Cause of Error

You may have included the $DESIGNONLY or $RUNONLY compiler directive (or both) in a source file which is not a package (.DPK) file.

Quick Fix

Remove these compiler directives from the source file where they appear.

Additional Information

These compiler directives affect the way the IDE will treat a package DLL. For that reason, they can only be contained in package source files (.DPK).

$WEAKPACKAGEUNIT & $DENYPACKAGEUNIT both specified

Possible Cause of Error

You may have specified both the $WEAKPACKAGEUNIT and the $DENYPACKAGEUNIT compiler directives in the same source file.

Quick Fix

Remove one or both of these compiler directives from the source file where they both appear.

Additional Information

If the {$WEAKPACKAGEUNIT ON} compiler directive appears in a unit file, the compiler omits that unit from DPLs if possible.

Do not use the {$WEAKPACKAGEUNIT ON} compiler directive in a unit with global variables, Initialization sections, or Finalization sections.

$WEAKPACKAGEUNIT <> cannot have initialization or finalization code

Possible Cause of Error

You may have used the $WEAKPACKAGEUNIT compiler directive in a unit that also contains an Initialization and/or a Finalization section.

Quick Fix

Either remove the $WEAKPACKAGEUNIT compiler directive or the Initialization/Finalization section(s).

Additional Information

The reason a unit containing the $WEAKPACKAGEUNIT compiler directive cannot contain initialization or finalization code (or global data, for that matter) is that multiple copies of the same weakly packaged units could potentially appear in the same application.

$WEAKPACKAGEUNIT <> contains global data

Possible Cause of Error

You may have used the $WEAKPACKAGEUNIT compiler directive in a unit that also contains global data.

Quick Fix

Remove either the $WEAKPACKAGEUNIT compiler directive or the global data.

Additional Information

The reason a unit containing the $WEAKPACKAGEUNIT compiler directive cannot contain global data (or Initialization/Finalization section(s), for that matter) is that multiple copies of the same weakly packaged units could potentially appear in the same application.

';' not allowed before 'Else'

Possible Cause of Error

You may have placed a semicolon directly before the reserved word *else* in an *if* statement.

Quick Fix

Remove the semicolon.

Additional Information

A semicolon denotes the end of an *if* statement. For example, the following will raise the error message under discussion:

```
if SunIsShining then
  PlayBaseball; { causes error }
else
  PlayBasketballIndoors;
```

The correct way to do it is:

```
if SunIsShining then
  PlayBaseball {no semicolon, no error}
else
  PlayBasketballIndoors;
```

< > already exists

Possible Cause of Error

You may have attempted to add a procedure, function, or property to the Members pane in an Automation object or Type Library that has already been declared therein.

Quick Fix

Remove the second declaration of the procedure, function, or property.

Additional Information

You must have a project open to create an Automation object.

< > can't be added to this package because another file with the same base name (<>) is already in the directory of the package

Possible Cause of Error

You may be attempting to insert a file into a package which is either already in the package or which has the same name as a file already in the package.

Quick Fix

If the package is already contained in the package, do not attempt to add it again. If you want to add a new version, first delete the original from the package. If the files differ in functionality but have the same name (and you need both of them), rename the one you attempted to add and then try again.

Additional Information

Packages made their debut with Delphi 3. There are two types of packages: design time and run time. See "Packages" in Delphi help for details.

< > expected but < > found

Possible Cause of Error

1. Based on the preceding code, the compiler was expecting to find one thing, but you supplied it with something "unexpected." For example, you may have tried to make an assignment with the equals sign (=), a la Basic, rather than colon equals (:=), writing something like:

```
ActiveControl = btnClose;
```

2. You may have omitted something necessary, such as the *end* reserved word in a case statement.

Quick Fix

1. Replace the "found" token with the one "expected."
2. Add the omitted element.

Additional Information

1. If you are coming to Delphi/Object Pascal from a language (such as Visual Basic) that uses "=" as both a comparison operator ("equals") and an assignment operator ("gets/is assigned"), you will have to retrain yourself. In Object Pascal, "=" must produce a Boolean result (True or False). For example, the following two statements using the "=" operator are valid:

    ```
    if ActiveControl = btnClose then
    BattenTheHatches := (ActiveControl = btnClose);
    ```

    as they both produce Boolean results (either True/Yes or False/No).

< > has no index for fields < >

Possible Cause of Error

1. You may be attempting to change a table's index via its IndexFieldNames property, either directly at design time or with code at run time, to an index that does not exist. For example, the following line:

    ```
    Table1.IndexFieldNames := 'PeanutGallery';
    ```

    will raise the error if an index on the PeanutGallery field has not been created.

2. You may have changed the TableName property of a TTable component, and the IndexFieldNames property is still set for the previous table.

Quick Fix

1. Create the index before attempting to change to it.
2. Delete the value from the IndexFieldNames property or change it to one appropriate to the current table.

Additional Information

1. The code that causes this error will still compile, because as far as the compiler "knows," you are going to create the index in code before calling it. In other words, this is a run-time error only.

    To create an index in code (as opposed to at table design time), use the AddIndex procedure.

    The IndexFieldNames and IndexName properties are mutually exclusive. When you set one, the other one is cleared.

<> has the descendent <> in the Repository and therefore cannot be removed

Possible Cause of Error

You may have inherited an object from one in the repository, then added the inherited object itself to the repository (presumably after making some changes to it), and finally attempted to remove the original object you inherited from.

Quick Fix

If you really want to delete an object from the repository, you must first remove any objects that inherit functionality from it.

Additional Information

This error message is caused by what is known in the database world as "referential integrity." You cannot remove a master record on which other records rely. The situation is similar here in that the inherited object in the repository relies on the one inherited from.

<> is a read-only file

Possible Cause of Error

1. You may be attempting to modify a file that is read-only.
2. You may be attempting to save a .PAS file while working with version control software (such as PVCS) without having checked out the file.

Quick Fix

1. You can change the file's read-only attribute from True to False using Microsoft Explorer or other file manipulation programs. In Explorer, follow these steps:
   a. Locate and then right-click the file in question.
   b. If the Read-Only check box is checked, click in it to "un-check" it.
2. Check out the file and then try again to save the changes to the .PAS file. Ensure that you do not check out the file in read-only mode.

Additional Information

1. Verify that you really want to modify the file. Perhaps it has been set to read-only (by you or someone else) for a good reason.
2. If you have made a modification which also affects the .DFM file (such as having changed a property of the form or its children), the presence of a checked out .DFM file will also be necessary when saving changes to a .PAS file.

< > is a reserved word

Possible Cause of Error

You may have attempted to use an Object Pascal reserved word to name an identifier.

Quick Fix

Rename the identifier. Give the identifier a meaningful name (to make the code easier to read and debug) beginning with either a letter or an underscore and continuing thereafter with any combination of letters, numbers, and underscores.

Additional Information

Delphi/Object Pascal reserves the following words for its own use:

Object Pascal reserved words

and, array, as, asm, begin, case, class, const, constructor, destructor, dispinterface, div, do, downto, else, end, except, exports, file, finalization, finally, for, function, goto, if, implementation, in, inherited, initialization, inline, interface, is, label, library, mod, nil, not, object, of, or, out, packed, procedure, program, property, raise, record, repeat, resourcestring, set, shl, shr, string, then, threadvar, to, try, type, unit, until, uses, var, while, with, xor

> **Note:** Not all of the reserved words above and directives below are available in all versions of Delphi (except, of course, Delphi 4, in which all of them are recognized).

Although Delphi will not prevent you from doing so, it is also advised that you do not name your identifiers using any of the following Object Pascal directives:

Object Pascal directives

absolute, abstract, assembler, automated, cdecl, contains, default, dispid, dynamic, export, external, far, forward, implements, index, message, name, near, nodefault, overload, override, package, pascal, private, protected, public, published, read, readonly, register, reintroduce, requires, resident, safecall, stdcall, stored, virtual, write, writeonly

> **Note:** *Private, protected, public, published,* and *automated* act as reserved words within object type declarations, but are otherwise treated as directives.

< > is already in the Repository. Replace it?

Possible Cause of Error

You may be attempting to place an object in the repository that is already there.

Quick Fix

Select the **Cancel** button.

Additional Information

Objects in the repository can be used for sharing among developers and projects. If you add an object from the repository to your project, you can either Copy, Inherit, or Use it. If you "copy," you get a separate copy with no further connection to the original which resides in the repository. If you "inherit," future changes to the object in the repository will also be reflected in your object. If you "use" it, you are taking custody of the original copy in the repository itself—changes you make are reflected in objects that are "inherited" from this object.

For more information, see "Sharing Objects in a team environment" in Delphi help.

< > is already in use by < >

Possible Cause of Error

1. You may be attempting to view the structure of or edit a database table in Database Desktop or perform some other operation (or "utility," as Database Desktop often refers to them) while the table is still open.
2. It may be that one or more TTables or a TDatabase component are open in the Delphi IDE.

Quick Fix

1. Close Database Desktop, if it has the table(s) in question open.
2. Close the table(s) by setting the Active property of TDatasets (TTable, TQuery, and TStoredProc components in all versions of Delphi; TClientDataset in Delphi Client/Server versions 3 and 4; TNestedTable in Delphi 4) to False, and the Connected property of TDataBase components to False.

Additional Information

If you have experienced abnormal termination of your application (a crash), it may be necessary to exit and then restart Delphi itself before being able to access the table for exclusive use.

< > is an invalid filename

Possible Cause of Error

You may have entered an extension for a filename which is not an appropriate extension for the type of file you are working with.

Quick Fix

Remove the extension so that the appropriate extension will be automatically appended, or change the extension to the appropriate one.

Additional Information

An example of what might cause this error is if you are using the ActiveX Control Wizard and attempt to save the project name with an extension other than .DPR.

Windows and Delphi depend on filename extensions to know what kind of information a file contains and how it should therefore be treated. If you change file extensions, the machine has no way of knowing what is a text file, source file, object file, project file, executable file, etc. (unless you specify the association yourself).

< > is an invalid PageIndex value. PageIndex must be between 0 and < >

Possible Cause of Error

You may have tried to assign the PageIndex property of a TTabSheet component to one that does not exist. For example, you may have written code similar to this:

```
TabSheet1.PageIndex := 3;
```

when there are only three pages (0, 1, and 2, but no 3).

Quick Fix

Change the page index assignment to one that already exists, or create it in the Form Editor or in code before making the assignment.

Additional Information

This error will not be caught at compile time, because for all the compiler "knows," you are going to create the referenced PageIndex in code before making it active via code similar to that above.

< > is not a type identifier

Possible Cause of Error

You may have declared a data type in a procedure or function that does not exist. At any rate, a type identifier was expected in the location the error occurred, but a recognized type name was not found there.

Quick Fix

Ensure that you are spelling the name of the type correctly.

Additional Information

An example of when you may get this error message is if you try to get by with a shortened version of a data type. For instance, you might try this:

```
var
  s: Str;            {you must declare string, not str}
  i: Int;            {you must declare integer, not int}
  tidy: Bool;        {however, this is fine...}
  wooly: Boolean;    {...as is the long form}
```

< > is not a unique name

Possible Cause of Error

You may have attempted to assign the same name to a database in Database Explorer or SQL Explorer (Delphi Client/Server edition) as one that already exists.

Quick Fix

Assign unique names to all database aliases.

Additional Information

All things must have unique names to be accurately and absolutely identified. People, for example, have names that distinguish them from one another. If the name is the same at a certain level of detail, for example if both the first name and the last name are the same (such as "John Smith"), then you must continue to another level of detail, such as middle name or even birth date or some other piece of information, to accurately and uniquely identify a person. Database aliases must also be uniquely identified, and in fact, are much simpler than humans in this respect. If their one-syllable name is unique, this is enough.

< > is not a valid component name

Possible Cause of Error

You may have assigned a component a name that is not allowed by the Object Pascal language.

Quick Fix

Assign the component a name that adheres to the following rules:

1. It must begin with a letter or an underscore (_) character.
2. Subsequent characters must be letters, numbers, or the underscore character.
3. Do not use an Object Pascal reserved word to name a component. Object Pascal reserved words are:

and, array, as, asm, begin, case, class, const, constructor, destructor, dispinterface, div, do, downto, else, end, except, exports, file, finalization, finally, for, function, goto, if, implementation, in, inherited, initialization, inline, interface, is, label, library, mod, nil, not, object, of, or, out, packed, procedure, program, property, raise, record, repeat, resourcestring, set, shl, shr, string, then, threadvar, to, try, type, unit, until, uses, var, while, with, xor

Additional Information

By default, Delphi assigns sequential names based on the type of the component, such as Button1, Button2, Timer1, etc. To make your code more readable (and thus maintainable), change these to more meaningful names. For example, you may name your components btnSave, btnClose, tmrSplash, etc.

You can use up to 63 characters to name a component.

Although it is possible to do so without receiving an error message, it is advised that you do not use the following Object Pascal standard directives:

absolute, abstract, assembler, automated, cdecl, contains, default, dispid, dynamic, export, external, far, forward, implements, index, message, name, near, nodefault, overload, override, package, pascal, private, protected, public, published, read, readonly, register, reintroduce, requires, resident, safecall, stdcall, stored, virtual, write, writeonly

Similarly, avoid using identifiers already defined in the Object Pascal language (such as *Writeln, Exit, String, Word,* etc.) to name your identifiers.

Do not change the names of components at run time. In other words, do not change them in code. Assign names to components only from within the IDE at design time (in the Object Inspector).

 Tip: If your attempts to change the name of a component are not accepted—the name keeps reverting to its "invalid" name—toggle the Num Lock key and try again.

< > *is not a valid date*

Possible Cause of Error

You may have attempted to add an invalid date to a database table or convert an invalid date from string format to date format.

Quick Fix

Ensure that the date entered or converted is valid.

Additional Information

Internally, the TDateTime value is stored as a Real number (to be more specific, a Double). The portion left of the decimal point represents the date (with the value 0 representing December 30, 1899, the value 368 representing January 1, 1901, etc.); the fractional portion to the right of the decimal point represents the time of day.

You can store dates prior to December 30, 1899, by using negative numbers (–1 represents December 29, 1899, etc.).

 Note: In Delphi 1, the internal value begins with the year 1 rather than 1899. To convert a Delphi 1 date to subsequent versions of Delphi, subtract 693594 from the Delphi 1 date. Although the original (Delphi 1) starting point seems more sensible, this change was made for compatibility with OLE Automation.

You can easily trap for this error by enclosing an attempt to typecast the value to a Date data type within a *try...except* block, like so:

```
var
  Fig: TDateTime;
try
  Fig := StrToDate(Edit1.Text);
except
  on EConvertError do ...
```

If you are using Delphi 3 or higher, consider using the TDateTimePicker component to retrieve date values from the user. The TDateTimePicker component does not allow the user to select invalid dates, and is thus a "no code" (no-brainer?) solution.

If you are using Delphi 4, take a look at the TMonthCalendar component.

< > is not a valid date and time

Possible Cause of Error

You may have tried to convert an invalid TDateTime value from a string or otherwise attempted to store an invalid value into a TDateTime variable.

Quick Fix

Verify that the TDateTime value you entered or converted is valid.

If you are directly storing a value in a TDateTime variable, use this format:

```
var
  TheDay: TDateTime;
begin
  TheDay := 30678.001 {12/28/1983 12:01:26}
```

If converting from a string, use this format:

```
var
  TheDay: TDateTime;
begin
    TheDay := StrToDateTime('12/01/1990 2:11 am');
```

Additional Information

It is not necessary to add the time portion of the value (the part to the right of the decimal point). For example, in the above examples, you could have assigned the values 30678 and '12/01/1990' (without the time portions, .001 and 2:11 am, respectively).

Internally, the TDateTime value is stored as a Double. The portion left of the decimal point represents the date (with the value 0 representing December 30, 1899, the value 368 representing January 1, 1901, etc.); the portion to the right of the decimal point represents the time of day.

You can store dates prior to December 30, 1899, by using negative numbers (−1 represents December 29, 1899, etc.).

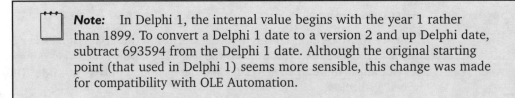

Note: In Delphi 1, the internal value begins with the year 1 rather than 1899. To convert a Delphi 1 date to a version 2 and up Delphi date, subtract 693594 from the Delphi 1 date. Although the original starting point (that used in Delphi 1) seems more sensible, this change was made for compatibility with OLE Automation.

You can easily trap for an invalid DateTime error by enclosing an attempt to type-cast the value to a Date data type within a *try...except* block, like so:

```
var
  Fig: TDateTime;
try
  Fig := StrToDateTime(Edit1.Text);
except
  on EConvertError do ...
```

< > *is not a valid floating point value*

Possible Cause of Error

You may be attempting to convert a value to a floating-point number that is not recognized as a floating-point value by the compiler. For example, if your code looks something like this:

```
var
  Trouble: Double;
begin
  Trouble := StrToFloat(Edit1.Text);
```

and the user enters any number in the Edit1 field, the value will be converted to a float and stored in the float variable. But if the user enters anything other than a number, the error message under discussion will display.

Quick Fix

Verify that the value is a valid floating-point value before assigning it to the variable. For example, you might try something like this:

```
var
  Trouble: Double;
try
  Trouble := StrToFloat(Edit1.Text);
except
  on EConvertError do ...
```

Additional Information

The Real, Single, Double, Extended, Comp, and Currency data types are all floating-point types.

If you attempt to assign an invalid value to a Real number at compile time (for example, assigning the Boolean value True to the variable Trouble), you will get the error "Incompatible types: < > and < >."

< > *is not a valid identifier*

Possible Cause of Error

1. You may have selected an OK button without supplying necessary information.

2. You may be attempting to save a unit file with an extension other than .PAS or a project file with an extension other than .DPR.

Quick Fix

1. Make a selection in the dialog box before selecting the OK button.

2. Use the default extensions (or none at all, in which case the appropriate extension will be automatically appended) for files that Delphi must manage.

Additional Information

One example (of many similar ones) where you would get this error message is if you are attempting to install a component, and then select OK in the dialog box without entering a value in the Unit filename edit box.

< > *is not a valid integer value*

Possible Cause of Error

1. You may be attempting to convert a value to an integer that is not recognized as an integer value by the compiler. For example, if your code looks something like this:

```
var
  CountOfMonteCarlo: Integer;
begin
  CountOfMonteCarlo := StrToInt(Edit1.Text);
```

and the user enters an integer in the Edit1 field, the value will be converted to an integer and stored in the integer variable. But if the user enters anything other than an integer, the above error message will display.

2. You may be opening a project in a version of Delphi that precedes the one used to last compile it, in which case a form may be referenced as the invalid integer value.

Quick Fix

1. Verify that the value is a valid integer value before assigning it to the variable. For example, you might try something like this:

```
var
   CountOfMonteCarlo: Integer;
try
   CountOfMonteCarlo := StrToInt(Edit1.Text);
except
   on EConvertError do ...
```

2. Select **OK** and proceed.

Additional Information

If you attempt to assign an invalid value to an integer at compile time (as opposed to at run time, as demonstrated in the example above—for example, assigning the value "Dracula" to the integer variable CountOfMonteCarlo), you will get the error "Incompatible types: < > and < >."

ShortInt, SmallInt, Integer, Byte, Word, and Cardinal are all integer types.

< > is not a valid time

Possible Cause of Error

You may be attempting to convert an invalid value from a string into a TDateTime variable or otherwise attempting to store an invalid value in a TDateTime variable.

Quick Fix

Ensure that the value entered or converted is valid.

If you are directly storing a value in a TDateTime variable, use this format:

```
var
   TheTimeOfOurLives: TDateTime;
begin
   TheTimeOfOurLives := 0.8125
```

If converting from a string, use this format:

```
var
   TheTimeOfOurLives: TDateTime;
begin
      TheTimeOfOurLives := StrToTime('7:30 pm');
```

Additional Information

Internally, the TDateTime value is stored as a Double. The portion left of the decimal point represents the date (with the value 0 representing December 30, 1899, the value 368 representing January 1, 1901, etc.); the portion to the right of the decimal point represents the time of day.

You can easily trap for an invalid DateTime error by enclosing an attempt to typecast the value to a Date data type within a *try...except* block, like so:

```
var
  TheTimeOfOurLives: TDateTime;
begin
  try
    TheTimeOfOurLives := StrToTime(Edit1.Text);
  except
    on EConvertError do begin
      ShowMessage('That_does_not_com_pute...' + #13#10 +
                  'no_such_time...beep...');
      ActiveControl := Edit1;
    end;
  end;
```

< > is not a valid value for field < >. The allowed range is < > to < >

Possible Cause of Error

You may have attempted to assign a value to a database field that is either less than the field's MinValue property or greater than the field's MaxValue property.

Quick Fix

Either enter a value within the range you have specified for the field or increase the allowable range by decreasing the MinValue property and/or increasing the MaxValue property.

Additional Information

All numerical TField descendents (which are created by Delphi when the underlying database fields are instantiated) have the MinValue and MaxValue property.

> **Note:** If you set the MinVal or MaxVal property in Database Desktop (as opposed to directly to a TField in the Delphi IDE), and assign a value that is too small or large, the error message is "[Maximum, Minimum] Validity Check failed."

< > must be saved before adding to Repository. Save now?

Possible Cause of Error

You may be attempting to add a form to the repository that has not been saved.

Quick Fix

Save the unit by selecting **File | Save**, and then save it to the repository by either:

Right-clicking on it and then selecting **Add to Repository**

-OR-

Selecting **Project | Add to Repository**.

Additional Information

If you are working in a team programming environment, you can set up a shared network directory as the Delphi Object Repository, from which all developers can draw. You can then map your copy of Delphi to that directory by selecting Tools | Environment Options, and then entering the location of this shared directory in the Shared Repository area at the bottom of the Preferences tab.

The default location for local copies of the Object Repository is

```
C:\Program Files\Borland\Delphi X\Objrepos.
```

< > or < > expected but < > found

Possible Cause of Error

1. You may have used a parenthesis where a bracket belongs, or vice versa.
2. You may have used a semicolon where a period belongs, or vice versa.

3. You may have supplied the wrong number of arguments to a procedure or function call (in which case the compiler will be expecting a comma rather than a closing/right parenthesis).

4. You may have left out the semicolon on the preceding line.

5. You may have inserted some code between the Unit and Interface parts of a unit. For example, you may have inserted a Var and/or Const section there.

6. You may be using a .PAS file which has omitted a necessary reserved word, for example, *unit*.

7. You may have attempted to declare a type in a Variable section, like this:

```
var
  TForm1 = class(TForm)
```

In that case, the specific error message will be " ',' or ':' expected but '=' found."

8. You may have prepended the unit name instead of the class name to a method (for example, defining a method in the Implementation part as Unit1.Some-Procedure rather than TForm1.SomeProcedure).

Quick Fix

1-6. Replace the existing ("found") token with the one expected.

7. Declare type declarations in Type sections only.

8. Replace the unit name with the class name.

Additional Information

Refer to Delphi help for information about the statement type, procedure, or function you are using.

{$R *.RES} missing or incorrect

Possible Cause of Error

You may have removed or modified the project (.DPR) file's compiler directive.

Quick Fix

Verify that your project's .DPR file contains the line:

```
{$R *.RES}
```

between its Uses and Begin...End sections. Select **View | Project Source** and add or modify this line if necessary.

Additional Information

The {$R *.RES} compiler directive specifies that the file with the same base name as the project and the extension .RES should be linked into the project. This resource file typically contains the project's application icon only.

Do not edit this resource file, as any changes you make will be lost the next time you recompile. Use a separate resource file to add additional resources.

> **Note:** If you are using Delphi 4, see "Resource .DLLs" in Delphi help for information on the resource .DLL wizard available with the newest version of Delphi.

> **Note:** Each unit (.PAS) file has the following compiler directive linking in the form (.DFM) file:
>
> {$R *.DFM}
>
> It is automatically placed directly after the *implementation* keyword. Do not remove this either.

16-Bit segment encountered in object file < >

Possible Cause of Error

A 16-bit segment has been found in an object (.OBJ) file linked to your program via the $L compiler directive.

Quick Fix

Use an object file that does not have a 16-bit segment definition.

Additional Information

Consult the documentation for the product that was used to create the object file for instructions on converting 16-bit segment definitions to 32-bit segment definitions.

A CoClass must have at least one default interface

Possible Cause of Error

You may have deselected the default menu item of an interface that is a member of a CoClass object.

Quick Fix

Follow these steps:

1. Decide which of the CoClass's interfaces (if there are more than one) you want to designate as its default interface.

2. With the affected CoClass highlighted in the left pane, select the Members page in the right pane.

3. If the interfaces are not listed, right-click within the Members page and select **Insert Interface**.

4. Select as many of the interfaces as you want from the list (shift-click to select multiple interfaces) and then select the **OK** button.

5. Highlight the interface you want to designate as the default interface for the CoClass object.

6. Right-click the interface member and select the Default menu item.

You will now be able to save the Type Library.

Additional Information

Besides simply fixing the syntax error generated by not having a default interface or interfaces for the CoClass object, you will no doubt also want to add procedures, functions, and properties to the interface (if you have not done so already). For specific information on doing this, see "Creating a new type library" in Delphi online help.

The Type Library Editor can be accessed by selecting File | New | ActiveX page | Type Library. Use the Type Library Editor to create and inspect type information for ActiveX controls and COM objects.

> **Note:** The Type Library Editor is also activated by selecting **File | New | ActiveX page | Automation Object**.

You must have a project open to select File | New | ActiveX page | Automation Object, as the Automation object created is specific to a project. This is not the case with selecting File | New | ActiveX page | Type Library.

A CoClass must implement at least one interface

Possible Cause of Error

You may be attempting to save a Type Library that contains a CoClass object with no linked interface(s).

Quick Fix

Add at least one interface to the CoClass object or delete the CoClass object. To add an interface to the CoClass object, follow these steps:

1. In the Type Library Editor, click the Interface icon (it looks like a red ping-pong paddle).
2. In the Type Library Editor, click the Members page to make it active.
3. Right-click within the Members page and select **Insert Interface** from the context menu.
4. Highlight the interface you want to add in the Insert Interface dialog box and then select the **OK** button.

You will now be able to save the Type Library.

Additional Information

Besides simply fixing the syntax error of not having an interface or interfaces linked to the CoClass object, you will also doubtless want to add procedures, functions, and properties to the interface. For specific information on doing this, see "Creating a new type library" in Delphi online help.

The Type Library Editor can be accessed by selecting File | New | ActiveX page | Type Library icon. Use the Type Library Editor to create and inspect type information for ActiveX controls and COM objects.

> **Note:** The Type Library Editor is also activated by selecting File | New | ActiveX page | Automation Object.

You must have a project open to select File | New | ActiveX page | Automation Object, as the Automation object created is specific to a project. This is not the case with selecting File | New | ActiveX page | Type Library.

A component class named < > already exists

Possible Cause of Error

While creating a new component with the New Component Wizard (select **File | New | Component** or **Component | New Component...**), you may have changed the entry in the Class Name edit box to the name of a component that already exists in your VCL. For example, you may have changed the name to "TBatchMove" (which already exists).

Quick Fix

Change the name in the Class Name edit box to one that is unique within your VCL.

Additional Information

By default, Delphi will select a name for you that does not conflict (or "collide") with components that already make up your VCL.

For example, if you select THeader as the ancestor type of the component you are about to create, Delphi will enter THeader1 in the Class Name edit box (if there already is a THeader1 in your VCL, it will be THeader2, etc.).

The phrase "your VCL" is used instead of "the VCL" because each user of Delphi is likely to have a unique collection of VCL components. Surely you will have the core Delphi VCL components that ship with Delphi (which even differ between various versions and editions of Delphi—editions as in Standard, Professional, Client/Server, and Enterprise), but you may also have third-party components installed on your system (such as those offered by Woll2Woll, TurboPower, Raize, Classic Software, etc.), shareware components, freeware components, as well as some of your own. Altogether, these comprise "your VCL."

A component named < > already exists

Possible Cause of Error

You may have attempted to give a component the same name as one that already exists.

Quick Fix

Provide each component with a unique name, preferably one that describes the component's purpose, such as mniAbout for a menu item that opens an About box, btnClose for a button that closes a form or dialog box, etc.

Additional Information

Delphi will automatically give each component you place on the form a unique name based on the type of component it is and an incrementing number. For example, if you placed three labels on a form, Delphi would give them the names Label1, Label2, and Label3. You can, of course, change them to something more descriptive if you want, but each component's name must be unique.

A component named < > already exists in a descendent form

Possible Cause of Error

You may have used the visual form inheritance feature available in Delphi from version 2 onward, and then renamed the form you inherited from (or a component on the form), using the name of a component that is already being used in the descendent form.

Quick Fix

Assign the original (ancestor) form and all components on it names unique to the project.

Additional Information

You can and probably will have components on the descendent form that have the same name as those on the ancestor form, but these are components that are first placed on the ancestor form (which are, including the name, inherited by the descendent form). In other words, components placed on the ancestor are inherited by the descendent form and even have the same name. Components placed on the descendent form are "overriding," or extending, the declaration of the ancestor form, and the ancestor cannot "reverse inherit" from the descendent.

For example, create a descendent form by following these steps:

1. Select **File | New**.
2. Select the tab with the same name as your project.

3. Select the form you want to inherit from.

4. Verify that the Inherit radio button is selected.

If you then place a TLabel component on the ancestor form, Delphi will assign the component the name Label1. The descendent form will then also have a Label1 in the exact same position on the form (it has inherited it from its ancestor). However, if you then placed a TLabel component directly on the descendent form (which Delphi would assign the name Label2), followed by placing another label on the ancestor form (which Delphi would assign the name Label3), and attempted to assign Label3 on the ancestor form the name Label2, you would get the error message under discussion.

A device attached to the system is not functioning

Possible Cause of Error

1. You may be attempting to install a package that requires a .DLL which is not in Delphi's search path. The missing .DLL may also be a package unit.

2. The package may have been compiled with a different version of Delphi than the one you are using.

Quick Fix

1. Verify that all required .DLLs, including packages, are available to your system and located in the correct place. They must be on Delphi's search path (Tools | Environment Options, Library tab, Library Path combo box), and packages especially should be in the \Windows\System directory.

2. If you are the author of the package, recompile the package in the version of Delphi into which you are attempting to install it. If you are not the author, see if you can get the appropriately compiled version from him, her, or them.

Additional Information

This is one of those error messages that does not really give you much of a hint as to the real problem.

A dispinterface type cannot have an ancestor interface

Possible Cause of Error

You may have specified a dispinterface as an ancestor for a dispinterface type.

Quick Fix

Do not declare another interface as the ancestor of a dispinterface type.

Additional Information

An interface type specified with dispinterface cannot specify an ancestor interface, as they are abstract interfaces.

Refer to "Dispatch Interfaces," "Creating and accessing Interfaces," and "Dual Interfaces" in Delphi online help for more information.

A dispinterface type requires an interface identification

Possible Cause of Error

You may have neglected to specify a GUID in a dispinterface type.

Quick Fix

Supply a GUID so that the dispinterface type is accessible.

Additional Information

A GUID is a 16-byte binary value that is guaranteed to be unique among all interfaces (GUID stands for Globally Unique IDentifier).

A field or method named < > already exists

Possible Cause of Error

Your .PAS file may contain a reference to the object or method you are attempting to add to the form, but there is no corresponding reference to it in the form's .DFM file. For example, you may have added Button1 to a form, then manually removed the reference to Button1 from the form (.DFM) file, and then added another button to the form—the .DFM and .PAS file are not synchronized, as the .PAS file believes there are two TButton controls, whereas the .DFM file only knows of one.

Quick Fix

First remove the reference in the .PAS file to the object or method which has no corresponding reference in the form's .DFM file, then add back the object or method to the .DFM file.

Additional Information

When you attempt to add an object or method to your form, Delphi attempts to give it the next available name for an instance of its class (for example, if you are dropping a button on the form, it will name it Button1 if there are no other buttons on the form, Button2 if there is one there already, etc.). If, however, there is a reference to a Button1 in the .PAS file (but not the .DFM file), the attempt to name the button Button1 (because there are no buttons referenced in the .DFM file) will cause the error message under discussion, as you cannot have two components named Button1 in the same .PAS file.

A module called < > is already installed

Possible Cause of Error

You may be attempting to install a component which you previously unsuccessfully tried to install.

Quick Fix

Follow these steps:

1. Close the message box by selecting the **OK** button.
2. In the Installed Units list box, highlight the unit you are attempting to install.
3. Select the **Remove** button.
4. Try again to install the component.

Additional Information

The "module" (component unit) was partially installed, therefore preventing you both from using it (because it was only "halfway there") or attempting to reinstall it (because it was already "halfway there").

This does not apply to Delphi 3 and 4, in which you install components into packages. There is no Installed Units list box in those versions of Delphi. To see which components you have installed by palette page in Delphi 3, select **Component | Configure Palette**. To see which components you have installed by package, follow these steps:

1. Select **Component | Install Packages**.
2. In the Design Packages section of the dialog box which then displays, highlight the package you want to inspect.
3. Select the **Components** button.

A page must be empty before it can be deleted

Possible Cause of Error

You may be attempting to delete a page from your component palette that still contains components.

Quick Fix

Delete any and all components from a page before attempting to delete the page itself. If you want to retain the component(s) but get rid of the page, drag the component(s) from the page you want to delete to another page; you can then delete the page itself.

Additional Information

Delphi 1 and 2

To remove a component, follow these steps:

1. Select **Component | Configure Palette...**.
2. In the Pages list box on the left side of the dialog box that displays, highlight the page which contains the component you want to delete. Its constituent components will display in the Components list box on the right.
3. Highlight the component you want to delete.
4. Select the **Delete** button.
5. Select the **OK** button.

Delphi 3

To remove a component altogether (as opposed to moving it to a different page), you will have to remove it from the package in which it resides first, and then remove the page on which the component displayed.

To remove a component from a package, follow these steps:

1. Select **Project | Options**, and then click the Packages page.
2. In the Design Packages section of the Packages page, highlight the package in which the component you want to delete resides (to see which components are contained in each package, select the **Components** button).
3. Select the **Edit** button (do not select the Remove button unless you want to get rid of the entire package).
4. Select **Yes** in the confirmation dialog box that displays.
5. Right-click the unit that you want to remove and select **Remove Unit** from the context menu.

Delphi 4

To remove a component, you must remove the package in which it resides. To do so, follow these steps:

1. Select **Project | Options**, and then click the Packages page.

2. In the Design Packages section of the Packages page, highlight the package in which the component you want to delete resides (to see which components are contained in each package, select the **Components** button).

3. Select the **Remove** button.

4. Select **Yes** in the dialog box that displays to confirm the removal of the package.

 Note: All the components in the package will be removed.

A reference to < > already exists in the Type Library

Possible Cause of Error

You may be attempting to create an ActiveX control based on a VCL component, and the ActiveX name given the control has already been used.

Quick Fix

Change the name in the New ActiveX Name edit box to one that is unique among components in your VCL.

Additional Information

When you derive an ActiveX control from a Delphi component using the ActiveX Control Wizard (File | New | ActiveX tab, ActiveX Control icon), the wizard creates a default name for the new ActiveX control by removing the T from the beginning of the component name and appending an X to the end. For example, if you derive an ActiveX control from a component in your library called TNavPanel, the ActiveX Control Wizard will generate the name NavPanelX for it. You can change this if you wish, and (as this error shows) if you already have created an ActiveX control based on the component and used this default name the first time, you will have to use another name on subsequent occasions.

A required .DLL file, < >, was not found

Possible Cause of Error

You may be trying to execute a program that was compiled to use run-time packages, and one (or more) of the packages, for example VCL30.DPL, is not installed on the machine or is not in the correct location.

Quick Fix

Ensure that all packages required are installed in the Windows System directory (C:\Windows\System).

Additional Information

In Delphi 4, VCL40.DPL is the main component library file. In Delphi 3, it is VCL30.DPL. These have replaced COMPLIB.DCL (Delphi 1) and CMPLIB32.DCL (Delphi 2).

When building applications using run-time packages, ensure that you install all the required packages on the target machines. You can do this using InstallShield, which is provided with most versions of Delphi.

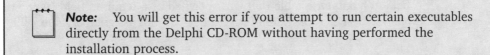

Note: You will get this error if you attempt to run certain executables directly from the Delphi CD-ROM without having performed the installation process.

A user transaction is already in progress

Possible Cause of Error

You may be attempting to begin a database transaction while an earlier one is still in progress. For example, this will cause the error message under discussion:

```
begin
  with Database1 do
    begin
      Connected := True;
      StartTransaction;
      try
        Query1.Active := True;
```

```
        StartTransaction; {remove this line to prevent the error message}
        Commit;
      except
        Rollback;
      end;
    end;
  end;
```

Quick Fix

Terminate a database transaction by either "committing" or "rolling back" before beginning another transaction.

Additional Information

See "StartTransaction" and "InTransaction" in Delphi help for more information.

A value must be specified for < >

Possible Cause of Error

A field in a database table that was specified as a required field (when the table was designed or thereafter in code) was not assigned a value.

Quick Fix

Ensure that all required fields are assigned values.

Additional Information

There are three basic levels of validation you can enforce on the data in a table: table-level, record-level, and field-level. Additionally, you can enforce character-level validation at the time the user is entering values using TField's EditMask property or through custom code you attach to one of the OnKeyX events.

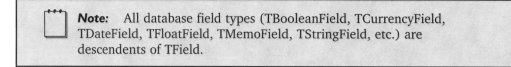

Note: All database field types (TBooleanField, TCurrencyField, TDateField, TFloatField, TMemoField, TStringField, etc.) are descendents of TField.

Table-level validation is provided at table design time by ensuring that the data type and size of the field is appropriate for the values with which the field is to be populated. For example, a field named DateOfBirth should use a Date data type, a field named MothersMaiden should contain a String (known as Alpha by Paradox, Char and VarChar by SQL server databases), etc.

You can (and it is recommended that you do) specify a field or column in a table as the primary key. This will prevent two records from being assigned the same value for this field. An example of where you might use this is the SSN field for an Employee table. Autoincrement fields are also commonly used as the primary key.

Using Database Desktop and Paradox tables, you specify a field as being primary at table design time by double-clicking in the Key column (or pressing any key when that column has the focus). If you create the table in code, you can use the AddIndex method and the ixPrimary Options parameter. See "TTable.AddIndex" in Delphi help for more information.

> **Note:** You can also specify a number of fields as constituting a composite primary key. That is, none of the individual fields or columns are guaranteed to be unique by themselves, but taken together, there are to be no two records with the same values in all of these fields. This is known as a "composite key." If you designate a field as a primary key in a Paradox table, it must be the first field in the table. If you designate multiple fields as a composite primary key, they must be consecutive fields beginning with the first field. In other words, fields 1, 2, and 3 can comprise a composite primary key, but fields 2 and 3 cannot (field 1 must be included in the key), nor can fields 1 and 3 (you cannot skip fields).

Additionally, you can designate fields as being Required to prevent a field from being left blank. To do this in Database Desktop with Paradox tables, select the 1. Required Field check box while the field which you want to designate as Required is highlighted in the Field Roster section.

If you create the table in code, you can use the TTable's FieldDefs.Add method and set the Required parameter to True. For example, if you are creating two field definitions, designating the first two as being required and the second two as not being required, you could do it this way:

```
Table1.FieldDefs.Add('OfDreams',ftString,20,True);
Table1.FieldDefs.Add('WC',ftBlob,256,True);
Table1.FieldDefs.Add('DepthOf',ftInteger,0,False);
Table1.FieldDefs.Add('Mrs',ftBytes,32,False);
```

The Add method's parameters are:

1. The Name you are assigning the field
2. The Data type you are assigning the field
3. The Size of the field (0 if size does not apply to the data type, such as an Integer field)
4. The Required flag

See "TDataSet.FieldDefs" in Delphi help for more information.

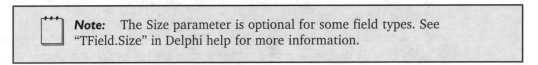

Note: The Size parameter is optional for some field types. See "TField.Size" in Delphi help for more information.

Table-level validation alone, however, does not prevent the user from entering a bogus value of the correct data type. For example, entering 10/15/1879 as a current employee's date of birth or the maiden name of a customer as K6%l3 ^ b6&n will be accepted as valid input (unless you have practiced defensive coding by preventing these types of "errors").

Note: "Field" and "Column" are sometimes used interchangeably in this book. Local databases, such as Paradox, dBase, and Access, usually use "Field," while SQL Server databases, such as Interbase, Oracle, MS SQL Server, usually use "Column."

Record-level validation is also provided at table design time when you designate a field as having a primary index (Delphi will ensure that you do not enter the same value in two of these fields), and/or as requiring a value (Delphi will not allow you to leave it blank), and/or when you designate minimum and maximum values that can be accepted for the field, etc.

Table- and record-level validation are enforced by Delphi when you attempt to move from the record you are inserting or editing to another record. If any of the entries (or lack thereof) violate the validation rules you have built into the database, you will receive appropriate error messages at this time.

> **Note:**   Delphi does not recognize all the record-level validation you may provide via Database Desktop. Delphi does support the Default value you supply in all cases, but if you instantiate the fields in the table*, the Required, Minimum Value, Maximum Value, and Picture you specified in Database Desktop are ignored in your Delphi application, as the instantiated fields have "new and improved" properties that Delphi refers to (where appropriate for the data type) for this information, namely Required, MinValue, MaxValue, and EditMask, respectively.
>
> As stated already, if you provided a default value for a column in Database Desktop, it is supported by your Delphi application even if you instantiate the fields at design time. However, if you assign a value to the corresponding TField descendent's DefaultExpression property, this value will take precedence over and "override" the default value you supplied in Database Desktop. For example, if you specify Not My as the default value in Database Desktop for a particular column, Not My will display in that column in new records you insert inside your Delphi application (although the user, of course, can change the value). If you assign San Andreas to the corresponding field's DefaultExpression property, though, the default value you set in Database Desktop (Not My) will be ignored and San Andreas will be used in its stead.
>
> * To instantiate your table's fields at design time, use the Fields Editor. See "Fields Editor" and "Persistent Field Components" in Delphi help for more information.

If you prefer to provide record-level validation in code, use TDataSet's Before-Post event (TTable, TQuery, and TStoredProc are all descendents of TDataSet, which are available in all versions of Delphi; TClientDataset is available in Delphi Client/Server version 3 and 4; TNestedTable in Delphi 4). For more information, see "TDataSet.BeforePost" in Delphi help.

If you so desire, you can also provide **Field-level validation** which is enforced after you enter a value for a field (as opposed to waiting until values for the entire row have been entered).

To enforce field-level validation, you can use a TField's OnValidate event. Using this method, you can catch an oversight right after it occurs rather than possibly several fields later.

For example, here is some code that can be assigned to a TField's OnValidate event to prevent an inappropriate value from being entered:

```
const
  crlf = #13#10; {carriage return/line feed}
  ...
procedure TForm1.Table1QuantityValidate(Sender: Tfield);
begin
  if Table1Quantity.Value < 1 then begin
    raise Exception.Create( 'Each item ordered requires,'  +crlf+
                            'a quantity of at least 1.'     +crlf+
                            'Otherwise we will go bankrupt '+crlf+
                            'and you will be out of a job.');
    Edit3.Color := clRed;
    Edit3.SetFocus;
  end;
end;
```

The exception which is created "on the fly" with the Exception.Create statement prevents the value from being entered into the field. The next two lines move the cursor to the control in which the user entered the value and then highlight it so the user can enter an appropriate value.

> **Note:** You can attach code to a control's OnExit event to return the color of the control to its previous setting, such as the default of clWindow.

There is yet another way you can implement field-level validation: using TField's CustomConstraint and ConstraintErrorMessage properties. CustomConstraint is a SQL statement that must evaluate to True for the entry to be valid. ConstraintErrorMessage is the message the user will see when the constraint fails (the entry is not valid).

To use these two properties to enforce the validation shown in the Table1QuantityValidate procedure above, set the CustomConstraint to **x > 0** and the ConstraintErrorMessage to **Each item requires a quantity of at least 1. Otherwise we will go bankrupt and you will be out of a job**.

There is also a read-only ImportedConstraint property which displays any constraints created on the server (if you are connecting to a SQL server database). You cannot alter this property, but you can add to the imported constraint by assigning a value to the CustomConstraint property. See "TField.CustomConstraint" and "TField.ConstraintErrorMessage" in Delphi help for more information.

> **Note:** The CustomConstraint, ConstraintErrorMessage, and ImportedConstraint properties made their debut with Delphi 3.

> **Note:** To validate data entered into non-data-aware controls, you can use the control's OnExit event to validate entries by typecasting the entry as the type of data you want it to be or by checking to see whether the entry falls within the boundaries you set.

If you want even more immediate feedback for your users as they enter data, especially data that demands a very precise format, you can use TField's Edit-Mask property. This is termed **character-level validation**. Whereas TField's OnValidate event enforces assignments made to a field as a whole, TField's EditMask property allows validation of the data on a character-by-character basis as it is being entered by the user.

The EditMask property provides several predefined masks for validating entries of phone numbers, zip codes, dates, and times. You can also create your own masks for specific types of entries required in your application. If you assign a field's value programmatically, validation by the EditMask is bypassed, since there is no data-aware control to enforce adherence to the mask. In this case, use TField's OnValidate event to validate the entry before it is posted to the table.

For more information, see "TField.EditMask" in Delphi help.

If all the valid entries for a particular field are known in advance or contained in a table, another way to ensure that all entries are valid is to use TDBLookupListBox and/or TDBLookupComboBox components. In this way, you can limit users to a list of values from which they can select. For more information, see "TDBLookupListBox" and "TDBLookupComboBox" in Delphi help.

A Win32 API function failed

See "EOutOfResources."

Abstract Method Error

Possible Cause of Error

I. You may be attempting to execute a virtual abstract method. For example, you may have created a TCustomGrid descendent without overriding

TCustomGrid's virtual and abstract DrawCell method and then attempted to call that method.

2. Similar to #1 above, you may be attempting to call TStringGrid's Delete or Insert methods.

Quick Fix

I. You must override and implement any abstract virtual methods before calling them. For the TCustomGrid example, override the DrawCell method in your component declaration, like this:

```
. . .
protected
  procedure DrawCell(ACol, ARow: Longint; ARect:
      TRect; AState: TGridDrawState); override;
. . .
```

and then in the implementation, like this:

```
procedure TGridIron.DrawCell(ACol, ARow: Longint;
        ARect: TRect; AState: TGridDrawState);
begin
  {do it your way}
end;
```

2. Do not call Delete or Insert on a string grid, as these abstract virtual methods are not overridden in the TStrings descendent (TStringGridStrings) class that the Rows and Columns properties use.

Additional Information

Virtual methods can be overridden in descendent classes. Abstract virtual methods <u>must</u> be overridden in descendent classes. Be aware of these types of situations when deriving from a TCustomX component, as well as the TStrings object.

Abstract Methods must be virtual or dynamic

Possible Cause of Error

You may be attempting to declare an abstract method but have omitted the *virtual* or *dynamic* directive.

Quick Fix

Add the *virtual* or *dynamic* directive to the end of the method's declaration, prior to the *abstract* directive.

Additional Information

For "normal" (non-abstract) methods, the default method type is Static. For abstract methods, you must specify either *virtual* or *dynamic*. Abstract methods must be overridden; they are not defined in the class wherein they are declared. That is why this type of class is often referred to as a "base" class (other classes inherit from the base class, using it as a base from which to begin). The following three declarations are all acceptable:

```
procedure Radio(Interference: Variant);        {static method}
procedure Reality(Memory: Extended); virtual; {virtual method}
procedure Fluid(Duo: Boolean);dynamic;         {virtual dynamic method}
```

However, declaring an abstract method like the following will produce the error message under discussion:

```
procedure Extrapolate(Interpolate: Extended); abstract;
```

To avoid the error, declare the method in one of the two following ways:

```
procedure Extrapolate(Interpolate: Extended); virtual; abstract;
procedure Extrapolate(Interpolate: Extended); dynamic; abstract;
```

> **Note:** The *abstract* directive must follow (not precede) the *virtual* or *dynamic* directive.

For more information on the differences between and the advantages/disadvantages of using static, virtual, and dynamic methods in various circumstances, see "Dispatching Methods" in Delphi help.

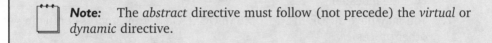

Access Violation (General Protection Fault)

Possible Cause of Error

This is a fairly generic, common, and serious error message.

1. You may be attempting to reference an object that does not exist yet or no longer exists. For example, you may be attempting to open a TTable in the main form's OnCreate event when the TTable is located in a form or module which has not been created yet (preferably a data module).

2. You may have created a component that references another component through one of its properties, but have not overridden the Notification method. For this reason, your component may still refer to a nonexistent component if you remove the referenced component from the form.

3. You may have placed a component on your form which fails to call "Inherited" in its constructor.

4. You may have published a property of data type Real in a component (in Delphi 1, 2, or 3, that is—Reals are allowed in Delphi 4, where they are implemented differently than in previous versions of Delphi). For example, the following will generate the error message under discussion (prior to Delphi 4):

```
unit NoRealityAllowed;
interface
uses WinTypes, WinProcs, Classes, Controls, Forms;
type
  TDontGetReal = class(TWinControl)
private
  FEstate: Real;
published
  Estate: Real read FEstate write FEstate;
end;
```

5. You may be passing an invalid parameter to a Windows API call. For example, you may be passing an invalid pointer as a buffer parameter.

6. You may be using pointers and are failing to allocate memory prior to accessing the pointer or are attempting to reference a pointer after the memory has been deallocated.

7. You may have a BDE SHAREDMEMLOCATION setting that is conflicting with other processes.

Quick Fix

1. Ensure that any objects you refer to have first been created and that you do not reference objects after they have been destroyed. For example, make sure that the form (or module) on which your object resides has been created (and has not been destroyed yet) when referencing any of its properties or methods.

2. Override the Notification method and set the property value to nil if the referenced component is removed from the form. For example, here are the pertinent parts necessary in implementing your Notification code:

```
TForTheTillerman = class(TComponent);
private
  FReferencedObject: TBird;
. . .
protected
```

```
      procedure Notification(AComponent: TComponent;
                  Operation: Toperation); override;
  . . .
  implementation
  . . .
  procedure TForTheTillerman.Notification(AComponent:
                  Tcomponent; Operation: Toperation);
  begin
    inherited Notification(AComponent, Operation);
    if (Operation = opRemove)
      and (AComponent = FReferencedObject) then
        FReferencedObject := nil;
  end;
```

3. If you have access to the component's source file (*.PAS), make sure that it overrides its ancestor's constructor in this way:

```
  public
    . . .
    constructor Create(AOwner: TComponent);
                                  override;
  . . .
  constructor TControl.Create(AOwner: TComponent);
  begin
    {this makes inherited methods and properties
      accessible and allocates memory for them}
    inherited Create(AOwner);
    . . .
```

4. If you need to use a "real" (floating-point) number in a component's Published section (in Delphi 1, 2, or 3), don't use the Real data type, but rather Single, Double, Extended, or Comp.

5. Refer to the Windows API help for information on the particular API call and the parameters and parameter types it expects. If you need more information than the minimalistic help file provides (a product of Microsoft, not Inprise!), see *The Tomes of Delphi 3: Win32 Core API* by John Ayres, et al, which provides a Delphi-centric view of Windows API calls with specific examples of how to use them from Delphi.

6. Allocate memory before referring to pointers, and deallocate the memory when you are finished with it. For example, you could allocate the memory in the unit's Initialization section, and free the memory in its Finalization section, like this:

```
  initialization
    New(ptrOne);
    New(ptrTwo);
    . . .
  end.
```

```
finalization
  Dispose(ptrOne);
  Dispose(ptrTwo);
  . . .
end;
```

If working with Delphi 1, there is no Finalization section available to you. You will have to dispose of the memory elsewhere, or create an exit procedure, like this:

```
procedure GarbageCollection; far;
begin
  Dispose(ptrOne);
  Dispose(ptrTwo);
  . . .
end;
initialization
  New(ptrOne);
  New(ptrTwo);
  . . .
  AddExitProc(GarbageCollection);
end.
```

7. If you are running Windows 95, enter a setting for SHAREDMEMLOCATION between 9000 and FFFF; if Windows NT, between 1000 and 7F00.

Note: If changing the settings via the BDE Configuration utility does not work, you can directly alter the system registry. To do so, follow these steps:

1. Select **Start | Run**.

2. Enter **RegEdit** and press **OK**.

3. Navigate to HKEY_LOCAL_MACHINE\Software\Borland\Database Engine\Settings\Init.

4. Edit the SHAREDMEMSIZE and/or SHAREDMEMLOCATION settings as noted above.

Additional Information

4. Note: The definition of the Real type has changed with Delphi 4, in which you can use Real types in the Published section. Formerly 48 bits, Real is now 64 bits and identical to a Double. If you need to use the old (48-bit) implementation of Real for backwards compatibility, use the $REALCOMPATIBILITY compiler switch.

Tip: If you have the "Break on Exception" flag set to True, you are more likely to be able to see where exactly in your code the problem is occurring. To verify that this option is set, select **Tools | Environment Options**. On the Preferences page, ensure that the Break on Exception check box in the Debugging section is on.

In Delphi 4, you can control how exceptions are handled on an exception-type by exception-type basis. Select **Tools | Debugger Options... | [Language Exceptions, OS Exceptions]** to modify these settings. See "Exceptions | Debugging" in Delphi 4 help for more information.

Note: You do not need to free forms which are created automatically by Delphi. Delphi will also handle the deallocation of the memory without your intervention. To see a list of the forms created automatically by Delphi, select **View | Project Manager** and then click the **Options** button. Forms that Delphi automatically allocates and deallocates memory for are in the Auto-Create Forms list. If any forms are listed in the Available Forms list, these are ones for which you should free memory. A project's main form is always created (and destroyed) automatically. In fact, all forms are by default created and destroyed automatically by Delphi.

Another way to see which forms are automatically created by Delphi is by selecting **View | Project Source** (**Project | View Source** in Delphi 4). All forms automatically created and destroyed by Delphi will be listed in the format:

```
Application.CreateForm(TForm1, Form1);
```

To create (and subsequently destroy) a form dynamically, follow these steps:

a. Select **View | Project Manager**.

b. Click the **Options** button.

c. In the Auto-Create Forms list box, select the form you want to create dynamically.

d. Click the right-arrow button to move the form to the Available Forms list.

e. Select the **OK** button.

f. Change the code you used to show the form to the following:

```
procedure TForm1.ShowAbout(Sender: Tobject);
begin
  About := TAbout.Create(Application);
  try
    About.ShowModal;
  finally
    About.Free;
    About := nil;
  end;
end;
```

However, if you attempt to show the About box before it is created, like this:

```
AboutBox.ShowModal:
AboutBox := TAboutBox.Create(Application);
AboutBox.Free;
```

or if you omit the Create call altogether, you will instead "create" the error message under discussion.

It is a good idea to dynamically create forms in code, especially when they may not be accessed every time your program is run. If you do not dynamically create your forms, they will all be automatically created by Delphi at startup. You will nearly always want Delphi to automatically create the main form for you, but you should consider postponing the creation of others until they are needed.

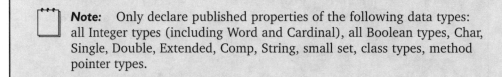

Note: Only declare published properties of the following data types: all Integer types (including Word and Cardinal), all Boolean types, Char, Single, Double, Extended, Comp, String, small set, class types, method pointer types.

> **Note:** The definition of the Real type has changed with Delphi 4, in which you can use Real types in the Published section. Formerly 48 bits, Real is now 64 bits and identical to a Double. If you need to use the old (48-bit) implementation of Real for backwards compatibility, use the $REALCOMPATIBILITY compiler switch or specify the old Real datatype by its new name Real48.

7. See "BDE Initialization Error $2501."

Ambiguous Overloaded Call to < >

Possible Cause of Error

You may have used a combination of method overloading and default parameters (both new with Delphi 4), and then made a call to the procedure or function which could apply to either of these overloaded methods. For example, if you declare the following overloaded methods:

```
procedure PTBoat(I: Integer; J: Integer = 0);
                               overload;
procedure PTBoat(Size: Integer); overload;
. . .
```

and then attempt to call either of them like this:

```
procedure TForm1.Button1Click(Sender: Tobject);
begin
  PTBoat(109)
end;
```

you will get this error message, as it is impossible for the compiler to determine which of the two procedures you are calling.

Quick Fix

You can call the method that uses default parameters by supplying the second parameter (even when its value is the same as the default value provided in its declaration), like this:

```
procedure TForm1.Button1Click(Sender: Tobject);
begin
  PTBoat(109,0) { calls second PTBoat method }
end;
```

Additional Information

The "workaround" shown above is not the recommended approach, as you would still be unable to call the "other" PTBoat method. It is best to avoid using same-named (overloaded) methods together with methods that use default parameters unless the method signatures differ enough so as to cause no confusion (human or machine) when calling either method.

An error occurred while attempting to initialize the Borland Database Engine (error <>)

If the error code is $2C08, see "Not initialized for accessing network files."

If the error code is $2C09, see "SHARE not loaded. It is required to share local files."

If the error code is $2108, see "Cannot locate IDAPI32.DLL."

If the error code is $2109, see "Cannot load IDAPI32.DLL."

Another file named <> is already on the search path

See "Another file with the same base name (<>) is already on the search path" below.

Another file with the same base name (<>) is already on the search path

Possible Cause of Error

You may be attempting to install a component into the VCL for which you already have a version installed (or a different component with the same name is already installed).

Quick Fix

If you are replacing an older version of a component with a new version, first remove the older version from your component library before installing the new version.

If the file is not a new version of an existing file, but has the same name as an existing file (and you want to retain the original, same-named file in your component library), simply change the name and attempt to install it again.

Additional Information

> **Note:**   Depending on your version of Delphi, the exact text of this error message may be "Another file named < > is already on the search path."

To remove an existing component from your component library, follow these steps:

Delphi 1 and 2

To remove a component, follow these steps:

1. Select **Component | Configure Palette...**.
2. In the Pages list box on the left side of the dialog box that displays, highlight the page that contains the component you want to delete. Its constituent components will display in the Components list box on the right.
3. Highlight the component you want to delete.
4. Select the **Delete** button.
5. Select the **OK** button.

Delphi 3

There are two methods you can use to remove a component in Delphi 3:

You can remove it from a particular palette:

1. Select **Component | Configure Palette**.
2. Highlight the palette page on which the component resides in the Pages list box.
3. Click on the component in the Components list box (it is not enough for the component to simply be highlighted—you must click it to avoid getting the "A Page Must Be Empty Before It Can Be Deleted" error message).
4. Select the **Delete** button.

or you can remove a component from a particular package:

1. Select **Project | Options**, and then click the Packages page.
2. In the Design Packages section of the Packages page, highlight the package in which the component you want to delete resides (to see which components are contained in each package, select the **Components** button).
3. Select the **Edit** button (do not select the Remove button unless you want to get rid of the entire package).
4. Select **Yes** in the confirmation dialog box that displays.
5. Right-click the unit that you want to remove and select **Remove Unit** from the context menu.

To locate the file with the same name as the one you are attempting to install, select **Tools | Environment Options...** and then inspect the Library path on the Library page to ascertain the search path Delphi is using. You can then search for the file in those directories using Windows Explorer's searching features.

Delphi 4

You can either hide a component so that it does not appear on the component palette, or you can delete the package in which it resides.

To prevent a component from appearing on a particular palette ("hide" it), follow these steps:

1. Select **Component | Configure Palette**.
2. Highlight the palette page on which the component resides in the Pages list box.
3. Click on the component in the Components list box (it is not enough for the component to simply be highlighted—you must click it to avoid getting the "A Page Must Be Empty Before It Can Be Deleted" error message).
4. Select the **Hide** button.

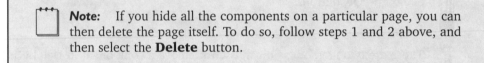

> **Note:** If you hide all the components on a particular page, you can then delete the page itself. To do so, follow steps 1 and 2 above, and then select the **Delete** button.

To remove a component from a particular package, follow these steps:

1. Select **Project | Options**, and then click the Packages page.
2. In the Design Packages section of the Packages page, highlight the package in which the component you want to delete resides (to see which components are contained in each package, select the **Components** button).
3. Select the **Remove** button.

Application is not licensed to use this feature

Possible Cause of Error

You may be attempting to run a demo program included with Delphi Client/Server from the Standard or Professional edition.

Quick Fix

If you do not own Delphi Client/Server, you will either have to desist from attempting to run the demo program, or purchase the Client/Server edition.

If you do own Delphi Client/Server and yet get this error message, you will first have to uninstall Delphi and then reinstall by following these steps:

1. Select **Start | Settings | Control Panel | Add/Remove Programs**.
2. On the Install/Uninstall page, select the version of Delphi that you have on your system.
3. Select the **OK** button and follow the prompts.
4. Reinstall Delphi Client/Server.

Additional Information

As the different editions of Delphi differ in features and components, you cannot necessarily "mix and match" projects created with different editions. This is also true between versions. That is, you cannot normally compile a project created in 32-bit Delphi in Delphi 1 (without some modification). Consult the Delphi home page on Inprise's web site (**http://www.inprise.com**) for specific information on the differences in features and components between the various editions of Delphi.

See "Your application is not enabled for use with this driver."

Arithmetic Overflow Error

Possible Cause of Error

You may be attempting to assign a number to an integer variable that is greater than the integer type's capacity to represent, or store. For example, you will get this error if you attempt to assign the value 256 to a variable of type Byte.

Quick Fix

When you declare variables, verify that they are suitable for all possible values you might want to store in them. For example, if a particular variable may hold values up to 100,000, do not use a Word variable type, but rather an Integer (LongInt in Delphi 1).

Additional Information

This exception is Runtime Error 215. This exception is only raised if you have enabled Overflow checking in the IDE or in code.

To enable Overflow checking in the IDE, follow these steps:

Delphi 1

Select **Options | Project**, and on the Compiler page, verify that the Overflow checking check box is checked (try saying that several times quickly).

32-bit Delphi

Select **Project | Options**, and on the Compiler page, verify that the Overflow checking (Q) check box is checked (try saying that several times quickly).

To turn on Overflow checking in code, add **{$Q+}** to the top of the unit(s) where you want it.

 Note: To see all the compiler directive settings in your unit, press **Ctrl+O+O** (that's the letter "Oh," not the numeral "Zero"). They will display at the top of your unit.

Array type required

Possible Cause of Error

You may be attempting to access an index while referencing an identifier which is not an array type.

Quick Fix

Ensure that you only access into indexes when referring to arrays.

Additional Information

The following will produce the error message under discussion because an attempt is made to assign to an element in the variable RuggedIndividualist, which is not an array, and thus has no elements to index into:

```
procedure IndexIntoTheArray(element: integer);
var
  RuggedIndividualist: integer;
begin
  RuggedIndividualist[1] := element;
end;
```

Assertion failed

Possible Cause of Error

A Boolean statement passed to the Assert function returned False.

Quick Fix

If the assertion should be True, go through your code to ascertain why it is failing.

Additional Information

If the statement needs to be True for the program to run effectively or to provide valid results, halt the program if an assertion fails.

Here is an example of how you can use the Assert procedure:

```
procedure ScrutinizePayCheck(amtpaid, amtexpected: Currency);
begin
  try
    assert(amtpaid >= amtexpected,'Dadburn it!
      What in Sam Hill''s goin'' on here!?!');
  except
    on EAssertionFailed do
      Halt;
  end;
end;
```

The optional string parameter is the error message displayed if the assertion fails.

Assignment to FOR-Loop variable < >

Possible Cause of Error

You may be attempting to assign a value to the loop control variable inside the *for* loop (in other words, after the *do*) in 32-bit Delphi.

Quick Fix

Remove the assignment to the *for* loop control variable following the *do* reserved word.

Additional Information

 Note: Assigning to the *for* loop control variable is legal in Delphi 1.

The "*for* loop control variable" is the variable (commonly an integer declared as "i") to which you assign an initial value as the starting number which partly determines how many times the *for* loop will execute. This value is usually initialized to 0. The final value, normally a variable, determines the number of iterations at which the *for* loop will stop. For example, here is a simple *for* loop with its elements noted in the comments:

```
procedure SimpleLoop(TimesToLoop: integer);
var
  i: integer; {i is the control loop variable}
  s: string;
begin
  s := '';
  for i := 0 to TimesToLoop do {0 is the initial
          value, TimesToLoop is the final value}
    s := s + IntToStr(i); {nonsense statement}
end;
```

The following, however, is not acceptable and will produce the error message under discussion:

```
procedure BadLoop(TimesToLoop: integer);
var
  i: integer;
begin
  for i := 0 to TimesToLoop do
    i := i + IntToStr(i); {assigning to control
                loop variable 'i' is not allowed}
end;
```

If you want to conditionally break out of a *for* loop based on the value of the *for* loop control variable, test the value and call the Exit or Break procedure if the value is beyond the range within which you want to perform the loop action. You can do this in the following way:

```
procedure SimpleLoop(TimesToLoop: integer);
var
  i: integer;
  s: string[10];
begin
  s := '';
```

```
    for i := 0 to TimesToLoop do
      begin
        if i > 10 then Break;
        s := s + IntToStr(i);
      end;
end;
```

At End of Table

Possible Cause of Error

You may have attempted to access the OldValue property of a field when adding or inserting a new record in CachedUpdates mode. Since there is no older version of this record, trying to access the old value is an impossibility.

Quick Fix

Before attempting to access the OldValue property, determine first if that is feasible by checking to see if the DataSet's state is dsEdit, like this:

```
if Table1.State = dsEdit then
  FogieVal := OldValue;
```

Alternatively, you can enclose the attempt to ready the OldValue in a *try...except* block, like this:

```
try
  GeezerVal := OldValue;
except
  MessageBox('no old value available -
              this is a new record');
  Abort;
end;
```

Additional Information

When using Cached Updates, the "cached" records are referred to as the "old values." This allows you to cancel edits made, returning the data to its prior condition (with the "old values" regaining their status as the current values).

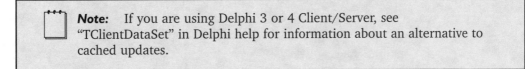

Note: If you are using Delphi 3 or 4 Client/Server, see "TClientDataSet" in Delphi help for information about an alternative to cached updates.

Bad global symbol definition: < > in object file < >

Possible Cause of Error

You may have linked an object (.OBJ) file into your program that contains a definition for a symbol that was not declared in Pascal as an external procedure. The symbol may have been declared as a variable.

Quick Fix

Ignore the error if the definition specified in the error message is not necessary for your purposes, or edit the .OBJ file.

Additional Information

If you receive this error message, the definition in the object (.OBJ) file causing the error will be ignored.

 Note: All compiler directives, except switch directives, must have at least one space between the directive name and the parameters.

The $L and $LINK directives are interchangeable and are used to link in procedures and functions written in other languages and declared therein as external.

The syntax used is:

```
$L[INK] [Filepath]FILENAME
```

For example, if you want to link in the file CBUILDER.OBJ that resides in the Delphi search path, you could enter either of the following:

```
$L CBUILDER
$LINK CBUILDER
```

If you do not prepend a path to the filename, Delphi will look in the same directory as the current module, followed by the path specified in Tools | Environment Options... | Library | Library Path.

Bad packaged unit format: < >.< >

Possible Cause of Error

The file named in the error message may be corrupt. It could be the result of an abnormal compiler termination during the writing of the package file, perhaps as a result of a loss of power at that time.

Quick Fix

Delphi 3

Move or delete the offending .DCP file named in the error message and recompile the package.

Delphi 4

Move or delete the offending .DCP file named in the error message and reinstall the package.

Additional Information

To recompile the package after deleting the .DCP file, follow these steps:

1. Select **Component | Install Packages...**.
2. Highlight the appropriate package in the Design Packages Checklist box.
3. Select the **Edit** button.
4. Select the **Yes** button in the confirm dialog box.
5. Select the Compile icon.

If you continue to receive the same error message after deleting the corrupt file and recompiling the package, contact Inprise. Refer to the back of your Delphi CD for the phone number or select **Help | Inprise Programs and Services** to link to their web site.

Bad unit format: < >

Possible Cause of Error

A compiled unit (.DCU) file has likely become corrupt.

Quick Fix

Recompile the unit source (.PAS) file to produce a new compiled unit (.DCU) file.

Additional Information

If the .DCU is a component file, follow these steps to recompile the unit source (.PAS) file to produce a new unit object (.DCU) file:

1. Select the following based on your version of Delphi:
   Delphi 1: **Options | Install Components**
   Delphi 2: **Component | Install**
   Delphi 3 and 4: **Component | Install Component**

2. Select the appropriate page in the Install Component dialog box (Into Existing Package or Into New Package), based on where you want to install the component.

3. Select the **Browse** button.

4. In the Unit File Name dialog box, navigate to and then highlight the .PAS file.

5. Select the **Open** button.

6. Select the **OK** button in the Install Component dialog box.

If the .DCU file is a regular unit object file (not a component file), follow these steps to recompile the unit source (.PAS) file to produce a new unit object (.DCU) file:

1. Delete the .DCU file (or move it to a file other than the file wherein the project to which it belongs exists).

2. Load the project of which the corresponding .PAS unit is a constituent part.

3. Recompile the project (F9).

If recompiling the source file does not solve the problem, uninstalling and then reinstalling Delphi may.

BDE Initialization Error $2501

Possible Cause of Error

You may be using the TDatabase or TSession component in a multi-tier application and need to modify the SHAREDMEMLOCATION and/or SHAREDMEMSIZE settings.

Quick Fix

Change the SHAREDMEMLOCATION and SHAREDMEMSIZE settings in the BDE Configuration utility (System page/System | Init node). Increase the setting for SHAREDMEMSIZE to 4096 or 8192 (it is 2048 by default).

If you are running Windows 95, enter a setting for SHAREDMEMLOCATION between 9000 and FFFF; if Windows NT, between 1000 to 7F00. Try 1000 first. After changing the setting, shut down all applications that use the BDE. It may be necessary to try several settings before finding one that works for you.

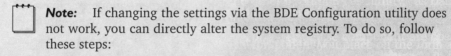

Note: If changing the settings via the BDE Configuration utility does not work, you can directly alter the system registry. To do so, follow these steps:

1. Select **Start | Run**.

2. Enter **RegEdit** and press **OK**.

3. Navigate to HKEY_LOCAL_MACHINE\Software\Borland\Database Engine\Settings\Init.

4. Edit the SHAREDMEMSIZE and/or SHAREDMEMLOCATION settings as noted above.

Additional Information

This error corresponds to "Insufficient Memory for this Operation."

See the BDE help file for more information.

Before you can deploy, you must complete the Web Deployment page of the Project|Web Deploy Options dialog

Possible Cause of Error

You may have selected Project | Web Deploy without supplying all the necessary information in the Projects page of the Web Deploy Options dialog box (there is no "Web Deployment" page, the text of the error message notwithstanding).

Quick Fix

Select OK to dismiss the error message and return to the Projects page of the Web Deploy Options dialog box (Project | Web Deploy Options). You must provide entries in the Target Dir, Target URL, and HTML Dir edit boxes.

Additional Information

Besides the required entries on the Projects page, there are also other options you can choose and specify there as well as on the Packages, Additional Files, and Code Signing pages of the Web Deploy Options dialog box.

The Web Deploy Options and Web Deploy menu items are unavailable if you don't have a project open or you are working with a "conventional" type of project.

Bitmap image is not valid

Possible Cause of Error

You may be loading a file into a TImage's Picture property that, although it has a .BMP extension, is not in actuality a .BMP file.

The .BMP file may be corrupt.

Quick Fix

Ensure that any file you attempt to load into a TImage component's Picture property is indeed a valid graphics file.

Additional Information

Delphi provides native support for four graphic file formats, namely .BMP (bitmap), .ICO (icon), .WMF (Windows MetaFile), and .EMF (Enhanced MetaFile).

It may be that somebody changed a file's extension so that it appears to be a bitmap file based on its file extension (but it is not in actuality a bitmap file).

Bits index out of range

Possible Cause of Error

You may have attempted to reference an element of a Boolean array which is greater than the size of the TBits object or less than 0. For example, both assignments to the variable *little* in the code snippet below cause this error message, as the first is trying to access an index beyond the size of the TBits object, and the second attempts to access an index less then 0:

```
procedure TForm1.BitsUnderOverExample(Sender: TObject);
var
  kibbles: TBits;
  little: Boolean;
begin
  kibbles := TBits.Create;
  try
    kibbles.Size := 7;
    little := kibbles.Bits[8];
    little := kibbles.Bits[-1];
  finally
    kibbles.Free;
end;
```

Quick Fix

Do not assign to a negative number or a number equal to or greater than TBits' Size property. If you do not explicitly set the Size property, it will automatically expand as necessary to hold the values you assign to the Bits array of Boolean.

Additional Information

The "Bits" referred to in the error message is the TBit object's array of Boolean values.

In the example above, attempting to assign to the element 7 in the array would also create the error message, as the index is 0-based (and thus a Size of 7 creates elements 0, 1, 2, 3, 4, 5, and 6 only).

 Tip: You can use TBits to store the values of multiple check boxes. See "TBits" in Delphi help for more information.

BLOb has been modified

Possible Cause of Error

1. Multiple applications may be accessing a table from a machine running Windows 95 that has either version 4.00.1111 or version 4.00.1113 of Microsoft's Virtual Network Redirector file (VREDIR.VXD).

2. You may be attempting to display the contents of a TBlob field (such as a Paradox Formatted Memo) in a TDBRichEdit control.

Quick Fix

1. Replace the "bad" version of VREDIR.VXD. The original release (4.00.950) and 4.00.1116 do not cause the problem. VREDIR.VXD should be located in C:\Windows\System. You can download an updated file from Microsoft's web site.

2. Use a Paradox Memo field (TMemo field in Delphi) instead of Formatted Memo if you want to display the contents in a TDBRichEdit control. You can then programmatically format the contents of the TRichEdit control.

Additional Information

1. All users may be affected if any user has the "bad" version of VREDIR.VXD (even if they personally have a "good" version of the file on their machine).

2. Here is a table of Paradox data types and their corresponding Delphi TField descendents:

Paradox data type	Delphi TField descendent
Alpha	TStringField
Autoincrement	TAutoIncField
BCD	TBCDField
Binary	TBlobField
Byte	TBytesField
Date	TDateField
Formatted Memo	TBlobField
Graphic	TGraphicField
Logical	TBooleanField
Long Integer	TIntegerField
Memo	TMemoField
Money	TCurrencyField
Number	TFloatField
OLE	TBlobField
Short	TSmallIntField
Time	TTimeField
Timestamp	TDateTimeField

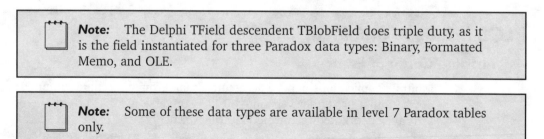

Note: The Delphi TField descendent TBlobField does triple duty, as it is the field instantiated for three Paradox data types: Binary, Formatted Memo, and OLE.

Note: Some of these data types are available in level 7 Paradox tables only.

Break or continue outside of loop

Possible Cause of Error

You may be calling the Break or Continue procedures outside of a *for*, *while*, or *repeat* loop.

Quick Fix

Only call Break or Continue inside *for*, *while*, and *repeat* loops. Extend a *for* or *while* loop, if necessary, by adding a Begin...End section after the *do* statement. (*Repeat* loops already consider the entire block between the *repeat* and *until* a composite statement and therefore do not need to be encased in a Begin...End block.)

Additional Information

The following will produce the error message under discussion:

```
procedure SaturdayNightAtTheMovies;
begin
  while WatchingMovie do
    EatPopcorn;
  if TheaterCatchesFire then
    Break;
end;
```

To prevent the error message, enclose the call to the Break or Continue procedure in a Begin...End pair, like this:

```
procedure SaturdayNightAtTheMovies;
begin
  while WatchingMovie do
  begin
    EatPopcorn;
    if TheaterCatchesFire then
      Break; {now this is part of the loop}
  end;
end;
```

The same, of course, applies to the Continue procedure. For more information about *for*, *while*, and *repeat* statements, see "Writing Loops" in Delphi help.

There are four flow control procedures that you may want to use in various circumstances: Continue, Break, Exit, and Halt. Additionally, the TApplication class has a Terminate procedure.

To explain these procedures in a nutshell, Continue kicks you back to the top of the loop; Break kicks you out of the loop; Exit kicks you out of the procedure or function; and Halt kicks you out of the entire program (as does Application.Terminate).

Now let's examine these flow control procedures in more detail:

A call to the Continue procedure returns the flow of control back to the top of the *for, while,* or *repeat* statement. In other words, the next iteration of the flow control statement is immediately begun when the Continue procedure is called. By way of example, note the comments in the code below:

```
function OneForTheThumb: Boolean;
var
  i: integer;
begin
  i := 0;
  Result := False;
  repeat
    Play(RegularSeasonGames);
    if not WinTheDivision then
      Continue; {continue over again}
    Play(Playoffs);
    if not WinThePlayoffs then
      Continue; {continue from the top}
    Play(ChampionshipGame);
    if not WinTheChampionshipGame then
      Continue; {once more with feeling}
    i := i + 1;
  until i = 5;
  Result := True;
end;
```

A call to the Break procedure causes the flow of control to "break out of" a *for, while,* or *repeat* loop and resume at the next statement after the loop.

By way of example, note the comments in the following example:

```
procedure ForAllTheTeaInChina(widgets: integer);
var
  i: integer;
  s: string;
begin
  for i := 0 to widgets do
    begin
      if i >= 1000 then
        Break;     {for loop is "broken out of"}
      s := IntToStr(i); {if i >= 1000, this line is skipped}
```

```
      end;
    Order('TsingTao', i * 2);
    Order('HotPepperBeefStick', i);
end;
```

> **Note:** Calling the Break procedure within a *try...finally* block will not bypass the code following the *finally* clause.

A call to the Exit procedure immediately passes control from the current procedure back to the calling procedure, where program execution will resume from the line following the call to the procedure that called Exit.

As an example, a call to Exit in the following code will cause the procedure CheckItOut to be exited and the line x will be called immediately thereafter:

```
type
  TGenre = (BaroqueChamber,Blues,CountryRock,
            Disco,Opera,Rap,Reggae,Rock,Soul);
. . .
procedure CheckItOut(MusicStyle: TGenre);
begin
  if MusicStyle in [Disco..Rap] then
    Exit {resumes at "CashItOut" line below}
  else if MusicStyle in [BaroqueChamber..CountryRock] then
    ListenToTheMusic
  else if MusicStyle in [Reggae..Soul] then
    DanceToTheMusic
  else
    ShowMessage('What in the world?');
end;
procedure DetermineCourseOfAction;
begin
  CheckItOut(Soul);
  CashItOut(Retirement);
end;
```

Calling TApplication's Terminate procedure causes an orderly shutdown of your program, but it does not necessarily stop your application immediately. Here is an example of how to use this procedure:

```
procedure StopInTheNameOfTheLaw;
begin
  if YouNeedToShutDownTheApp then
    Application.Terminate; {This performs an immediate shutdown
                            of your program}
end;
```

See "Application | Terminate" in Delphi help for more information.

Calling the Halt procedure causes an abnormal termination of the program and returns to the operating system. Here is an example of the use of this procedure:

```
procedure StopInTheNameOfTheLaw;
begin
  if YouNeedToQuitNowAndIMeanNow then
    Halt; {This performs an immediate shutdown of your program}
end;
```

"Normal" termination of a program takes place automatically when the main form closes (you do not need to call it).

Breakpoint is set on line that may have been removed by the optimizer or contains no debug information. Run anyway?

Possible Cause of Error

You may be attempting to set a breakpoint on a line in your source file for which the compiler did not generate code; therefore, it cannot stop there.

Quick Fix

Remove the breakpoint. Set breakpoints only on lines that generate code, such as assignment statements.

Additional Information

Delphi's optimizer may have "removed" the line in question (obviously not by deleting the lines you have written, but just as far as the compiler is concerned) because the code is never called in your application.

One example of where you might see the error message under discussion is if you attempt to run to a location in the Interface section of a unit. Normally you would not try this; other examples (within the Implementation section) are the first line of a procedure, a variable declaration line(s), etc.

> **Note:** In Delphi 3 and 4, it is easy to see on which lines it is permissible to set breakpoints. They are marked with a blue diamond in the "gutter" at the left of the code window.

In the following procedure, the lines which produce the error message under discussion (if you set a breakpoint on them) are noted in the comments with a "not here!" comment:

```
procedure SaturdayNightAtTheMovies; {not here!}
begin
  while WatchingMovie do
  begin           {not here!}
    EatPopcorn;
    TheaterCatchesFire := OLearysCowIsHere;
    if TheaterCatchesFire then
      Break;
  end;            {not here!}
end;
```

Note: Breakpoints are used to pause program execution at a location(s) designated by you while debugging. You can then view the values your variables contain at that point in your program's "life."

Using Delphi's integrated debugging environment, you can not only set breakpoints, but also add watches, evaluate and modify variables, and examine the call stack.

For more information about these tools, see "Using Breakpoints," "Setting Breakpoints," "Working with Breakpoints," "Modifying Breakpoint Properties," "Watching Expressions," "Evaluating and Modifying Expressions," "Pausing the Program," "Navigating to Function Calls," "Viewing Function Calls," "Running to the Cursor Location," "Starting a Debugging Session," "Stepping Through Code," and "Restarting the Program" in Delphi help.

Note: If you are using Delphi 3 or 4, you benefit from another debugging tool called Tool-Tip Expression Evaluation. This works like a dynamic "watch window." When your application is stopped while debugging, simply hold the mouse over any variable or property name in the code editor. A pop-up window displays the current value of the variable or property.

Note: If you are using Delphi 4, you can also take advantage of a CPU window, Event Log, and Modules Windows. Select **View | Debug Windows** to examine these options.

Call to Application.CreateForm is missing or incorrect

Possible Cause of Error

You may have modified the project (.DPR) file's Application.CreateForm( ) line.

Quick Fix

Ensure that the project file (select **View | Project Source**—Project | View Source in Delphi 4—to inspect the project file's source code) contains the following syntax in loading at least the program's main form (there may be multiple similar lines opening a variety of forms):

```
Application.CreateForm(TForm1, Form1);
```

Additional Information

 Note: .DLLs are also contained in .DPR files, but they do not have a corresponding form and so do not contain a call to create the project's main form as shown above.

All subsequent forms (other than the main form) can be loaded dynamically as needed. This amortizes the cost of opening the forms over a greater period of time, and some forms (such as the About box, if you have one) may not be opened at all.

To create (and subsequently destroy) a form dynamically, follow these steps:

1. Select **View | Project Manager**.
2. Click the **Options** button.
3. In the Auto-Create Forms list box, select the form you want to create dynamically.
4. Click the right-arrow button to move the form to the Available Forms list.
5. Select the **OK** button.
6. Change the code you used to show the form to the following:

```
procedure TForm1.ShowAbout(Sender: Tobject);
begin
  About := TAbout.Create(Application);
  try
    About.ShowModal;
  finally
    About.Free;
```

```
        About := nil;
      end;
    end;
```

However, if you attempt to show the About box before it is created, like this:

```
AboutBox.ShowModal:
AboutBox := TAboutBox.Create(Application);
AboutBox.Free;
```

or if you leave out the Create call altogether, you will instead create the error message under discussion.

It is a good idea to dynamically create forms in code, especially when they may not be accessed every time your program is run. If you do not dynamically create your forms, they will all be automatically created by Delphi at startup. You will always want Delphi to automatically create the main form for you, but you might consider postponing the creation of others until they are needed.

Call to RegisterClass is missing or incorrect

Possible Cause of Error

The text of the error message notwithstanding, the real source of the problem may be that you commented out or deleted the final *end*. (the one that should be terminated with a period, or dot, rather than a semicolon appended) in a unit.

Quick Fix

Ensure that the final *end*. is intact and not commented out. Verify that every *begin* has a matching *end*, and that all comments begun with a left curly brace ({) are paired with a matching right curly brace (}).

Additional Information

The RegisterClass procedure is distinct from the RegisterComponents procedure, which is used in component units to specify the name of the component and the page on which it is to be placed (or, if the page does not exist, the page which will be created to house the component).

Can't change value while socket is active

Possible Cause of Error

1. You may be attempting to change the value of the Address, Host, Port, or Service properties of a TClientSocket component while its Active property is set to True.

2. You may be attempting to change the value of the Port or Service properties of the TServerSocket component while its Active property is set to True.

Quick Fix

1, 2. Turn the Active property to False, make the change(s), and then set the Active property back to True.

Additional Information

The TClientSocket component is new with Delphi 4, as are all the components on the Internet page. Previous versions of Delphi had an Internet page on the component palette, but these were ActiveX controls; the new set of components are native Delphi controls.

Can't load [complib.dcl, cmplib32.dcl, vcl30.dpl, vcl40.dpl]

Possible Cause of Error

1. You may have moved or deleted the file named in the error message.

2. The Delphi VCL may have become corrupted due to changes you made to the VCL source code.

3. You may have unsuccessfully attempted to install a component into your VCL.

4. You may be attempting to install a component which references another component or a .DLL which is not available or not on the computer's search path.

Quick Fix

> **Note:** The following are the filenames and default locations for the various versions of Delphi:
>
> Delphi 1: **COMPLIB.DCL** in C:\Borland\Delphi\BIN
> Delphi 2: **CMPLIB32.DCL** in C:\Program Files\Borland\Delphi 2\BIN
> Delphi 3: **VCL30.DPL** in C:\Windows\System
> Delphi 4: **VCL40.DPL** in C:\Windows\System

1. Check to ensure that your component library file resides in the appropriate location based on your version of Delphi. If you find the file elsewhere, move it to the expected location given above and attempt to recompile the library (Delphi 1 and 2) or package (Delphi 3) or reinstall the package (Delphi 4). If the file already is in the correct location but you receive this error message anyway, follow these steps:

    a. Make a backup copy of the file (COMPLIB.DCL, CMPLIB32.DCL, VCL30.DPL, or VCL40.DPL) and store it in a safe place.

    b. Delete the "original" copy of the file you just backed up.

    c. If you had previously made changes to the file, Delphi will have created a backup of the file prior to recompilation, replacing the first letter of the extension with a tilde (~) and truncating the last letter of the extension. In Delphi 1, this file is COMPLIB.~DC; in Delphi 2, it is CMPLIB32.~DC, etc. If you have the file appropriate to your version of Delphi on your system, you can rename the file as appropriate for your version of Delphi and restore it to its former exalted position as Delphi's component library file. If you had not made previous changes to the file, or the backup file no longer exists, copy the file from the Delphi CD to the location appropriate for your version of Delphi.

> **Note:** In Delphi 3 and 4, you should not attempt to modify this file. When you add components, install them into the dclusr package (Dclusr40 in Delphi 4) or a new package you create. If you need to reinstall VCL30.DPL or VCL40.DPL, copy it from the Delphi CD to the C:\Windows\System directory.

> **Note:** You will have to reinstall all the components you added to your component library file if you restore from the CD, but if you do not have an older version of the file, this is your only recourse.

2. Rebuild or reinstall the component library.

3. Follow steps a-c above to reinstall the last good copy of the VCL.

4. Be sure to deploy all required modules with any components or programs you distribute.

Additional Information

In Delphi 1, the component library's filename was named COMPLIB.DCL. Its size was 1,036 KB. In Delphi 2, the component library file was renamed CMPLIB32.DCL. Its size was 4,636 KB. In Delphi 3 and 4, there are no files with a .DCL extension. Instead of one single unit containing the entire VCL, several packages consisting of related components are provided. The "main" package, which contains the most common components and units you will need for a typical Delphi project, are contained in a .DPL (Delphi package library) file. In Delphi 3, VCL30.DPL is 1,257 KB. In Delphi 4, VCL40.DPL is 1,753. There are approximately 25 .DPL files in a full installation of Delphi 3. Delphi 4 introduces the .BPL file, of which there are 38 in the Client/Server version (as well as .DPL files).

Note: Other things that may pose a problem are not having enough virtual memory, which may be due to a lack of sufficent RAM and/or hard disk space, or a fragmented hard drive. Ensure that virtual memory is set up correctly on your system*. Purchase more RAM if possible. Leave at least 10 percent of your hard drive free. Defrag the hard drive if it needs it. If all else fails, uninstall and then reinstall Delphi. Don't forget to (re)install any appropriate patches for your version of Delphi. To get the latest patches, visit Inprise's web site at **http://www.inprise.com**.

*If you seem to be having problems with virtual memory settings, you can allow Windows to automatically adjust virtual memory for you by following these steps:

1. Select **Start | Settings | Control Panel**.

2. Double-click the System icon.

3. Select the Performance Page.

4. Select the **Virtual Memory** button.

5. Check the Let Windows manage my virtual memory settings radio button.

Note: The extension for the component library file has changed from .DCL (Delphi Component Library) in Delphi 1 and 2 to .DPL (Delphi Package Library) in Delphi 3 and 4.

Can't load package <>.<>

Possible Cause of Error

1. It may be that the package referenced in the error message (or a package or .DLL that it relies on) is not installed, or not installed in the correct location.

2. You may be attempting to load a package that relies on another package or .DLL that, while it <u>does</u> exist on your system (and in the correct location), is not the expected version.

Quick Fix

1. Ensure that all required packages and .DLLs are located in the current directory or on the Windows or network search path (preferably in the \Windows\System directory).

2. If you make changes to a package that another package depends on, recompile <u>both</u> packages (the one that is required by the other one first).

Additional Information

Delphi packages are specialized .DLLs (with a .DPL extension) that made their debut with Delphi 3. See "About Packages" in Delphi help for more information.

Can't write .EXE file. Disk full?

Possible Cause of Error

You may not have enough RAM or virtual memory available.

Quick Fix

Try these progressively more "drastic" solutions in sequence until one of them works:

1. Exit Delphi; restart Delphi; try to compile the application again.

2. Exit Windows; restart Windows (warm boot); restart Delphi; attempt to compile the application again.

3. Exit Windows; turn off the computer (cold boot); wait a couple of minutes; restart the computer (and Windows); restart Delphi; attempt to compile the application again.

4. If hard disk space is at a minimum (less than 10 percent of the total size of the drive is free), delete all unnecessary files. Once you have freed up space on your hard drive (for use as virtual memory), defrag your hard drive and then try to compile the application again.

5. Verify that virtual memory is configured correctly on your system (see "Additional Information" below).

6. Buy more RAM.

Additional Information

If you seem to be having problems with virtual memory settings, you can allow Windows to automatically adjust virtual memory for you by following these steps:

1. Select **Start | Settings | Control Panel**.
2. Double-click the System icon.
3. Select the Performance Page.
4. Select the **Virtual Memory** button.
5. Check the Let Windows manage my virtual memory settings radio button.

Cannot add a session to the form or data module while session < > has AutoSessionName enabled

Possible Cause of Error

You may already have a TSession component on a form or data module with its AutoSessionName property set to True.

Quick Fix

If you are going to add multiple TSession components to a form or data module, you must set their AutoSessionName property to False.

Additional Information

In a typical application, you will not need to even place a single TSession component on your form or data module. A TSession component is needed for database connectivity, but it is created for you automatically, similar to the Application component which is automatically created for you for each program you develop.

If you are creating multi-threaded applications or if you are accessing Paradox tables residing in various places on a network, though, you can drop additional TSession components on your form or data module to facilitate operating under these special circumstances.

The purpose of the AutoSessionName property is to guarantee developers of multi-threaded applications that sessions spawned for each thread are unique at run time. The AutoSessionName property, when set to True, automatically generates a unique name for each new session.

See "AutoSessionName" in Delphi help for more information.

Cannot assign to a read-only property

Possible Cause of Error

You may be attempting to assign a value to a read-only property.

Quick Fix

Either add a *write* specifier for the property in question, or refrain from attempting to assign a value to it if it should remain read-only.

Additional Information

A property must have either a *read* specifier, a *write* specifier, or both. It is common practice to read from a private field (which, by convention, begins with the letter "F"), and to write to a procedure whose name begins with the word "Set." Here is an example of some possible ways to declare properties:

```
private
  FScottFitzgerald: String;
  FLeeBailey: Boolean;
  FAOSchwarz, FDR: Currency;
  FPSantangelo: Extended;
  procedure SetFee(i: Integer);
  procedure SetPrice(c: Currency);
public
  {this property is read-only}
  property ScottFitzgerald: String; read FScottFitzgerald;
  {this property is write-only}
  property LeeBailey: Boolean; write SetFee;
  {this property can both be
  read from and written to}
  property AOSchwarz: Currency; read FAOSchwarz; write SetPrice;
```

If you declare a property like ScottFitzgerald (which is a read-only property, as it has no *write* specifier in its declaration), and then attempt to write to it, like this:

```
ScottFitzgerald := 'The very rich are different than you and I';
```

you will get the error message under discussion.

Cannot break, continue, or exit out of a finally clause

Possible Cause of Error

You may have placed a call to Break, Continue, or Exit in the *finally* part of a *try...finally* statement.

Quick Fix

Remove the offending call from the *finally* part of the *try...finally* statement.

Additional Information

The *finally* part of a *try...finally* statement is guaranteed to always execute in full. Therefore, you cannot add flow control procedures such as Break, Continue, or Exit that would attempt to potentially prevent some of the code in the *finally* part from executing.

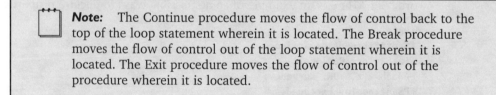

Note: The Continue procedure moves the flow of control back to the top of the loop statement wherein it is located. The Break procedure moves the flow of control out of the loop statement wherein it is located. The Exit procedure moves the flow of control out of the procedure wherein it is located.

Cannot change the size of an icon

Possible Cause of Error

You may be attempting to change the size of an icon. For example, the following code will generate this error:

```
Image1.Picture.Icon.Width := 23;
```

Quick Fix

Do not attempt to change the size of icon (.ICO) files. TIcon's height and width properties are read-only and uniform for all icons in Windows (32 pixels square for regular icons, 16 pixels square for small icons).

Additional Information

You can create icons (among other things) in Delphi's ImageEditor. Select **Tools | Image Editor** and then **File | New... | Icon File**.

You can also create .DCR files for custom components that you create. These need to be 24 pixels square. To do so, select **Tools | Image Editor**, then **File | New... | Bitmap File**, change both the width and height files to **24**, and select VGA (16 colors) unless you are positive all users of your component use Super VGA (256 colors) systems. 16-color images will be acceptable on systems configured for 256 colors, but 256-color images on systems configured for 16 colors may look bad.

Cannot change Visible in OnShow or OnHide

Possible Cause of Error

1. You may have been attempting to change a form's FormStyle property in its OnActivate or OnShow events. For example, the following will generate the error message under discussion:

```
procedure TForm1.FormShow(Sender: Tobject);
begin
  FormStyle := fsStayOnTop;
end;
```

2. You may have been attempting to set a form's Visible property during the form's OnActivate, OnShow, or OnHide events. For example, the following will produce the error message under discussion:

```
procedure TForm1.FormActivate(Sender: Tobject);
begin
  Visible := false;
end;
```

Quick Fix

1. Do not change a form's FormStyle property during the OnActivate or OnShow events.

2. Do not change a form's Visible property during the OnActivate, OnShow, or OnHide events.

Note: The Visible property of all forms is False by default. Delphi automatically sets them to True when the form is displayed. Normally, you will not need to set this property at all.

Additional Information

If you set a form's Visible property to True at design time, it will display immediately at run time. Delphi will automatically display your application's main form at startup, and all other forms when their Show or ShowModal methods are called. If you set the Visible property of all the forms in your application to True at design time, they will all display as soon as the application starts, which could leave you with a very cluttered desktop and confused user.

If you want a form to display in response to a particular event (a button click, for example) and remain on the screen while you work in other forms, you can do it this way:

```
procedure TForm1.Button12Click(Sender: Tobject);
begin
  Form3.Show;
end;
```

If you want the form to display but require a response from the user before he can continue working with other forms, you can do it this way:

```
procedure TForm1.Button12Click(Sender: Tobject);
begin
  Form3.ShowModal;
end;
```

This shows the form "modally," which is similar to a dialog box, which requires a response from the user, even if it is just to close the dialog box, before the user can resume working with other forms. An example of this type of form, or "dialog box," are Delphi's wrapper components for the "Windows common dialogs" on the Dialogs page of the Visual Component Palette (TOpenDialog, TSaveDialog, etc.).

You can also create forms dynamically, as they're needed. This conserves system resources and is especially useful when you have forms which may not be used on a given execution of your application, such as an About box.

To create a form dynamically, follow these steps:

1. Select **View | Project Manager**.
2. Click the **Options** button.
3. In the Auto-Create Forms list box, select the form you want to create dynamically.

4. Click the right-arrow button to move the form to the Available Forms list.

5. Select the **OK** button.

6. Change the code you used to show the form to the following:

```
procedure TForm1.Button12Click(Sender: Tobject);
begin
  Form3 := TForm3.Create(Application);
  try
    Form3.ShowModal;
  finally
    Form3.Free;
    Form3 := nil;
  end;
end;
```

> **Note:** If you omit step 6, you will get an access violation, as you would be trying to show a form that has not been created (for which no memory has been allocated).

Cannot connect, < > must contain a valid ServerName or ServerGUID

Possible Cause of Error

You may have attempted to set the Connect property of a TDCOMConnection, TMIDASConnection, or TRemoteServer property to True without having specified a valid value for the ServerName or ServerGUID property.

Quick Fix

Enter a valid GUID in the ServerGUID property in this format:

{00000002-0000-0000-C000-000000000046}

or enter the name of a registered server in the ServerName property.

Additional Information

If you provide a value for both the ServerName and ServerGUID properties, as long as one of them is valid, this error message will not display.

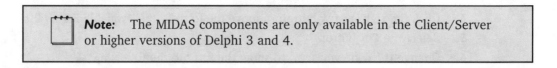

> **Note:** The MIDAS components are only available in the Client/Server or higher versions of Delphi 3 and 4.

Cannot connect to database < >

Possible Cause of Error

You may have attempted to connect to a database by one of the following methods:

a. You attempted to set a TDataBase component's Connected property to True, either at design time or at run time (in code).

b. You called a TDataBase or TTable component's Open method.

c. You attempted to set a TTable's Active property to True, either at design time or at run time (in code), and then selected the Cancel button as a response to the DataBase Login dialog box.

Quick Fix

Supply the password when the DataBase Login dialog box displays, and then select the OK button.

Additional Information

> **Note:** If you selected OK in the DataBase Login dialog box without entering the correct password, you would get the error message "Unknown user name or password. Unavailable database. Alias < >." See the "Unknown user name or password" entry for more information.

You can avoid continually entering a password while you're developing your application by either setting the password in code or via the TDataBase component's Parameter Overrides section.

To set the password in code, add a line like the following at a point in code prior to any attempt to access the database (for example, in the form's OnCreate event).

```
Session.AddPassword('Kennwort');
```

To set the password using the TDataBase component's Parameter Overrides, follow these steps:

1. Double-click the TDataBase component.

2. Verify that the correct Name and Alias are displayed.

3. Deselect the Login Prompt check box.

4. Select the **Defaults** button.

5. Add the password to the Password= line in the Parameter Overrides list box.

   Alternatively, you can supply an event handler for the OnLogin event. See "OnLogin" in Delphi help for more information.

 Note: If the database contains sensitive information, remember to remove these passwords before deployment. Otherwise, anybody with access to the source code could discover the password.

Cannot copy a Repository Project to a directory underneath itself

Possible Cause of Error

You may have attempted to copy a project you selected from the Repository to a directory beneath the directory in which the Repository project resides.

Quick Fix

Save your new project to a different directory.

Additional Information

An example of how the error under consideration might occur is if you were to follow these steps:

1. Create a directory called Logjam beneath the Delphi 3\Objrepos\Logoapp directory in Delphi 3 or 4, namely:

   `C:\Program Files\Borland\Delphi X\Objrepos\Logoapp\Logjam.`

2. Subsequently select **File | New**.

3. Select the Win 95 Logo Application icon from the Projects page.

4. Attempt to save the new project (based on the Repository Project "Logoapp") to the directory named above.

Cannot create cursor handle

Possible Cause of Error

1. You may have attempted to call a TQuery component's Open method when the SQL statement does not return a result set. As an example, the following would produce this error message:

```
with Query1.SQL do
  begin
    Add('INSERT VALUES');
    Add('(Aaron, Mays, Murray)');
    Add('INTO RBIHRKINGS');
    Open; {Replace this with ExecSQL}
  end;
```

2. The TQuery component's SQL property may be empty.

Quick Fix

1. If the SQL statement used by the TQuery component does not return a result set (it is not a SQL SELECT statement), use TQuery's ExecSQL method instead.
2. Assign a valid SQL SELECT statement to the SQL property.

Additional Information

If you are using the SQL property to insert, update, or delete from a table, use the ExecSQL method. TQuery's Open method is for SELECT statements only.

Cannot create file < >

Possible Cause of Error

1. You may have attempted to save a file using the SaveToFile method to a location which does not exist. For example, you may have tried something like:

```
Image1.Picture.SaveToFile('C:\dotbumps\road.BMP');
```

without first having a "dotbumps" directory on your C drive.

2. You may have attempted to modify and then save a read-only file using the SaveToFile method. For example, if the file snapshot.txt is a read-only file, the following would generate the error message under discussion:

```
var
  Annotate: TStrings;
. . .
Annotate := TStringList.Create;
```

```
try
  Annotate.LoadFromFile('C:\standing\snapshot.txt');
  Annotate.Add('As of ' + DateTimeToStr(Now) +
               ', standings are as follows...');
  . . .
  Annotate.SaveToFile('C:\standing\snapshot.txt');
finally
  Annotate.Free;
. . .
```

Quick Fix

1. Ensure that any directory to which you save a file with the SaveToFile method has already been created. You can do this by first creating the directory and then saving the file to it. For example, to continue with the above scenario, you can do this:

```
CreateDir('C:\dotbumps');
Image1.Picture.SaveToFile('C:\dotbumps\road.BMP');
```

2. Ensure that any file you attempt to write to is not write-protected (read-only).

Additional Information

The TPicture class's SaveToFile and LoadFromFile methods can be used with graphics files. The TStrings abstract class's SaveToFile and LoadFromFile methods can be used with TStrings properties, such as TQuery's SQL property, as well as other TStrings descendents, such as TStringList.

By way of example, here are some ways that SaveToFile can be used:

```
procedure TForm1.Button3Click(Sender: Tobject);
var
  Liszt: TStrings;
begin
  Liszt := TStringList.Create;
  try
    Liszt.Add('Franz, Hungary');
    CreateDir('C:\Composers');
    {Use SaveToFile on TStrings descendent TStringList}
    Liszt.SaveToFile('C:\Composers\FLiszt.txt');
    {Use SaveToFile on TQuery's SQL property}
    Query1.SQL.SaveToFile('st8ments.txt');
    {Use SaveToFile on Tpicture to save bitmap;
     assume Pitchers directory already created}
    Image1.Picture.SaveToFile('C:\Pitchers\vase.BMP');
```

```
finally
  Liszt.Free;
. . .
```

> **Note:** If you do not specify a directory in the string parameter that you pass the SaveToFile method (as in the SQL statement above), the file will be saved in the current directory.

Cannot create form. No MDI forms are currently active

Possible Cause of Error

1. You may have attempted to create an MDI child form (a form with its Form-Style property set to fsMDIChild) before the main form (its parent, with a FormStyle property of fsMDIForm) has been created.

2. You may have designated a form as an MDI child by setting its FormStyle property to fsMDIChild while the main form's FormStyle property is not set to fsMDIForm. This includes setting the main form's FormStyle property to fsMDIChild.

Quick Fix

1. Ensure that the child form's parent form (the form with its FormStyle property set to fsMDIForm) is created before any child forms.

2. If any forms are designated as MDI child forms (by setting the FormStyle property to fsMDIChild), the project's main form's corresponding value must be fsMDIForm.

Additional Information

1. If you create forms dynamically (in code at run time), the parent form must be created first in an MDI application.

   MDI stands for Multiple Document Interface. The alternate style of applications is SDI (Single Document Interface). An MDI application contains one form with its FormStyle property set to fsMDIForm and one or more other forms with their FormStyle property set to fsMDIChild. In an MDI application, the child forms are always contained within the boundaries of the parent form.

   An example of an MDI application is the Windows 3.x File Manager. You could open multiple windows within the framework of File Manager, and then cascade or tile them, or move them anywhere within the boundaries of the File Manager window itself, but not outside of it.

An example of an SDI application is Delphi. Delphi is comprised of multiple free-floating forms (the Object Inspector, the Component Palette, the Code window, etc.) which are not contained within or constrained by other windows.

> **Note:** There are times when you may want to switch a project's main form to a different one than what you began with (at design time). An example of this is if you used the Database Form Wizard to create a database form and instructed it to create a main form but later opted to use a different form as the project's main form (the one that displays first when the program is run). You would do this in the following way:
>
> 1. Select **View | Project Manager**.
> 2. Click the **Options** button.
> 3. Select the form you want to promote to the main form from the Main Form combo box. Delphi will move the form you just promoted as the project's main form to the first one listed in the project source (.DPR) file.

Cannot debug project unless a host application is defined. Use the Run|Parameters... dialog box

Possible Cause of Error

1. You may have created an ActiveForm or ActiveX library and tried to run it without specifying an application from which to access the library.
2. You may have attempted to directly execute a .DLL by selecting Run | Run or pressing the F9 key.

Quick Fix

1. Follow these steps:
   a. Select **Run | Parameters**.
   b. In the Host Application combo box, either:
      Select the host application (executable) from the list.
      - OR-
      Enter the path to the host application.

-OR-

Navigate to the host application using the **Browse** button.

2. In Delphi 4, you can add a .DLL to a project by selecting Project | Add to Project..., and then indirectly "run" the .DLL by running the .EXE which calls it. See "Project Manager," "Remote debugging," and "Resource .DLLs" in Delphi help for more information.

Additional Information

ActiveForms and ActiveX creation made their debut with Delphi 3. Active-Forms can be deployed on the World Wide Web (WWW); ActiveX controls also have a web "connotation," but are not just for the web. By creating Delphi components and then converting them to ActiveX components, you can make them available not just to fellow Delphi developers, but also to those using any development environment which supports ActiveX controls, such as C++ Builder, Visual C++, IntraBuilder, Internet Explorer, Visual Basic, Power-Builder, etc.

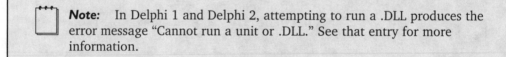

Note: In Delphi 1 and Delphi 2, attempting to run a .DLL produces the error message "Cannot run a unit or .DLL." See that entry for more information.

Cannot enable AutoSessionName property with more than one session on a form or data module

Possible Cause of Error

You may have attempted to set a TSession component's AutoSessionName property to True when there is one or more additional TSession components on the form or data module.

Quick Fix

Leave the AutoSessionName property set to False if you use more than one TSession component on a form or data module.

Additional Information

If you use more than one TSession component in your application, you cannot set the AutoSessionName property of any of them to True. Delphi can automatically set the name of the session for you when using a single TSession component, and guarantee that sessions spawned at run time are uniquely named.

When the AutoSessionName property is set to False (as it must be if there is more than one TSession component on the form), you must set the Session-Name property yourself, either at design time or at run time (in code).

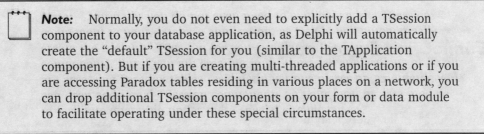

Note: Normally, you do not even need to explicitly add a TSession component to your database application, as Delphi will automatically create the "default" TSession for you (similar to the TApplication component). But if you are creating multi-threaded applications or if you are accessing Paradox tables residing in various places on a network, you can drop additional TSession components on your form or data module to facilitate operating under these special circumstances.

See "Cannot modify SessionName while AutoSessionName is enabled" for more information about restrictions to bear in mind when working with the TSession component.

Cannot find <> on the search path

Possible Cause of Error

You may be attempting to view the source code of a unit in the Package Editor, but it does not reside in Delphi's search path.

Quick Fix

Locate the file and place it in Delphi's search path, or alter the search path to include the current location of the file.

Additional Information

To locate the file using Windows Explorer, follow these steps:

1. In the directory pane on the left, highlight the area you want to search; to search your entire machine, select the standalone computer icon (named "MyComputer" by default).
2. Select **Tools | Find | Files or Folders...**.
3. Enter the name of the file in the Named combo box (for example, **Misplaced.PAS**).
4. Select the **Find Now** button.

To place the file in Delphi's search path, you may first want to see which directories constitute Delphi's search path. To do so, follow these steps:

1. Select **Tools | Environment Options**.
2. Select the Library page.
3. Inspect the entry in the Library Path combo box.
4. Either move the file into one of these directories, or add the directory in which the file resides to the path.

Cannot find Engine configuration file

Possible Cause of Error

IDAPI.CFG (Windows 3.x) or IDAPI32.CFG (32-bit Windows/Delphi) may not be where it should be.

Quick Fix

If using Delphi 1/Windows 3.x, ensure that the location of IDAPI.CFG (C:\IDAPI by default) matches that shown in the [IDAPI] section of WIN.INI for the CONFIGFILE01 entry.

If necessary, move the file to match the entry in WIN.INI or change the entry in WIN.INI to match the location of the file.

If using 32-bit Delphi and Windows 95, ensure that the location of IDAPI32.CFG (C:\Program Files\Borland\Common Files\BDE by default) matches that shown in the system registry.

If necessary, move the file to match the entry in the system registry or change the entry in the system registry to match the location of the file.

Additional Information

Things have changed with the advent of the system registry as used in 32-bit Windows. Prior to Windows 95, the Borland Database Engine configuration file (IDAPI.CFG) was located by default in the IDAPI directory on the C: drive. WIN.INI pointed to the location of the file; this way, you could move the file, as long as you updated its new location in WIN.INI so that programs that needed to refer to it could look in WIN.INI and find IDAPI.CFG.

In 32-bit Delphi, the location of the database engine configuration file is now pointed to by the system registry. To see this, follow these steps:

1. Select **Start | Run**.
2. Enter **regedit** in the Open combo box and select the **OK** button (or press the **Enter** key).

3. Navigate to HKEY_LOCAL_MACHINE\Software\Borland\Database Engine.

4. The data for CONFIGFILE01 will display the path where the configuration file is supposed to be located.

Cannot find implementation of method < >

Possible Cause of Error

You may have deleted (or commented out) a method from the Implementation part without deleting the method's declaration in the Interface part, leaving a reference to it on the Object Inspector's events page. You then attempted to re-create the method by double-clicking the event handler on the right side of the Object Inspector's events page (or on an object to create its default event handler).

Quick Fix

Clear the method's event handler reference from the right side of the form's event page and remove the method's declaration from the unit's Interface section.

Additional Information

If you delete both the method from the Implementation section of the unit and the method's declaration in the Interface part (leaving the reference to the event on the Object Inspector's events page), and then attempt to re-create the event handler, you will not receive an error message, but Delphi will not create the skeleton of the event handler for you either. As in the case above, you must clear the method's event handler reference from the right side of the form's event page before you can recode the method.

Note: To remove an event handler you have coded, remove everything between the *begin* and *end* in the method's definition in the Implementation section. Delphi will automatically remove all traces of the method for you (no muss, no fuss).

Cannot focus a disabled or invisible window

Possible Cause of Error

1. You may have attempted to call the SetFocus method for a control whose Visible or Enabled property is set to False. For example, the following will generate this error if no text is selected in the RichEdit component:

```
procedure DisableAndFocus(Sender: Tobject);
begin
  Button1.Enabled := RichEdit1.SelLength > 0;
  ... {other processing}
  Button1.SetFocus;
end;
```

The same would be true if the Visible property was being tested in a similar fashion and it equated to False. For example, if there was no text data on the clipboard, the following code would generate the error message under discussion:

```
procedure HideAndFocus(Sender: Tobject);
begin
  Button1.Visible := Clipboard.HasFormat(CF_TEXT);
  ... {other processing}
  Button1.SetFocus;
end;
```

2. You may have used a TPageControl component in Delphi 2 (they were not available in Delphi 1, and this no longer occurs in Delphi 3 or 4) and set the ActiveControl property to a control that was not visible at the time the project was last closed.

Quick Fix

1. Verify that a control's Visible and Enabled properties are both set to True before attempting to set focus to them.

2. Open the form as text and remove the line where the ActiveControl is set. You can do this either of these two ways:

> Right-click the form and select **View as Text** from the context menu
> -OR-
>
> Select **File | Open**, set the filter to show .DFM files, open the form file in question, and remove the ActiveControl line as noted above.

Additional Information

This error message may be confusing because of a possible difference in definition between what you may normally think of as a window and what Windows/Delphi considers to be a window. In this case, what is meant by a window is a "windowed control" (one that is assigned a window handle/can receive focus/can be a parent to other controls). In this context, a button is a window, an edit box is a window—in fact, all components that descend from TWinControl are in this sense "windows."

Cannot hide an MDI Child Form

Possible Cause of Error

You may be attempting to hide an MDI child form in any of the following ways:

```
procedure TMDIChild.FormClose(Sender: TObject; var Action: TCloseAction);
begin
  Action := caHide; { default is caMinimize }
end;

procedure TMDIChild.Button1Click(Sender: Tobject);
begin
  Hide; {You can run, but you can't hide}
end;

procedure TMDIChild.Button1Click(Sender: Tobject);
begin
  Visible := False; {This does the same thing}
end;
```

Quick Fix

Do not assign the caHide constant to the FormClose event's Action variable, call the form's Hide method, or set the form's Visible property to False for an MDI child form. If you want to at least temporarily remove the form, call its Close method.

This will close the form:

```
procedure TMDIChild.Button1Click(Sender: Tobject);
begin
  Close;
end;
```

Additional Information

TForm's Hide method sets the Visible property to False.

When closing an MDI child form, caMinimize is the default value assigned to the Action parameter. If you do not want the child form to be minimized, you can set the Action parameter to caFree to deallocate the memory allocated for the form.

```
procedure TMDIChild.FormClose(Sender: TObject; var Action: TCloseAction);
begin
  Action := caFree;
end;
```

Cannot inherit from form < >. It contains a component with a blank name property

See "Error Creating Form: Cannot inherit from form < >. It contains a component with a blank name property."

Cannot initialize local variables

Possible Cause of Error

You may have attempted to assign a value to a local variable at the time that you declared it. For example, the following will generate the error message under discussion:

```
procedure TForm2.Button1Click(Sender: Tobject);
var
  ThisIsThis: Boolean = True;
. . .
```

The following will also generate the error message under discussion (notwithstanding the wording of the error message, making it seem that the error is only generated within a Var section):

```
procedure TForm2.Button1Click(Sender: Tobject);
const
  ThisIsThis: Boolean = True;
. . .
```

Quick Fix

Do not assign values to variables in the Var section of a procedure or function.

Do not assign a data type to a constant in the Const section of a procedure or function.

To initialize the variable ThisIsThis to True (as attempted in the procedure above), do it this way:

```
procedure TForm2.Button1Click(Sender: Tobject);
var
  ThisIsThis: Boolean;
begin
  ThisIsThis := True;
  . . .
```

or this way if the value will not change:

```
procedure TForm2.Button1Click(Sender: Tobject);
const
  ThisIsThis = True;
  . . .
```

Additional Information

What the error message refers to as "initialized variables" are otherwise called "typed constants." Typed constants are actually a hybrid constant/variable. Like constants, you can (outside of local Var sections) assign them a value at the same time as you declare them. Like variables, their values can change at run time. And also like variables (and unlike constants), you specify their data type at the time they are declared (that is why they are referred to as being "typed").

> **Note:** Variables declare their name and data type; constants declare their name and value; and typed constants declare their name, data type, <u>and</u> value.

Here are examples of typical variables, constants, and typed constants as declared in a unit's Interface section, showing their similarities and differences:

```
unit Aryan;
interface
var
  tf: TextFile;
  ThisIsThis: Boolean = True; {This is a Typed
    Constant - legal here in a global section}
const
```

```
        crlf = #13#10;
        Satz = 'Das fesche Umherstolzieren +crlf+ des Hahns ist ein
                 bekannter Anblick';
implementation
. . .
```

> **Note:**   The typed constant ThisIsThis in the example above could also
> have been placed in the Const section. Its name might indicate that it
> actually belongs in the Const section, but since a typed constant is in
> actuality an initialized variable (as the text of the error message
> implies), the Var section is a good place for it.

Cannot initialize multiple variables

Possible Cause of Error

You may be attempting to declare more than one initialized variable (or
"typed constant") using one assignment. For example, the following will generate the error message under discussion:

```
interface
var
  QueSeraSera, WhateverWillBeWillBe: Boolean = True;
  . . .
```

To initialize both typed constants to True, you must do it this way:

```
interface
var
  QueSeraSera: Boolean = True;
  WhateverWillBeWillBe = True;
  . . .
```

Quick Fix

Initialize each typed constant on its own line.

Additional Information

You can declare multiple variables on one line, like this:

```
var
  i,j,k,l: integer;
```

or like this:

```
var
  aBeam: array[0..3] of integer;
```

but you cannot initialize them (assign the variables values on the same line, making them typed constants).

 Note: Typed constants cannot be used in local procedures or functions. See "Cannot initialize local variables" above for more information.

Cannot Load IDAPI Service Library

Possible Cause of Error

1. If you are using the MS Access driver and Access 95 or Microsoft Office 95 were not used to install the DAO engine, a necessary system registry entry may be missing.

2. IDPROV32.DLL may not be in the expected location.

3. If you get this error in a multi-tier application, STDVCL[32,40].DLL and/or DBCLIENT.DLL may not be registered on the server.

4. Your system registry may be set to read-only.

5. You may be attempting to access Access tables but do not have Microsoft's DAO installed on your machine (or you have an outdated version of it).

6. A .DLL required by IDAPI may be missing or corrupt.

Quick Fix

1. Add the entry to the system registry by following these steps:

   a. Select **Start | Run...** from the Windows desktop.

   b. Enter **regedit** in the Open combo box and select the **OK** button.

   c. Navigate to HKEY_LOCAL_MACHINE\Software\Microsoft\ Shared Tools\DAO.

   d. Right-click the Path entry, select **Modify** from the context menu, and then set the Value Data edit box to the location of **DAO3032.DLL**.

2. Locate the IDPROV32.DLL file, and move it to the BDE directory on the server. The default location is:

```
C:\Program Files\Borland\Common Files\BDE
```

Note: If IDPROV32.DLL is not in your system, reinstall the BDE.

3. Verify that IDPROV32.DLL is in the BDE .DLL directory (as specified in WIN.INI or the system registry, as appropriate for the operating system). Additionally, DBCLIENT.DLL and STDVCL[32,40].DLL need to be installed and registered in the \Windows\System[32] directory.

 To register servers on your system, you can use the Turbo Register Server utility (TRegSvr) which is a Delphi demo program located by default in

```
C:\Program Files\Borland\Delphi X\Demos\ActiveX\TRegSvr.
```

To do so, follow these steps (this example shows STDVCL32.DLL as the file to register):

1. Open the TRegSvr.DPR file.

2. Compile and run the project (press **F9**).

3. Activate a DOS session/Open a DOS window.

4. Enter the following at the prompt:

```
TRegSvr STDVCL32.DLL
```

5. Press the **Enter** key.

Turbo Register Server accepts three switches:

-u   to unregister a Server or Type Library
-q   to operate in quiet mode
-t   to register a Type Library (this is the default action, so if this is what you are doing, you can simply type the program name followed by the server name, as shown in the example above).

4. Set the entire system registry to read/write, or at least the entry for the .DLL in question.

5. Install DAO, and then add the entry for the Access driver included in your version of DAO into the BDE Configuration utility (Configuration | Drivers | Native | MSAccess | DLL 32), for example, IDDA3532.DLL.

If you are not using the latest version of the BDE, download it from **www.inprise.com**. Open the BDE Configuration utility and change the entry for the Access driver from IDDAO32.DLL to IDDA3532.DLL (or whatever the newest version of the Access driver is).

6. Verify that you have completed a full install of the BDE and any and all middleware you need in order to connect to the database you are using.

Additional Information

1. Delphi 4 has native support for Access 97.

6. If you cannot determine the cause of this message, you can resort to the "drastic measure" of reinstalling the BDE (select "Full Install") from the Delphi CD and/or reinstalling any and all database drivers and middleware relative to the database to which you are connecting.

See "Class not registered" for more information.

Cannot load IDAPI[32].DLL

Possible Cause of Error

1. You may be missing one or more BDE files. The BDE may not have been installed at all.

2. The BDE may not be correctly configured. One problem may be that you may have an incorrect entry in WIN.INI (Delphi 1) or system registry (32-bit Delphi) for the CONFIGFILE01 key.

3. You may have done only a partial install of the BDE.

4. You may have used InstallShield Express to install an application that uses the BDE, and the .DLL path system registry entry was not made.

Quick Fix

1. Install the BDE on all computers that will execute database programs created with Delphi (unless you are using a third-party replacement for the BDE, in which case you would presumably not get this error message).

See Deploy.TXT for specific information on deploying applications for your particular version of Delphi. It is located by default in the \Delphi directory.

2. Make sure that the location specified by the value in the Configfile01 entry in WIN.INI or the system registry points to the location of your configuration file (IDAPI[32].CFG).

Here are the specifics:

Delphi 1

Locate the DLLPATH setting beneath the [IDAPI] section (in C:\Windows\WIN.INI) and verify that the setting is correct. By default, it is:

```
[IDAPI]
DLLPATH = C:\IDAPI
```

If the DLL path in WIN.INI corresponds to the default setting of C:\IDAPI, but IDAPI.DLL is elsewhere, either a) Move IDAPI.DLL to the location set in WIN.INI, or b) Change the WIN.INI setting to the path where IDAPI.DLL resides.

32- bit Delphi

Locate the system registry setting for the location of the BDE .DLLs. This setting should be in HKEY_LOCAL_MACHINE\Software\Borland\Database Engine\DLLpath.

If the DLL path setting in the system registry corresponds to the default setting of C:\Borland\Common Files\BDE, but IDAPI32.DLL is elsewhere, either a) Move IDAPI32.DLL to the location set in the System registry, or b) Change the system registry setting to the path where IDAPI32.DLL resides.

3. Reinstall the BDE, this time selecting Full install.

4. Edit the system registry as shown below under Additional Information. Enter the path to IDAPI32.DLL in the DLLPATH setting (by default \borland\common files\bde).

Additional Information

> **Note:** This error is seen as "An error occurred while attempting to initialize the Borland Database Engine (error $2109)."

To edit the system registry, follow these steps:

1. Select **Run** from the Start menu.

2. Enter **regedit** in the edit box and click the **OK** button.

3. Navigate your way to HKEY_LOCAL_MACHINE\Software\Borland\ Database Engine\DLLpath.

4. Right-click on **DLL Path** in the right pane.

5. Select **Modify** from the context menu.

6. Edit the path in the Value Data edit box.

> **Note:** Here is how these system registry settings look after a default (Delphi 4) installation:
>
> ```
> DEFAULT          (value not set)
> CONFIGFILE01     "C:\Program Files\Borland\Common
>                   Files\BDE\IDAPI32.CFG"
> DLLPATH          "C:\Program Files\Borland\Common Files\BDE\"
> RESOURCE         "0009"
> SAVECONFIG       "WIN32"
> USE COUNT        "3"
> ```

3. A partial install places a "stripped-down" version of the BDE in the directory of the program that will use the BDE.

Cannot load language driver

Possible Cause of Error

Your language driver may be missing or the system registry entry may be incorrect.

Quick Fix

To inspect the setting, follow these steps:

1. Select **Start | Run**.
2. Enter **RegEdit** and press **OK**.
3. Navigate to My Computer\HKEY_LOCAL_MACHINE\Software\ Borland\Database Engine\Settings\System\INIT\LANGDRIVER.

Your entry depends on your physical location (USA, Europe, Japan, etc.), or more specifically, the location for which the computer was configured. For example, if you are located in the United States of America, the LANGDRIVER data value entry should be DBWINUS0.

Verify that the entry is correct. If necessary, edit the System registry entry. If the entry is correct, verify that the appropriate language driver exists on your system (in \Program Files\Borland\Common Files\BDE). For example, the file corresponding to the DBWINUS0 entry is USA.BLL. If the appropriate language driver (.BLL) file is missing, copy it from the Delphi CD-ROM to the location given above.

Additional Information

> **Note:** This is BDE Initialization error $3E06.

Cannot load package < >. It contains unit < > which is also contained in package < >

Possible Cause of Error

1. You may be attempting to load a package that contains a unit that is already present in your library.

2. You may be attempting to recompile an existing package after installing a component into it which is already contained in the VCL.

Quick Fix

1. If the package contains no additional units that you need, simply refrain from further attempts to load the "redundant" package.

2. Select **OK** to close the error message, and then **No** when asked whether to save changes. You still may "lose" the package into which you installed the component. If that is the case, simply reinstall the package (this time without the additional component).

Additional Information

1. If both packages contain components you need, you can create a new package which comprises the pieces from both packages that you want.

Cannot locate IDAPI[01,32].DLL

Possible Cause of Error

You may have opted for a partial installation when you installed Delphi.

Delphi 1

It may be that the IDAPI01.DLL file was never installed, or has been moved or deleted, or the [IDAPI] section in WIN.INI is missing or incorrect.

32-Bit Delphi

It may be that the IDAPI32.DLL file was never installed, or has been moved or deleted, or the system registry setting is missing or incorrect.

Quick Fix

Ensure that the BDE is installed and configured correctly. If it is not installed, install it. See "Deploy.TXT" for information on installing the BDE for your particular version of Delphi (Deploy.TXT is located by default in the \Delphi directory). If it is installed, it may not be configured correctly. See the following section which deals with your version of Delphi.

Delphi 1

Verify that the location to which the WIN.INI file points for the IDAPI .DLL corresponds with the actual location of IDAPI01.DLL. Find the [IDAPI] section. The CONFIGFILE01 and DLLPATH entries refer to C:\IDAPI by default.

32-Bit Delphi

Verify that the location to which the system registry points for the IDAPI .DLL corresponds with the actual location of IDAPI32.DLL.

To inspect this, run Regedit and navigate to HKEY_LOCAL_MACHINE\ Software\Borland\Database Engine.

The default location pointed to by the CONFIGFILE01 and DLLPATH entries is:

```
C:\Program Files\Borland\Common Files\BDE\IDAPI32.CFG
```

Additional Information

> **Note:** This is the error message "An error occurred while attempting to initialize the Borland Database Engine (error $2108)."

Delphi 1

To inspect and possibly edit the WIN.INI file, navigate to it in the Windows directory, open it, and then search for the [IDAPI] section. It should look something like this:

```
[IDAPI]
DLLPATH=C:\IDAPI
CONFIGFILE01=C:\IDAPI\IDAPI.CFG
```

If there is no [IDAPI] entry, or if it lacks the settings for DLLPATH and/or CONFIGFILE01, add them and point them to the locations of the IDAPI .DLLs (IDAPI01.DLL, et al) and the IDAPI.CFG file, respectively.

If the entries appear to be in order, either move the files to the location pointed to in the entries, or change the entries to correspond with the location of the files.

32-Bit Delphi

To inspect and possibly edit the system registry, follow these steps:

1. Select **Run** from the Start menu.
2. Enter **regedit** in the edit box and click the **OK** button.
3. Navigate your way to HKEY_LOCAL_MACHINE\Software\Borland\ Database Engine\DLLpath.
4. Right-click on **DLL Path** in the right pane.
5. Select **Modify** from the context menu.
6. Edit the path in the Value Data edit box.

Note: Here is how these system registry settings look after a default installation with Delphi 4:

```
DEFAULT         (value not set)
CONFIGFILE01    "C:\Program Files\Borland\Common
                Files\BDE\IDAPI32.CFG"
DLLPATH         "C:\Program Files\Borland\Common Files\BDE\"
RESOURCE        "0009"
SAVECONFIG      "WIN32"
USE COUNT       "3"
```

How to Create an Alias Using the BDE Config Tool

In Delphi 1, the BDE Config Tool is BDECFG.EXE. In Delphi 2, it is BDECFG32.EXE. In Delphi 3 and 4 it is BDEADMIN.EXE. In any version, it should be available by selecting Start | Programs | Borland Delphi X | BDE [Configuration, Administrator]. Alternatively, you can add it to Delphi's Tools menu for quicker access while working in Delphi (Tools | Configure Tools | Add).

To create an alias with the BDE Config Tool, follow these steps:

1. Select **Start | Programs | Borland Delphi X | BDE [Configuration, Administrator]**.
2. With the Databases tab active and the Databases item highlighted in the hierarchical view, select **Object | New...**.

3. Verify that the Type setting corresponds to the type of database you have created or will create (Standard for Paradox, dBASE, and ASCII, Access for MS Access, etc.).

4. If you selected a Standard driver (to create a Paradox database, for instance), set the Path to the location of the database (ServerName for Interbase and Oracle; Database Name for MS SQL Server and MS Access, Sybase, and Informix; DB2 DS2 for DB2). If using Path, you can enter a DOS path, as in:

```
K:\HallOfFame\Baseball
```

or, in 32-bit Delphi, you can use UNC (Universal Naming Convention), which is of the format:

```
\\ServerName\ShareName\ShareDir.
```

> **Note:** Normally, the Path setting will point to a shared network directory. You can later change the path, if so desired, without requiring that changes be made to all the client machines, as they still will refer to the same alias.

Cannot make a visible window modal

Possible Cause of Error

You may have called a form's ShowModal method after it was already displaying.

Quick Fix

Do not call a form's ShowModal method unless you are creating it dynamically.

Additional Information

When a form is created automatically by Delphi (such as all forms are by default and an application's main form always is), Delphi changes the form's Visible property from False to True.

The only time you should (and must) call either a form's Show or ShowModal method is when creating the form dynamically. Creating forms dynamically is recommended for forms which may not be opened every time an application is instantiated (such as an About box).

To create a form dynamically, follow these steps:

1. Select **View | Project Manager**.
2. Select the **Options** button.
3. Highlight the form you want to create dynamically in the Auto-Create Forms list box.
4. Move it to the Available Forms list box by clicking the right arrow.
5. Select the **OK** button.
6. Add code patterned after the following to the event of your choice (replace *AboutBox* with the form's instance variable name and *TAboutBox* with the form's class name):

```
procedure TForm1.AboutBoxClick(Sender: Tobject);
begin
  AboutBox := TAboutBox.Create(Application);
  try
    AboutBox.ShowModal;
  finally
    AboutBox.Free;
    AboutBox := nil;
  end;
end;
```

> **Note:** If you display a window "modally" (as most dialog boxes are, such as TOpenDialog and TSaveDialog), the user must respond to it before resuming other activities within the program. Windows that are not modal, such as a floating toolbar, can remain open throughout the run of an application.

Cannot modify a read-only dataset

Possible Cause of Error

You may be attempting to edit a TTable component whose ReadOnly property is set to True.

Quick Fix

Ensure that the TTable's ReadOnly property is set to False before attempting to edit the table.

Additional Information

You cannot change a TTable's ReadOnly property while the table is open (Active property is True), so you may have to first close the table, change the ReadOnly property, and then make the change, insertion, or deletion.

```
with TableTennis do begin
  Active := False;
  ReadOnly := False;
  Active := True;
  Insert;
  InsertRecord(['Gump','Forrest','PingPong',1]);
end;
```

Cannot modify SessionName while AutoSessionName is enabled

Possible Cause of Error

You may be attempting to assign a new value to a TSession component's SessionName property when its AutoSessionName property is set to True.

Quick Fix

Either refrain from editing the automatically generated name for the TSession component or first set the AutoSessionName property to False before changing the SessionName property.

Additional Information

The TSession component is similar to TApplication in that you normally don't have to concern yourself with creating one, as Delphi creates them for you automatically, as needed. But if you are creating multi-threaded applications or if you are accessing Paradox tables residing in various places on a network, you can drop additional TSession components on your form or data module to facilitate operating under these special circumstances. For more information, see "AutoSessionName" and "Managing Multiple Sessions" in Delphi help.

Cannot open component library <Path>\Complib.dcl

Possible Cause of Error

You may have installed a component which links a .DLL statically, and the .DLL cannot be found.

Quick Fix

Copy a backup version of your component library (COMPLIB.DCL) to
\Delphi\bin (Delphi 1).

Rectify the problem with the .DLL before installing the component again.

Additional Information

Where possible, use dynamic linking of .DLLs (using LoadLibrary and GetProc-
Address) rather than static linking. See "External reserved word | External
declarations" and "GetProcAddress function" in Delphi help for more
information.

Cannot open file < >

Possible Cause of Error

1. You may be attempting to open a file whose content is not of the format necessary for the attempted action. For example, if you attempt to load a file
   which you expect to be a graphic, and it is in fact a text file, you will get the
   error message under discussion.

2. You may be attempting to open a file that does not exist using the LoadFrom-
   File method (or at least does not exist in the location you have specified).

Quick Fix

1. Verify that the file you are attempting to open is indeed of the type you
   expect.

2. Ensure that the file is located in the directory you have given, and that you
   have spelled the name of the directory as well as the filename accurately.

Additional Information

1. It may be that the file's extension has been changed so that it appears to be a
   type of file that it is not. For example, the file ShapesOfThingsToCome.TXT
   may have had its extension changed from .TXT to .BMP. Attempts to load this
   file into a TImage component's Picture property will cause this error. As the
   saying goes, "A text file by any other extension is still a text file" (and vice
   versa—"a BLOb file with a text file extension is still a BLOb file").

2. The LoadFromFile method can be used on TPicture objects and TStrings and
   its descendents (such as TStringList).

Cannot open module because it is a dependent of < >, which is open as text

Possible Cause of Error

While attempting to compile a project, you may have a form (.DFM) file open "As Text."

Quick Fix

Revert the form file to Form View and compile again.

Additional Information

To return a form that is displaying its textual representation (.DFM file) to its visual representation (Form View), follow these steps:

1. Right-click inside the code window of the .DFM file.
2. Select **View As Form** from the context menu.

Cannot override a static method

Possible Cause of Error

You may have appended the *override* directive to a method which was not declared as *virtual* in the ancestor class.

Quick Fix

Either remove the *override* directive in the descendent class or add a *virtual* or *dynamic* directive in the ancestor class.

Additional Information

You can override methods in ancestor objects that have been declared using the *virtual*, *dynamic*, or either *virtual* or *dynamic* and *abstract* directives.

For example, if the ancestor object declaration looks like this:

```
type
  A = class
    procedure WorkHard; virtual;
    procedure PlayHard; dynamic;
    procedure StudyHard; virtual; abstract;
    procedure RunHard; dynamic; abstract;
```

```
  procedure Leotard;
end;
```

you can override the WorkHard, PlayHard, StudyHard, and RunHard methods, but you cannot override the Leotard method, as it is declared as Static (the default). You can create a method of the same name (Leotard) in your descendent class, but you will have to refrain from appending the *override* directive to it, and it will not inherit any of the functionality of the same-named method in the ancestor class.

So, the following is allowable in a descendent class:

```
type
  AA = class(A)
    procedure WorkHard; override;
    procedure PlayHard; override;
    procedure StudyHard; override;
    procedure RunHard; override;
    procedure Leotard; {No relation to method in class A}
  end;
```

Cannot perform this operation on a closed database

Possible Cause of Error

You may have attempted to call a TDataBase component's StartTransaction method without first setting its Connected property to True or calling its Open method. For example, you may have done something like this:

```
with Database1 do begin
  StartTransaction;
  Table1.FieldByName('Mister').Value := 'Magoo';
```

Quick Fix

Set the Connected property to True, either at design time or in code, or call the TDatabase component's Open method, before calling StartTransaction. For example, to fix the example shown above, you can do this:

```
with Database1 do begin
  Connected := True;
  StartTransaction;
```

```
try
  try
    Table1.FieldByName('Mister').Value := 'T';
. . .
  finally
    Commit;
  end;
except
  Rollback
end;
```

or this:

```
with Database1 do begin
  Open;
  StartTransaction;
  try
    try
      Table1.FieldByName('Mister').Value := 'Coffee(Joe DiMaggio)';
. . .
    finally
      Commit;
    end;
  except
    Rollback
  end;
```

Additional Information

If you set a TDatabase component's Connected property to True (either at design time or at run time before you reference the database) and set its KeepConnections property to True also, you will avert ever receiving this error, as the database will always be open.

Note: By setting KeepConnections to True, you may improve performance by maintaining a connection to the database even if various of its constituent tables set their Active properties to False. Whether it will really be advantageous to you depends on the exact nature of your program. See "KeepConnections" in Delphi help for more information.

Cannot perform this operation on a closed dataset

Possible Cause of Error

1. You may have attempted to refresh, edit, empty, delete, or search a TDataset component that was not open or active.

   For example, you will produce the error message under discussion if you try either of the following:

   ```
   Table1.Close;
   Table1.Refresh;
   ```

   -OR-

   ```
   Table1.Active := False;
   Table1.Edit;
   ```

2. An "auxiliary" dataset that is required by another dataset may be inactive or closed. For example, you may have a lookup table that must be open before its values can be accessed.

Quick Fix

1, 2. Open all necessary datasets before performing any of the above actions.

Additional Information

2. If you are using a calculated field in a table, it may be referencing another table during the OnCalcFields event which has not been created yet. All tables must exist before being referenced. The creation order of nonvisible components is at first determined by the order in which you placed the components on the form. If the referenced TTable was placed on the form after the TTable which does the referencing, you can alter the creation order by selecting **Edit | Creation Order** and using the arrow buttons to move the referenced TTable(s) above the referencing TTable(s).

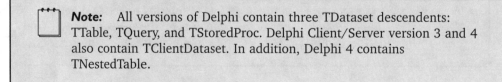

Note: All versions of Delphi contain three TDataset descendents: TTable, TQuery, and TStoredProc. Delphi Client/Server version 3 and 4 also contain TClientDataset. In addition, Delphi 4 contains TNestedTable.

Cannot perform this operation on an active session

Possible Cause of Error

You may be attempting to set a TSession component's AutoSessionName property to True or modify its SessionName property while its Active property is set to True.

Quick Fix

First set the Active property to False before attempting to change the AutoSessionName property to True or modify its SessionName property.

Additional Information

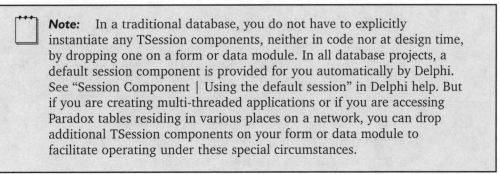

Note: In a traditional database, you do not have to explicitly instantiate any TSession components, neither in code nor at design time, by dropping one on a form or data module. In all database projects, a default session component is provided for you automatically by Delphi. See "Session Component | Using the default session" in Delphi help. But if you are creating multi-threaded applications or if you are accessing Paradox tables residing in various places on a network, you can drop additional TSession components on your form or data module to facilitate operating under these special circumstances.

For more information about sessions, see "Managing Database Sessions," "Managing Multiple Sessions," "Naming a Session," "Working with a Session Component," "Using the default session," and "Using a session component in Data Modules" in Delphi help.

Cannot perform this operation on an empty dataset

Possible Cause of Error

You may have attempted to call a TTable's Delete method when it contains no records.

Quick Fix

Before calling the Delete method, verify that the table is not already empty. For example, you could do this:

```
if Table1.IsEmpty then
  Exit
else
  Table1.Delete;
```

or this:

```
if not Table2.IsEmpty then
  Table2.Delete;
```

Additional Information

TDataset's Delete method will only delete the current record.

To delete all the records from a table, use the EmptyTable method.

To delete not only all the records but also the table itself (the structure information), use the DeleteTable method. The TTable must be closed first before calling DeleteTable (call TTable's Close method or set its Active property to False).

To selectively delete records that match a certain criteria, use a TQuery component and set its SQL property based on the following:

```
DELETE FROM BogusData {to delete all records}
DELETE FROM Airwaves
WHERE ContentType = SoapOpera {to delete all records with a ContentType
                              value of Soap Opera}
```

Cannot perform this operation on an open database

Possible Cause of Error

1. You may have attempted to set a TTable's Exclusive property to True while its Active property was True.

2. You may have tried to assign a value to a TTable's TableName property with its Active property set to True.

3. You may have attempted to assign a value to a TDatabase's Alias or Database-Name property while the Database's Connected property was set to True.

4. You may have attempted to assign a TSession component's Active or AutoSessionName property to True while the TDatabase component's Connected property is set to True.

Quick Fix

1-4. Ensure that the TTable or TDatabase is not active before attempting such operations. You can do this using these method calls:

```
Table1.Close; {for a TTable component}
Database1.Close; {for a TDataBase component}
```

or by setting properties:

```
Table1.Active := False; {for a TTable component}
Database1.Connected := False; {for a TDataBase component}
```

> **Note:** Remember to open the database/set its Active property back to True before attempting to access it subsequent to closing it/setting the Active property to False. If you get this error at design time, you can set the Active property to False in the Delphi IDE, perform the operation, and then set the Active property back to True (although it is usually preferable to leave the property set to False at design time, opening tables only as necessary).

Additional Information

Attempting to set the table's Active property to True while the Exclusive property is True produces the error message "Table is Busy."

Cannot perform this operation on an open dataset

Possible Cause of Error

1. You may have attempted to modify a TTable's Exclusive, ReadOnly, Database-Name, TableName, TableType, or SessionName property while the table was open.

2. You may have called a TQuery's Unprepare method while the query was active.

Quick Fix

1. Close the TTable before modifying any of the properties noted above.

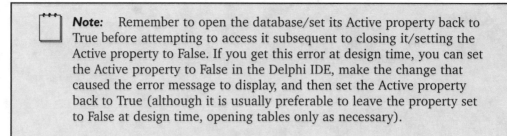

Note: Remember to open the database/set its Active property back to True before attempting to access it subsequent to closing it/setting the Active property to False. If you get this error at design time, you can set the Active property to False in the Delphi IDE, make the change that caused the error message to display, and then set the Active property back to True (although it is usually preferable to leave the property set to False at design time, opening tables only as necessary).

2. Close the TQuery before calling Unprepare.

Additional Information

You can close a TDataset (from which both TTable and TQuery descend) by setting the Active property to False:

```
Table1.Active := False;
```

-OR-

```
Query1.Active := False;
```

or by calling its Close method:

```
Table1.Close;
```

-OR-

```
Query1.Close;
```

1. You need to set a TTable's Exclusive property to True before performing certain activities, such as adding indexes with the AddIndex method. Therefore, you must first close the TTable, add the indexes, and then open the table again.

Cannot perform this operation with table open

Possible Cause of Error

You may have attempted to delete a table in Database Desktop while the table was open.

Quick Fix

Close the table before deleting it.

Additional Information

You can perform many operations on "local," or desktop, databases, such as Paradox, dBASE, MS Access, etc., using Database Desktop. See "Database Desktop" in Delphi help.

Cannot perform utility while table is in use

Possible Cause of Error

You may be attempting to perform an action, such as editing or restructuring a table in Database Desktop, while the table is open.

Quick Fix

Close the table by setting the Active property of the TTable to False and the Connected property of TDatabase components to False, and then try again.

Additional Information

The table may be open either in a running application or in the Delphi IDE, if a TTable's Active property is set to True or the Connected property of a TDatabase component is set to True.

Cannot read a write-only property

Possible Cause of Error

You may be attempting to access the value of a property which is write-only. For example, you may be trying to write to a property like this:

```
Table1.CanModify := True;
```

Quick Fix

Only attempt to modify properties which can be written to, in other words those that are not read-only. For example, you can read from the CanModify property's value like this:

```
if Table1.CanModify = True then
  {carry out conditional processing}
```

but you cannot assign to it, as shown above.

Additional Information

If a property is read-only, it is declared like this:

```
property Required: Boolean read FRequired;
```

and is normally declared in a class's Public section.

If a property can both be read from and written to, it is declared like this:

```
property NetFileDir: string read GetNetFileDir
                            write SetNetFileDir;
```

> **Note:** Read-only properties are much more common than write-only properties. Both are rare compared to properties that are both readable and writable.

It is common for a property to access a private field from which to read the internal value and a private method from which to write the value. Here is an example section from the Dbtables.PAS unit where the TTable component is declared, showing the DatabaseName property and its related private field and procedure:

```
TTable = class(TDBDataSet)
  private
    ...
    FDatabaseName: string;
    ...
    procedure SetDatabaseName(const Value: string);
    ...
  protected
    ...
  public
    ...
  published
    property DatabaseName: string read FDatabaseName
                                  write SetDatabaseName;
end;
```

Here is the definition of the SetDatabaseName method:

```
procedure TDatabase.SetDatabaseName(const Value: string);
begin
  if csReading in ComponentState then
    FDatabaseName := Value
  else if FDatabaseName <> Value then
  begin
```

```
      CheckInactive;
      ValidateName(Value);
      FDatabaseName := Value;
   end;
end;
```

As can be seen, when the user accesses the DatabaseName property, the value is read from the internal private field FDatabaseName. When a user assigns a value to the DatabaseName property, the SetDatabaseName method is passed the value to which the user is attempting to set the DatabaseName.

Cannot Run a Unit or DLL

Possible Cause of Error

1. You may have attempted to execute an application from the Delphi IDE without having its project file (.DPR) open. For example, you may have one or more units which are part of a project open, but did not open the project itself.

2. You may have attempted to run a .DLL.

Quick Fix

1. Open the project source (.DPR file) of which the unit is a part before attempting to run the application.

2. While .DLLs are executables, they cannot be executed directly. Call the .DLL from an .EXE in order to run it.

Additional Information

You can execute an application without having all its constituent units open in the IDE (as long as the .DPR file is open), but not vice versa. Expressed another way, if you open a project file and run it, it will load the unit (.PAS) files that comprise the project. The opposite, though, is not true—a unit will not load the .DPR of which it is a constituent part. A unit may belong to multiple projects, and therefore would not necessarily "know" which project to load.

> **Note:** If you are attempting to test a library (.DLL) file, you must load an application that calls it and execute the .DLL indirectly from the calling program.

> **Note:** You can compile a .DLL by selecting Compile | Compile (Project | Compile in Delphi 3 and 4). If you attempt to execute (run) the .DLL, though, you will get the error message under discussion in Delphi 1 and Delphi 2, and "Cannot debug project unless a host application is defined. Use the Run | Parameters...dialog box" in Delphi 3 and 4. See that entry for more information.

Cannot write EXE or DLL to disk

Possible Cause of Error

You may have executed the module (.EXE or .DLL) and then attempted to compile the project while the module was still resident in memory.

Quick Fix

Shut down the instance of the program before attempting to recompile it. If necessary, reboot Windows to clean the executable or .DLL out of memory.

Additional Information

This may also occur after crashing the program from within the IDE. Shut down Delphi and restart it, and then attempt to compile the project/program again.

Cannot Write to Engine Configuration File

Possible Cause of Error

IDAPI.CFG (Windows 3.x) or IDAPI32.CFG (32-bit Windows/Delphi) may not be where it should be.

Quick Fix

Delphi 1/Windows 3.x

Ensure that the location of IDAPI.CFG (C:\IDAPI by default) matches that shown in the [IDAPI] section of WIN.INI for the CONFIGFILE01 entry.

If necessary, move the file to match the entry in WIN.INI or change the entry in WIN.INI to match the location of the file.

32-bit Delphi/Windows 95

Ensure that the location of IDAPI32.CFG (C:\Program Files\Borland\Common Files\BDE by default) matches that shown in the system registry.

If necessary, move the file to match the entry in the system registry or change the entry in the system registry to match the location of the file.

Additional Information

> **Note:** This is BDE Error 8453.

Capability Not Supported

Possible Cause of Error

1. You may have a syntax error in a SQL statement. You may be attempting to do something in a "local," or desktop, database which can only be done in a "back end," or SQL Server, database. For example, you may be attempting to use a nested SELECT statement on a Paradox table.

2. You may be using SQL SELECT syntax that is not supported for a live result set while the TQuery component's RequestLive property is set to True.

3. You may have attempted to modify a TStoredProc component's StoredProc-Name property while the DatabaseName property refers to a "local," or desktop, database.

4. You may have omitted the table name in a SELECT statement (providing the column name only). For example, you may have a SELECT statement similar to:

```
SELECT Candy
FROM Sees
WHERE Chocolate = DarkRaspberry
```

5. You may be attempting to use cached updates on a table which contains TBlob fields.

Quick Fix

1. Check the SQL statements and syntax that are supported and used by the database format you are using. See your database documentation for further details.

2. If you do <u>not</u> need a live result set, change the TQuery component's RequestLive property from True to False.

If you <u>do</u> need a live result set, your query cannot contain any of the following:

➤ "Aggregate" functions (SUM, COUNT, AVG, MIN, MAX, etc.)

➤ JOINs, UNIONs, INTERSECTs, or MINUS operations

➤ An ORDER BY clause

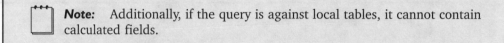

> **Note:** Additionally, if the query is against local tables, it cannot contain calculated fields.

3. Do not attempt to modify the StoredProcName property while the TStored-Proc component's DatabaseName property references a "local," or desktop, database.

4. Include the table name in the SELECT statement, and enclose the column name in quotation marks. For example:

```
SELECT Sees."Chocolate"
FROM Sees
WHERE Sees."Chocolate" = DarkRaspberry
```

5. Refrain from using Cached Updates in combination with TBlob fields.

Additional Information

1. Although SQL is the "lingua franca" of both desktop and server databases, the dialects and "vocabulary" differ between the various implementations of it. For example, Oracle uses PL/SQL, MS SQL Server uses Transact SQL, etc.

3. If you are using a "local," or desktop, database (such as Paradox, dBASE, MS Access, etc.), you cannot use stored procedures. They are a feature of SQL Server databases only (such as Interbase, Oracle, MS SQL Server, Sybase, Informix, etc.).

If all else fails, try using a string variable in the WHERE clause. For example,

```
var
  WhereVar: String;
  . . .
  WhereVar:= 'Kelvin Caleb Mordecai Immerfort Purify Shannon';
  . . .
  Query1.SQL.Add('SELECT * from "RUNTHE"');
  Query1.SQL.ADD('WHERE Whatever = ' + WhereVar);
```

> **Note:** Uppercase SQL statements when accessing Oracle databases.

5. If you are using the Client/Server version of Delphi, version 3 or higher, see "TClientDataSet" in Delphi help for an alternative to Cached Updates.

Circular datalinks are not allowed

Possible Cause of Error

You may be attempting to use a TTable component as its own lookup table by setting the TTable component's MasterSource property to the TDataSource component that references the TTable component.

Quick Fix

Assign a value from the MasterSource properties drop-down list as the TData-Source to use to link to another TTable component as a source of lookup information.

Additional Information

Delphi will not display a TDataSource component that refers to a TTable component in that TTable component's own MasterSource property drop-down list. This is a preventive measure against this error message. You can, though, type in anything you want, and if you enter the name of such a TDataSource in a TTable's MasterSource property, you will generate the error message under discussion.

For more information about using lookup tables and the MasterSource property, see "TTable.MasterSource" in Delphi help.

Circular Unit Reference [to < >]

Possible Cause of Error

You may have placed two units in each other's Interface section Uses clause.

Quick Fix

Move at least one of the references from the referencing unit's interface Uses section to the Uses section in the Implementation part (directly below the *implementation* reserved word). For example, if the error message is caused by Unit1 and Unit2 simultaneously referencing each other in each one's Interface Uses section, so that Unit1 currently appears like this:

```
unit Unit1;
interface
uses
  Windows, Messages, SysUtils, Classes,
  Graphics, Controls, Forms, Dialogs, Unit2;
type
  TForm1 = class(TForm)
  private
    { Private declarations }
  public
    { Public declarations }
  end;
var
  Form1: TForm1;
implementation
{$R *.DFM}
```

change it so that it looks like this:

```
unit Unit1;
interface
uses
  Windows, Messages, SysUtils, Classes,
  Graphics, Controls, Forms, Dialogs;
  {removed Unit2}
type
  TForm1 = class(TForm)
  private
    { Private declarations }
  public
    { Public declarations }
  end;
var
  Form1: TForm1;
implementation
uses Unit2; {added the reference to Unit2 here}
{$R *.DFM}
```

Additional Information

You can also move both references to each unit's Implementation part (you must move at least one; you can move both).

The only units which need to be included in the Interface part's Uses section are those whose classes are referenced within that (Interface) section. All others can be placed in the Implementation part's Uses section.

The Uses section in the Interface section is automatically added for you. You will have to manually add the Uses section in the Implementation part.

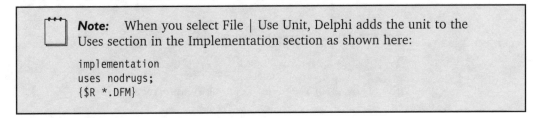

Note: When you select File | Use Unit, Delphi adds the unit to the Uses section in the Implementation section as shown here:

```
implementation
uses nodrugs;
{$R *.DFM}
```

Class, interface and object types only allowed in type section

Possible Cause of Error

You may have attempted to declare a class type variable outside a type section. For example, you may have tried something like this:

```
var
  ts: class(TFont);
```

Quick Fix

Only declare class types inside class sections, like this (an example of a class type):

```
type
  TForm1 = class(TForm)
```

or like this (an example of an enumerated type):

```
TFormerResidences = (California,NewYork,Montana, Alaska,Oklahoma,Wisconsin);
```

Additional Information

➤ If you attempt to declare a class type in a Variable section, like this:

```
var
  TForm1 = class(TForm)
```

you will get the error message " ',' or ':' expected but '=' found."

➤ If you attempt to declare a class type in a Const section, like this:

```
const
  TForm1 = class(TForm)
```

you will get the error message "Expression expected but 'CLASS' found."

➤ If you attempt to declare a class type in a local procedure or method, like this:

```
procedure TryToDeclareALocalFormClass;
type
  TForm1 = class(TForm)
```

you will get the error message "Local class, interface, or object types not allowed."

Class < > not found. [Ignore the error and continue?]

Possible Cause of Error

1. You may have modified a form's .DFM file and changed an object from one type to another (for example, a TButton to a TBitBtn), and Delphi cannot reconcile the difference.

2. You may have used a unit or component in this project which you subsequently moved out of Delphi's search path, uninstalled, or deleted.

3. You may be loading a project in a version of Delphi that predates the version used to last compile the project.

4. You may have altered the field declaration of a component in a .PAS file directly (that is, not via the Object Inspector, changing the component's Name property), and then responded by selecting the Yes button to the message "Field < > does not have a corresponding component. Remove the declaration?"

Quick Fix

1. Inspect the form's .DFM file by right-clicking the form and selecting **View As Text** from the context menu. Verify that the object definitions therein coincide with what is actually on the form.

2. If you still want to use the missing class, you will have to reintroduce Delphi to it either now or later. If you want to wait until later (or you don't need the class at all), simply elect to ignore the error. To reunite the class with Delphi, follow the appropriate course of action based on what caused the problem:

   ➤ If you moved the file the project needs, move it back to a directory in Delphi's search path or add the directory it currently resides in to Delphi's search path (select **Tools | Environment Options...**, then the Library page and Library Path combo box).

➤ If the class is a component that you uninstalled, reinstall it.

➤ If the file has been deleted, see if you can get another copy from wherever you got the original (the Delphi CD, a third-party book's CD, a web site, etc.).

➤ If you removed a directory from Delphi's search path which contains units that you need, add the directory back or move the file to a location referred to in Delphi's search path.

3. You can ignore the error, and the parts of the project which are not specific to the later version of Delphi will open. If the project is one that you created yourself, you probably still have access to the newer version of Delphi. If this is the case, load the project in the newer version to retain use of the class referred to in the error message.

4. Select the **OK** button. In design mode, remove the component that was not found, and then add it again.

Additional Information

If you elect to "ignore the error and continue," Delphi will remove the reference to the missing class from the .DFM file. Its declaration will still exist in the .PAS file, though. When you then try to compile the project, which now contains a discrepancy between the description provided by the .PAS file and the description provided by its corresponding .DFM file, you may get the error message "Field < > does not have a corresponding component. Remove the declaration?" If you select Yes, the declaration is then also removed from the .PAS file.

1. Normally, editing the object in the .DFM file will also cause it to change on the form. This is what is meant when people refer to Delphi as being a "two-way tool."

After changing a component from one type to another in the .DFM file, when you attempt to compile the project you may get the message "Field < > should be of type < > but is declared as < >. Correct the declaration?." Select **Yes** to allow Delphi to reconcile the reference.

3. An example of this happening would be if you create a project in Delphi 3 or 4 that uses a TChart component, and then attempt to load that project into Delphi 2 (or Delphi 1).

4. See the "Field < > does not have a corresponding component. Remove the declaration?" entry for more information.

Class already has a default property

Possible Cause of Error

You may have attempted to assign a default property to a class which already has a default property defined.

Quick Fix

Remove one of the "default" declarations. You can only have one default property.

Additional Information

When declaring an array property for a class, you can define it as the default property for the class, like this:

```
type
  TCircus = class
    . . .
    property Clowns[Index: Integer]: String read FBozo write SetBozo;
                                  default;
    . . .
var
  Circus: TCircus;
```

The advantage of doing this is that you can then access or assign to that array property in code without having to specify the property name. For example, with the property declared above, you could assign a value to it like this:

```
Circus[i] := Bozo;
```

In other words, as it is the default property, it is not necessary to "spell out" the property name when assigning to it, like this:

```
Circus.Clowns[i] := Bozo;
```

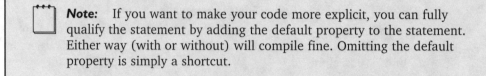

> **Note:** If you want to make your code more explicit, you can fully qualify the statement by adding the default property to the statement. Either way (with or without) will compile fine. Omitting the default property is simply a shortcut.

However, if you were to try the following, you would get the error message under discussion:

```
type
  TCircus = class
  . . .
    property Clowns[Index: integer]: String read
               FBozo write SetBozo; default;
    property Animals[Index: integer]: String
       read FAnimals write SetAnimals; default;
            {attempting to add a second default property not allowed}
  . . .
```

> **Note:** Do not confuse the *default* directive you can use with an array property of a class (as discussed here) with the default storage specifier used to help determine which of a form's values are stored. The default storage specifier is used to save storage space and loading time in connection with streaming data to and from the form (.DFM) file. The difference between the *default* directive and the default storage specifier is made obvious by the presence or absence of a specified default value. For more information, see "Storage Specifiers" and "Default Property Values" in Delphi help.

> **Note:** In Delphi 4, you can now supply procedures and functions with default parameters. See "default parameters" in Delphi help for more information.

Class does not have a default property

Possible Cause of Error

You may have attempted to assign to a class variable using an array expression when the class type has no default property. For example, you may have written something like:

`TCollection[i] := BostonHarbor;`

or:

`BeatlesParaphernalia := TCollection;`

whereas the TCollection class has no default property (although it does have an array property, namely Items).

Quick Fix

Specify all non-default properties explicitly in any statements that reference them.

Additional Information

Default properties are array properties whose name can be omitted in assignment statements. For more information, see the preceding entry "Class already has a default property."

Class not registered

Possible Cause of Error

1. You may be trying to run an application which contains an ActiveX (.OCX) control that has not been installed and registered on your system.

2. You may have attempted to set the Connected property of a TDCOMConnection, TOLEEnterpriseConnection, or TRemoteServerConnection component to True whose server (represented by the ServerName or ServerGUID property) has not been registered on your system.

Quick Fix

1. Ensure that you install and register all ActiveX controls before referencing them.

2. Ensure that you install and register all servers before referencing them.

Additional Information

1. Although ActiveX (.OCX) controls are a type of .DLL, it is not enough for the file simply to exist in the right location, as is the case with .DLLs. ActiveX controls are identified by their GUID (Globally Unique IDentifier), not by their filename, and this GUID must be registered with Windows (in the system registry) before the ActiveX control can be referenced.

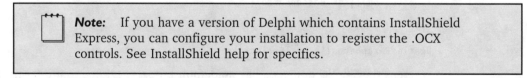

Note: If you have a version of Delphi which contains InstallShield Express, you can configure your installation to register the .OCX controls. See InstallShield help for specifics.

To "manually" register an ActiveX control (a .DLL with an .OCX extension), first copy it to the \Windows\System directory and then follow these steps:

a. Open a DOS Window.

b. Change to the \Windows\System directory.

c. Enter the following at the prompt and then press the **Enter** key:

```
Regsvr32 <libraryname>
```

For example, if the type library in question is IDataBroker, you would enter the following (as it is defined in STDVCL32.DLL):

```
Regsvr32 STDVCL32
```

(In Delphi 4, the corresponding file is STDVCL40.DLL, so the line would read: Regsvr32 Stdvcl40.)

 Note: Alternatively, you can use the Turbo Register Server utility (TRegSvr) which is a demo program located by default in

```
C:\Program Files\Borland\Delphi X\Demos\ActiveX\TRegSvr.
```

To do so, follow these steps:

1. Open the TRegSvr.DPR file.

2. Compile and run the project (press **F9**).

3. Activate a DOS session/Open a DOS window.

4. Navigate to the directory in which TRegSvr exists.

5. Enter the following at the prompt:

   ```
   TRegSvr STDVCL32.DLL
   ```

6. Press the **Enter** key.

Turbo Register Server accepts three switches:

-u   to unregister a Server or Type Library
-q   to operate in quiet mode
-t   to register a Type Library (this is the default action, so if this is
      what you are doing, you can simply type the program name
      followed by the server name, as shown in the example above)

Delphi 3 and 4

In Delphi 3 and 4, you can register and unregister ActiveX controls you create via menu items, specifically Run | Register ActiveX Server and Run | Unregister ActiveX Server. These menu items are available when an ActiveX control project or ActiveX Library is open in the IDE.

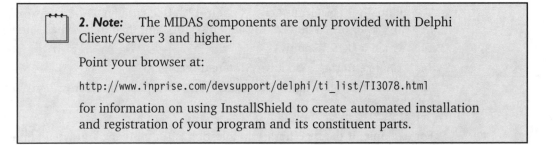

2. Note: The MIDAS components are only provided with Delphi Client/Server 3 and higher.

Point your browser at:

`http://www.inprise.com/devsupport/delphi/ti_list/TI3078.html`

for information on using InstallShield to create automated installation and registration of your program and its constituent parts.

See "DAX Error: Class not Registered."

Class type required

Possible Cause of Error

1. You may have referenced a non-class type as the argument of an exception block's Raise statement. For example, you may have done something like this:

```
var
  b : Byte;
  aRuckus: String;
begin
  try
    b := StrToInt(Edit1.Text);
  except
    on Cain do raise aRuckus('Holy Cow!');
  end;
end;
```

2. You may have used two Interface types in the declaration of an ActiveForm class type, like this:

```
TActiveFormX = class(IActiveFormX, IActiveFormX)
```

Quick Fix

1. When using the *try...except on...*<exception object> *do* construct, use a prede-fined exception type. This can be either an Object Pascal exception object or a user-defined one.

2. You need to use a class type followed by an Interface type in the declaration of an ActiveForm class type, like this:

```
TActiveFormX = class(TActiveForm, IActiveFormX)
```

Additional Information

1. Here is an example of using a predefined Object Pascal exception (EDivByZero):

```
function DivideThePie(Pieces, Recipients: Integer): Integer;
begin
  try
    Result := Pieces div Recipients;
  except
    on EDivByZero do Result := 0;
  end;
end;
```

Here is an example of declaring and using a user-defined exception object (ESoMuchTrouble):

```
type
  ESoMuchTrouble = class(Exception);
  . . .
if Problems > BreakingPoint then
  raise ESoMuchTrouble.Create('That was the straw that broke the
                              camel''s back');
```

For more information about exceptions, see "Exception Declarations," "Predefined Exceptions," and "Exception" in Delphi help.

2. See "Interface type required" for this error message's "opposite number" (this is an example of how to keep a programmer busy).

Clipboard does not support Icons

Possible Cause of Error

You may have attempted to place an icon on the clipboard. For example, you may have tried something like this when the Picture referred to is an .ICO file:

```
Clipboard.Assign(Image1.Picture);
```

Quick Fix

Do not attempt to place icons (files with an .ICO extension) on the clipboard.

Additional Information

You <u>can</u> place bitmaps (files with a .BMP extension) and metafiles (files with a .WMF extension) on the clipboard.

In other words, the same exact code could in one instance produce the error message under discussion (if an icon is assigned to the Picture property) and in another instance work fine (if a bitmap or metafile is assigned to the Picture property).

Code Insight™ features are disabled while debugging

Possible Cause of Error

You are attempting to use Code Insight™ features while your program is running in the Delphi IDE. For example, you may have attempted to take advantage of Code Completion features by pressing Ctrl + Spacebar while stepping through your code.

Quick Fix

Only use Code Insight features at design time without the program running.

Additional Information

Code Insight is not available in Delphi 1 and 2. For more information, see "Code Insight" in Delphi help.

Code Segment Too Large

Possible Cause of Error

You may have placed too much code within a single unit in your project.

Quick Fix

Move some of the code to another unit, and add a Uses section directly after the *implementation* reserved word that references the second unit. For example, if you named this second unit SecondCodeBucket, you would reference it from the original unit like this:

```
implementation
uses SecondCodeBucket;
{$R *.DFM}
```

Additional Information

This is normally a Delphi 1 problem, as the code segment under Windows 3.x is limited to 64 K.

COINITIALIZE has not been called

Possible Cause of Error

You may be using multi-threading in a COM application, but have not called CoInitialize for each thread.

Quick Fix

Call CoInitialize in every thread in a COM application.

Additional Information

> **Note:** This is a descendent of EOLESys Error.

You also need to call CoUninitialize when through with each thread.

Column not a BLOb

See "Unknown SQL Error."

Comma Expected

Possible Cause of Error

You may not be providing enough parameters to a procedure or function.

Quick Fix

If the procedure or function wherein you receive this error message is an Object Pascal method, look it up in Delphi help to determine the amount and type of parameters the method expects. If the procedure or function's declaration is contained within the project's units (it is a custom procedure or function), inspect its declaration to determine this information.

Additional Information

Actually, Delphi is probably expecting not only a comma, but also at least one more parameter following the comma. As the comma is the first thing expected that is missing, the missing comma is reported as the problem.

Compilation terminated; too many errors

Possible Cause of Error

There are too many errors present in the current project.

Quick Fix

Comment out a large block of code to reduce the number of "live" errors and then fix the errors one at a time until you can remove the comments (and work on the errors contained therein).

Additional Information

You may be trying to do too much at once or have waited too long before attempting to compile. As you develop your program, periodically check the validity of your code by selecting Project | Syntax Check, and resolve the errors as you proceed, rather than waiting until the "end" for a "debug-o-rama."

Component already installed

Possible Cause of Error

The component you are attempting to install is already a part of your VCL.

Quick Fix

Select **Revert** in the Install dialog box.

Additional Information

If you get this error message, and subsequently have no VCL at all (the library could not load as it became corrupted), reinstall it from the Delphi CD.

Delphi 1

Reinstall COMPLIB.DCL to:

`C:\Borland\Delphi\BIN.`

Delphi 2

Reinstall CMPLIB32.DCL to:

`C:\Program Files\Borland\Delphi 2\BIN.`

Delphi 3 and 4

Reinstall VCL30.DPL (Delphi 3) or VCL40.DPL (Delphi 4) to \Windows\ System and VCL30.DCP (Delphi 3) or VCL40.DCP (Delphi 4) to \Program Files\Borland\Delphi X\Lib.

You may need to reinstall Delphi. If so, first uninstall your existing installation of Delphi.

Connection error—no server available

Possible Cause of Error

You may be attempting to use the "Delphi Connection" in ReportSmith without providing both a TReport component as well as either a TTable component or a TQuery component (with their Active property set to True).

Quick Fix

Provide a TReport component and either a TTable component or a TQuery component, setting the Active property of the table or query component to True.

Additional Information

You must have both ReportSmith and a Delphi TReport component to incorporate ReportSmith reports in your Delphi application. ReportSmith was provided with both Delphi 1 and Delphi 2. The Delphi 3 CD contains Delphi 1, so you can install ReportSmith from there if desired (not to be confused with the TReport component—ReportSmith is a reporting tool, TReport is Delphi's encapsulation of/interface to that tool). Although the TReport component is not installed by default with Delphi 3, it _is_ still available. Follow these steps to install it on your component palette:

1. Select **Component | Configure Palette....**
2. Select **Data Access** from the Pages list.
3. Scroll all the way to the bottom and locate the TReport component.
4. Highlight the TReport component.
5. Select the **Add** button. The TReport component will be added to your Data Access component palette page.

Connection in use by another statement

Possible Cause of Error

1. You may be attempting to open or execute a query while the result set of a previous query is still pending. In other words, the entire result set has not been retrieved yet.
2. You may be attempting to execute a stored procedure after a prior stored procedure failed.
3. You may have called Unprepare on a TQuery before the entire result set was returned.

Quick Fix

1. Ensure that the previous query has finished processing before running a new query. To do so, call TQuery's Last method. You can then call First to move to the top of the result set if so desired. For example:

```
with Query1 do
begin
  Open;
  Last;
  First;
end;
```

Alternatively, you can call the FetchAll method:

```
with Query1 do
begin
  Open;
  FetchAll;
end;
```

2. Call TStoredProc's Unprepare method following the execution of the first stored procedure and prior to execution of the second one, like this:

```
with StoredProc1 do begin
  Prepare;
  try
    ExecProc;
  finally
    Close;
    Unprepare;
  end;
end;
```

```
with StoredProc1 do begin
  StoredProcName := 'SafewayMosaic';
  Prepare;
  try
    ExecProc;
  finally
    Close;
    Unprepare;
  end;
end;
```

3. Add a call to Last before calling Unprepare:

```
with Query1 do
begin
  Last;
  Close;
  Unprepare;
end;
```

Additional Information

> **Note:** Make sure you are through with the results of the query or stored procedure and have closed it before you call Unprepare. If you call Unprepare on an open query, you will get the error message "Cannot perform this operation on an open dataset."

3. Calling TQuery.Unprepare frees resources that the TQuery component allocated. Delphi will call Prepare and Unprepare for you implicitly if you do not call them explicitly. Call Prepare each time the "Select" part of a SQL statement changes. If the "Select" part never changes, call Prepare once before the query runs the first time. Each call to Prepare should have a corresponding call to Unprepare.

Note: This error usually seems to occur while accessing MS SQL Server or Sybase databases.

Constant expression expected

Possible Cause of Error

You may have attempted to assign the address of a local (stack) or dynamic (heap) variable to a pointer constant. For example, the following will generate this error message:

```
procedure TForm1.Button1Click(Sender: TObject);
var
  i: integer;
  const ptr: Pointer = @i;
```

Quick Fix

To assign the address of a variable to a pointer constant, the variable must be global:

```
{ Interface section }
var
  Form1: Tform1;
  s: string = 'It''s Howdy Doody Time!';
. . .
procedure TForm1.Button1Click(Sender: TObject);
var
  const ptr: Pointer = @s;
```

Additional Information

See "Pointers" in Delphi help for more information.

Constant expression violates subrange bounds

Possible Cause of Error

1. You may be attempting to assign to an element of an array which does not exist. For example, the following will produce the error message under

discussion, as it attempts to access an element that is beyond the declared bounds of the array:

```
type
  Rays = array[0..3] of string;
end;
...
procedure Radiation;
var
  FamousRays: Rays;
begin
  FamousRays[0] := 'Ray Bolger';
  FamousRays[1] := 'Ray Konopka';
  FamousRays[2] := 'Ray Krok';
  FamousRays[3] := 'Ray Lischner';
  FamousRays[4] := 'Ray Snethen'; {This causes the error as FamousRays
                                    has no element 4}
end;
```

2. You may have assigned a variable a value that is either too small or too large for its data type. For example, you may be assigning a negative number to a variable of data type Byte, which only accepts integers from 0 to 255.

Quick Fix

1. Ensure that you do not try to assign a value to an array element beyond the length of the array as declared.

2. Ensure that the values you assign are compatible with the data type of the variable to which you are assigning them.

Additional Information

See "Subrange Types" in Delphi help for more information.

Constant object cannot be passed as var parameter

Possible Cause of Error

1. You may have attempted to pass a constant parameter to a procedure or function expecting a variable parameter. For example, the following will generate this error message:

```
procedure GiveMeAPointer(var malleable: string);
var
  owwhoooWerewolvesOfLondon: Integer;
begin
```

```
    owwhoooWerewolvesOfLondon := Form1.InstanceSize;
    malleable := malleable + ' ' + IntToStr(owwhoooWerewolvesOfLondon);
end;
procedure BigShovel(const Immutable: string);
begin
  GiveMeAPointer(Immutable);
end;
procedure RoyalMountainKingMineOrangeMonster;
begin
  BigShovel('Hitachi');
end;
```

because the actual parameter Immutable is a constant parameter, but the parameter malleable is a variable parameter.

2. You may have attempted to pass a class property to a procedure or function that expects a variable. For example, you may have tried something like the following:

```
type
  TTime = class
  private
    FWound: string;
  public

    . . .
  published
    property Wound: string read FWound
                    write SetWound;
  end;
. . .
procedure TForm1.HealAll(Sender: Tobject);
var
  Sage: TTime;
begin
  Sage := TTime.Create;
  Wound := 'Bury My Heart at Wounded Knee';
  delete(Sage.Wound, 1, Length(Sage.Wound));
```

Quick Fix

1. If you want to modify the value of the parameter, remove the *const* reserved word from the parameter declaration in the calling procedure. If you do <u>not</u> want the value to be modifiable, remove the *var* reserved word from the parameter declaration in the called procedure.

2. Assign the property's value to a variable, and then pass that variable to the procedure or function. For example, to solve the problem created by the code above, you could do this:

```
procedure TForm1.HealAll(Sender: Tobject);
var
  s: String;
  Sage: TTime;
begin
  Sage := TTime.Create;
  Wound := 'Bury My Heart at Wounded Knee';
  s := Sage.Wound;
  delete(s, 1, Length(s));
  Sage.Wound := s;
```

Additional Information

1. Be consistent with the way you declare your variables. They can be declared as constant (const), variable (var), or value (the default), but once they are declared as one type, do not attempt to change them to another. For more information about parameter types, see "Passing Parameters" in Delphi help for more information.

2. Look up the procedure or function in Delphi help to ascertain what types of arguments it expects and in which order. If it is a third-party procedure or function, consult the documentation or source code. If it is one of your own procedures or methods, consult your own code. Of course, in this case you might alternatively decide to alter the declaration of the procedure or function.

Constant or type identifier expected

Possible Cause of Error

You may have declared a local variable of a type that the compiler does not recognize as a type. In other words, the compiler "knows" the symbol you used as the type, but it does not apply in this context (it is not a valid type). For example, the following will generate the error message under discussion:

```
var f: Text;
```

Quick Fix

Ensure that the types you assign your variables are built-in Object Pascal types or user-defined types that the current module has access to, either in that they have previously been declared in the current unit or in a unit accessible through the current unit's Uses section.

Additional Information

The following produces the error message "Undeclared Identifier: Tex":

```
f: Tex;
```

As noted above, the following will produce the error message "Constant or Type Identifier Expected":

```
f: Text;
```

You can, though, use the Text type by prepending it with "System" like so:

```
f: System.Text;
```

You can also use:

```
f: Textfile;
```

> **Note:**   Many controls have a property called Text, such as TMemo and TRichEdit, but Text cannot be used as a data type.

Constant out of range

Possible Cause of Error

1. You may have assigned a value to a subrange type which is either greater than or less than the bounds of the subrange type. To be more specific, you may have declared a subrange type and then made an assignment to it like this:

```
var
  OctoberRoster: 1..25;
begin
  OctoberRoster := 0;
```

2. You may have assigned a value to an Object Pascal type that is too large or too small for that data type to store. For example, the Byte data type can store values between 0 and 255. You will get the error message under discussion if you try to store something less than 0 or greater than 255 in a Byte variable, like this:

```
const
  Under, Over: Byte;
begin
  Under: -1;
  Over := 256;
```

Quick Fix

1, 2. Ensure that you remain within the limits of all Object Pascal and user-defined subrange types in all assignments you make.

Additional Information

Rather than dealing with the problem after it has arisen (reactively), you can deal with it proactively by preparing for and preventing the problem from occurring. Here is one way you can do that:

```
const
  Under, Over: Byte;
begin
  if StrToInt(Edit1.Text) in [0..255] then
    Under := StrToInt(Edit1.Text);
```

Alternatively, instead of explicitly checking for a problem, you can code defensively and "reactively" (as opposed to proactively) handle an error if and when it arises, like this:

```
const
  Under, Over: Byte;
begin
  try
    Under := StrToInt(Edit1.Text);
  except
    on exception do {trap and handle error}
  end;
end;
```

Constants cannot be used as open array arguments

Possible Cause of Error

You may have a syntax error in a method such as TDataSet's InsertRecord. For example, the following will generate the error message under discussion:

```
Table1.InsertRecord('Jenny Lind','Calaveras', 'California',50,1200);
```

Quick Fix

Add brackets to the array of values:

```
Table1.InsertRecord(['Jenny Lind','Calaveras', 'California',50,1200]);
```

Additional Information

In addition to the example given above, the custom procedure SendAryOfInts produces the error message under discussion:

```
procedure busywork(aoi: array of integer);
var
  li: longint;
  i: integer;
begin
  for i := low(aoi) to high(aoi) do
    ext := ext + aoi[i];
end;
procedure TForm1.SendAryOfInts(Sender: Tobject);
begin
  busywork(12,24,36,48); {This produces error,
          as attempt to send "literal values"}
end;
```

Again, simply add brackets to the procedure call:

```
busywork([12,24,36,48]);
```

Constructing Instance of < > containing abstract methods

Possible Cause of Error

1. You may be creating an instance of a class that contains abstract methods. An example of when this might happen is if you create a TStrings variable like this:

```
var
  CoffeeStrings: TStrings;
  . . .
  CoffeeStrings := TStrings.Create;
```

2. You may be creating an object that inherits one or more virtual abstract methods that are not being overridden in descendent classes.

Quick Fix

1. It is best to avoid creating instances of abstract classes, as it makes it too easy to accidentally call one of those abstract methods (which, by definition, have no implementation).

2. If you are not going to override the method in all descendent classes, make the method virtual (only), not virtual and abstract, in the ancestor.

   If you do intend the method to be virtual and abstract, be sure to implement it in all descendent classes.

Additional Information

1. You may want to declare a variable of TStrings but instantiate it as a TStrings descendent, TStringList for example, like this:

```
var
  CoffeeStrings: TStrings;
  . . .
  CoffeeStrings := TStringList.Create;
```

In this way you take advantage of being able to assign values to and from the TStringList you created (CoffeeStrings) with other TStrings descendents.

2. Virtual methods <u>may</u> but do not have to be overridden in descendents. If you redeclare them and use the *override* directive, you can inherit the functionality in the ancestor by calling:

```
inherited <methodname>
```

in the body of the descendent's method definition. You can then extend (add additional functionality to) the method in the descendent with descendent-class-specific code.

If you redeclare the method name without the *override* directive, you are replacing the method in the ancestor (see "Method < > hides virtual method of base class < >").

If you declare a method as virtual, you must also define it in the same unit, although you can define an empty method body, like this:

```
public
  procedure OverrideMe; virtual;
  . . .
implementation
  . . .
  procedure TForm1.OverrideMe;
  begin
  end;
```

If you declare a method virtual and abstract, descendent classes <u>must</u> override and implement it (or they will get the compiler warning under discussion).

Do not define a method declared virtual and abstract in the unit in which it is introduced (override and define it in descendent classes).

Constructors and Destructors must have register calling convention

Possible Cause of Error

You may have appended a calling convention reserved word other than *register* to a constructor or destructor's declaration. For example, any of the following will produce the error message under discussion:

```
constructor Create(AOwner: TComponent);
                    override; pascal;
destructor Destroy; override; stdcall;
constructor Create(AOwner: TComponent);
                    override; safecall;
destructor Destroy; override; cdecl;
```

Quick Fix

Remove the *pascal*, *stdcall*, *safecall*, or *cdecl* directive.

Additional Information

Register is the default calling convention for methods, and is the only one allowed for constructors and destructors. You do not have to explicitly append the *register* reserved word.

For more information on this subject, see "Calling Conventions," "Constructors and Destructors," and "Method Calling Conventions" in Delphi help.

Constructors and Destructors not allowed in OLE automation section

Possible Cause of Error

You may have declared a constructor or destructor in the Automated section of a class declaration.

Quick Fix

Move the constructor and/or destructor out of the Automated section.

Additional Information

Constructors and destructors are normally declared in the Public section.

The Automated section was introduced in Delphi 2, giving Delphi five "visibility specifiers," namely *Private*, *Protected*, *Public*, *Published*, and *Automated*. The Automated section is retained in Delphi 3 and 4 for backwards compatibility with Delphi 2.

For more information, see "Automated Components" in Delphi help.

CONTAINS clause is incorrect

Possible Cause of Error

The Contains clause in the Package Editor may have a syntax error. The following are not allowed and could cause the error message under discussion:

1. Adding invalid units to the Contains clause.
2. Including filename extensions (for example, .PAS) in the Contains clause.
3. Omitting the semicolon from the last file unit listed in the Contains clause.

Quick Fix

1. Ensure that all units you add are valid. To be valid, they must exist, be spelled correctly, and be on Delphi's search path. To inspect Delphi's search path, select **Tools | Environment Options... | Library | Library Path**.
2. Remove any filename extensions you may have added to the unit's names.
3. Ensure that you end the Contains clause with a semicolon.

Additional Information

The Package Editor's Contains page reflects the units in the Contains clause of the package source file (.DPK). An example .DPK file appears below:

```
package W8snM;
{$R *.RES}
{$R 'W8snMsrs.DCR'}
{$ALIGN ON}
{$ASSERTIONS ON}
{$BOOLEVAL OFF}
{$DEBUGINFO ON}
```

```
{$EXTENDEDSYNTAX ON}
{$IMPORTEDDATA ON}
{$IOCHECKS ON}
{$LOCALSYMBOLS ON}
{$LONGSTRINGS ON}
{$OPENSTRINGS ON}
{$OPTIMIZATION ON}
{$OVERFLOWCHECKS OFF}
{$RANGECHECKS OFF}
{$REFERENCEINFO ON}
{$SAFEDIVIDE OFF}
{$STACKFRAMES OFF}
{$TYPEDADDRESS OFF}
{$VARSTRINGCHECKS ON}
{$WRITEABLECONST ON}
{$MINENUMSIZE 1}
{$IMAGEBASE $00400000}
{$DESCRIPTION 'GeekO Components Weights & Measures Component Suite'}
{$DESIGNONLY}
{$IMPLICITBUILD ON}
requires
  vcl30;
contains
  AreaM,
  CubicM,
  DryM,
  LinearM,
  LiquidM,
  W8snMsrs,
  W8s;
end.
```

Control < > has no parent window

Possible Cause of Error

1. You may be attempting to display (or perform some other action on) a component which does not have a parent. For example, the following will produce the error message under discussion, as no parent has been assigned to the TBitBtn variable:

```
procedure TForm1.OrphanBitBtn(Sender: Tobject);
var
  Oliver: TBitBtn;
begin
```

```
    Oliver := TBitBtn.Create(Self);
    Oliver.SetFocus; {Setting focus to a control
                  without a parent causes error}
  end;
```

2. You may be attempting to access a control whose parent's window handle has not yet been allocated. For example, the form on which the control resides may not have been created yet.

Quick Fix

1. Assign a parent to a control before you attempt to display it or perform any other action on it. For example, assigning the form (which is referred to as Self, since the assignment is taking place in a method of the form) as the parent prevents the error:

```
procedure TForm1.ChildBitBtn(Sender: Tobject);
var
  Junior: TBitBtn;
begin
  Junior:= TBitBtn.Create(Self);
  Junior.Parent := Self; {Assign Form1 as parent}
  Junior.SetFocus; {This works like a charm now}
end;
```

2. Ensure that a control has had its window handle allocated before referencing it.

Additional Information

1. Do not confuse the parent and owner of a control. A control can, but need not, have the same control as both its owner and its parent.

An owner handles the creation and destruction of its owned components, and thus has to do with memory allocation and deallocation.

A parent, on the other hand, is a windowed control that visually contains the control. The parent thus has to do with the surface on which the child control is displayed.

A control may have the same owner as its parent. For example, a TBitBtn could have a TPanel as its parent, and both the TBitBtn and the TPanel would have a TForm as their owner.

As mentioned already, a control's parent may also be its owner. This need not be the case, though. The form could be the owner of the TBitBtn, but a TPanel could be the parent of the TBitBtn. Here is an example of that being the case:

```
procedure TForm1.ParentNotSameAsOwner(Sender: Tobject);
var
  Junior: TBitBtn;
begin
  Junior:= TBitBtn.Create(Self);
  Junior.Parent := Panel1; {Assign Panel1 as parent}
  Junior.SetFocus; {This still works like a charm}
end;
```

2. See "Creation Order" in Delphi help for more information.

Controls cannot be added to a data module

Possible Cause of Error

You may be attempting to add a visual component (a control) to a data module.

Quick Fix

Only add nonvisual components to data modules.

Additional Information

Although they are most useful as such, data modules are not just for housing data access components. You can place any nonvisual components on data modules, for example, TTimer components and Dialog components (such as TOpenDialog, TSaveDialog, etc.).

Corrupt table/index header

Possible Cause of Error

1. You may be attempting to set the IndexName or IndexFieldNames property of a TTable component which has a corrupt index.

2. You may be attempting to instantiate the fields of a table at design time (using the Fields Editor), but the table has a corrupt index.

3. You may be attempting to set a TTable's Active property to True, but the table has a corrupt index.

4. You may be attempting to open a table in Database Desktop which has a corrupt index.

Quick Fix

1-4. Delete and then re-create the index file.

Additional Information

If you receive this error in Database Desktop, it may be preceded by "Unable to open table."

If the table in question is a Paradox table, the index file which is corrupt probably has a .PX extension. Here is a list of the auxiliary files that you can (indirectly) create with Paradox and what they are used for:

<Tablename>.PX

This file contains the table's primary key information, and is probably the one that has become corrupt. If you designate a field or group of fields as the primary key, this file is created.

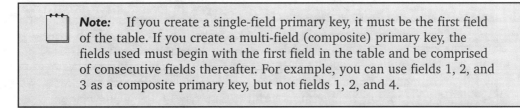

> **Note:** If you create a single-field primary key, it must be the first field of the table. If you create a multi-field (composite) primary key, the fields used must begin with the first field in the table and be comprised of consecutive fields thereafter. For example, you can use fields 1, 2, and 3 as a composite primary key, but not fields 1, 2, and 4.

> **Note:** The following data types cannot be included in a primary key: Binary, Byte, Formatted Memo, Graphic, Logical, Memo, and OLE.
>
> The Logical/TBooleanField type contains too few possible values (two) to be a valid primary key. A primary key's value must be unique within the table, and so your table would be limited to a maximum of two records. You <u>can</u>, however, create a secondary (non-unique) index on a Logical/TBooleanField, in order to sort the table by the N and Y values contained therein. See "Secondary Indexes" and "Creating Secondary Indexes" in Database Desktop help for more information.
>
> The Memo/TMemoField type is potentially very large, which could have a severe negative impact on performance, as the primary key values would have to be compared with one another and sorted accordingly.
>
> The other data types listed above are comprised of data which cannot be compared for indexing/sorting purposes (for example, how would you determine the relational positions of two bitmaps, one of Bullwinkle the Moose and the other of Marilyn Monroe?).

\<Tablename\>.X*nn*

Files with the .X*nn* extension (where *nn* is a hexadecimal number) contain secondary index information.

\<Tablename\>.Y*nn*

Files with the .Y*nn* extension (where *nn* is a hexadecimal number) contain secondary index information.

\<Tablename\>.VAL

Files with the .VAL extension contain information you provided through Database Desktop regarding validity checks, such as whether a column is required to contain a value (allowed to be null) or not, minimum and maximum values allowed for a column, default value for a column, and "picture" validation.

Select **Validity Checks** from the Table properties combo box in Database Desktop to access this feature.

Note: Delphi supports the default value you supply in all cases, but if you instantiate the fields in the table*, the Required, Minimum Value, Maximum Value, and Picture you specified in Database Desktop are ignored in your Delphi application. The reason for this is that the instantiated fields have "new and improved" properties that Delphi refers to (where appropriate for the data type) for this information. These properties are Required, MinValue, MaxValue, and EditMask, respectively.

As stated already, if you provided a default value for a column in Database Desktop, it is supported by your Delphi application even if you instantiate the fields at design time. However, if you assign a value to the corresponding TField desendent's DefaultExpression property, this value will take precedence over and "override" the default value you supplied in Database Desktop. For example, if you specify Not My as the default value in Database Desktop for a particular column, Not My will display in that column in new records you insert inside your Delphi application (although the user, of course, can change the value). If you assign San Andreas to the corresponding field's DefaultExpression property, though, the default value you set in Database Desktop (Not My) will be ignored and San Andreas will be used in its stead.

* To instantiate your table's fields at design time, use the Fields Editor. See "Fields Editor" and "Persistent Field Components" in Delphi help for more information.

<Tablename>.MB

Files with the .MB extension contain data from Memo and Graphic (TMemoField and TGraphicField) columns.

Could not create output file < >

Possible Cause of Error

1. You may have specified a directory that does not exist as one in which to store output files.

2. You may have specified a directory which is write-protected as one in which to store output files.

3. You may be trying to run an executable that is still running or is already running in another instance of Delphi.

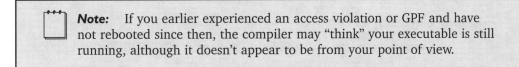

Note: If you earlier experienced an access violation or GPF and have not rebooted since then, the compiler may "think" your executable is still running, although it doesn't appear to be from your point of view.

Quick Fix

1. Ensure that the directory in which your output file is supposed to be created exists.

2. Remove the Read Only flag from the directory. To do so using Windows Explorer, right-click the directory, select **Properties** from the context menu, and then deselect the Read Only check box.

3. If you experienced a GPF and have not rebooted, do so.

Additional Information

By default, Delphi will store the output files in the same directory as the project (.DPR) file. Examples of output files are executables (.EXE), compiled units (.DCU), and map files (.MAP).

If you want to store the output files somewhere other than the project directory for a particular project, follow these steps:

1. Create, if necessary, the directory in which you will store the output file(s).

2. Ensure that the directory is not write-protected.

3. Select **Project | Options**.

4. Select the Directories/Conditionals page.

5. Enter the fully qualified path to the directory in the Output Directory combo box, for example, I:\Separate\Output.

6. Select the **OK** button to close the Project Options dialog box.

Note: When creating packages in Delphi 3, you can specify the locations for the .DPL and .DCP files you create by selecting Tools | Environment Options, the Library page, and then supplying values in the DPL Output Directory and DCP Output Directory combo boxes.

In Delphi 4, the DPL output directory combo box has been replaced with the BPL output directory combo box.

Could not find IDataBroker in type library

Possible Cause of Error

You may be missing a necessary file, namely STDVCL[32,40].DLL, which should be in the \Windows\System directory.

Quick Fix

If STDVCL[32,40].DLL is in your system, but not in your Windows\System directory, move it there. If it does not exist in your system at all, copy it from the Delphi CD to the \Windows\System directory and register it.

To register the .DLL (after copying it to the \Windows\System directory), follow these steps:

1. Open a DOS Window.

2. Change to the \Windows\System directory.

3. Enter the following at the prompt and then press the **Enter** key:

```
Regsvr32 <libraryname>
```

For example, if the Type Library in question is IDataBroker, you would enter the following (as it is defined in STDVCL32.DLL):

```
Regsvr32 STDVCL32
```

(In Delphi 4, the corresponding file is STDVCL40.DLL, so the line would be: Regsvr32 STDVCL40.)

> **Note:** Alternatively, you can use the Turbo Register Server utility (TRegSvr) which is a demo program located by default in
>
> `C:\Program Files\Borland\Delphi X\Demos\ActiveX\TRegSvr.`
>
> To do so, follow these steps:
>
> 1. Open the TRegSvr.DPR file.
>
> 2. Compile and run the project (press **F9**).
>
> 3. Activate a DOS session/Open a DOS window.
>
> 4. Navigate to the directory in which TRegSvr exists.
>
> 5. Enter the following at the prompt:
>
>   `TRegSvr STDVC132.DLL`
>
> 6. Press the **Enter** key.
>
> Turbo Register Server accepts three switches:
>
> -u   to unregister a Server or Type Library
> -q   to operate in quiet mode
> -t   to register a Type Library (this is the default action, so if this is what you are doing, you can simply type the program name followed by the server name, as shown in the example above).

Additional Information

STDVCL[32,40].DLL has a corresponding type library file, STDVCL.TLB, which is located by default in C:\Program Files\Borland\Delphi X\BIN.

Could not find interface < > in type library

Possible Cause of Error

The Type Library referenced by name in the error message may not have been registered.

Quick Fix

Register the Type Library referenced in the error message by following these steps:

1. Open a DOS Window.
2. Change to the C:\Windows\System directory.
3. Enter **Regsvr32 <libraryname>** at the prompt.
4. Press the **Enter** key.

For example, if the Type Library in question is IDataBroker, you would enter the following (as it is defined in STDVCL32.DLL):

```
Regsvr32 STDVCL32
```

(In Delphi 4, the corresponding file is STDVCL40.DLL, so the line would be: Regsvr32 STDVCL40.)

Additional Information

The default location of STDVCL[32,40].DLL is:

```
C:\Program Files\Borland\Delphi X\BIN.
```

STDVCL[32,40].DLL contains the interface declarations for Borland's standard VCL.

 Note: See the example program TRegSvr to examine the "low level" view of the registration process. It is located by default in:

```
C:\Program Files\Borland\Delphi X\Demos\ActiveX\TRegSvr
```

Could not find object. Cannot load an IDAPI service library. File: ODBC32.DLL

Possible Cause of Error

You may be attempting to load the default parameter overrides in a TData-Base component editor with an unrecognized alias entered in the Alias Name combo box.

Quick Fix

Select an alias from the Alias Name combo box. If necessary, create a new BDE alias before setting the default parameter overrides.

Additional Information

To create a BDE alias, follow these steps:

1. Select **Database | Explore**.
2. In SQL Explorer/Database Explorer, select **Object | New...**.

3. Select the driver type you want from the combo box (select Standard if you are working with Paradox or dBASE tables) and select the **OK** button.

4. The new alias will display in the Database page in the left pane with a default name such as "Standard1."

5. Right-click the new alias, select **Rename** from the context menu, and enter the name you want to give the alias.

6. In the Definition page in the right pane, select the appropriate driver from the Default Driver combo box.

7. Enter the path to the database in the Path edit box.

8. Select **Object | Exit**, and then **Yes** to save the changes you just made.

Could not initialize IDAPI

Possible Cause of Error

1. The BDE .DLLs may have been moved or deleted.

2. The WIN.INI file or system registry may have been modified.

Quick Fix

1, 2. Check to see that the BDE .DLLs exist and are in the location specified by the WIN.INI file (Delphi 1) or the system registry (Delphi 2 and 3). If they are not in the expected location but are elsewhere in your system, either move them to the expected location or edit the WIN.INI/system registry setting to use them from their current location. If they are not on your system at all, copy them from the Delphi CD.

Additional Information

Each PC which uses the BDE needs the BDE .DLLs and an IDAPI configuration file. In Delphi 1, the IDAPI configuration file is named IDAPI.CFG. In 32-bit Delphi, it is IDAPI32.CFG. In Delphi 1, the location of IDAPI.CFG is pointed to in the [IDAPI] section of the WIN.INI file. By default, these settings are:

```
DLLPATH=C:\IDAPI
CONFIGFILE01=C:\IDAPI\IDAPI.CFG
```

In 32-bit Delphi, the location of the .DLLs and the configuration file is held in the system registry. The system registry setting can be found by selecting Start | Run, entering Regedit in the Open combo box, selecting the OK button, and navigating to HKEY_LOCAL_MACHINE\Software\Borland\Database Engine.

Its default entries are:

`C:\Program Files\Borland\Common Files\BDE\IDAPI32.CFG`

for the DLL Path (BDE .DLLs), and

`C:\Program Files\Borland\Common Files\BDE\IDAPI32.CFG`

for CONFIGFILE01 (the Configuration file).

Could not find interface IDataBroker in type library

Possible Cause of Error

The Type Library which defines DataBroker may not have been registered properly during installation of Delphi.

Quick Fix

Register STDVCL[32,40].DLL using REGSVR32.EXE or TREGSVR.

Additional Information

DataBroker is defined in Borland's standard VCL Type Library, located by default in \Program Files\Borland\Delphi X\bin.

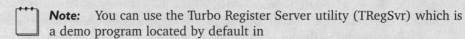

Note: You can use the Turbo Register Server utility (TRegSvr) which is a demo program located by default in

`C:\Program Files\Borland\Delphi X\Demos\ActiveX\TRegSvr`

to register servers. To do so, follow these steps:

1. Open the TRegSvr.DPR file.

2. Compile and run the project (press **F9**).

3. Activate a DOS session/Open a DOS window.

4. Navigate to the directory in which TRegSvr exists.

5. Enter the following at the prompt:

   `TRegSvr STDVCL32.DLL`

6. Press the **Enter** key.

Could not load <>. The OLE control may possibly require support libraries that are not on the current search path or are not present on your system

See "The OLE control may possibly require support libraries that are not on the current search path or are not present on your system."

Could not load RLINK32.DLL

Possible Cause of Error

The file RLINK32.DLL may not be located within Delphi's search path.

Quick Fix

Locate RLINK32.DLL. Its default location is:

```
C:\Program Files\Borland\Delphi X\BIN
```

If it is not in the default location but is elsewhere on your system, ensure that it is on Delphi's search path. Select **Tools | Environment Options**, then the Library page and Library Path combo box to inspect or modify Delphi's search path.

If it is not on your system at all, copy it from the Delphi CD.

Additional Information

Whenever possible, it is best to keep files in their default locations. Do not arbitrarily move files. Do not delete files if you don't know their purpose—the file may be one vital to the operation of your system, to Delphi, and/or to your sanity.

See "Error 0: RLINK32 Error opening file <TypeLibrary>.tlb."

Could not load StdOle version 1.0 type library

Possible Cause of Error

The STDOLE.TLB or STDOLE2.TLB may have been moved or deleted.

Quick Fix

Locate the file and move it into the \Windows\System directory.

If the file is not on your system at all, copy it from the Delphi CD to \Windows\System.

Additional Information

Delphi 1 uses STDOLE.TLB. 32-bit Delphi uses STDOLE2.TLB.

Could not load Type Library

Possible Cause of Error

You may have deleted a Type Library file.

Quick Fix

If you deleted a Type Library file, but have not emptied the Windows Recycle Bin (trash can), follow these steps:

1. Right-click the Recycle Bin.
2. Select **Open** from the context menu.
3. Right-click the file you want to restore (a Type Library file in this case).
4. Select **Restore** from the context menu.

If the file is no longer on your system (not even in the Recycle Bin), try to reinstall it from its original source (the Delphi CD, if that's where it came from).

Additional Information

The most important Type Library file that ships with Delphi 3 is STDVCL32.TLB, which is an interface to the standard VCL controls. The corresponding file in Delphi 4 is STDVCL40.DLL.

Could not load unit < > symbol information for < > Do you want to try to find this file yourself?

Possible Cause of Error

You may get this error while working with the ActiveX Control Wizard, after selecting a VCL component to inherit from. It may be that the file is indeed where it should be (notwithstanding the error message), but there is an error in the file.

Quick Fix

If there is an error in the VCL component you are attempting to derive from, fix this error before attempting to derive an ActiveX control from this component.

Additional Information

If the file cannot be loaded due to an error, you may have made changes to it after it was installed into the VCL. The compiler messages window will display any errors it encountered. Right-click on the error message and select **Edit Source**. This will take you directly to the line that is causing the error in the file. Fix the error, close and save the .PAS file, and then try again to create the ActiveX control.

Data Base Error Database access resulted in error

Possible Cause of Error

You may have attempted to access the Query Builder in Delphi Client/Server by right-clicking a TQuery component and selecting Query Builder... from the context menu, but you neglected to supply a valid password after supplying the alias name and selecting the OK button.

Quick Fix

Supply a valid password in the password edit box and try again.

Additional Information

The Query Builder is only available in the Client/Server version of Delphi.

> **Note:** The Query Builder in Delphi 4 is a completely new version of the tool.

Data Segment Too Large

Possible Cause of Error

1. You may have declared too many large unit global variables (that is, variables global to the unit). These are stored in the data segment.

2. You may be using data structures which consume a large amount of data segment space, for example, strings in Delphi 1 (strings consume 256 bytes in Delphi 1, unless you explicitly declare them as being smaller), large arrays, or records which contain numerous and/or large fields (such as strings). For example, you may be declaring a record such as:

```
TRecording = record
  Number: Integer;
  Hits:   Integer;
  Title:  String;
  Artist: String;
end;
var
  Platter, Album, Disc, CD, Music, Tunes, Toons: TRecording;
```

3. You may have declared numerous typed constants.

Quick Fix

1. Try to avoid using unit global variables as much as possible. Use local variables where possible. If you need to share global variables between multiple units, use a Globals unit specifically for this.

2. If your problem stems from too many strings in Delphi 1 (in 32-bit Delphi simply use long strings, which are 4-byte pointers), you can decrease the amount of space they consume by explicitly declaring their size, such as:

```
TRecording = record
  Number: Integer;
  Hits:   Integer;
  Title:  String[24];
  Artist: String[16];
end;
```

-OR-

You can use string resources for string constants your program will use. This is particularly easy beginning with Delphi 3, which introduces the *resourcestring* reserved word. The string constants are automatically stored in a resource file and dynamically loaded when referenced. You might use them something like this:

```
resourcestring
  KnockKnock = '%s who?';
  Excuse = 'The reason %s  doesn''t %s is %s';
  WeatherDialog = '%s enough for ya?';
  ElvinBishop = 'There ain''t no %s like %s %s';
```

As for string variables, you can reduce the size of memory allocated by declaring their size as the maximum length you want to allow for the particular string variable. In other words, if you declare a string that will contain a person's last name, it is not necessary to allocate the default 256 bytes for it*. In a case like this you could do the following:

```
var
  Surname: String[20];
```

This allocates 21 bytes instead of 256, a significant savings in memory.

Note: If you are working with Delphi 1 or 2 (prior to the addition of *resourcestring*), you can create string tables in resource files. To do so, follow these steps:

1. Create a text file with contents based on the following:

```
STRINGTABLE
BEGIN
  1, "String Cheese"
  2, "String of Pearls"
  3, "String of Fish"
  4, "Stringent"
END
```

2. Save the file with an .RC extension, such as STRINGY.RC.

3. Compile the .RC file into a Delphi resource (.RES) file at the DOS command line like this:

```
brc -r STRINGY.RC
```

4. Add the resource file to your unit with the following:

```
{$R STRINGYS.RES}
```

5. Use the Windows API LoadStr call to retrieve the string you want:

```
Label1.Caption := LoadStr(1)
```

If your problem stems from too many large data structures (other than strings), you can convert them to pointers, which only consume four bytes each, like this:

```
TptrRecording = ^TRecording;
TRecording = record
  Number: Integer;
  Hits:   Integer;
  Title:  String;
  Artist: String;
end;
. . .
var
  ptrPlatter, ptrAlbum, ptrDisc, ptrCD,
  ptrMusic, ptrTunes, ptrToons: TptrRecording;
```

If you use pointers, you will have to allocate and deallocate the memory for them. In Delphi 1, you can use an Initialization section and an exit procedure. In 32-bit Delphi, you can use both an Initialization and a Finalization section. Here is an example for Delphi 1 (using an exit procedure):

```
procedure SanitaryEngineer; far;
begin
  Dispose(ptrPlatter);
  Dispose(ptrAlbum);
  . . .
end;
initialization
  New(ptrPlatter);
  New(ptrAlbum);
  . . .
  AddExitProc(SanitaryEngineer);
end.
```

You then retrieve the values in the pointer by dereferencing it. For example, to retrieve the value from the Artist field, do it this way:

```
ptrPlatter^.Artist := 'Hootie and the Blowfish';
```

3. Use initialized variables instead of typed constants. For example, instead of typed constants, which are declared like this:

```
const
  StringCheeseString: String = 'Wisconsin Wonder';
  TypedTypeTypTip: Integer = 17;
```

use initialized variables, which are declared like this:

```
const
  StringCheeseString = 'Wisconsin Wonder';
  TypedTypeTypTip = 17;
```

Additional Information

This is primarily a Delphi 1 problem; more specifically, a Windows 3.x problem, wherein the data segment is limited to 64 K.

2. You can include as many string tables as you want, and the numbers used in them to designate the strings need not be consecutive.

---

*Note: In 32-bit Delphi, the long string is the default type, but you can still declare short strings by:

Explicitly declaring the variable as shortstring

-OR-

Adding the compiler directive {$H-} to the top of your unit(s)

-OR-

Using the technique shown above (explicitly restricting the string to a particular size).

---

3. Typed constants are added to a program's data segment. Initialized variables, on the other hand, are not. If you are not going to reassign the value of a typed constant, use an "untyped constant," or initialized variable, instead. Replace typed constants with initialized variables for compatibility with future versions of Delphi.

Data Structure Corruption

Possible Cause of Error

1. You may be attempting to make more than 255 changes within a single database transaction.
2. You may be using version 3.00 or 3.10 of the BDE.

Quick Fix

1. Limit the number of changes within a single database transaction to no more than 255.
2. Download the newest version of the BDE from:

   `www.inprise.com/devsupport/bde/bdeupdate.html`

Additional Information

Paradox limitations are shown below. For similar information regarding general BDE and dBASE limitations, see **http://www.inprise.com/devsupport/bde/ti_list/TI2751.html**.

127	Tables open per system
254	Tables open per system (BDE 4.01 and greater)
64	Record locks on one table (16-bit) per session
255	Record locks on one table (32-bit) per session
255	Records in transactions on a table (32-bit)
512	Open physical files (DB, PX, MB, X??, Y??, VAL, TV)
1024	Open physical files (DB, PX, MB, X??, Y??, VAL, TV) (BDE 4.01 and greater)
300	Users in one PDOXUSRS.NET file
255	Number of fields per table
255	Size of character fields
2	Billion records in a table
2	Billion bytes in .DB (Table) file
10800	Bytes per record for indexed tables
32750	Bytes per record for non-indexed tables
127	Number of secondary indexes per table
16	Number of fields in an index
255	Concurrent users per table
256	Megabytes of data per BLOb field
100	Passwords per session
15	Password length
63	Passwords per table
159	Fields with validity checks (32-bit)
63	Fields with validity checks (16-bit)

Data Type too large: exceeds 2 GB

Possible Cause of Error

You may have attempted to declare a user-defined data type that is too large. For example, the following type declaration produces this error message:

```
TDeviantVariants = array[0..135000000] of variant;
```

as does this:

```
TSoMuchTrouble = array[0..1333333333] of integer;
```

Quick Fix

You must decrease the size of the type. For example, the following will compile:

```
TTexasSizedArray = array[0..100000000] of variant;
```

as does this:

```
TAlaskaSizedArray = array[0..200000000] of integer;
```

Additional Information

200,000,000 integers and 100,000,000 variants should be enough in most cases. If necessary, declare two separate types, like this:

```
TAlaska      = array[0..200000000] of integer;
TAlaskaAnnex = array[0..200000000] of integer;
```

(Declaring one array with the <u>combined</u> size of the two shown above results in the error message under discussion.)

Database name missing

Possible Cause of Error

You may have attempted to set a TDatabase component's Connected property to True without having first assigned a value to the DatabaseName property.

Quick Fix

Assign a value to the TDatabase component's DatabaseName property before attempting to set its Connected property to True.

Additional Information

The TDatabase component is similar to the TSession component in that one is instantiated for you "behind the scenes" when necessary with properties set to default values.

It can be to your advantage to explicitly create a TDatabase component at times, especially when connecting to a SQL server database (such as Interbase, Oracle, MS SQL Server, Informix, etc.).

You can improve performance in such cases by setting the TDatabase component's KeepConnection property to True, preventing multiple time-consuming connection initializations during the life of the program.

A TDatabase component also allows you to use transaction processing by calling TDatabase's StartTransaction method followed by either Commit or Rollback, depending on the success or failure of the transaction.

Here is an example of using database transactions:

```
begin
  with Database1 do
    begin
      StartTransaction;
      try
        Query1.Active := True;
        Commit;
      except
        Rollback;
      end; {except block}
    end;   {with block}
end;
```

For more information on database transactions, see "Handling Transactions" in Delphi help.

Dataset not configured for network access

Possible Cause of Error

You may have set the BDE's NetDir setting to a local drive.

Quick Fix

The NetDir setting/directory must be a shared network directory to which all users who will access the tables have read, write, and create rights.

Additional Information

Two TSession properties, NetFileDir and PrivateDir, are specific to applications that work with Paradox tables. NetFileDir specifies the directory that contains the Paradox network control file, PDOXUSRS.NET. This file governs sharing of Paradox tables on network drives. All applications that need to share Paradox tables must specify the same directory for the network control file (typically a directory on a network file server).

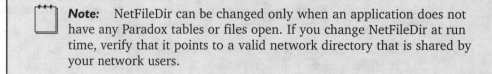

Note: NetFileDir can be changed only when an application does not have any Paradox tables or files open. If you change NetFileDir at run time, verify that it points to a valid network directory that is shared by your network users.

Dataset not in edit or insert mode

Possible Cause of Error

You may be either attempting to edit a value in a table, or attempting to insert a new record while the dataset is in a mode other than edit or insert.

Quick Fix

Place the dataset in edit or insert mode before making modifications or additions to it. For example, if you want to edit the current record of the Pizza table's MonthlySpecial field, you could do the following:

```
with Pizza do
begin
  Edit;
  PizzaMonthlySpecial.AsString := 'Italian Garlic';
  Post;
end;
```

Additional Information

For the above syntax to work (PizzaMonthlySpecial.AsString), the field needs to be instantiated at design time using the Fields editor. Otherwise, you will need to assign a value to the field using TDataset's Fields, FieldValues, or FieldByName properties.

The possible states, or modes, of a TDataset are:

dsBrowse, dsCalcFields, dsCurValue, dsEdit, dsFilter, dsInactive, dsInsert, dsNewValue, dsOldValue, and dsSetKey

DAX Error: Class not registered

Possible Cause of Error

You may not have a necessary file, for example DBCLIENT.DLL, installed and registered on the client machine(s).

Quick Fix

Install and register the file on the client machine(s).

Additional Information

To register the file (after copying it to the \Windows\System directory), follow these steps:

1. Open a DOS window.

2. Change to the \Windows\System directory.

3. Enter the following at the prompt and then press the **Enter** key:

```
Regsvr32 <filename>
```

For example, if the file in question is DBCLIENT.DLL, it would be:

```
Regsvr32 DBCLIENT.DLL
```

 Note: Alternatively, you can use the Turbo Register Server utility (TRegSvr) which is a demo program located by default in

```
C:\Program Files\Borland\Delphi X\Demos\ActiveX\TRegSvr.
```

To do so, follow these steps:

1. Open the TRegSvr.DPR file.

2. Compile and run the project (press **F9**).

3. Activate a DOS session/Open a DOS window.

4. Navigate to the directory in which TRegSvr is located.

5. Enter the following at the prompt:

```
TRegSvr DBCLIENT.DLL
```

6. Press the **Enter** key.

Turbo Register Server accepts three switches:

-u   to unregister a Server or Type Library
-q   to operate in quiet mode
-t   to register a Type Library (this is the default action, so if this is what you are doing, you can simply type the program name followed by the server name, as shown in the example above)

See "Class not registered."

DAX Error: Name not unique in this context

See "Name not unique in this context."

DAX Error: Unexpected failure

Possible Cause of Error

The application server may have raised an exception during initialization.

Quick Fix

Add exception handling to your application server.

Additional Information

By trapping errors in the application server, you can determine the specific nature of the problem that is being encountered.

DCOM not installed

Possible Cause of Error

You may have attempted to set the Connected property of a TMIDASConnection component to True while its ConnectType property was set to ctDCOM and its UseBroker property was set to False without first installing DCOM.

Quick Fix

If necessary, download and install DCOM from Microsoft's web site.

Additional Information

Windows NT 4, Windows 98, and IE4 (Internet Explorer 4) all include DCOM.

Debug process is already running

Possible Cause of Error

1. You may have a watch window open and are stepping or tracing through your code faster then the watch window can update itself.
2. You may have terminated a program in the Delphi IDE that generated an exception without using Run | Program Reset and subsequently attempted to compile or run it.

Quick Fix

1. Wait until the watch window has updated its display before stepping or tracing further.
2. After a run-time exception, select **Run | Program Reset**.

Additional Information

2. By selecting Run | Program Reset after experiencing exceptions, Delphi releases resources allocated by calls to the VCL and clears your program's variable settings.

   However, resetting a program from the Delphi IDE in this way (Run | Program Reset) does not necessarily release all Windows resources allocated by your program.

   If you continually experience instability for no apparent reason, select **File | Close All**, then **File | Exit**, and finally restart Delphi and try to compile the project again.

Debug session in progress. Terminate?

Possible Cause of Error

You may have selected Project | Build All, Project | Compile, or Project | Syntax Check while your project is currently running or paused.

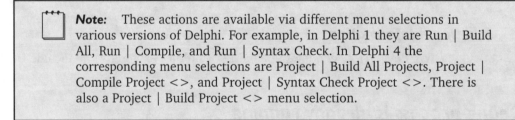

> **Note:** These actions are available via different menu selections in various versions of Delphi. For example, in Delphi 1 they are Run | Build All, Run | Compile, and Run | Syntax Check. In Delphi 4 the corresponding menu selections are Project | Build All Projects, Project | Compile Project < >, and Project | Syntax Check Project < >. There is also a Project | Build Project < > menu selection.

Quick Fix

Select **Cancel** when you receive this error message and then select **Run | Program Reset**.

Additional Information

If you are experiencing unusual exceptions or error messages, select **File | Close All**, then **File | Exit**, then start Delphi again. If you continue to have problems, close and then restart Windows.

Debugger kernel error. Error code: < >

Possible Cause of Error

1. Your program may be attempting to load a .DLL (either a "regular" .DLL or a package, which is a Delphi-specific .DLL with a .DPL extension) that it is unable to find. It either does not exist on your system, or is not in the current directory or the search path.

2. It may be that a procedure or function that you are attempting to access in a .DLL is not available due to a spelling or case mismatch error.

3. It may be that a procedure or function that you are attempting to access in a .DLL is not available due to unidentical parameter signatures (a mismatch of parameter numbers, types, or sequence).

4. You may be stepping through your code too fast while monitoring several complex variables in the watch window.

Quick Fix

1. Ensure that any required .DLLs are accessible. By convention, .DLLs (including .DPLs, or packages) are installed in the \Windows\System directory. In the world of computers, it is usually good to go by convention unless you have an excellent reason not to.

2. Verify that any procedures or functions in .DLLs you call match those in the .DLL in question in spelling and case. Exported procedure and function names are case-sensitive in 32-bit Windows.

3. Verify that you are calling procedures and functions with the same number and type of parameters, and in the same sequence.

4. Allow all the values in the watch window to update before continuing to step through your code, or delete some of the watches.

Additional Information

Attempt to run the program from Windows Explorer. You may get a more descriptive error message, detailing which .DLL is missing (provided that is the problem).

Remember, too, that you cannot "mix and match" 16-bit and 32-bit .DLLs.

Declaration expected but < > found

Possible Cause of Error

1. You may have entered something other than a valid Object Pascal declaration in a location where the compiler expects to find a declaration.

   To be more specific, you may get this error message if you use an Object Pascal reserved word or begin a declaration with anything other than an underscore or an alpha character (a..z, A..Z). Numbers are allowed after the first character; other characters are not allowed at all.

   For example, these declarations are <u>not</u> allowed:

   ```
   string: string;    {Object Pascal reserved word}
   1string: string;   {begins with a number}
   +1string: string   {the + character cannot be used}
   ```

2. You may have deleted or omitted something that is necessary. For example, removing the Begin and End section from a .DLL will produce the error message under discussion.

3. You may have added a Finalization section to a unit without first supplying an Initialization section.

Quick Fix

1. Use a legal Object Pascal name for the declaration. These declarations are fine:

   ```
   stringy: string;
   a1string: string;
   _1string: string;
   ```

2. Add back the necessary declaration.

3. Add an Initialization section prior to the Finalization section.

Additional Information

3. If you use a Finalization section, you must also use an Initialization section. You can initialize variables, allocate memory, etc., in the Initialization section. The Finalization section is a good place to deallocate memory and free other resources.

Declaration of < > differs from previous declaration

Possible Cause of Error

1. A declaration of a procedure or function in the Implementation part differs from its previous declaration.

2. A method you are attempting to override may have a different signature (number, type, or order of parameters) than the original which you are attempting to override.

3. You may be attempting to override a virtual method, but are using a different calling convention than the one used by the overridden method.

Quick Fix

1. Refer to the original declaration of the procedure or function and use that signature in its implementation also.

2. When overriding a virtual method, you must use the same parameter list (number, type(s), name(s), and order of parameters).

3. Use the same calling convention in your overridden method as used in the original, overridden method.

Additional Information

3. Look up "calling conventions" in Delphi's online help for more information.

Note: If you use the "far" calling convention, you do not need to duplicate the parameter part of the declaration in the definition. Here is an example of going "far":

```
procedure fa(so, la, ti, do: String) far;
. . .
procedure Tform1.fa; {look ma, no parameters!}
var
  tsom: String;
begin
  tsom := so+la+ti+do+' thread';
end;
. . .
procedure TForm1.Edelweiss(Sender: Tobject);
begin
  fa('sew',' a',' needle',' pulling');
end;
```

Declaration of class < > is missing or incorrect

Possible Cause of Error

1. You may have modified or deleted the class name (descendent) from a unit's Interface section. For example, modifying a form's type declaration from:

   ```
   TForm1 = class(TForm)
   ```

   to:

   ```
   TPanel1 = class(TForm)
   ```

   will generate this error message.

2. You may have removed the reference to the type's ancestor from the Type declaration, like this:

   ```
   TForm1 = class { (Tform) is missing }
   ```

Quick Fix

1, 2. Revert the declaration to that automatically generated by Delphi, namely:

```
TForm1 = class(TForm)
```

Additional Information

You can declare a <u>new</u> type without specifying an ancestor, like this:

```
TBill = class
```

If you do, the ancestor will be the "ultimate" ancestor of all classes, TObject. You cannot, though, as shown above, implicitly change a form's ancestor from, for example, a TForm to a TObject.

DEFAULT clause not allowed in OLE automation section

Possible Cause of Error

The Default clause is not allowed in OLE Automated sections.

Quick Fix

Remove the Default clause from the OLE Automated section.

Additional Information

Delphi 2 and above has five visibility specifiers: *Private*, *Protected*, *Public*, *Published*, and *Automated*. A class's properties can specify a storage specifier of *stored*, *default*, or *nodefault*. These storage specifiers are not allowed in the Automated section, though.

The *index* specifier, which allows multiple properties to share the same access methods, is also not allowed in an Automated section.

Default property must be an array property

Possible Cause of Error

You may have declared a non-array property as the default property of the class. For example, the following property declaration generates the error message under discussion:

```
property Twiggy: String read FTwiggy
            write FTwiggy; default;
```

Quick Fix

Remove the *default* designation from the non-array property. You can only designate an array property as the class's default property. For example, the following is acceptable:

```
type
  TComputer = class
  . . .
  property Clones[Index: Integer]: String
    read FNetPC write SetNetPC; default;
```

Additional Information

> **Note:** Do not confuse the *default* directive you can use with an array property of a class (as discussed here) with the default storage specifier used to help determine which of a form's values are stored. The default storage specifier is used to save storage space and loading time in connection with streaming data to and from the form (.DFM) file. The difference between the *default* directive and the default storage specifier is made obvious by the presence or absence of a specified default value. For more information, see "Storage Specifiers" and "Default Property Values" in Delphi help.

The advantage of specifying a default array property is that you can then access or assign to that array property in code without having to specify the property name. For example, with the property declared above, you could assign a value to it like this:

```
var
  PC: TComputer;
  . . .
Clones[i] := Compaq;
```

In other words, as it is the default property, it is not necessary to "spell out" the property name when assigning to it, like this:

```
Computer.Clowns[i] := PackardBell;
```

 Note: If you want to make your code more explicit, you can fully qualify the statement by adding the default property to the statement. Either way (with or without) will compile fine. Omitting the default property is simply a shortcut.

Default values must be of ordinal, pointer, or small set type

Possible Cause of Error

You may have declared a property containing a default storage specifier whose data type is incompatible with those acceptable as default values. For example, the following produces this error, as a String data type cannot have a default value assigned to it:

```
property Nanook: string read FZappa write FZappa
                default 'great oogly moogly';
```

Quick Fix

Remove the default storage specifier and the corresponding default value. Do not declare default values for string, floating-point, or array properties.

Additional Information

As the text of the error message under discussion indicates, default property values must be of ordinal, pointer, or small set type. In practical terms, this usually means integers, Booleans, and enumerated types. As an example of what is acceptable and commonly used, here is an excerpt from Delphi's Buttons unit:

```
{ Enumerated type used later as a property type with a default storage
specifier }
type
  TButtonLayout = (blGlyphLeft, blGlyphRight,
            blGlyphTop, blGlyphBottom);
. . .
TSpeedButton = class(TGraphicControl)
  { Default storage specifier used with Boolean property }
  property AllowAllUp: Boolean read FAllowAllUp
            write SetAllowAllUp default False;
  { Default storage specifier used with Integer property }
  property GroupIndex: Integer read FGroupIndex
              write SetGroupIndex default 0;
  . . .
  { Default storage specifier used with enumerated type declared above }
  property Layout: TButtonLayout read FLayout
        write SetLayout default blGlyphLeft;
```

Delphi has three storage specifiers. Besides the one under discussion (*default*), there are also *nodefault* and *stored*. Normally, all property values are stored, and there is no default value for a given property. The only way to specify a default value is by using the *default* storage specifier. The only way to prevent a value from being stored is to use the *stored* storage specifier followed by a Boolean function whose return value determines whether the property is stored or not. Here is another excerpt from Delphi's Buttons unit showing the *stored* storage specifier in use:

```
TBitBtn = class(TButton)
. . .
private
  function IsCustom: Boolean;
  function IsCustomCaption: Boolean;
. . .
published
  . . .
  property Cancel stored IsCustom;
  property Caption stored IsCustomCaption;
  . . .
function TBitBtn.IsCustom: Boolean;
begin
  Result := Kind = bkCustom;
end;
```

```
. . .
function TBitBtn.IsCustomCaption: Boolean;
begin
  Result := CompareStr(Caption,
    LoadResString(BitBtnCaptions[FKind])) <> 0;
end;
```

> **Note:**   As properties normally do not have a default property, the *nodefault* property is not usually necessary, but can be used when redeclaring a property whose previous declaration used the *default* directive.

See "Storage Specifiers" in Delphi help for more information.

Destination must be indexed

Possible Cause of Error

You may be attempting to append, update, or delete records from an indexed table to, in, or from an unindexed table with the TBatchMove component. For example, if the Source table contains a primary key, and the Destination table does not, and you call the TBatchMove component's Execute method (either at run time or at design time in the Delphi IDE*) while the TBatchMove component's Mode property is set to batAppendUpdate, batDelete, or batUpdate, you will get the error message under discussion.

Quick Fix

Ensure that the table referred to in the TBatchMove component's Destination property has an index corresponding to one in the table referenced by the Source property.

Additional Information

> **Note:**   You can use the batAppend and batCopy modes when the destination is not indexed, for example when working with an ASCII table as the destination.

In order to update or delete specific records from a table, Delphi must be able to match the records in the Destination table with the records in the Source table. If the Destination and Source tables do not have corresponding indexes, this is impossible and you will get the error message under discussion.

> **Note:** The indexes must be of the same data type to correspond to each other, but they need not have the same name. In fact, they do not need to be of the same size (for data types which accept sizes as part of their definition). If, for example, you are working with Paradox tables, and the data type of the indexed fields is Alpha, one field can be created with a size of 20 and the other a size of 18. Of course, this could lead to values being truncated if the Destination field's size is smaller then the Source field's size.

---

*To execute the BatchMove operation at design time, follow these steps:

1. Set the TBatchMove component's Source property to a TDataset component.
2. Set the TBatchMove component's Destination property to a TTable component.
3. Set the TBatchMove component's Mode property to the one you desire or require (batAppend, batAppendUpdate, batCopy, batDelete, or batUpdate).
4. Right-click the TBatchMove component.
5. Select **Execute** from the context menu.

See "TBatchMove" in Delphi help for more information.

Directory Is Busy

Possible Cause of Error

Multiple applications (or multiple instances of the same application) may be attempting to use the same directory as their private directory.

Quick Fix

Either deploy each application so that it executes in its own separate directory and/or set the TSession component's PrivateDir property at application startup (before any tables are accessed). Each user's private directory should be inaccessible to other users; it can be either on the user's local hard drive or on the network if local hard drive space is limited. For example, to have the program create a directory on the user's local hard drive, you could do this before the tables are accessed:

```
var
  Extension, ExecName, MineAllMine : String;
  ExtensionPos: Integer;
. . .
ExecName := ExtractFileName(Application.ExeName);
Extension := ExtractFileExt(Application.ExeName);
ExtensionPos := Pos(Extension, ExecName);
Delete(ExecName,ExtensionPos,4);
MineAllMine := 'C:\Temp\' + ExecName;
if not DirectoryExists(MineAllMine) then
  CreateDir(MineAllMine);
if DirectoryExists(MineAllMine) then
  Session.PrivateDir := MineAllMine
else
  raise Exception.Create('For some reason, the private directory ' +
                 MineAllMine + ' was not created. Beats the heck out
                 of me why not, though!');
end;
```

> **Note:** To use the DirectoryExists function, you will have to add FileCtrl to your Uses clause (if it is not already there).

Additional Information

> **Note:** If you are using an additional TSession component (one session is created for you automatically), each session must have its own private directory.

This is a nonissue if each user is running his own local copy of the executable, as the Private Directory is implicitly set to the current directory. Unless you have changed it, this will be the directory in which the executable resides.

> **Note:** Do not set the PrivateDir setting to the root drive; always specify a subdirectory.

If multiple users are accessing the same program on a network (all running a single executable on a shared network drive), they will each need to have their Private Directory explicitly set to a different directory than the others. Otherwise, all the temporary files will try to use the same directory (the one in which the .EXE resides), and there will be conflicts (specifically, they will get the error message under discussion).

> **Note:** Unless you explicitly specify otherwise, the application's startup directory will be the private directory.

Directory is controlled by other .NET file

Possible Cause of Error

1. You may be attempting to access a table that is currently being accessed by someone else whose Paradox NetDir setting differs from yours. Each user must share the same netdir file (PDOXUSRS.NET) to enable concurrent access for the table.

2. There may be renegade, or stray, network directory file(s) (PDOXUSRS.NET) or lock (*.LCK) files on your system. These are sometimes left behind after an abnormal termination of your program (a crash).

3. You may not have Local Share set to True while accessing a directory on a peer-to-peer LAN.

Quick Fix

1. Configure each user's machine so that they all use the same NetDir setting (the network directory is the one in which the PDOXUSRS.NET file resides). You can do so by following the steps appropriate for your version of Delphi:

   #### *Delphi 1*

   If each user has their own copy of the BDE on their machine, you can use the BDE Configuration utility to assign the net file directory. To do so, follow these steps:

   a. Open the BDE Configuration utility.

   b. With the Paradox entry highlighted in the Driver Name list box, enter the complete path to the shared network directory wherein to store the network control file (PDOXUSRS.NET) in the NetDir setting.

   c. Select **File | Exit** and save your changes.

If any users do not have a copy of the BDE Configuration utility, ensure that the actual location of your IDAPI.CFG file (C:\IDAPI by default) matches that shown in the [IDAPI] section of WIN.INI for the CONFIGFILE01 entry.

If necessary, move the file to match the entry in WIN.INI or change the entry in WIN.INI to match the location of the file.

Delphi 2

If each user has their own copy of the BDE, you can use the BDE Configuration utility to assign their Paradox net file directory. To do so, follow these steps:

a. Open the BDE Configuration utility (BDECFG32.EXE) by selecting **Start | Programs | Delphi | BDE Configuration**.

b. With the Paradox entry highlighted in the Driver Name list box, enter the complete path to the shared network directory wherein to store the network control file (PDOXUSRS.NET) in the NetDir setting.

c. Select **File | Exit** and save your changes.

See "32-bit Delphi" below.

Delphi 3 and 4

If each user has their own copy of the BDE, you can use the BDE Administration utility to assign their Paradox net file directory. To do so, follow these steps:

a. Open the BDE Configuration utility (**Start | Programs | Delphi X | BDE Administrator**).

b. Select **Object | Open Configuration...**.

c. Open IDAPI32.CFG.

d. Navigate to Configuration | Drivers | Native | Paradox | Net Dir.

e. Enter the complete path for the directory wherein you want the network control file to reside. Select a shared network directory to which all users of the Paradox tables in question have read, write, create, and delete rights.

f. Select **Object | Exit** and then **Yes** to save the changes you made.

32-Bit Delphi

If any users do not have a copy of the BDE Configuration/Administration utility, you can consult the system registry to ensure that the location of IDAPI32.CFG (C:\Program Files\Borland\Common Files\BDE by default) matches that shown in the system registry. The DLLPATH system registry key is located in HKEY_LOCAL_MACHINE\Software\Borland\Database Engine.

If necessary, move the file to match the entry in the system registry or change the entry in the system registry to match the location of the file.

> **Note:** Another way to set the network file directory in 32-bit Delphi—but doing so dynamically as the program runs rather than creating a persistent system registry setting—is to assign the shared network directory you are going to use for the network control file to the Session's NetFileDir property. For example, you could do something like this:
>
> ```
> const
>   SharedNetDir := 'K:\LanCon\';
> . . .
> implementation
> . . .
> procedure TForm1.OnCreate(Sender: Tobject);
> begin
>   if DirectoryExists(SharedNetDir) then
>     Session.NetFileDir := SharedNetDir;
>   else
>     ShowMessage('Couldn't connect to shared
>       Paradox network net file directory');
> end;
> ```
>
> Alternatively, you can set the NetDir to the same directory as that of the executable:
>
> ```
> Session.NetFileDir := ExtractFilePath(ParamStr(0));
> ```
>
> Make sure that you set the NetFileDir property prior to any attempt to access the tables, either directly or indirectly. It is a good idea to close all tables before the program closes, and then open them soon after startup or as necessary.

2. Have all users exit all programs that access the tables in question. Search for and delete stray PDOXUSRS.NET and *.LCK files.

> **Note:** The .LCK file causing the problem is probably in the directory on the server which contains the data.

3. Set the Local Share setting to True in the BDE Configuration utility.

Additional Information

The directory in which the network control file (PDOXUSRS.NET) resides must be a shared network directory where all users who need access to the tables have read, write, and create rights. You can think of the network control file as a "traffic cop." Potential conflicts can be avoided if all drivers/users look to the same traffic cop/network control file for direction. If drivers/users are looking at different traffic cops/network control files, the results will not be pretty.

32-Bit BDE

Borland recommends that the UNC naming convention be used for all 32-bit BDE network connections. Doing so obviates the need for mapped drives. UNC uses the syntax:

```
\\(server name)\(share name)\(path)+(file name)
```

For example, using UNC, your BDE alias and NetDir paths may be something like:

```
\\BobRiggs\Cher\YBRoad\H2OGate
```

16-bit BDE

UNC is not supported. Avoid long filenames (and spaces in file and directory names). Each client must reference the location of the net file in the same way. In other words, each client's path setting must be identical except for the drive letter used. For example, the NetDir might be set on client one as:

```
T:\BobRiggs\Cher\YBRoad\H2OGate
```

and on client two as:

```
U:\BobRiggs\Cher\YBRoad\H2OGate
```

If multiple users will be sharing the same copy of an .EXE (i.e., one that resides on a shared network drive) that accesses Paradox tables, they will also need to set their Paradox PrivateDir setting to a location that only they have access to. For example, they can set PrivateDir to a directory on their own hard drive by assigning to the PrivateDir property of the TSession component. An example of how this could be done follows:

```
var
  Extension, ExecName, GomerPyle : String;
  ExtensionPos: Integer;
```

```
. . .
ExecName := ExtractFileName(Application.ExeName);
Extension := ExtractFileExt(Application.ExeName);
ExtensionPos := Pos(Extension, ExecName);
Delete(ExecName,ExtensionPos,4);
GomerPyle := 'C:\Temp\' + ExecName;
if not DirectoryExists(GomerPyle) then
  CreateDir(GomerPyle);
if DirectoryExists(GomerPyle) then
  Session.PrivateDir := GomerPyle
else
  raise Exception.Create(Gol-lee, the private directory ' +
                    GomerPyle + ' was not created. Aw, sarge!');
end;
```

 Caution: Do not set the PrivateDir setting to a root directory on a drive; always specify a subdirectory.

 Note: It may be that the BDE configuration has not been changed from the default setting, which specifies the root of the hard drive (C:\) as the directory in which to create and store the network control file. Do not specify a root directory as the NetDir directory. Specify a subdirectory other than the directory that contains the tables or executable.

Disk Error

Possible Cause of Error

You may have made changes to a file, and then attempted to check it into a version control system, such as PVCS, without having first checked out the file in writeable mode.

Quick Fix

If you want the changes made to be applied to the file, you must check it out in writeable mode.

Additional Information

PVCS is not shipped with Delphi, but Delphi Client/Server does have native support for it. See "PVCS" in Delphi help for more information.

Note: If you prefer, you can instead use an alternate version control system. One example of an alternative program of this type is Microsoft Visual Source Safe.

Disk full

Possible Cause of Error

You may be attempting to install a component whose associated resource file (.DCR) is corrupted.

Quick Fix

Delete the .DCR file (it has the same name as the component but the .DCR rather than .PAS or .DCU extension).

Additional Information

.DCR files contain palette bitmaps for the corresponding component. These are a nice feature to allow you to visually distinguish between components on your palette as well as on your forms and data modules. If a .DCR file is not provided, or if one is provided but you do not use it, the component will use its ancestor's bitmap.

Even if components share the same bitmap, there are ways to differentiate them from each other. On the component palette, hold your cursor over the bitmap until the hint displays the name of the component. With the component on a form or data module, its type will display in the Object Inspector. For example, if you created a descendent of the TBatchMove component and named it TSoftBatchMove, the drop-down list box at the top of the Object Inspector would display "SoftBatchMove1: TSoftBatchMove" while your descendent component has focus.

Disk write error

Possible Cause of Error

You may have called one of the following procedures when the disk to which you are attempting to write is full or has become full as a result of the operation:

➤ CloseFile

➤ Flush

➤ Write

➤ Writeln

Quick Fix

Keep at least 10 percent of your hard drive free. Delete unnecessary files. Back up files which are seldom or never accessed to removeable media (and then delete them from your system).

Additional Information

Failing to leave ample "breathing room" on your hard drive can indirectly cause many seemingly unrelated errors. Your system uses this for virtual memory, for one thing. The more free hard drive space, the more virtual memory is available. If you start getting odd error messages that do not seem to make sense, check your available hard drive space.

Dispid < > already used by < >

Possible Cause of Error

You may be attempting to use a dispid that is already assigned to another procedure of the class. For example, the following will produce the error message under discussion:

```
automated
  procedure OnClick; dispid 1;
  procedure OnKeyPress(var Key: Smallint);
                                  dispid 1;
```

Quick Fix

Use a unique dispid for each method. For instance, in the example shown above, simply replace one of the "dispid 1" clauses with a number other than 1, such as "dispid 2."

Additional Information

Method and property declarations in an Automated section can optionally have a *dispid* directive. If a *dispid* directive is used, it must be followed by a constant integer. If you do not explicitly specify a *dispid* directive with its corresponding number, the compiler will automatically generate a unique id for you.

See "Automated Components" in Delphi help for more information.

Dispid clause only allowed in OLE automation section

Possible Cause of Error

A *dispid* directive has been appended to a property which is not in the class's Automated section. For example, the following will generate the error message under discussion:

```
Public
  . . .
  property rillest8: integer read getF14 dispid 3;
```

Quick Fix

Only append the *dispid* directive to properties and methods in a class's Automated section.

Additional Information

Dispid directives can only be used in an Automated section. See "Automated Components" in Delphi help for more information.

Division by zero

Possible Cause of Error

You may be attempting to divide a number by zero. For example, if the variable *Divisor* evaluates to 0, the following will generate this error message:

```
var
  Dividend, Divisor, Quotient: integer;
begin
  . . .
  Dividend := StrToInt(Edit1.Text);
  Divisor := StrToInt(Edit2.Text);
  Quotient := Dividend div Divisor;
```

Note: Besides the *div* operator, you may be using the / (division operator for Real numbers) or *mod* operator.

Quick Fix

Ensure that the divisor is not 0 before dividing by it, or enclose the division operation in a *try...except* block. For example, to prevent the division operation from taking place if the divisor is 0, you can do something like this:

```
. . .
Dividend := StrToInt(Edit1.Text);
if StrToInt(Edit2.Text) > 0 then
  begin
    Divisor := StrToInt(Edit2.Text);
    Quotient := Dividend div Divisor;
  end;
else
  begin
    ShowMessage('Enter a value greater than 0 '
          +#13#10+ ' in the Divisor edit box');
    Edit2.SetFocus;
  end;
```

To enclose the operation in a *try...except* block, you can do something like this:

```
. . .
  Dividend := StrToInt(Edit1.Text);
  Divisor := StrToInt(Edit2.Text);
try
  Quotient := Dividend div Divisor;
except
  on EDivByZero do
    ShowMessage('Enter a value greater than 0 '
          +#13#10+ ' in the Divisor edit box');
    Edit2.SetFocus;
  end;
end;
```

Additional Information

If you are dividing by Real numbers, you need to use the "forward slash" operator, as opposed to the *div* operator, which is used when dividing integers.

Duplicate case label

Possible Cause of Error

This error message occurs when there is more than one case label with a given value in a case statement.

Quick Fix

Ensure that there is only one occurrence of each value in a case statement.

Additional Information

Specifying more than one action to take in the event of a particular case label cannot be "understood" by the compiler as it is ambiguous. The following example, where the case label "walton" is accounted for twice, causes the error message under discussion:

```
function GetFirstName(shagger: outfielders): string;
var
  FirstName: string;
begin
  case shagger of
  anderson:          FirstName := 'Brady';
  carter:            FirstName := 'Joe';
  davis:             FirstName := 'Eric';
  hammonds,walton:   FirstName := 'Jeffrey';
  surhoff:           FirstName := 'B.J.';
  tarasco:           FirstName := 'Tony';
  walton:            FirstName := 'Jerome';
  end;
  Result := FirstName;
end;
```

You <u>can</u> specify multiple case constants on one line, but none of them can be used more than once within the same case statement. For example, the following two case statements are valid:

```
function GetFirstInitial(shagger: outfielders): string;
```

```
var
  FirstName: char;
begin
  case shagger of
  anderson,surhoff:      FirstInitial := 'B';
  davis:                 FirstInitial := 'E';
  carter,hammonds,walton: FirstInitial := 'J';
  tarasco:               FirstInitial := 'T';
  end;
  Result := FirstName;
end;
....
function StartersEvaluation(innings: integer): string;
var
  outing: string;
begin
  case InningsPitched of
  1..3:          outing := 'Bombed';
  4   :          outing := 'Poor';
  5,6 :          outing := 'Decent';
  7,8 :          outing := 'Good';
  9   :          outing := 'Excellent';
  end;
  Result := outing;
end;
```

Duplicate database name < >

Possible Cause of Error

You may have assigned the same name to a TDatabase component's Database-Name property as one that is already on the form.

Quick Fix

Select unique names for all components.

Additional Information

For code clarity and ease of maintenance, it is a good idea to be descriptive in the name you use for components and component properties, such as TDatabase component's DatabaseName property. Delphi will not prevent you from supplying the name "DB" or "BigIron" or "q" to the DatabaseName property, but it may not be the best to use as far as code clarity and maintenance is concerned.

Duplicate field name < >

Possible Cause of Error

You may be attempting to use the same name for multiple database fields. For example, you may be creating fields like this:

```
with Table1 do begin
. . .
  with FieldDefs do begin
    Clear;
    Add('Outstanding', ftBoolean, 0, True);
    Add('Outstanding', ftString, 30, False);
  end;
```

Alternatively, you may be creating the fields multiple times. For example, the following will work fine the first time:

```
with Table1 do begin
. . .
  with FieldDefs do begin
    Clear;
    Add('Baseball', ftBoolean, 0, True);
    Add('Force', ftString, 30, False);
  end;
```

but fail on subsequent executions as the fields Baseball and Force already exist.

Quick Fix

Rename the duplicated field name to something unique. In the first example given above, for example, you could rename the second field SafeSliding.

Additional Information

See "CreateTable" in Delphi help for information on creating tables in code.

Duplicate implements clause for interface < >

Possible Cause of Error

You may have declared two delegate properties for the same interface. For example, the following will give you this error message:

```
property SomeInterface: ISomeInterface read
    ReadItAndWeep implements ISomeInterface;
property SomeOtherInterface: ISomeInterface read
    ReadItAndRejoice implements ISomeInterface;
```

Quick Fix

Remove one of the delegate interface properties (or change the name of one of the interfaces to another available interface).

Additional Information

See "Implements getter must be register calling convention" and "Read or Write clause expected but identifier < > found" for more information on what is not allowed while delegating properties to implement interfaces.

 Note: The *implements* directive is new with Delphi 4.

Duplicate resource

Possible Cause of Error

1. You may have a unit or a class within a unit that has the same name as a unit or class that already exists within the visible scope of the program. It could be one of Delphi's or another of your own units that you have duplicated.

2. You may be using components that have same-named resources in their .DCR files.

3. You may have attempted to manually add a resource to your project's .RES file.

Quick Fix

1. Locate the duplicate unit or class name, and then rename it. To do this with a unit, follow these steps:

   a. With the unit highlighted, select **File | Save As...**.

   b. Provide a unique name for the unit.

   c. Modify the references to the unit to reflect the new name. If it is a class name that is the culprit, simply edit it directly in the code window.

2. If the components are your own, or if you have the source code to them, inspect the .DCR files to see which two elements have the same name. Rename one of the resources and try again. To rename a resource using Delphi's Image Editor, follow these steps:

   a. Select **Tools | Image Editor**.

   b. Select **File | Open**.

   c. Navigate to and then open the resource file (.DCR).

   d. In the tree-view, navigate to the element you need to change.

   e. With the element highlighted, right-click on it and select **Rename** from the context menu.

   f. Enter a new name.

   g. Select **File | Exit**, and then **Yes** to save the change you made.

3. If you want to add additional resources, use a separate resource file, giving it a name that does not conflict with the project name or any of the unit names. Add your custom resource file(s) to Delphi. For example, to add a resource file you have created named Whatever.res, enter a line like:

   ```
   {$R Whatever.Res}
   ```

Additional Information

1. Pare your Uses clauses of any units that are no longer needed.

3. The project's resource file, which is automatically created by Delphi, is not intended to be modified. See "EResNotFound."

   If all else fails, try deleting all the *.DSM, *.DOF, and *.DSK files.

   See "Error Creating Form: Duplicate resource [Type:,Name:]."

Duplicate session name < >

Possible Cause of Error

You may have assigned the same SessionName property to two TSession components.

Quick Fix

Assign a unique name to each TSession component. Delphi can handle this for you automatically if you set the AutoSessionName property to True.

Additional Information

Normally, you do not need to add a TSession component to your database applications. A default TSession component is automatically created for you (similar to the TDatabase component). But if you are creating multi-threaded applications or if you are accessing Paradox tables residing in various places on a network, you can drop additional TSession components on your form or data module to facilitate operating under these circumstances.

 Note: Even if you do explicitly add TSession components to your application, you do not have to explicitly set the SessionName property, as they have an AutoSessionName property. For more information, see "AutoSessionName" in Delphi help.

Dynamic method or message handler not allowed here

Possible Cause of Error

You may have specified a message handling method or a dynamic method as a property's read accessor or write mutator. For example, either of the following property declarations will generate the error message under discussion:

```
private
  function Dynamo: Integer; dynamic;
  procedure wmuserchanged(var Message: TMessage);
    message WM_USERCHANGED;
. . .
published
  property propwash: integer read dynamo;
  property improper: integer write wmuserchanged;
```

Quick Fix

Replace the property's accessor function(s) with a private field or a method. Do not use message handling methods or dynamic methods as accessor functions for properties. For example, you could replace the above with something like this:

```
private
  FDynamite: Integer;
  procedure SetProper(NewProper: Integer);
. . .
published
  property propwash: integer read FDynamite;
  property proper: integer write SetProper;
```

Additional Information

See "Creating Properties" and "Dynamic Methods" in Delphi help for more information.

Dynamic method or message handlers not allowed in OLE automation sections

Possible Cause of Error

You may have declared a dynamic method or a message handling method in a class's Automated section. For example, either one of the following declarations will generate this error message:

```
automated
  procedure dynamo; dynamic;
  procedure wmvscrollclipboard(var Message:
     integer); message WM_VSCROLLCLIPBOARD;
```

Quick Fix

Remove the dynamic methods and/or message handling methods from the Automated section.

Additional Information

Trying to declare a message handling method as they normally appear (with TMessage as the variable, as opposed to an Integer, as shown above) results in the error message "Illegal type in OLE automation section: TMessage" being generated.

EAccessViolation

See "Access Violation."

EBitsError

See "Bits Index out of Range."

EClassNotFound

Possible Cause of Error

You may have directly modified a form's .DFM file, and it cannot now reconcile the contents of the .DFM file with the .PAS file.

Quick Fix

Inspect the .DFM file by right-clicking on the form and selecting View As Text from the context menu. Verify that the form's object definitions coincide with what is actually on the form.

Additional Information

Many new students have experienced this on failing to find their way around campus.

EComponentError

Possible Cause of Error

1. You may have given a component a name that is not unique.
2. You may have given a component a name that is not valid.
3. You may be attempting to call the RegisterComponents method outside the Register procedure in a component unit.

Quick Fix

1. Always use unique names within a namespace. If unit abc contains a component called AlphabetSoup, and so does unit xyz, they will have a difficult time coexisting.

2. In Object Pascal, identifiers (such as component names) must begin with either a letter or an underscore and each subsequent character must be a letter, an underscore, or a numeral.

3. Only call RegisterComponents from within the Register procedure of a component's unit.

Additional Information

3. The Register procedure and its call to RegisterComponents are created for you automatically when you use the Component Wizard.

EConvertError

Possible Cause of Error

You may be attempting to convert a value of one type to that of another type, but the conversion is not possible as attempted.

Quick Fix

Only convert types from one to another when the value in question can be translated, or converted, to the other type. This requires that the types being converted from and to have a corresponding conversion function, and that the value to be converted can be represented in the destination data type. For example, attempting to convert a String to a Boolean would not work, nor would attempting to translate a Float to a BLOb. In addition, sometimes the type of conversion is acceptable, but the value itself is not. As an example, attempting to convert the String value 'Parsley, Sage, Rosemary and' to a TTime value will not do anything—useful, anyway; in fact, it will generate the error message under discussion. However, converting the String value '10:09' to a TTime value using the StrToTime conversion function <u>does</u> work fine.

Additional Information

This is the generic class of error that is raised when there is a problem attempting to convert or typecast one data type into another.

You can use the EConvertError exception class as a data validation tool. For example, to verify that a date entered by a user is a valid date before storing it, you could do something like this:

```
try
  DayTripDay := StrToDate(Edit1.Text);
except
  on EConvertError do
```

```
MessageDlg('The value you entered does not
            evaluate to a valid date as used
               on Earth', mtError, mbOK, 0);
end;
```

> **Note:** Some of the more useful conversion functions available in
> Object Pascal/Delphi are: StrToCurr, StrToDate, StrToTime,
> StrToDateTime, StrToInt, StrToFloat, IntToString, DateToStr,
> DateTimeToStr, FloatToDecimal, FloatToStr, and VarToStr.

EDivByZero

See "Division by zero."

EFCreateError

Possible Cause of Error

You may have given a file an invalid name.

Quick Fix

Use valid Object Pascal names for all identifiers. Begin the name with either a
letter or an underscore and follow with additional letters, underscores, and
numerals.

Additional Information

This exception is a descendent of EStreamError, which is the base class of all
stream exceptions.

EFilerError

Possible Cause of Error

You may have attempted to register a class with the streaming system using
the RegisterClass procedure while there is a different class with the same
name already registered.

Quick Fix

Ensure that classes you create are unique, not only in functionality, declaration, and implementation, but also in name.

Additional Information

Attempting to register the same class more than once via a call to Register-Class does not cause a problem; it is just ignored. Different classes with the same name, though, raise this error.

This error is the base class from which the following errors descend: EClass-NotFound, EInvalidImage, EMethodNotFound, and EReadError.

EGPFault

See "Access Violation."

EInOutError

Possible Cause of Error

You may have attempted to append to a file that does not exist.

Quick Fix

Guard against this possibility by checking to see if the file exists, and if not, creating it "on-the-fly" like this:

```
var
  tF: TextFile; {or sT: System.Text}
begin
  AssignFile(tF,'TrueFun.txt');
  if FileExists('TrueFun.txt') then
    Append(tF)
  else
    Rewrite(tF);
  . . .
```

or like this:

```
var
  sT: System.Text; { or tF: TextFile}
begin
  AssignFile(sT,'SoTrue.txt');
  try
```

```
    System.Append(sT)
except
  on EInOutError do
    Rewrite(sT);
. . .
```

You can also guard against EInOutErrors on closing files (unable to save) like this:

```
procedure TForm1.CloseButtonClick(Sender:
                                  TObject);
begin
  . . .
  try
    CloseFile(globalLog);
  except
    on EInOutError do
      if MessageDlg('Problem with saving the file. Exit anyway?', mtError,
                    [mbYes,mbNo], 0) = mrNo then
        Exit; {the procedure, not the program}
  end;
end;
```

Additional Information

For the EInOutError to be available, you must have the I/O checking compiler directive set, either in the Delphi IDE or in code. To set it in the Delphi IDE, follow these steps:

1. Select **Project | Options...**.
2. Select the Compiler tab.
3. Check I/O checking in the Runtime Errors section.
4. Select the **OK** button.

To turn on I/O checking in code, add **{$I+}** or **{$IOCHECKS ON}** to the top of the unit in which you want to activate I/O checking. You will not need to do this unless it has been turned off, since it is "on" by default.

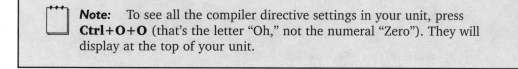

Note: To see all the compiler directive settings in your unit, press **Ctrl+O+O** (that's the letter "Oh," not the numeral "Zero"). They will display at the top of your unit.

EIntOverflow

See "Arithmetic Overflow Error."

EInvalidCast

See "Invalid typecast"

EInvalidGraphic

Possible Cause of Error

You may have attempted to load a file other than a .BMP, .ICO, or .WMF into an object expecting a valid Delphi graphic. For example, both of the following lines would generate this error, as .JPG and .GIF are not native Delphi graphics formats:

```
Image1.Picture.LoadFromFile('Kangaroo.jpg');
Image1.Picture.LoadFromFile('ChoosyMothersChoose SkippyNot.gif');
```

Quick Fix

Only load bitmaps (.BMP), icons (.ICO), and metafiles (.EMF and .WMF) into a TPicture object.

Additional Information

See "TImage," "TPicture," "TGraphic," "TBitmap," "TIcon," and "TMetafile" in Delphi help for more information.

EInvalidGraphicOperation

Possible Cause of Error

You may have attempted to perform an invalid operation on a graphic object. For example, attempting to resize an icon will generate this error:

```
Image1.Picture.Icon.Height := 36;
```

Quick Fix

Do not attempt to modify an icon's default size of 32 x 32 pixels for regular icons, 16 x 16 pixels for small icons.

Additional Information

See the "Cannot change the size of an icon" error message for more information.

EInvalidOp

See "Invalid floating point operation."

EInvalidOperation: Cannot create form. No MDI forms are currently active

See "Cannot create form. No MDI forms are currently active."

EInvalidOperation: Cannot make a visible window modal

See "Cannot make a visible window modal."

EInvalidPointer

See "Invalid pointer operation."

Element 0 Inaccessible—use "Length" or "SetLength"

Possible Cause of Error

You may be attempting to access or set the value of element 0 in a variable of type String in 32-bit Delphi. For example, this attempt to store element 0 in the byte variable LengthByteContents will generate the error message under discussion:

```
procedure Bight;
var
  s : String;
  LengthByteContents : Byte;
```

```
begin
  s := 'Cheese';
  LengthByteContents := s[0];
end;
```

This attempt to set element 0 will also generate the error message under discussion:

```
program Produce;
var
  s: String;
  LengthByteSize: Integer;
begin
  LengthByteSize := 25;
  s[0] := LengthByteSize;
end;
```

Quick Fix

Use the Length function and SetLength procedure to accomplish the same things in 32-bit Delphi. To store the length of a string variable in an integer variable, do this:

```
procedure FindStringLength;
var
  s : String;
  StrLength : Integer;
begin
  s := 'HowMuchIsThatPCInTheWindow';
  StrLength := Length(s);
end;
```

To set the length of the string, do this:

```
procedure SetStringLength(s: String;
        ArbitraryNumber: Integer );
begin
  SetLength(s, ArbitraryNumber);
end;
```

Additional Information

The native 32-bit Delphi string type, Long String, does not store the length of the string in element 0 as is the case in Delphi 1. This is why attempting to get or set the length of the string via element 0 does not work and is not allowed.

> **Note:** The SetLength procedure works differently in Delphi 1 and 32-bit Delphi. In Delphi 1, where short strings are used, the SetLength procedure sets the length byte element (0) to the value in the second parameter. This variable must be between 0 and 255.
>
> In 32-bit Delphi, where long strings are used by default, the SetLength procedure reallocates the amount provided in the second parameter to the string specified by the first parameter. See "SetLength" in Delphi help for more information.

You can assign any valid element of a string (other than 0) to another string, for example:

```
var
  s,t: string;
begin
  s := 'Are you just stringing me along?';
  t := s[1];
end;
```

'END' expected but < > found

Possible Cause of Error

You may have added something superfluous to a statement, such as a right parenthesis where none is needed.

Quick Fix

Remove the offending item that was "found."

Additional Information

You may wonder why the message is not " ';' expected but < > found." Prior to an *end*, the semicolon is unnecessary (although harmless); therefore the compiler does not "expect" it.

'End' expected but implementation found

Possible Cause of Error

You may have omitted the *end* that is needed to terminate a type declaration in the Interface part.

Quick Fix

Terminate type declarations with the *end* reserved word.

Additional Information

A type declaration must have the following structure:

```
type
  WhateverYouWant = class
    FWhateverYouWant: Boolean;
    procedure WhateverYouSay(widget: Integer);
  end; {don't forget to add this end at the end}
```

END. missing at end of module

Possible Cause of Error

1. You may have unmatched *begin* and *end* pairs.
2. You may have neglected to add the *end* reserved word following a case statement, *try...finally* block, or *try...except* block.
3. There may indeed be a final *end*, but the compiler cannot see it for some reason. For example, you may have a left curly brace ({) in your code somewhere which is causing everything after it to be "commented out" if it does not have a complementary right curly brace (}) to terminate the "commented out" section.

Quick Fix

1. Ensure that each *begin* has a corresponding *end*.
2. Append an *end* to each case statement, *try...finally* block, and *try...except* block.
3. If you have an unmatched left curly brace ({), either remove it if you don't want to "comment anything out," or add a right curly brace (}) to the end of the section that you do want to "comment out."

Additional Information

> **Note:** You can also comment code in 32-bit Delphi with the "C style" double forward slashes. For example:
>
> ```
> //This is commented out. Explain the code here.
> ```
>
> Get in the habit of adding an *end* as soon as you code a *begin*, a case statement, a *try...finally* block, or a *try...except* block. Then go back and fill in the "meat" of the statement. Also, indent your code in such a way that the various *begin...end* blocks visually stand out so that you can see which *begin* belongs with which *end*.

> **Note:** Beginning with Delphi 3, code templates are available. See "code templates" in Delphi help for details or select **Tools | Environment Options**, and select the Code Insight page. The Code Template section displays a list of predefined templates and a window that displays them. For example, the tryf (try finally) code template is this:
>
> ```
> try
>   |
> finally
> end;
> ```
>
> The vertical bar, or "pipe," shows where the cursor is located after using this code template—right where you want it to be to start coding your *try...finally* block.
>
> To use a code template, follow these steps:
>
> 1. In the code window, press **Ctrl + J**.
> 2. Highlight the code template you want from the list.
> 3. Press the **<Enter>** key.

EOLEError

See "Class not registered."

EOleSys—Class not Registered

See "Class not registered."

EOleSys—Operation Unavailable

Possible Cause of Error

You may be calling a method of an OLE Automation server that is not running. For example, the following will generate this error if Word is not running at the time of the call:

```
procedure TForm1.StartThatHog(Sender: TObject);
var
  Ovari: OleVariant;
begin
  Ovari := GetActiveOleObject('Word.Basic');
  Ovari.FileNew;
  Ovari.Insert('OLE! Death In The Afternoon');
end;
```

Quick Fix

Ensure that the OLE Automation server is running before attempting to access its methods. You can do this with the CreateOLEObject method:

```
procedure TForm1.StartThatHog(Sender: TObject);
var
  Ovari: OleVariant;
begin
  Ovari := CreateOLEObject('Word.Basic');
  Ovari.FileOpen('SunNumTu');
  Ovari.Insert('Morgan Tell MacKenzie Immerfort Purify "Sluggo" Shannon');
end;
```

Additional Information

If you are going to use the OLE Automation server more than just once in your application, you can prevent multiple "loadings" and "unloadings" of the server by declaring the OleVariant variable globally and instantiating it in the form's OnCreate event.

EOutOfMemory

Possible Cause of Error

You may have attempted to allocate more memory than you have available.

Quick Fix

If possible, equip your computer with at least 32 MB of RAM. Keep at least 10 percent of your hard disk space free so that it can be used for virtual memory.

Additional Information

See "Out of Memory" for more information.

EOutOfResources

Possible Cause of Error

1. You may be (directly or indirectly) attempting to allocate a window handle, but the maximum number of handles is already being used.

2. A Windows API function you directly or indirectly called may have failed.

3. Despite the message, there may be a bug in the video driver you are using, especially if you are operating in high-color (32 KB or 64 KB colors) mode.

Quick Fix

1. Keep the number of windowed controls (descendents of TWinControl) to a minimum. Use graphical controls where possible (they do not require a handle). Create as many forms as possible dynamically. See "Dynamically creating forms" below.

2. Consult the Win32 help file (Win32.HLP) that ships with Delphi for information on the particular API call. If that does not prove enlightening, you might consider purchasing *The Tomes of Delphi 3: Win32 Core API* by John Ayres, et al.

3. Switch to the standard Windows VGA driver, or to a less powerful mode of your video driver. If you do not know how to do this, consult the Windows documentation for instructions.

Additional Information

3. An example of this is a call to TWinControl's GetDeviceContext, which in turn calls the Windows API function GetDC.

Tips for preserving resources:

➤ Move as many forms as possible from the Auto-Create to the Available (dynamic) list. See "Dynamically creating forms" below.

➤ Where possible, use graphical components in place of windowed components. Graphical components do not need a Windows handle. For example, if you want to display a string of read-only text, use a TLabel as opposed to a TEdit control.

Dynamically creating forms

To create (and subsequently destroy) a form dynamically, follow these steps:

1. Select **View | Project Manager**.

2. Click the **Options** button.

3. In the Auto-Create Forms list box, select the form you want to create dynamically.

4. Click the right-arrow button to move the form to the Available Forms list.

5. Select the **OK** button.

6. Change the code you used to show the form to the following:

```
procedure TForm1.ShowAbout(Sender: Tobject);
begin
  About := TAbout.Create(nil);
  try
    About.ShowModal;
  finally
    About.Free;
  end;
end;
```

ERangeError

See "Range check error."

EReadError

Possible Cause of Error

Your .PAS file and .DFM file may be out of sync. Specifically, the .DFM file may contain a reference to something that no longer exists in the .PAS file.

Quick Fix

Delete existing references from the form (.DFM) file to methods or properties which you deleted from the unit (.PAS) file.

Additional Information

If you delete an existing event handler, Delphi will prompt you when you compile "The <> method referenced by <>.<> does not exist. Remove the reference?" If you select No, you will get this error. By selecting Yes, Button1Click (or whatever method or property you removed) is removed from the form (.DFM) file.

See "Invalid property value" or "Error reading <>.<>: <>" (depending on the more specific error message that accompanied the generic EReadError message).

ERegistryException

See "Failed to get data for <>."

EResNotFound

Possible Cause of Error

1. You may have deleted or modified the form files' resource {$R *.DFM} directive.
2. You may have changed the name of the main form in code.

Quick Fix

1. Restore the {$R *.DFM} directive to the form's unit (.PAS) file. If you do not have a Uses clause in the Implementation section, it belongs after the *implementation* reserved word, like this:

```
implementation
{$R *.DFM}
```

If you do have a Uses clause in the Implementation section, it belongs after the Uses clause, like this:

```
implementation
uses ItsNoggin, TimeWisely, HardlyAnyOil;
{$R *.DFM}
```

2. Although you <u>can</u> do it, it is generally best to refrain from changing the names of objects in code.

Additional Information

The {$R *.DFM} directive links the form (.DFM) file to the unit (.PAS) file. It is a necessary part of every form unit. A plain unit (created with New | Unit as opposed to New | Form) does not contain the {$R *.DFM} directive, and is, in fact, quite minimal at the outset:

```
unit Unit2;
interface
{A "plain" unit contains: 1) no Uses section with several units
automatically added, as a form unit does 2) no type declaration
automatically added, as with a form unit 3) no instance variable
automatically added, as with a form unit}
implementation
{4) no {$R *.DFM} directive automatically added, as with a form unit}
end.
```

If all else fails, compare the form (.DFM) file with the unit (.PAS) file and make sure that all components, properties, and methods declared in one are also in the other. To view the .DFM (form) file as text, right-click on the form at design time and select **View as Text** from the context menu. When you are finished viewing the .DFM file, reverse the process (right-click in the code window and select **View as Form** from the context menu).

Error 0—RLINK32 Error opening file <TypeLibrary>.tlb

Possible Cause of Error

You may be attempting to create an Automation server, ActiveForm, or ActiveX control, and your OLE .DLLs are out of date.

Quick Fix

Install Internet Explorer from the Delphi CD or copy the .DLLs directly from \Runimage\DelphiX0\Windows\System32.

Additional Information

See "Could not load RLINK32.DLL."

Error 2—File not found

See "File <> not found."

Error 4—Too many open files

See "Too many open files."

Error 68—Circular Unit Reference

See "Circular Unit Reference."

Error 76—Constant out of range

See "Constant out of range."

Error 94—"." Expected

See " "." Expected."

Error 101—Disk write error

See "Disk write error."

Error 102—File not assigned

See "File not assigned."

Error 103—File not open

See "File not open."

Error 104—File not open for input

See "File not open for input."

Error 105—File not open for output

See "File not open for output."

Error 200—Division by zero

See "Division by zero."

Error 201—Range check error

See "Range check error."

Error 202—Stack overflow error

See "Stack overflow."

Error 203—Heap overflow error

See "EOutOfMemory."

Error 204—Invalid pointer operation

See "Invalid pointer operation."

Error 207—Invalid floating point operation

See "Invalid floating point operation."

Error 210—Abstract Method Error

See "Abstract Method Error."

Error 215—Arithmetic overflow error

See "Arithmetic Overflow Error."

Error 216—Access Violation

See "Access Violation."

Error 219—Invalid Typecast

See "Invalid typecast."

Error 220—Invalid Variant Typecast

See "Invalid variant type conversion."

Error 227—Assertion failed

See "Assertion failed."

Error Creating Cursor Handle

Possible Cause of Error

This error usually occurs when Delphi does not receive a result set when it is expecting one.

1. You may have attempted to set a TQuery component's Active property to True or call its Open method while the TQuery's SQL property contains a SQL statement that does not return a result set (in other words, it is not a SELECT statement, but rather an INSERT, UPDATE, or DELETE statement).

2. You may have attempted to set a TStoredProc component's Active property to True or call its Open method when it has no value assigned to the StoredProc-Name property.

Quick Fix

1. If you are using a TQuery component, and the SQL statement is not a SELECT statement, use the ExecSQL method rather than the Open method. For example, if the TQuery is named Query1, use:

```
Query1.ExecSQL;
```

instead of:

```
Query1.Open;
```

2. Assign a value to the StoredProcName property before attempting to set the Active property or call its Open method. The DataBaseName property must be assigned an alias that describes a SQL Server database, such as Interbase, Oracle, MS SQL Server, Sybase, Informix, etc. Stored procedures are not a feature of desktop databases, such as Paradox, dBASE, MS Access, etc.

Additional Information

2. Stored procedures are compiled SQL statements that execute on the server. They are much faster than "local" SQL, and are one of the main advantages that SQL Server databases have over local (desktop) databases.

Error Creating Form: Cannot inherit from form <>. It contains a component with a blank name property

Possible Cause of Error

You may have inherited a form from the current project which contains a component with a blank Name property.

Quick Fix

Ensure that you name all components. Delphi will only allow you to have a component without a name until you attempt to refer to the component, either directly or indirectly.

Additional Information

Delphi 2 introduced visual form inheritance. Even in Delphi 1, a form could inherit from an ancestor, but this had to be done in code. In 32-bit Delphi, you can "visually" inherit forms you create.

Follow these steps to create an ancestor form:

1. Create a form that incorporates all the common elements that you want to include in descendent forms.

   If you only want to make the form available to the current project, you need do nothing else. The ancestor form is automatically available to be inherited from.

   If you want to make the form available to other projects (as opposed to only the current project), follow these additional steps:

2. Right-click the form and select **Add To Repository**.

3. Provide a title for the form in the Title edit box.

4. Optionally, provide a description in the Description edit box.

5. Select or enter the page on which you want the form to appear in the Object Repository in the Page combo box.

6. Optionally, enter your name in the Author edit box.

7. Optionally, select an icon to represent the form.

8. Select the **OK** button.

To inherit a form, follow these steps:

1. Select **File | New**.

2. Select the form you want to inherit from the page on which it is found.

If you inherit from a form that contains a button named Button1, the button on the inherited form will be exactly the same as the ancestor button (the one on the form you're inheriting from). All properties, including event handlers, will be inherited. For example, if the ancestor form has a button with the Caption property set to Belly, the Tag property set to 7, and the OnClick event handler is:

```
procedure TForm1.Button1Click(Sender: Tobject);
begin
  Close;
end;
```

the inherited form's button will also have the caption "Belly," and the Tag property 7, and the OnClick event handler will inherit the ancestor form's event handler:

```
procedure TForm2.Button1Click(Sender: Tobject);
begin
  inherited;
end;
```

Error Creating Form: Cannot inherit from form < >. Contains a component < > that does not support inheritance

Possible Cause of Error

Using 32-bit Delphi's visual form inheritance features, you may have attempted to inherit from a form which contains a TTabbed Notebook component.

Quick Fix

Replace the TTabbedNotebook with a TPageControl.

Additional Information

You will only get this error in 32-bit Delphi (Delphi 1 does not support visual form inheritance). 32-bit Delphi provides the TPageControl component, which can be used in place of the TTabbedNotebook component.

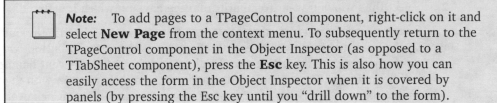

> **Note:** To add pages to a TPageControl component, right-click on it and select **New Page** from the context menu. To subsequently return to the TPageControl component in the Object Inspector (as opposed to a TTabSheet component), press the **Esc** key. This is also how you can easily access the form in the Object Inspector when it is covered by panels (by pressing the Esc key until you "drill down" to the form).

Error creating form: Cannot open file < >.DFM

Possible Cause of Error

You may be attempting to open a .PAS file, and its corresponding form (.DFM) file contains errors, has become corrupt, or is not in the same location as the .PAS file you are attempting to open.

Quick Fix

Try to locate the .DFM file specified in the error message and move it to the directory where the rest of your project resides.

If the file was already in the same directory with the rest of your project, open the .DFM file in a text editor (such as Notepad) and check it for errors.

Additional Information

If the .DFM file is not in the directory with the rest of your project, you can search your entire computer using Windows Explorer by following these steps:

1. In the directory pane on the left, highlight the area you want to search; to search your entire machine, select the standalone computer icon (named "MyComputer" by default).

2. Select **Tools | Find | Files or Folders...**.

3. Enter the name of the file in the Named combo box (for example, **Misplaced.PAS**).

4. Select the **Find Now** button.

The form (.DFM) file is the textual representation of the form. It contains definitions of which objects are on the form, where these objects are located (on the form), and their properties along with their values.

This information is saved so that the form can be "re-created" when you open it. If the form contains errors, has become corrupt, or has been moved, Delphi will not be able to re-create the form for you, as it does not know how to "assemble" it. It no longer has the "blueprint." This saving and loading of the form is referred to as "streaming."

After displaying this error message, your project, along with the corresponding .PAS file (the code behind the form), will still open. However, any attempt to view the visual representation of the form will fail, as the .DFM file and its information is necessary to do this.

Error Creating Form: Duplicate resource [Type:,Name:]

Possible Cause of Error

You may be loading a project in a version of Delphi that predates the version that the project was compiled in. For example, you may be opening a project created with Delphi 2 in Delphi 1.

Quick Fix

Select the **OK** button, and then **Build All**. To build all in Delphi 1 and 2, select **Compile | Build All**. In Delphi 3, select **Project | Build All**. In Delphi 4, **Project | Build <>**. All the units will be recompiled for the currently running version of Delphi.

 Note: Delphi 4 also has a Project | Build All Projects menu item, when you have multiple projects open simultaneously.

Alternatively, you can delete the project's .RES file (the file with the project's name and the .RES extension). The next time you compile, the appropriate .RES file will be re-created, based on the version of Delphi you are using.

Additional Information

16-bit and 32-bit resources are like water and vinegar—they don't mix. That is, you cannot use 16-bit resources in 32-bit Delphi, nor can you use 32-bit resources in 16-bit Delphi (Delphi 1).

See "Duplicate Resource."

Error creating Process

Possible Cause of Error

You may be referencing .DLLs in Windows NT by specifying the extension (.DLL). For example, the following will generate the error in NT:

```
procedure HawaiianPunch; external 'pineappl.DLL';
```

although that is the proper way to do it in other versions of Windows.

Quick Fix

In Windows NT, reference the .DLL without the extension. For example, the following is the proper syntax for Windows NT:

```
procedure HawaiianPunch; external 'pineappl';
```

Additional Information

If this is not the problem, try to execute the program outside of the Delphi IDE. Windows may give you a more detailed error message, such as the name of a .DLL that is needed.

Error Creating Variant Array

Possible Cause of Error

You may have attempted to create a variant array of strings using the varString data type. For example, the following will generate this error message:

```
procedure TForm1.Button1Click(Sender: Tobject);
var
  Roster: Variant;
begin
  Roster := VarArrayCreate([0,40],varString);
  . . .
```

Quick Fix

Use the varOLEStr data type to create a variant array of strings, like this:

```
procedure TForm1.Button1Click(Sender: Tobject);
var
  Roster: Variant;
begin
  Roster := VarArrayCreate([0,3],varOLEStr);
. . .
```

Additional Information

See "VarArrayCreate" and "VarArrrayOf" in Delphi help for more information.

Error Creating Window

Possible Cause of Error

You may have too many windowed controls in memory at the same time.

Quick Fix

There really is no quick fix for this. Remove any extraneous controls you may have. See the "Additional Information" section below for tips on how to "win back" some of the window handles you are using.

Additional Information

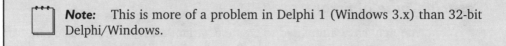

Note: This is more of a problem in Delphi 1 (Windows 3.x) than 32-bit Delphi/Windows.

This error is usually caused by your application using up all windows handles available. Each windowed control (controls that can receive input focus—in other words, descendents of TWinControl) is a "window" and requires a window handle.

Use graphical controls (descendents of TGraphicControl) where possible. For example, use a TLabel to display text rather than a TEdit, and a TBevel rather than a TPanel if all you need to do is provide visual separation between areas of your form.

Create as many forms as possible (besides the main form) dynamically, particularly those that may not necessarily be opened in every run of your application—for example, an About box.

To create (and subsequently destroy) a form dynamically, follow these steps:

1. Select **View | Project Manager**.

2. Click the **Options** button.

3. In the Auto-Create Forms list box, select the form you want to create dynamically.

4. Click the right-arrow button to move the form to the Available Forms list.

5. Select the **OK** button.

6. Change the code you used to show the form to the following:

```
procedure TForm1.ShowAbout(Sender: Tobject);
begin
  About := TAbout.Create(nil);
  try
    About.ShowModal;
  finally
    About.Free;
  end;
end;
```

However, if you attempt to show the About box before it is created, like this:

```
AboutBox.ShowModal:
AboutBox := TAboutBox.Create(Application);
AboutBox.Free;
```

or if you leave out the Create call altogether, you will instead create the error message under discussion.

It is a good idea to dynamically create forms in code, especially when they may not be accessed every time your program is run. If you do not dynamically create your forms, they will all be automatically created by Delphi at startup. You will almost always want Delphi to automatically create the main form for you, but you might consider postponing the creation of others until they are needed.

Error in module <>: Call to Application.CreateForm is missing or incorrect

See "Call to Application.CreateForm is missing or incorrect."

Error in module <>: CONTAINS clause is incorrect

See "CONTAINS clause is incorrect."

Error in module <>: Declaration of class <> is missing or incorrect

See "Declaration of class <> is missing or incorrect."

Error in module <>: 'END.' missing at end of module

See " 'END.' missing at end of module."

Error in module <>: Implementation part USES clause incorrect

See "Implementation part USES clause incorrect."

Error in module <>: Incorrect field declaration: class <>

See "Incorrect field declaration: class <>."

Error in module <>: Requires clause is incorrect

See "REQUIRES clause is incorrect."

Error in module <>: USES clause is missing or incorrect

See "USES clause is missing or incorrect."

Error loading type library/dll

Possible Cause of Error

STDVCL[32,40].DLL may be missing, in the wrong location, or unregistered.

Quick Fix

Verify that STDVCL[32,40].DLL is in \Windows\System and has been registered.

Additional Information

 To register servers on your system, you can use the Turbo Register Server utility (TRegSvr) which is a Delphi demo program located by default in

`C:\Program Files\Borland\Delphi X\Demos\ActiveX\TRegSvr.`

To do so, follow these steps (this example shows STDVCL32 as the file to register):

1. Open the TRegSvr.DPR file.

2. Compile and run the project (press **F9**).

3. Activate a DOS session/Open a DOS window.

4. Navigate to the directory in which TRegSvr exists.

5. Enter the following at the prompt:

   ```
   TRegSvr STDVCL32.DLL
   ```

6. Press the **Enter** key.

Turbo Register Server accepts three switches:

-u   to unregister a Server or Type Library

-q   to operate in quiet mode

-t   to register a Type Library (this is the default action, so if this is what you are doing, you can simply type the program name followed by the server name, as shown in the example above)

Error Opening Component Library

Possible Cause of Error

You may have installed a component that links in a DLL statically (that is, via external statements) that cannot be found.

Quick Fix

Uninstall the offending component.

If the component is one you have written, replace the external calls (static loading of the .DLLs) with calls to the LoadLibrary and GetProcAddress functions (dynamic loading).

Additional Information

It only seems right to load a .DLL (Dynamic Link Library) dynamically, rather than statically.

Error reading <>.<>: <>

Possible Cause of Error

1. It may be that components referenced in the form (.DFM) file are no longer available. You may have uninstalled these components after using them in a project. This is most likely to happen with third-party components.

2. You may be opening a project in a version of Delphi which predates the one used to compile the project. In this case, one or more messages may display, saying that a certain "property does not exist."

3. You may have manually edited the form (.DFM) file independent of the .PAS file, perhaps changing one object type to another. If so, there will be properties that one object has and the other does not, causing this problem.

4. Delphi may be unable to find a necessary configuration file, such as IDAPI32.CFG.

Quick Fix

1. Select **OK**, then reinstall the components that the form file references.

2. Select **OK**. The reference to the nonexistent property will be removed from the .DFM file.

3. Select **OK**, then follow these steps:

   a. Right-click on the form that contains the nonexistent property and select **View As Text**.

   b. Edit the .DFM file that then displays to revert it to its original state.

   c. Right-click on the .DFM file and select **View As Form**.

   d. Select **File | Close All**, and save your changes.

   e. Reopen the project.

4. Ensure that the location of IDAPI32.CFG matches that given in the system registry. By default the location is:

   ```
   C:\Program Files\Borland\Common Files\BDE.
   ```

   The system registry retains information on where it expects to find IDAPI32.CFG. To see where this is for your machine, follow these steps:

   a. Select **Start | Run**.

   b. Enter **regedit** in the Open combo box and select the **OK** button (or press the **Enter** key).

   c. Navigate to HKEY_LOCAL_MACHINE\Software\Borland\Database Engine.

The data for CONFIGFILE01 will display the path where the configuration file is located. If it differs from the location of your copy of IDAPI32.CFG, either move the file to the location pointed to by the system registry setting (recommended), or change the system registry setting to match the current location of the file.

Additional Information

See "Stream Read Error."

Error reading <Database>.SessionName. Duplicate database name '<>'

Possible Cause of Error

You may have the TDatabase component's HandleShared property set to False.

Quick Fix

Set the HandleShared property of the TDatabase component to True.

Additional Information

See "HandleShared" in Delphi help for more information.

Error reading <Session>.SessionName. Duplicate session name '<>'

Possible Cause of Error

You may have the TSession component's AutoSessionName property set to False.

Quick Fix

Set the AutoSessionName property of the TSession component to True.

Additional Information

See "AutoSessionName" in Delphi help for more information.

Error reading symbol file

Possible Cause of Error

1. The project's symbol file (.DSM) may be corrupt or out of sync with the project.

2. You may be opening a project last compiled in Delphi 1 in 32-bit Delphi and the project contains a 16-bit symbol (.DSM) file.

3. You may have moved a project to a different directory or machine.

Quick Fix

1. Select the **OK** button to dismiss the error message and then select **Compile | Build All**.

2. Select the **OK** button to dismiss the error message and then select **Project | Build All**.

3. Delete the project's .DSM and .DSK files, or simply ignore the message (select **OK** to dismiss the message).

Additional Information

To prevent this error message from displaying, you can delete the .DSM file before or after moving the project.

> **Note:** Before you open a Delphi 1 project in 32-bit Delphi, delete the symbol (.DSM), resource (.RES), and compiled unit (.DCU) files. New 32-bit resource and compiled unit files will be automatically generated when you next compile.

You create some files in each Delphi project that must not be deleted, in particular the .PAS, .DFM, and .DPR files. Other files, though, will be automatically regenerated each time you compile, so you can safely delete them. These include, depending on your version of Delphi, <projectname>.OPT, <projectname>.DSK, <projectname>.DSM, <projectname>.RES, and <projectname>.DOF. Additionally, the automatically saved last versions of form (.DFM), project (.DPR), Pascal (.PAS), and, in Delphi 3 and 4 (where appropriate), type library (.TLB) files are saved with an extension beginning with a tilde (~) followed by the first two letters of the normal extension. For example, backup .PAS files have the extension .~PA. In this way, you can always revert to the last version of one of these files, if need be, by changing the extension back to its regular format.

> **Note:**   Of course, deleting files will cause you to lose whatever settings they hold. For example, if you set the program icon and subsequently delete the project's corresponding .RES file, the icon will revert to the default "torch" icon. See ".DSK" and ".RES" as well as any other file types in which you have interest in Delphi help for specific information on what each contains.

Error saving I(Interface): The parameter is incorrect

Possible Cause of Error

You may be attempting to create an Automation server, ActiveForm, or ActiveX control, and your OLE .DLLs are out of date.

Quick Fix

Install Internet Explorer from the Delphi CD (not available on all copies of Delphi) or copy the OLE .DLLs directly from \Runimage\DelphiX\Windows\System32.

Additional Information

See "Could not load RLINK32.DLL" and "Error 0: RLINK32 Error opening file <TypeLibrary>.tlb."

Error setting debug exception hook

Possible Cause of Error

1. You may be experiencing a minor glitch in Delphi.
2. One or more compiled unit (.DCU) files may be corrupt.

Quick Fix

1. Select **OK**; either **Ctrl+F2** or **Alt+R+E**; and then **Project | Build All**.
2. If you have the corresponding source (.PAS) files, delete the compiled unit (.DCU) files and rebuild. The compiled units will be regenerated automatically from the source files.

Additional Information

Never delete a project's .DPR (project), .PAS (Pascal source), or .DFM (form) files. Most other files can be regenerated automatically by Delphi without any intervention or interaction necessary on your part. Of course, deleting files that contain settings you have specified for your application will require that you specify these settings again. An example of this type of file is the project's resource file, which has the same base name as the project/executable followed by an .RES extension. This file holds the application's name as it will appear below the icon, the icon itself, and the project's help file. Deleting such files is sometimes necessary (see "Error reading symbol file") and only a nuisance (as opposed to a disaster) to reconstruct.

EStackOverflow

See "Stack overflow."

EStringListError

See "List index out of bounds."

EThread

Possible Cause of Error

1. You may have a main thread which has called the WaitFor method, followed by another thread which called the Synchronize method.

2. You may have a thread that called the Synchronize method, followed by the main thread calling the WaitFor method.

Quick Fix

1, 2. Remove the WaitFor main thread call and/or the Synchronize call by the other thread.

Additional Information

Threaded applications are not used in Delphi 1. See "OnIdle" in Delphi help for information on an alternate way of performing background processing.

EVariantError

Possible Cause of Error

You may have attempted to reference a value from a result set that was Null. For example, the following will generate this error message if the value of the ExpendableIncome field for the current record is Null:

```
var
  i: Integer;
begin
  i := Query1['ExpendableIncome'];
```

Quick Fix

You can test the result to see if it is Null, and only assign it to the variable if it is not, like this:

```
if not VarIsNull(Query1['ExpendableIncome']) then
  i := Query1['ExpendableIncome']
else
  i := 0;
```

 If the value in the result set is a String, use the VarToStr function, which converts Null string values to empty strings. For example, you could code it like this:

```
s := VarToStr(Query1['VBTestimonials']);
```

Additional Information

TDataset's FieldValues property returns a Variant, as can be deduced from the above code. It is less convenient but faster to reference the fields in a result set in their native format, for example:

```
bs := Query1['VBTestimonials'].AsString;
```

FieldValues is the default property of TDataset; for that reason, it is not necessary to explicitly reference it. In other words, the following two assignments perform the same action:

```
i := Query1['ExpendableIncome'];
i := Query1.FieldValues(['ExpendableIncome']);
```

See "TDataset.FieldValues" in Delphi help for more information.

Except or Finally expected

Possible Cause of Error

You have omitted the *finally* or *except* reserved word after using the *try* reserved word. For example, the following will generate this error message:

```
procedure TForm1.SickoAndEgbertClick(Sender:
                                     Tobject);
var
  TwoThumbsUp: String;
begin
  try
    TwoThumbsUp := 'Waylon and Willie meet Godzilla';
  end; {with or without this 'end' the error message is the same}
end;
```

Quick Fix

Whenever you use the reserved word *try*, you must add either the reserved word *finally* or the reserved word *except*.

Additional Information

try...finally statements are usually used to ensure that resources you allocate are always freed (the *finally* part is <u>always</u> executed). That is why *try...finally* blocks are often referred to as "resource protection blocks." A typical *try...finally* block might be:

```
var
  Feed: TStrings;
begin
  Feed := TStringList.Create;
  try
    Feed.Add('PurinaHyenaChow');
    Feed.Add('PurinaPteradactylChow');
    Feed.Add('PurinaChowChow');
    Feed.Add('CiaoBaby');
  finally
    Feed.Free;
  end;
end;
```

try...except blocks are usually used to provide specific responses to specific errors. An example of the use of a *try...except* block is:

```
try
  Dividend := StrToInt(Edit1.Text);
  Divisor := StrToInt(Edit2.Text);
  Quotient := Dividend div Divisor;
except
  on EDivByZero do
    ShowMessage('Enter a value greater than 0 '
          +#13#10+ ' in the Divisor edit box');
    Edit2.SetFocus;
  end;
end;
```

Expression expected but < > found

Possible Cause of Error

1. You may have omitted something. For example, the following statement (which leaves out the second operand, which should appear after the plus sign) generates this error message:

```
LblIntegerAddition.Caption := IntToStr(1+);
```

2. You may be attempting to assign a fraction to a real/floating-point number (or a time value to a TDateTime variable), but have forgotten to prepend a number prior to the decimal point. You must include some number, even if it is a zero, for the compiler to accept this assignment. For example, this assignment will generate the error message under discussion:

```
MediocreBattingAvg := .246;
```

3. You may have attempted to declare a class within a Constant section, like this:

```
const
  TForm1 = class(TForm)
```

in which case the specific error message would be "Expression expected but 'CLASS' found."

Quick Fix

1. Provide the expression at the place where the compiler generated the error message. In this example, delete the plus sign (+) or add another integer. **IntToStr(1);** or **IntToStr(1+2);** are both fine.

2. Prepend a numeral (such as 0) to the decimal point in this way:

```
MediocreBattingAvg := 0.246;
```

3. Do not declare types in a Constant section.

Additional Information

3. Types must be declared in a Type section, and instances of the type in a Var section, as Delphi does for you automatically when you create a form:

```
type
  TForm1 = class(TForm)
. . .
var
  Form1: TForm1;
```

> **Note:** There are many error messages of the type "<> expected but <> found" or "<> or <> expected but <> found," such as "Declaration expected but <> found," " 'END' expected but <> found," " 'End' expected but implementation found," etc.

External exception C0000008

Possible Cause of Error

You may be using SQL Net client version 2.3.3.

Quick Fix

You have several options to remedy this problem; use any of the following. The first is that recommended by Oracle support.

a. In Regedit, navigate to HKEY_LOCAL_MACHINE\SOFTWARE\ ORACLE\OTRACE73 and rename or remove this entry.

b. Remove Oracle Trace Collection Services 7.3.3.x.x using Oracle's Installer.

c. In Delphi, select **Tools | Options | Preferences | Debugging**, and deselect Integrated Debugging.

d. Use a previous version of the Oracle SQL Net client (pre-2.3.3).

Additional Information

NT 4 reports all exceptions raised during debugging (even exceptions that would normally be ignored).

> **Note:** What is meant by "external" is that the exception is raised external to Delphi. See the Windows.PAS unit for the declaration of many of these error codes.

Failed to get data for < >

Possible Cause of Error

You may have attempted to retrieve data from the system registry into a variable of a data type which differs from the data type of the value retrieved. For example, the following will generate this error message if the value ThirdBase stored in the system registry is an Integer (or, in fact, anything other than a String):

```
function GoSeeCal: String;
var
  ReggiesTree: TRegistry;
begin
  ReggiesTree := TRegistry.Create;
  try
    ReggiesTree.RootKey := HKEY_CURRENT_USER;
    ReggiesTree.OpenKey('\drmtmale\Baltimore Orioles', False);
    Result :=
        ReggiesTree.ReadString('ThirdBase');
  finally
    ReggiesTree.Free;
  end;
end;
```

Quick Fix

Verify that the value you are reading from the system registry is of the same type as the variable or property to which you are going to store or assign it. You can enclose the assignment in a *try...except* block to trap for this error, like this:

```
function GoSeeCal: string;
var
  ReggiesTree: TRegistry;
begin
  ReggiesTree := TRegistry.Create;
  try
```

```
        ReggiesTree.RootKey := HKEY_CURRENT_USER;
        try
          ReggiesTree.OpenKey('\drmtmale\Baltimore Orioles', False);
          Result :=
              ReggiesTree.ReadString('ThirdBase');
          except
            on ERegistryException do
              Result := ''; {include additional exception handling if desired}
          end;
        finally
          ReggiesTree.Free;
        end;
      end;
```

Additional Information

This error message is a descendent of ERegistryError.

The system registry is much more flexible than the "legacy" .INI files used prior to 32-bit Windows (and still available in 32-bit Windows). Whereas you can only store three data types in .INI files (Bool[ean], Integer, and String), the system registry supports 9 types: Binary, Bool[ean], Currency, Date, DateTime, Float, Integer, String, and Time.

Fatal Error: <>: Required Package '<>' not found

See "Required package <> not found."

Field <> cannot be used in a filter expression

Possible Cause of Error

1. You may be attempting to filter a calculated field.
2. You may be attempting to filter a field whose data type does not allow filtering (such as a graphic).

Quick Fix

1, 2. Only refer to static data fields whose values can be quantified via SQL-type filter expressions.

Additional Information

1. In the Country Paradox table that ships with Delphi, the following is allowable in a filter expression:

   ```
   Name = 'Bolivia' or 'Brazil' or 'Paraguay'
   ```

   because Name is one of the data fields in the table.

   However, if you create a calculated field (for example, Density, based on the Population and Area fields), the following filter expression is not allowed in the Dataset's Filter property and will generate the error message under discussion:

   ```
   Density > 6
   ```

2. A filter that attempts to match strings or numerical values will not work with certain data types (such as TGraphicField and TMemoField), and thus fields of these types will generate the error message under discussion if you use them in a filter expression. An example is the following filter using the Biolife Paradox table that ships with Delphi:

   ```
   Graphic > 8
   ```

Field < >.< > does not have a corresponding component. Remove the declaration?

Possible Cause of Error

1. You have a reference in your .PAS file that has no corresponding reference in the .DFM file.

2. You may get this error message after first receiving the "Class < > not found. Ignore the error and continue?" error message and then proceeding with the loading of the project (after ignoring the error message).

3. You may have manually removed the reference to the field from the .DFM file.

4. You may have modified the field declaration in the .PAS file. For example, you may have changed:

   ```
   type
     TForm3 = class(TForm)
       Label1: Tlabel;
   ```

   to:

   ```
   type
     TForm3 = class(TForm)
       abel1: Tlabel; {removed the L from Label1}
   ```

5. You may have attempted to manually add a class type to the Published part of your unit file, like this:

```
type
  TForm1 = class(TForm)
    Image1: TImage;
    Chloro: Form; {This line causes the error}
    private
    { Private declarations }
    public
    { Public declarations }
  end;
```

Quick Fix

1. Select **Yes** to remove the declaration.
2. If you want to then reinsert the reference in the .DFM file, it is easiest to add the component back to your form, which will automatically reinsert the reference in the .DFM file.
3. Reinsert the reference in the .DFM file that you removed.
4. Restore the field declaration to match the component's name in the Object Inspector.
5. When adding class types, do not add them to the Published part of a form's unit (.PAS) file. This is acceptable:

```
type
  TForm1 = class(TForm)
    Image1: TImage;
    private
      Concrete: Form;
    public
    { Public declarations }
  end;
```

Additional Information

5. It is more common to add class types to a Type declaration in a component unit than in a form unit. This is how "composite" components are created.

See "Class < > not found. Ignore the error and continue?" and "Error reading < >" for more information about related error messages and conditions.

Field < > is not indexed and cannot be modified

Possible Cause of Error

You may be attempting to search a field in a local table (Paradox or dBASE) that is (a) not indexed or (b) <u>is</u> indexed, but the TTable's IndexFieldNames property is not set for a (single or composite) primary key, or the IndexField property is not set for a secondary key. For example, the following code will generate this error message if either of these possibilities (a or b) is the case:

```
with Table1 do
begin
  SetRangeStart;
  FieldByName('Ballyard').AsString := 'Camden';
  SetRangeEnd;
  FieldByName('Ballyard').AsString := 'Wrigley';
  ApplyRange;
end;
```

Quick Fix

When accessing local (Paradox or dBASE) tables, ensure that the fields on which you are searching are indexed and that the TTable component's Index-Name property is set to that field.

If you want to search by a (single or composite) primary key, set the Index-FieldNames property to the field(s). If it is a composite primary key, separate each field name with semicolons. You can set this either in the IDE or in code, like this:

```
IndexFieldNames := 'Prime;Secondary;Tertiary';
```

If you want to search by a secondary key, set the IndexField property. You can set this either in the IDE or in code, like this:

```
IndexName := 'SecondaryIndx';
```

Additional Information

If you are using a SQL server database (Interbase, Oracle, MS SQL Server, etc.), you can set a range on any field, indexed or not. In this case, set the TTable component's IndexFieldNames property to the field or fields on which you want to set the range.

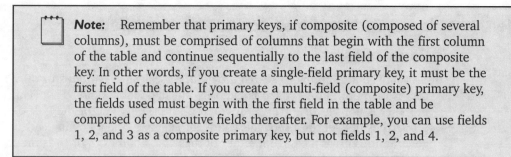

> **Note:** Remember that primary keys, if composite (composed of several columns), must be comprised of columns that begin with the first column of the table and continue sequentially to the last field of the composite key. In other words, if you create a single-field primary key, it must be the first field of the table. If you create a multi-field (composite) primary key, the fields used must begin with the first field in the table and be comprised of consecutive fields thereafter. For example, you can use fields 1, 2, and 3 as a composite primary key, but not fields 1, 2, and 4.

Field < > is not of the expected type

Possible Cause of Error

After instantiating fields at design time, you may have modified the structure of the table by deleting a field (or fields), or modifying a field's name, data type, or size.

Quick Fix

Remove the "outdated" definition of the table's field(s) and replace it or them with the current information. You can do this by following these steps:

1. Double-click the TTable component which contains/contained the field that was deleted/modified.
2. Right-click in the list of fields and select **Delete** from the context menu.
3. Right-click in the now empty window and select **Add Fields** to instantiate the new definitions of the fields.

Additional Information

> **Note:** The exact text of the error message notwithstanding, it is not necessary to change a field's data type to get this error message. You may have changed its name or size instead.

Sometimes you may have "stray" references to components or their properties in your form (.DFM) file. You can always inspect the form file by right-clicking on the form and selecting View as Text from the context menu. Search for any components or properties that no longer belong or whose settings do not correspond with what they should be. For example, an instantiated database field is represented like this:

```
object Table1RptFileName: TStringField
  FieldName = 'RptFileName'
  Required = True
  Size = 6
end
```

If the properties do not correspond to the field's current properties, remove or modify this entry as necessary.

Field < > must have a value

Possible Cause of Error

You may have attempted to post a record to the database, but the table contains a required (or NOT NULL if a SQL Server database) field which has not had a value assigned to it.

Quick Fix

Provide a value for all required (or NOT NULL) fields before attempting to post the record.

Additional Information

The field named in the error message was designated as a required field when you created a "local" (Paradox, dBASE, etc.) table using Database Desktop, or when the table was created with Object Pascal code. Alternatively, if you are using a SQL Server database (Interbase, Oracle, MS SQL Server, etc.), the field was designated as "required" when you defined it as NOT NULL.

If you want to check for and handle this occurrence yourself (as opposed to allowing Delphi to handle it, providing you with the above error message), you can perform record-level validation using the TTable component's Before-Post event, field-level validation using the TField's OnValidate event, or character-level validation using TField's EditMask property. If any of these validation checks fail, you can set the cursor to the "offending" field and highlight it. For information on how to perform all these validity checks, see "A value must be specified for < >."

You can designate a TField that you instantiate at design time as being required via its Required property. You can also provide a default value for TField descendents via the DefaultExpression property. If you do this, a field will by default have a value, so you wouldn't have to worry about getting the error message under discussion unless the default value was deleted.

If you create a table in code, you can designate a field as required by setting the fourth parameter of the FieldDefs.Add method to True. The parameters are the name of the field (String), its data type (TFieldType), its size (Word), and whether or not it is required (Boolean). For example, you might declare a field like this:

```
FieldDefs.Add('MrsLeppard',ftString,20,True);
```

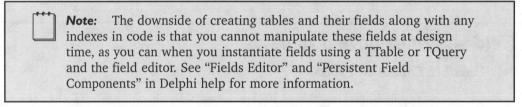

> **Note:** The downside of creating tables and their fields along with any indexes in code is that you cannot manipulate these fields at design time, as you can when you instantiate fields using a TTable or TQuery and the field editor. See "Fields Editor" and "Persistent Field Components" in Delphi help for more information.

See "A value must be specified for <>" for information on data validation (table, record, field, and character level).

Field <> not found

Possible Cause of Error

1. You may have referenced a field, perhaps in a TDataset's Filter property, which does not exist in the dataset (a calculated field, for example).

2. You may have changed a TTable component's TableName property, and a field from the previous TableName setting is still being referenced in the Filter property.

3. After instantiating fields using the Field Editor, you may have changed a TTable component's TableName property.

4. You may have specified the name of a field in a call to AddIndex which does not exist in the underlying dataset. For example, the following will generate this error if there is no field in Table1 named City:

```
Table1.AddIndex('City','City',[]);
```

5. You may have removed some fields from a TTable that you had earlier explicitly instantiated using the Fields Editor.

Quick Fix

1. Ensure that any fields referenced are spelled correctly and are part of the dataset in question.

2. Delete the value in the Filter property or set it to a filter appropriate to the current table.

3. After instantiating fields at design time via the Fields Editor, delete them before changing the TTable component's TableName property.

4. Verify that the field on which you are attempting to create an index exists in the table. You may need to correct your spelling, change the Table property of the TTable component, or alter the table.

5. Remove the TFields' declarations from the form (.DFM) file. You will then get the message "Field < > does not have a corresponding component. Remove the declaration?" Select **Yes** each time.

Additional Information

1. You cannot reference a lookup or calculated field in a TDataset's Filter property. For example, if the table KnightsOfTheRound has a field named Address which references a field named CurrentAddress in a lookup table, the following would generate the error message under discussion in KnightsOfTheRound's Filter property:

```
CurrentAddress = 'Tower of London'
```

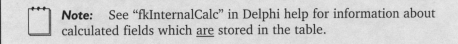

> **Note:** See "fkInternalCalc" in Delphi help for information about calculated fields which <u>are</u> stored in the table.

3. To "un-instantiate" fields you have instantiated using the Fields Editor, follow these steps:
   a. Double-click the TTable component to activate the Fields Editor.
   b. Right-click within the Fields Editor and select **Select All**.
   c. With all the fields highlighted, right-click within the Fields Editor and select **Delete**.

4. See "AddFieldDefs" in Delphi help for information on creating fields in code.

5. To view the form (.DFM) file, right-click the form and select **View As Text** from the context menu. The TField information therein will be of the form:

```
object Table1CustNo: TFloatField
  FieldName = 'CustNo'
end
object Table1Company: TStringField
  FieldName = 'Company'
  Size = 30
end
```

To revert to the "normal" view after editing the form file, right-click within the editor and select **View As Form** from the context menu.

Field <>.<> should be of type <> but is declared as <>. Correct the declaration?

Possible Cause of Error

You may have replaced the declaration of a component so that the component type is now declared as being something else. For example, if you placed a TEdit on a form, it would be declared as:

```
type
  TForm1 = class(TForm)
    Edit1: TEdit;
```

If you then changed the TEdit to anything other than TEdit, such as the following:

```
type
  TForm1 = class(TForm)
    Edit1: CoffeeEdit;
```

you would get the error message under discussion.

Quick Fix

Do not alter the code that Delphi automatically generates for you.

Additional Information

See "Class <> not found."

Field definition not allowed after methods or properties

Possible Cause of Error

1. You may be attempting to add a field (or fields) to a class declaration after declaring a method or property.
2. You may have appended the *index*, *stored*, *default*, or *nodefault* directives after a function in an Automated section. For example:

```
automated
  function yowza: string; index;
```

Quick Fix

1. Field definitions must be declared before methods and properties.
2. Do not use these directives in an Automated section.

Additional Information

Here is an example of the correct order in which to declare a field and a method:

```
private
  FAppraisedValue: Currency;
  . . .{0 to N additional fields}
  procedure ShowListing;
  . . .{0 to N additional methods}
```

Field in group by must be in result set

Possible Cause of Error

You may have a SQL statement that references a field in a GROUP BY clause that is not included in the SELECT clause. For example, you may have something like:

```
SELECT Title, Protagonist, Rating, Count(*)
FROM Movies
WHERE Protagonist = 'DeNiro'
OR Protagonist = 'Sinise'
GROUP BY Rating
```

Quick Fix

If you use a GROUP BY clause in your SQL statement, include all the fields from the SELECT part in the GROUP BY part (excluding computed columns, such as those created with the COUNT, SUM, MIN, MAX, and AVG aggregate functions). For example, the above statement would need to be amended to the following:

```
SELECT Title, Protagonist, Rating, Count(*)
FROM Movies
WHERE Protagonist = 'DeNiro'
OR Protagonist = 'Sinise'
GROUP BY Title, Protagonist, Rating
```

Additional Information

The exact SQL syntax required/allowed depends on the database type that you are accessing and the version of the BDE you are using. For specifics, see your server documentation (if using a SQL server "back-end" database) or the "Local SQL" help file that ships with Delphi (if using Paradox or dBASE).

Field in order by must be in result set

Possible Cause of Error

You may be attempting to sort by a field that either does not exist or was not specified in the SELECT clause of the SQL statement.

Quick Fix

Verify that the field you are attempting to sort by (using the ORDER BY clause) is in a table specified in the FROM clause of the SQL statement, that the field is included in the SELECT clause of the SQL statement, and that the field name is spelled correctly.

Additional Information

In order to sort by a particular field, the field must be in the result set that is returned by the SQL statement. For example, the following SQL statements will produce the error message under discussion:

```
SELECT Peaches, Strawberries
FROM Fruitstand
ORDER BY Bananas
```

The field this statement attempts to order by is not stated in the SELECT clause. You can rectify this by either explicitly or implicitly adding the field Bananas to the SQL statement's SELECT clause.

To explicitly add the Bananas field to the SQL statement's SELECT clause, do this:

```
SELECT Peaches, Strawberries, Bananas
FROM Fruitstand
ORDER BY Bananas
```

To implicitly add the Bananas field (as well as all other fields in the table) to the SQL statement's SELECT clause, do this:

```
SELECT *
FROM Fruitstand
```

```
ORDER BY Bananas
```

You do not have to limit your selection criteria to a single table as long as the tables you select from are "related" to one another by a common field. For example, if you wanted to find out what years the same city won both the football championship (Super Bowl) and the baseball championship (World Series), you could do this:

```
SELECT B.ThatChampionshipSeason
FROM Baseball B, Football F
WHERE B.City = F.City
AND B.ThatChampionshipSeason =
    F.ThatChampionshipSeason
ORDER BY B.ThatChampionshipSeason
```

Field index out of range

Possible Cause of Error

1. You may be attempting to access the index of a table using an index element that is greater than the highest index element number that the table has defined. For example, the following will generate this error message:

```
with Table1 do
  for i := 0 to IndexFieldCount do
    . . .
```

2. You may be using TTable's FindKey or FindNearest methods with dBASE tables and expression indexes.

3. You may be attempting to index a calculated field whose FieldKind property is fkCalculated.

4. You may have a Master/Detail table relationship without having set the Detail table's IndexName property to match that of the Master table.

Quick Fix

1. Remember that index elements are normally zero-based. The above example needs to be altered to account for this by deducting 1 from the IndexField-Count property if the *for* loop's control variable begins with 0:

```
with Table1 do
  for i := 0 to IndexFieldCount-1 do
    . . .
```

2. Use the TTable component's GoToNearest method with dBASE tables and expression indexes.

3. If you want to sort by a calculated field, change the field's FieldKind property from fkCalculated to fkInternalCalc.

4. Set the Detail table's foreign key (which matches the Master table's primary key) as its IndexName property.

Additional Information

1. Remember that indexes, like most array properties, are zero-based.

3. Calculated fields are not actually stored in the database unless you set the FieldKind property to fkInternalCalc.

Field name already exists. Rename one of the fields

Possible Cause of Error

You have assigned two fields the same name in Database Desktop. For example, you may have two fields that are named Address.

Quick Fix

Change the name of one of the fields with a duplicated field name. In the example given above, change the second Address field to Address2 (or change the first field to Address1 and the second to Address2).

Additional Information

The Type, Size, and Key attributes of the fields do not have to match to receive this error message—as long as two names are the same, this error message will be generated.

Field not found in table

Possible Cause of Error

1. You may be attempting to add an index to a table, but have specified a field in TTable's AddIndex method that does not exist. For example, the following will generate this error message if you have misspelled the field Geeko as Gecko:

```
with Table1
  AddIndex('Chipheads','Gecko',[]);
```

2. You may be attempting to add an expression index to a dBASE table, but have not specified ixExpression in AddIndex's final parameter. For example, the following will generate this error message:

```
with Table1
  AddIndex('CityState','city+state',[]);
```

Quick Fix

1. Verify that the field you specify exists in the table.

2. Add the ixExpression TOptions constant to TTable's AddIndex method in its third (Options) parameter, like this:

```
with Table1
  AddIndex('CityState','city+state',[ixExpression]);
```

Additional Information

The first parameter you pass TTable's AddIndex method is the name of the index, the second is the name of the field(s), and the third is a set of TIndexOptions. Valid entries depend on the type of table you are indexing. See "AddIndex" in Delphi help for more information.

Field or method identifier expected

Possible Cause of Error

You may have specified an identifier that is not a field or method as the read or write access specifier of a property. For example, the following will generate this error message (unless "fajdlskdfajlsk" is a field or method name):

```
property rates: string read fajdlskdfajlsk write FRates;
```

Quick Fix

Use a field or method that has previously been declared as a part of the class. For example, this will work:

```
...
private
  FRates;
public
  . . .
published
  property Rates: string read FRates write
                           SetRates;
```

Additional Information

By convention, fields used in properties begin with "F," and methods used in properties begin with "Get" for read and "Set" for write.

It is common to use a field in the read access specifier and a method in the write access specifier. Nevertheless, you can specify either a field or a method in both the read and write parts of a property declaration. For example, a typical property may be declared like this:

```
property RealEstate: Currency read FRealEstate
                        write SetRealEstate;
```

although it is allowable to use the same field for both the read and the write access specifiers, like so:

```
property RealEstate: Currency read FRealEstate
                        write FRealEstate;
```

or to use (different) methods for both the read and write access specifiers, like so:

```
property RealEstate: Currency read GetRealEstate
                        write SetRealEstate;
```

Field types do not match

Possible Cause of Error

You may have selected Table Lookup in Database Desktop and attempted to link two fields that are not of the same length.

Quick Fix

To link two tables for table lookup capability, you must select two fields (one from each table) that are identical in data type and (if applicable) size.

Additional Information

The names of the two fields do not matter, as long as they match from Database Desktop's perspective (same data type, same size if applicable to the data type). For example, you can use any Number field from table A to link to any other Number field from table B, no matter what you named the fields. If you want to link two tables on Alpha fields, though, they must not only both be Alpha fields but you must have assigned them the same size when designing the tables. For example, two Alpha fields with a length of 12 can be used as the link between two tables to facilitate table lookup. However, attempting to use two Alpha fields, one with a length of 12 and the other with a length of 15, for this purpose will produce the error message under discussion.

Field value required

Possible Cause of Error

You may have failed to assign a value to a required field. For example, if the first field in a table is required, the following will generate this error message:

```
Table1.InsertRecord([Null, Now, 'Filet Mignon', 'Medium', 'Italian',
                    'Zinfandel', 'Cheesecake', 'Kenya AA']);
```

Failing to provide required values when entering data "manually" at run time will also produce this error.

Quick Fix

Ensure that you assign values to all required fields.

Additional Information

See "Field <> must have a value" for techniques on assuring that all necessary information is provided.

File <> not found

Possible Cause of Error

You may have entered the name of a nonexistent file in a dialog box that prompted you for a filename.

Quick Fix

Enter the name of a filename that exists and is suitable for whatever action you are about to take on it/with it.

Additional Information

One example of many that could display this error message is if you attempt to install a component, and then enter the name of a nonexistent component in the Unit filename edit box.

You may find it advantageous to use Browse buttons, where available, to navigate to the file you want to use. That way you can only select valid files, eliminating guesswork, misspellings, etc.

File access denied

Possible Cause of Error

1. The file you are attempting to access may have been designated read-only via Microsoft Explorer or another such program.

2. You may be attempting to open a file for writing whose FileMode property is set to 0 (read-only).

Quick Fix

1. Verify that you are authorized to access the file. Change the file's read-only flag from True to False in Microsoft Explorer by following these steps:

   a. Locate and then right-click on the file.

   b. Select **Properties** from the context menu.

   c. If the Read-Only check box is checked, click in it to "uncheck" it.

2. Change the FileMode variable to 2 prior to accessing the file, if necessary, like this:

```
var tF: TextFile;
begin
  FileMode := 2;
  AssignFile(tF, 'AchtDrei.txt');
  . . .
```

Additional Information

See "FileMode" in Delphi help for more information.

File extension < > is not valid. Expecting < >

Possible Cause of Error

You are attempting to use a file as or for something for which it is not suitable or intended (or the file's extension has been inadvertently changed so that the file appears to be unsuitable for the current action).

Quick Fix

Only select appropriate files for each type of operation. For example, only select files with the extension .DPK when creating a new package.

Additional Information

Based on a file's extension, it "tells" the outside world what kind of file it is, and therefore what it can do. For example, a .DPK file cannot produce sounds, and a .WAV file cannot be used as a package file.

File is Locked. Table: < > User: < >

Possible Cause of Error

You may be attempting to open a table that another user has open in Exclusive mode.

Quick Fix

You can check for the table's status before accessing it, like this:

```
if not Table1.Exclusive then
    . . .
```

Additional Information

You must place a table in Exclusive mode before you can perform certain operations, such as creating indexes. Make sure that you always turn Exclusive mode "off" when you're done so you don't unnecessarily prevent other users from accessing the table.

If you try to open a table in Exclusive mode, and somebody else has the table open already, you will receive the error message "Table is busy." See that entry for more information on dealing with that occurrence.

See "Exclusive lock" in Delphi help for more information.

File not assigned

Possible Cause of Error

You may have failed to call AssignFile before calling Rewrite, Reset, Append, Rename, or Erase. For example, the following will generate this error message:

```
var tex: TextFile;
begin
  Rewrite(tex);
  Writeln(tex, 'I think I forgot something');
  CloseFile(tex);
end;
```

Quick Fix

Remember to call AssignFile before attempting to Rewrite, Reset, Append, Rename, or Erase a file:

```
var tex: TextFile;
begin
  AssignFile(tex, 'McMurtry.txt');
  try
    Rewrite(tex);
    Writeln(tex, 'Lonesome Dove');
    . . .
  finally
    CloseFile(tex);
  end;
end;
```

Additional Information

> **Note:** This is "I/O Error 102."

> **Note:** See "Text files" and "$I" in Delphi help for information about using text files and toggling Input/Output checking on and off.

File not found < >

Possible Cause of Error

1. You may have a unit in your Uses section whose spelling does not match that of the actual unit, the unit does not exist on your system, or it cannot be found because it is not located in Delphi's search path (or references a unit of which this is true).

2. You may be attempting to install a component into a package, and a unit that the component unit references is not found in the path. This can happen with a "registration" unit (a unit that contains the Register procedure for several components that it lists in its Uses clause) when one of the units it references is not in Delphi's path.

3. In Delphi 3, you may be attempting to use a TReport (ReportSmith) component, but have not yet added Report.DCU's path to Delphi's search path.

4. A resource file may be missing.

5. You may be attempting to open a text file that does not exist, using either the Append or Reset procedure.

6. You may be attempting to install a component using the .DCU file instead of the .PAS file.

7. You may have included a .DPK file in the Contains section of another .DPK (package unit) file.

Quick Fix

1. Verify that you spelled the unit name correctly, if you manually entered the unit name. If you are no longer using the unit, remove it from the USES list. Otherwise, verify that the directory wherein the unit's corresponding .DCU file resides is in Delphi's search path (see Quick Fix #2 directly below).

2. Add the path where the file resides to your path or move the file into the Delphi path (which can be inspected by selecting Tools | Environment Options, selecting the Library tab, and viewing the entry in the Library combo box).

3. In a default installation of Delphi 3, the Report.DCU file should be placed in both of the following locations:

```
C:\Program Files\Borland\Delphi X\LIB\DELPHI2
C:\Program Files\Borland\Delphi X\SLib
```

The TReport component is not installed by default. It is still available in Delphi 3 (but not in Delphi 4), and you can install it by following these steps:

a. Select **Component | Configure Palette....**

b. Select **Data Access** from the Pages list.

c. Scroll all the way to the bottom and locate the TReport component.

d. Highlight the TReport component.

e. Select the **Add** button. The TReport component will be added to your Data Access component palette page.

4. Locate the resource and move it to the project's directory.

5. Do not use the Reset procedure on files that do not or may not exist at the time you call Reset.

6. Using a .DCU file to install a component normally works fine, but if the .DCU was compiled using an earlier version of Delphi, you will need to install it using the .PAS file.

7. If you have included the name of a package unit file (.DPK) in the Contains section of another package file, remove it.

Additional Information

I. In this event, Delphi will be looking for a file with the name as it appears in the Uses section with an extension of .DCU (Delphi compiled unit).

If you want to open a file for writing using the Append procedure, it is recommended that you prepare for the file's nonexistence at the time of the call by exercising "defensive programming." For example, you could use this type of code to prevent errors caused by nonexistent files:

```
procedure TForm1.btnWriteToTextFileClick(Sender:
    Tobject);
var
  tF: TextFile;
begin
  AssignFile(tF,'sexyexe.txt');
  if FileExists(ChangeFileExt(Paramstr(0),'.txt')) then
              Append(tF)
  else Rewrite(tF);
  WriteLn(tF,DateTimeToStr(Now));
  CloseFile(tF);
end;
```

File not open

Possible Cause of Error

I. You may be attempting to perform some operation on a file that has not been opened, such as reading from it or writing to it. For example, the following code will cause this error message:

```
var
  Textilefile: TextFile;
begin
  AssignFile(Textilefile, 'bellbottoms.txt');
  Writeln(Textilefile, 'On the hips of the hippies in the sixties');
  CloseFile(Textilefile);
end;
```

2. You may have attempted to write to a file that does not exist or exists but is read-only. For example, using the Append procedure to write to a file that does not exist or attempting to write to a text file opened with the Reset procedure will generate this error message. By way of example, the following code generates this error when attempting to write to the read-only (because it is a text file opened with the Reset procedure):

```
var
  JSBach: Textfile;
begin
  AssignFile(JSBach,'Meisterstuecke.txt');
  try
    Reset(JSBach);
    Writeln(JSBach,'Air on a G String');
    Writeln(JSBach,'Jesu, Joy of Man''s Desiring');
    . . .
  finally
    CloseFile(JSBach);
  end;
end;
```

3. If you have created some procedures that directly intercept Windows messages (message handling methods), you may be trying to access a text file within a Windows message that is either dispatched before your text file can be created (WM_CREATE, for example) or after your text file has closed (WM_DESTROY, for example). To illustrate, you might override the Windows WM_KEYDOWN message by declaring a procedure using this syntax:

```
procedure wmkeydown(var Message: TMessage);
                    message WM_KEYDOWN;
```

You then define the procedure in your form unit's Implementation part like this:

```
procedure Tform1.wmkeydown(var Message);
begin
  inherited { call inherited to inherit the built-in functionality }
  { Do whatever you want here whenever the WM_KEYDOWN message is sent.
    For example, to keep track of which events are happening when,
    you might do something like this: }
  Writeln(tf, 'KeyDown message sent');
end;
```

Attempting to write to a text file within certain events (the WM_CREATE and WM_DESTROY events, among others) will produce the error message under discussion.

Quick Fix

1. You need to call Rewrite, Reset, or Append before writing to the file, like this:

    ```
    var
      Textilefile: TextFile;
    begin
      AssignFile(Textilefile, 'corduroy.txt');
      try
        if FileExists('corduroy.txt') then
          Append(Textilefile)
        else
          Rewrite(Textilefile);
        Writeln(Textilefile, 'On the hips of the hippies in the sixties');
      finally
        CloseFile(Textilefile);
      end;
    end;
    ```

2. Verify that the file exists before attempting to write to it, and use Append or Rewrite rather than Reset, like this:

    ```
    var
      JSBach: Textfile;
    begin
      AssignFile(JSBach,'Meisterstueck.txt');
      try
        if FileExists('Meisterstueck.txt') then
          Append(JSBach)
        else
          Rewrite(JSBach);
        Writeln(JSBach,'Air on a G String');
        Writeln(JSBach,'Jesu, Joy of Man''s Desiring');
      finally
        CloseFile(JSBach);
      end;
    end;
    ```

3. Do not attempt to write to a file inside an event that occurs before the text file has been created. If you want to have a text file available (say, for example, as a debug, log, or error file), you can assign it in your main form's OnCreate event and then close it in the main form's OnDestroy event.

Additional Information

>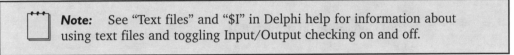
> **Note:** This is "I/O Error 103."

Use the Append procedure to append data to a file. Use the Rewrite procedure to overwrite/replace any existing data. Use Reset to open a file for reading.

> **Note:** See "Text files" and "$I" in Delphi help for information about using text files and toggling Input/Output checking on and off.

File not open for input

Possible Cause of Error

1. You may be attempting to read from a text file that has not been opened for reading. For example, the following code will generate this error as the Reset procedure has not been called:

```
var
  cookie: TextFile;
  s      : String;
  i      : Integer;
begin
  i:=0;
  AssignFile(cookie,'history.txt');
  try
    while not eof(cookie) do
      begin
        readln(cookie, s);
        cbxSitesVisited.items[i]:= s;
        inc(i);
      end;
  finally
    CloseFile(cookie);
  end;
end;
```

2. You may have used a Read or Readln statement without supplying the variable name of the text file to read. For example, the following will generate this error message:

```
Readln(s);
```

Quick Fix

1. Before attempting to read from a file, call the Reset procedure. To fix the example given above, add the call prior to the *while* loop, like this:

```
. . .
AssignFile(cookie,'history.txt');
try
  Reset(cookie);
  while not eof(cookie) do
  . . .
```

2. Add the name of the text file variable, like this:

```
readln(SomeTextFile, s);
```

Additional Information

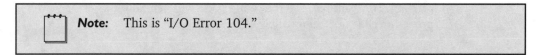

> **Note:** This is "I/O Error 104."

1. Use the Append procedure to append data to a file. Use the Rewrite procedure to overwrite/replace any existing data. Use Reset to open a file for reading.

2. Windows programs require the file variable as well as the string variable into which to read the line.

> **Note:** See "Text files" and "$I" in Delphi help for information about using text files and toggling Input/Output checking on and off.

File not open for output

Possible Cause of Error

1. You may be using Delphi 1 and the Writeln procedure without having added the WinCRT unit to your Uses clause.

2. You may be attempting to write to a text file opened with the Reset procedure.

Quick Fix

1. Add WinCRT to the Uses section of your unit.

2. Open files for writing with Append or Rewrite, not Reset. You cannot append to a file that does not exist, so you can use the following logic to write to a file the first time or prepare for the eventuality of the file being missing:

```
. . .
AssignFile(SingSing,'nail.txt');
if FileExists('nail.txt') then
  Append(SingSing)
else
  Rewrite(SingSing);
```

Additional Information

> **Note:** This is "I/O Error 105."

Use the Append procedure to append data to a file. Use the Rewrite procedure to overwrite/replace any existing data. Use Reset to open a file for reading.

> **Note:** See "Text files" and "$I" in Delphi help for information about using text files and toggling Input/Output checking on and off.

File or directory does not exist

Possible Cause of Error

You may have specified a table in a SQL statement which does not exist. For example, with a TQuery's DatabaseName property set to DBDEMOS, the following SQL statement will generate this error message:

```
SELECT *
FROM ANIMULES
```

Quick Fix

Be sure that the table you specified actually exists in the location you specified. It may be a simple spelling problem which can be fixed in the above case with:

```
SELECT *
FROM ANIMALS
```

Additional Information

If you are working with local (standard) aliases and have not specified the type of table you are attempting to access, Delphi will first search for a Paradox table, then dBASE, then an ASCII (text) file.

File type not allowed here

Possible Cause of Error

1. You may have attempted to declare a variable of type File of File, File of Text, or File of Textfile.
2. You may have attempted to pass a file type as a value parameter. For example, the following will generate this error:

```
procedure LegoMania(Technik: file);
```

Quick Fix

1. Do not attempt to declare variables of these types.
2. Do not pass file types as value parameters. Try this instead:

```
procedure LegoMania(var Technik: file);
```

Additional Information

You <u>can</u> pass a file type as a var or const parameter. See "Parameters" in Delphi help for more information. By default, parameters are passed by value.

Fixed column count must be less than column count

Possible Cause of Error

You may have set the FixedCols property of a TStringGrid or TDrawGrid to a number higher than the number of columns in the grid.

Quick Fix

Do not set the FixedCols property to a value equal to or greater than the number of columns the grid contains. If you allow the user to set the number of columns, ensure that the number of columns is not exceeded. For example, you could do something like this:

```
procedure TForm1.Button14Click(Sender: Tobject);
const
  crlf = #13#10;{or make this a global constant}
  procedure Whatchemacolumn(ColNum: Integer);
  begin
    if ColNum < StringGrid1.ColCount then
      StringGrid1.FixedCols := ColNum
    else
      MessageDlg('You must set the number'+crlf+ 'of fixed columns
                  less than'+crlf+ 'the total number of columns',
                  mtInformation,[mbOK],0);
  end;
begin
  Whatchemacolumn(StrToInt(Edit1.Text));
end;
```

Additional Information

You must have at least one column that is not fixed.

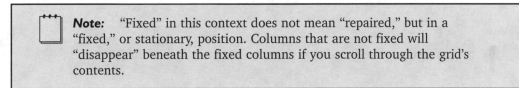

Note: "Fixed" in this context does not mean "repaired," but in a "fixed," or stationary, position. Columns that are not fixed will "disappear" beneath the fixed columns if you scroll through the grid's contents.

Fixed row count must be less than row count

Possible Cause of Error

You may have set the FixedRows property of a TStringGrid or TDrawGrid to a number higher than the number of rows in the grid.

Quick Fix

Do not set the FixedRows property to a value equal to or greater than the number of rows the grid contains. If you allow the user to set the number of rows, ensure that the number of rows is not exceeded. For example, you could do something like this:

```
procedure TForm1.Button14Click(Sender: Tobject);
const
  crlf = #13#10;{or make this a global constant}
  procedure PrettyMaidsAllInARow(RowNum: Integer);
  begin
    if RowNum < StringGrid1.RowCount then
      StringGrid1.FixedRows := RowNum
    else
      MessageDlg('You must set the number'+crlf+ 'of fixed rows
                  less than'+crlf+ 'the total number of rows',
                  mtInformation,[mbOK],0);
  end;
begin
  PrettyMaidsAllInARow(StrToInt(Edit1.Text));
end;
```

Additional Information

You must have at least one row that is not fixed.

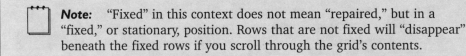 **Note:** "Fixed" in this context does not mean "repaired," but in a "fixed," or stationary, position. Rows that are not fixed will "disappear" beneath the fixed rows if you scroll through the grid's contents.

For Loop control variable must have ordinal type

Possible Cause of Error

You may have attempted to use a data type as the control variable of a *for* loop that is not an ordinal type (Boolean, Char, WideChar, Integer, enumerated, subrange). For example, the following will generate this error message:

```
var
  flcv, WinnieThePooh: String;
```

```
begin
  WinnieThePooh := '';
  for flcv := 'a' to 'z' do
    WinnieThePooh := WinnieThePooh+flcv;
```

Quick Fix

Use an ordinal type as the control variable of *for* loops. It is customary to use an integer declared as "i." To perform the *for* loop attempted above, you could do this:

```
var
  i: integer;
  s: string;
begin
  s:='';
  for i := Ord('a') to Ord('z') do
    s := s+Chr(i);
```

Additional Information

The Chr function actually takes a byte rather than an integer, but as long as you pass it a positive value less than 256, an integer value will work. To ensure that you do not assign a bogus value, you can first use the Ord function, as shown above. The same thing would be accomplished by:

```
for i := 97 to 122 do
```

but that makes the code less readable and the possibilities for mistakes greater. See "Ord" and "Chr" in Delphi help for more information.

FOR-Loop variable < > cannot be passed as var parameter

Possible Cause of Error

You may have attempted to pass the control variable of a *for* loop to a procedure or function which declares the accepted control variable as a var parameter. For example, the following will generate this error message:

```
function KoolAndTheGang(var intgr: integer): string;
begin
  intgr := intgr+1;
  Result := IntToStr(intgr);
end;
. . .
procedure PassKoolAnEye;
```

```
begin
  for i := ord('a') to ord('z') do
    KoolAndTheGang(i);
end;
```

Quick Fix

Do not attempt to externally modify the *for* loop control variable.

Additional Information

See "For statements" in Delphi help for more information.

Form <> links to form <> which cannot be found in the current project. Do you wish to remove/redirect the links to another form?

Possible Cause of Error

1. You may have added an existing form which relies on another form that is not included in the project. If the first form mentioned in the error message (the one that <u>is</u> in the project) contains data-aware controls, the second form mentioned in the error message (which is not in the project) may be a data module which contains the first form's corresponding non-visible data components (TDatabase, TTable, TQuery, TStoredProc, TDataSource, etc.).

2. You may have attempted to save a form which has a linked form that is not loaded.

Quick Fix

1, 2. If you don't need to retain the link between the two forms, select **Yes** and then select **Remove Link**. If you do need to retain the link, load the second form mentioned in the message.

Additional Information

See "Form <> references another form and cannot be saved until <> is loaded"; also, see "Data Modules" in Delphi help for more information.

Form <> references another form and cannot be saved until <> is loaded

Possible Cause of Error

You may have gotten the error message "Form <> links to form <> which cannot be found in the current project. Do you wish to remove/redirect the links to another form?" and answered No or Cancel (you did not remove or redirect the link).

Quick Fix

Load the second form mentioned in the error message into the current project.

Additional Information

See "Form <> links to form <> which cannot be found in the current project. Do you wish to remove/redirect the links to another form?"

Function needs result type

Possible Cause of Error

You may have omitted the result type (or the colon between the function name and result type) from a function you declared. For example, the following will generate this error message:

```
function junction(s: string);
```

as will this:

```
function Calc(x,y: integer); integer;
```

Quick Fix

Add the result type to the function declaration. For example, if the function returns a Boolean result, declare it like this:

```
function junction(s: string): boolean;
```

Additional Information

Procedures perform an action (or actions). Functions usually do the same, but they also return a result. If you teach your dog to roll over and to fetch, you could compare the roll to a procedure and the fetch to a function (the dog retrieves your slippers or the newspaper).

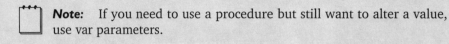

Note: If you need to use a procedure but still want to alter a value, use var parameters.

General SQL Error—connection does not exist

Possible Cause of Error

You may be attempting to perform database operations in a thread to which a Session component has not been assigned.

Quick Fix

Assign a Session component to each thread that accesses database components.

Additional Information

See "Session name missing" and "Cannot enable AutoSessionName property with more than one session on a form or data module."

General SQL Error—FROM keyword not found where expected

Possible Cause of Error

You may have neglected to add one or more comma separators between field names in a SELECT list. For example, the following will generate this error message:

```
SELECT First, Second, Third Fourth
FROM ORDINALS
```

Quick Fix

Add a comma after all fields except the last one in the list.

Additional Information

See "<> expected but <> found."

General SQL error. The [Commit,Rollback] Transaction request has no corresponding begin transaction

Possible Cause of Error

1. You may be calling Commit or Rollback, but have not explicitly begun the transaction with a call to StartTransaction. For example, you might be doing something like this:

```
begin
  with Database1 do
    begin
      Connected := True;
      try
        Query1.Active := True;
        Commit;
      except
        Rollback;
      end;
    end;
end;
```

2. You may be working with MS SQL Server and are experiencing a deadlock.

Quick Fix

1. Begin each transaction with a call to StartTransaction, and end each transaction with either a call to Rollback (if there is a problem) or Commit. For example, you might do it this way:

```
begin
  with Database1 do
    begin
      Connected := True;
      StartTransaction;
      try
        Query1.Active := True;
        Commit;
      except
        Rollback;
      end;
    end;
end;
```

2. After dismissing the error message, try again to make and post your changes.

Additional Information

2. MS SQL Server rolls back transactions that experience deadlocks.

General SQL Error : SQL is too complex

See "SQL is too complex."

GOTO <> leads into or out of TRY statement

Possible Cause of Error

You may have a *goto* statement that "goes to" or is contained within a guarded block of code (a *try...finally* or *try...except* block).

Quick Fix

Remove the *goto* statement from the guarded block or do not "go to" the guarded block of code.

Additional Information

goto statements are considered "bad form" (poor programming practice). Do not use *goto* statements unless you can find no other recourse.

Grid Index Out of Range

Possible Cause of Error

You may be looping through a dataset and are reaching the end of file (EOF) while displaying the dataset in a DBGrid.

Quick Fix

Call TDataset's DisableControls method while iterating through the dataset, like this:

```
with RegretTable do
begin
  DisableControls;
  try
```

```
      First;
      while not EOF do
      begin
        . . .
        Next;
      end;
    finally
      EnableControls;
end;
```

Additional Information

If calling DisableControls does not work in your situation, add the following code either:

In the form's OnCreate event if the table is open in the Delphi IDE

-OR-

Immediately after opening the table whose content the DBGrid displays:

```
DBGrid1.HandleNeeded;
```

GROUP BY is required when both aggregate and non-aggregate fields are used in result set

Possible Cause of Error

You may be attempting to use one or more aggregate functions in a SQL statement, but have neglected to add a GROUP BY section. For example, the following will generate this error message:

```
SELECT DIM, SUM(TSINGTAO)
FROM
CHINESEFOOD
```

Quick Fix

Whenever you use a SQL aggregate function, such as SUM, AVG, MIN, MAX, or COUNT, you must group by all the other (non-aggregate) fields. For example, the above SQL statement should be:

```
SELECT DIM, SUM(TSINGTAO)
FROM
CHINESEFOOD
GROUP BY DIM
```

Additional Information

Specific SQL syntax and features differ among vendors. Consult your database documentation for information pertinent to the database you are using. If you are using local tables, consult Localsql.hlp, which ships with Delphi (installed by default to: C:\Program Files\Borland\Common Files\BDE).

High cannot be applied to a long string

Possible Cause of Error

You may be porting an application from Delphi 1 to 32-bit Delphi in which the program uses the High function on a string. For example, the following will generate this error message in 32-bit Delphi:

```
var
  i: integer;
  s: string;
begin
  s := 'esszet';
  i := high(s);
```

Quick Fix

You cannot apply the High function to long strings. You can, though, use it with short strings, which are still available in 32-bit Delphi. You can use a short string in 32-bit Delphi by assigning a length (up to 255) in the string declaration or by using the ShortString type. The above example will work by simply appending the length you want to use to the string declaration or declaring the string as type ShortString. In other words, either of the following will work:

```
s: string[24]; { or any other positive integer up to and including 255 }
s: shortstring;
```

Alternatively, if you want to leave your code as is, you can turn off the use of long strings as the default string type in 32-bit Delphi by selecting Project | Options | Compiler | Syntax Options, and deselecting the Huge Strings check box. Another way of accomplishing the same thing is to include the {$H-} compiler directive at the top of the unit.

Additional Information

See "Open string parameters" and "High function" in Delphi help for more information.

> **Note:** To see the current compiler directives for a unit, select **Ctrl+O+O** (the letter O, not the numeral 0). The compiler directives set for the unit will then be visible at the top of the unit.

Higher table level required

Possible Cause of Error

You are attempting to add or utilize some functionality that is available only with a higher-level Paradox table. One or more of the following may be true in your case:

1. You may have attempted to add a unique index in code to a Paradox table below level 7. For example, the line below produces this error message with a Paradox 4 or 5 table:

```
Table1.AddIndex('NewIndex','Name_Last',[ixUnique]);
```

2. You may have attempted to add a descending index in code to a Paradox table below level 7. For example, the line below produces this error message with a Paradox level 4 or 5 table:

```
Table1.AddIndex('Wf','Waterfall',[ixDescending]);
```

3. You may be referencing a Paradox table whose path contains long filenames.

4. You may be attempting to add a Long Integer, BCD, Time, Timestamp, Logical, Autoincrement, or Bytes field to a pre-level 7 Paradox table. These data types are new to Paradox 7. For example, if the table is pre-level 7, the following will generate this error message:

```
FieldDefs.Add('OttoInque', ftAutoInc, 0, True);
```

Quick Fix

1, 2. One option is to add the index in the Database Desktop rather than in code (when you subsequently save the modified table structure, Database Desktop will automatically elevate the table level to the lowest level necessary to accommodate your changes). If you don't want to restructure the table, set the default table level to the highest available level in the BDE Configuration or Admin utility. To accomplish this, follow these steps:

Delphi 1 or 2

a. Select **Tools | BDE Config**.

b. Select **Paradox** in the Driver Name list box.

c. Change the LEVEL setting to that desired (for example, from 4 or 5 to 7).

d. Select **File | Exit**.

e. Select **Yes** to save changes.

Delphi 3 and 4

a. Select **Start | Programs | Borland Delphi X | BDE [Configuration, Administration]**.

b. Select the Configuration tab in the Drivers and System pane.

c. Expand the Drivers node in the tree-view list.

d. Expand the Native node in the tree-view list.

e. Select either **Paradox** or **dBASE**, as appropriate.

f. Select the highest level from the LEVEL drop-down list in the Definition pane.

g. Select **Object | Exit**.

h. Select **Yes** to save the change.

All subsequent tables will be created with the level you chose.

3. Either revert to 8.3 filenames and short directory names without spaces, or increase the level of your Paradox table to 7. Follow the steps above to increase the table level.

4. You need to set the level of your Paradox table to 7. See the steps above to accomplish this.

Additional Information

A "quick-and-dirty" way to elevate a Paradox table to level 7 from Database Desktop is to add a descending index. As descending indexes were not supported in Paradox until version 7, saving the database after adding the descending index will save it as a Paradox 7 database.

However, unless the index needs to be added in code (that is, you don't know the field for which you are going to create an index at design time), it's kind of silly to add an index you may not need (the descending index) in Database Desktop in order to create one you do need in code.

So there are two scenarios wherein you will find it necessary to add an index to a table in Database Desktop:

1. You want to add an index but you are using a Paradox 3.5, 4, or 5 table (you cannot add an index in code with these tables).

2. You need to add an index in code, but your Paradox table is pre-level 7 and so you need to elevate or promote it to level 7 by adding a descending index.

To add an index in Database Desktop, follow these steps:

a. Select **Tools | Database Desktop**.

b. Select **File | Open | Table...**.

c. Navigate to and open the table to which you want to add an index.

d. Select **Tools | Utilities | Restructure...** (or click the icon of the wrench and table).

e. Select **Secondary Indexes** from the Table Properties combo box.

f. Select the **Define** button.

g. Highlight the field to which you want to add an index in the Fields list box.

h. Click the right-pointing arrow between the Fields and Indexed Fields list boxes.

i. Select any of the check boxes in the Index Options section that you want to apply to the index. These index options are Unique, Case Sensitive, Descending, and Maintained. Maintained is selected by default. (This is where you could select Descending to "force" a Paradox 4 or 5 table to be promoted to a Paradox 7 table.)

j. Select the **OK** button.

k. Provide a name for the index in the Save Index As dialog box. You will now be able to set the table's IndexName property in code to the one you just created.

l. Select the **Save** button in the Restructure window.

m. Select **File | Close**.

You will now be able to change to the index you added in code:

```
Table1.Exclusive := True;
Table1.IndexName := 'Sub7Index';
```

Also, you will now be able to create new indexes in code with your Paradox 7 table:

```
Table1.Exclusive := True;
Table1.AddIndex('Paradox7Index','City',[ixUnique]);
```

Of course, if you need to create the indexes in code, you may want to wait until run time to specify the field to index and possibly the name of the index also:

```
Table1.Exclusive := True;
Table1.AddIndex(Edit1.Text,Edit2.Text,[]);
```

Indexes you set in code like this are persistent.

I/O Error 102

See "File not assigned."

I/O Error 103

See "File not open."

I/O Error 104

See "File not open for input."

I/O Error 105

See "File not open for output."

Identifier expected but array found

Possible Cause of Error

You may have declared an array as the return value of a function. For example, the following will generate this error message:

```
function Three41(i: integer): array[0..3] of char;
```

Quick Fix

Declare a type for the array you want to use, and then declare your new array type as the function's return type. For example, to fix the example above, try something like this:

```
type
  ThreeForOne = array[0..3] of char;
. . .
function Three41(i: integer): ThreeForOne;
```

Additional Information

See "Arrays" in Delphi help for more information.

Identifier expected but number found

Possible Cause of Error

You may have used a parenthesis while attempting to declare a subrange type. For example, the following will generate this error message:

```
type
  TSillySubrange = (4 * 8)..255;
```

Quick Fix

Avoid beginning a subrange declaration with a parenthesis. The compiler will think you are endeavoring to declare an enumerated type. Instead, do it this way:

```
type
  TSoberSubrange = 32..255;
```

Additional Information

You <u>can</u> use expressions in the declaration of subrange types, as long as you avoid beginning the declaration with a parenthesis. For example, the following are acceptable to the compiler:

```
type
  TSeriousSubrange = 32..255;
type
  TSuaveSubrange = 32..((32 * 8) -1);
```

Identifier expected but < > found

Possible Cause of Error

1. You may have declared a Type, Variable, or Constant section without declaring anything beneath them.

2. You may have attempted to use a reserved word as an identifier.

3. You may have prepended the dot scoping operator (.) to the name of an array property (before the square brackets). For example:

```
Label1.Caption := ListBox1.Items.[0];
```

Quick Fix

1. Remove the empty section or add one or more valid identifiers to it.
2. Do not use reserved words for anything but that for which they are "reserved" for.
3. Remove the dot scoping operator (.) from the statement.

Additional Information

Identifiers are the names given types, variables, constants, procedures, functions, units, programs, and fields in records.

See "Identifier expected but array found" and "Identifier expected but number found." See also "Identifiers" in Delphi help for more information.

Identifier redeclared: < >

Possible Cause of Error

1. You may be attempting to use a name that is already being used within the same scope. It may be a variable, constant, type, field (member of a class), method, or a redundant unit in a Uses section. For example, the following will generate this error message, because the variable ThirtySix is declared twice:

```
function BrickHouse(ThirtySix, TwentyFour, ThirtySix: integer): integer;
```

2. You may have added the System unit to the Uses section of one of your units. In this case, the error message is "Identifier redeclared: System."

Quick Fix

1. Remove or rename the "redeclared" item.
2. Remove System from your Uses clause, as it is implicitly declared for all units.

Additional Information

1. You cannot have two global variables with the same name. You also cannot have two local variables (within the same scope) with the same name.

   You can have a global and as many local variables (as long as each are unique within their scope) as you want that use the same name, though. For example, you could have a global variable named Expendable Income and simultaneously declare a variable with the same name within a procedure or function (in which case the global variable is eclipsed by the local variable).

> **Note:** In Delphi 4, overloaded methods are allowed. That is, a class can have multiple methods with the same name. However, these methods must be distinguishable from each other by having different numbers and/or types of arguments. Also, they must be defined with the new *overload* keyword. For example, you could define three different implementations of a method PayCheck like this:
>
> ```
> procedure PayCheck(Wage: Currency); overload;
> procedure PayCheck(Salary, Commission: Currency); overload;
> procedure PayCheck(Salary, Bonus, ProfitSharing: Currency); overload;
> ```
>
> It is possible to create ambiguous method signatures by combining method overloading and default parameters (when you assign default parameters, it is optional whether the parameter is specified or not). For example, the following declarations would be ambiguous:
>
> ```
> procedure Fuzzy(I: Integer; J: Integer = 0);
>                                 overload;
> procedure Fuzzy(Size: Integer); overload;
> ```
>
> If you tried to call one of the methods like this:
>
> ```
> Fuzzy(Wuzzy);
> ```
>
> you would receive the error message "Ambiguous Overloaded Call to <>," as it would be impossible for the compiler to know which method was being called (are you calling the first Fuzzy, leaving out the default parameter, or the second Fuzzy?). Of course, the purpose of using a default parameter is to optionally omit the default parameter, but to do so you must ensure that there is no ambiguity relative to overloaded methods.

Illegal character in input file: <> (<>)

Possible Cause of Error

I. You may have begun a declaration with an ampersand, tilde, slash, backslash, etc. For example, the following will generate this error message:

```
type
  Proto = &
```

2. You may have added something to the {$R *.RES} section in the project source (.DPR) file.

3. You may have left a curly brace (}) at the end of a line.

Quick Fix

1. Give the variable a legal Object Pascal name (begin with an underscore or alphabetic character; thereafter continue to use underscores, alphabetic characters, and numbers only).

2. Verify that the project source file's {$R *.RES} statement has not been altered.

3. Remove any curly braces (}) you may have at the end of lines.

Additional Information

This error message is encountered most often in connection with string constants or comments.

Illegal message method index

Possible Cause of Error

You may have declared a message method with a value less than 1. For example the following will generate this error message:

```
procedure WMChar(var Message: TWMChar);
                          message -34;
```

Quick Fix

Do not use a negative number (or zero) as the message method index. If you are capturing a Windows message, use its corresponding constant as declared in the Messages.PAS unit. For example, the above declaration should be:

```
procedure WMChar(var Message: TWMChar);
                  message WM_CHAR;
```

Additional Information

You can also refer to the WM_CHAR message by its hexadecimal value:

```
procedure WMChar(var Message: TWMChar);
                  message $0102;
```

or by its decimal value:

```
procedure WMChar(var Message: TWMChar);
                        message 34;
```

See "Message Handlers" in Delphi help and Delphi's MESSAGES.PAS unit for more information.

IMPLEMENTATION part is missing or incorrect

Possible Cause of Error

You may have altered, removed, or commented out a unit's *implementation* reserved word.

Quick Fix

Ensure that the *implementation* reserved word exists between the Interface section and the actual Implementation part.

Additional Information

See "Implementation reserved word | Positioning a procedure or function in your code" and "Implementation reserved word | The Structure of a Unit" in Delphi help for more information.

Implementation part USES clause incorrect

Possible Cause of Error

You may have a syntax error within the Implementation part's Uses clause.

Quick Fix

Verify that there is one comma between all units referenced in the Uses clause and a semicolon at the end.

Additional Information

You can have one or two Uses clauses in a unit. You will have one in the Interface section of the unit similar to this:

```
unit EdStates;
interface
uses
```

```
      Windows, Messages, SysUtils, Classes,
      Graphics, Controls, Forms, Dialogs;
type
  TForm1 = class(TForm)
. . .
```

You can also have a Uses clause in the Implementation section of your unit:

```
. . .
implementation
uses EdArabEm;
{$R *.DFM}
. . .
```

Implements getter must be register calling convention

Possible Cause of Error

You may have specified a calling convention other than the default register for the accessor (getter) method of a delegate interface property. For example, the following will generate this error message:

```
type
  ISomeInterface = interface
    procedure RollOver;
    function FetchMySlippers: Boolean;
  end;
  TSomeClass = class(TObject, ISomeInterface)
    FSomeInterface: ISomeInterface;
    function ReadItAndWeep: ISomeInterface;
                                stdcall;
    property SomeInterface: ISomeInterface read
      ReadItAndWeep implements ISomeInterface;
  end;
```

Quick Fix

Remove the stdcall (or other) calling convention you specified for the accessor/getter function.

Additional Information

See "Implementing Interfaces by delegation" in Delphi help for more information.

> **Note:** The *implements* directive is new with Delphi 4.

Incompatible types: < > and < >

Possible Cause of Error

1. You may be attempting to assign a property or variable of one type a value of an incompatible type. For example, you may be trying to assign a string to an integer or a bitmap to a Boolean.

2. You may be attempting to assign a TField descendent (such as TStringField, TFloatField, etc., which Delphi creates when you instantiate the fields in a Dataset) to a variable of a different data type. You cannot (directly) assign a TStringField to a variable of type String. By way of illustration, neither of the following assignments are allowed (Capital is a TStringField and Area is a TFloatField. Both are from the Country Paradox table that ships with Delphi):

    ```
    {This will generate "Incompatible types: String and TStringField"}
    StringGrid1.Cells[0,0] := Table1Capital;
    {This will generate "Incompatible types: Extended and TFloatField"}
    StringGrid1.Cells[0,0] := FloatToStr(Table1Area);
    ```

3. You may be passing a value to a procedure or function that is not the same as the parameter declared for the procedure or function. For example, the following will generate this error message:

    ```
    procedure TypeConfusion(i: integer);
    . . .
    procedure SendString;
    var
      s: string;
    begin
      TypeConfusion(s);
    {pass an integer, not a string}
    ```

4. You may have declared a function's result type of one data type and are attempting to return a result of a different data type. For example, the following function will generate the error message under discussion:

    ```
    function mpd(var i: integer): boolean;
    begin
      i := i+1;
    ```

```
  Result := IntToStr(i);
{result should be boolean, not string}
end;
```

5. You may have used an operator that is reserved for one data type on operands of another data type. For example, the following will generate this error message, as the "/" operator is for use with real (floating-point) numbers, not integers:

```
i := 3 / 0;
```

6. You may have attempted to assign a graphic control (a descendent of TGraphicControl) to a property that requires a "windowed" control (one that has a windows handle and can thus receive focus; a descendent of TWinControl). For example, the following will produce this error ("Incompatible types: TWinControl and TLabel"):

```
ActiveControl := Label1;
```

7. It may also be that a property's Read or Write clause references a field or method whose parameter type differs from that of the property. For example, the following will generate the "Incompatible types" error message, as a Boolean property is attempting to write to a procedure which takes a string:

```
private
  FEmUpJoe: boolean;
  procedure SetEmUpJoe(s: string);
public
  { Public declarations }
published
  property EmUpJoe: boolean read FEmUpJoe
                        write SetEmUpJoe;
end;
```

8. You may have used the TextOut procedure without prepending Canvas to it. For example, this will generate the error message under discussion:

```
procedure TForm1.FormMouseDown(Sender: TObject;
      Button: TMouseButton; Shift: TShiftState;
                              X, Y: Integer);
begin
  TextOut(X,Y,IntToStr(X)+' '+IntToStr(Y));
end;
```

9. You may be attempting to assign a "regular" procedure or function (one that is not a member of the class, but rather a global or local procedure or function) to a method pointer. For example, the following will generate this error message:

```
procedure TForm1.Button2Click(Sender: Tobject);
  procedure RegularGuy(Sender: TObject);
  begin
```

```
    Label1.Caption := 'You clicked Button 1!';
  end;
begin
  Button1.OnClick := RegularGuy;
end;
```

Quick Fix

1. Assign the value to a variable of the same data type or convert the value to be stored before making the assignment.

2. There are two ways you can assign the value from a TField descendent to a variable. You can append the Value property to the name of the field you are retrieving the value from; alternatively, you can convert the value to the type to which you are assigning it with the AsX property. Here are some examples of assignment statements that are valid:

```
{ This works }
StringGrid1.Cells[1,1] := Table1Capital.Value;
{ So does this }
StringGrid1.Cells[0,0] := Table1Capital.AsString;
```

Sometimes, the AsX conversion property does not work, depending on the variable you are trying to assign to and the TField descendent whose value you are attempting to retrieve. For example, the following statement produces the error message under discussion:

```
{"Incompatible types: String and Double"}
StringGrid1.Cells[1,1] := Table1Area.AsFloat;
```

In any case, using the AsVariant conversion property (on any TField descendent) will work:

```
StringGrid1.Cells[1,1] := Table1Capital.AsVariant;
```

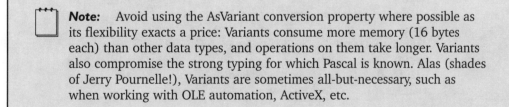

Note: Avoid using the AsVariant conversion property where possible as its flexibility exacts a price: Variants consume more memory (16 bytes each) than other data types, and operations on them take longer. Variants also compromise the strong typing for which Pascal is known. Alas (shades of Jerry Pournelle!), Variants are sometimes all-but-necessary, such as when working with OLE automation, ActiveX, etc.

3. Ensure that the data type of the variable you pass a procedure or function matches that in the procedure or function's declaration.

4. Ensure that the return result of the function matches the return type the function declares.

5. Use *div* with integer operands, and "/" with real (floating-point) operands.

6. Do not attempt to make a graphical control the form's active control.

7. Ensure that the types of properties and their read and write fields or methods match. In the example shown above, either change the private field and property type from Boolean to string, or change the Write method's parameter type from string to Boolean.

8. Prepend Canvas to the call to TextOut, like this:

```
procedure TForm1.FormMouseDown(Sender: Tobject;
      Button: TMouseButton; Shift: TShiftState;
                              X, Y: Integer);
begin
  Canvas.TextOut(X,Y,IntToStr(X)+' '+IntToStr(Y));
end;
```

9. Only assign methods (a procedure or a function that is a member of the class) to method pointers. You could accomplish the above by rearranging the code this way:

```
type
  TForm1 = class(TForm)
    Button1: TButton;
    Label1: TLabel;
    Button2: TButton;
    procedure Button1Click(Sender: TObject);
    procedure Button2Click(Sender: TObject);
  private
    . . .
  public
    procedure HandCodedMethod(Sender: TObject);
  end;
. . .
procedure TForm1.HandCodedMethod(Sender: TObject);
begin
  Label1.Caption := 'You clicked Button 1!';
end;
procedure TForm1.Button2Click(Sender: TObject);
begin
  Button1.OnClick := HandCodedMethod;
end;
```

Additional Information

1. Delphi/Object Pascal has many built-in functions that enable you to convert between data types, such as from integer to string and vice versa, etc. For

example, you can assign a string to an integer variable by using the StrToInt conversion function, like this:

```
SomeIntegerVariable := StrToInt(Edit1.Text);
```

but attempting to assign the string contained in an edit box directly to an integer variable, like this:

```
SomeIntegerVariable := Edit1.Text;
```

would cause the above error message. For more information on other conversions, see "Conversions" in Delphi online help.

2. When the Country Paradox table that ships with Delphi was created, the Capital field was given the data type Alpha and the Area field was given the data type Number. If you instantiate these fields in Delphi using the Fields Editor (see "Fields Editor" in Delphi help), they will be converted from their native Paradox types to the Object Pascal data types TStringField and TFloatField, respectively.

Here is a table of Paradox data types and their corresponding Delphi TField descendents:

Paradox data type	Delphi TField descendent
Alpha	TStringField
Autoincrement	TAutoIncField
BCD	TBCDField
Binary	TBlobField
Byte	TBytesField
Date	TDateField
Formatted Memo	TBlobField
Graphic	TGraphicField
Logical	TBooleanField
Long Integer	TIntegerField
Memo	TMemoField
Money	TCurrencyField
Number	TFloatField
OLE	TBlobField
Short	TSmallIntField
Time	TTimeField
Timestamp	TDateTimeField

Note: The Delphi TField descendent TBlobField does triple duty, as it is the field instantiated for three Paradox data types: Binary, Formatted Memo, and OLE.

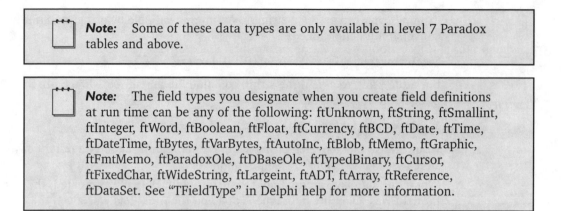

> **Note:** Some of these data types are only available in level 7 Paradox tables and above.

> **Note:** The field types you designate when you create field definitions at run time can be any of the following: ftUnknown, ftString, ftSmallint, ftInteger, ftWord, ftBoolean, ftFloat, ftCurrency, ftBCD, ftDate, ftTime, ftDateTime, ftBytes, ftVarBytes, ftAutoInc, ftBlob, ftMemo, ftGraphic, ftFmtMemo, ftParadoxOle, ftDBaseOle, ftTypedBinary, ftCursor, ftFixedChar, ftWideString, ftLargeint, ftADT, ftArray, ftReference, ftDataSet. See "TFieldType" in Delphi help for more information.

9. The specific error message in this case is "Incompatible types: method pointer and regular procedure."

Incompatible types: Parameter lists differ

Possible Cause of Error

You may have assigned a function to a function type (or a procedure to a procedure type) whose signatures do not match. For example, the following will generate this error message:

```
procedure Cream(Clapton, Bruce, Baker: integer);
type
  TYearsAfter = procedure(Lee, Alvin: integer);
const
  DesertRoseBand: TYearsAfter = Cream;
```

Quick Fix

To assign a function or procedure to a function or procedure type, their signature (number, data type, and sequence of parameters) must be identical (although the names of the parameters can differ). For example, the following will work fine:

```
function Kool(a,b,c: integer): integer;
type
  TAndTheMGs = function(x,y,z: integer): integer;
const
  Stylistics: TAndTheMGs = Kool;
```

Additional Information

See "Procedural Values" in Delphi help for more information.

Incorrect field declaration: class < >

Possible Cause of Error

You may have modified a field's class declaration with an invalid Pascal identifier. For example, in a unit that originally contained:

```
type
  TForm1 = class(TForm)
    Button1: TButton;
```

you may have modified the class declaration (the TButton part) so that it reads something like:

```
type
  TForm1 = class(TForm)
    Button1: TZip^per;
```

Quick Fix

It is not generally a good idea to modify the code that Delphi automatically generates for you.

Additional Information

If you modify the class declaration, but use a valid Pascal identifier, you will get the error message "Field < >.< > should be of type < > but is declared as < >. Correct the declaration?" See that error message's entry for more information.

Incorrect method declaration in class < >

Possible Cause of Error

You may have added a storage specifier to a method. For example, the following will generate this error message:

```
procedure Button607Click(Sender: TObject); stored;
```

Quick Fix

Storage specifiers are meant for properties in the Published section of a component. Do not declare storage specifiers to methods or outside the Published section.

Additional Information

If you receive this error message, and this is not the reason for it, try a "build all" (select **Project | Build All**).

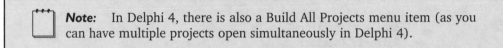

Note: In Delphi 4, there is also a Build All Projects menu item (as you can have multiple projects open simultaneously in Delphi 4).

If the error message persists, try deleting the files Delphi automatically generates, especially if you have moved the project from one machine or version of Delphi to another. These files include, depending on your version of Delphi and the options you have selected, <projectname>.OPT, <projectname>.DSK, <projectname>.DSM, <projectname>.RES, and <projectname>.DOF.

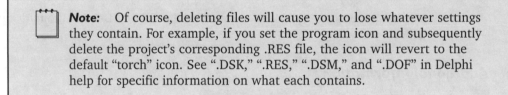

Note: Of course, deleting files will cause you to lose whatever settings they contain. For example, if you set the program icon and subsequently delete the project's corresponding .RES file, the icon will revert to the default "torch" icon. See ".DSK," ".RES," ".DSM," and ".DOF" in Delphi help for specific information on what each contains.

See "Storage specifiers" in Delphi help for more information.

Index already exists

Possible Cause of Error

You are attempting to add an index in code to a table which already has an index by that name.

Quick Fix

Verify that any indexes you create do not already exist. For example, you could proceed this way:

```
if not Table1.FieldByName('City').IsIndexField then
  Table1.AddIndex('sittee','City',[]);
```

Additional Information

If you attempt to add an index identical to one that already exists using the Database Desktop, you will be prompted "An index named < > already exists. Overwrite?" If you attempt to create an index on a field for which you already have an index, but you give the index a different name, you will receive the error message "An index of this type already exists." So, Database Desktop won't let you get away with this error.

INDEX clause not allowed in OLE automation section

Possible Cause of Error

The Index clause is not allowed in the Automated section.

Quick Fix

Remove the Index clause from the Automated section.

Additional Information

Delphi 2 and above has five visibility specifiers: *Private, Protected, Public, Published,* and *Automated*. A class's properties can specify a storage specifier of *stored, default,* or *nodefault*. These storage specifiers are not allowed in the Automated section, though.

> **Note:** The *index* specifier allows multiple properties to share the same access methods.

INDEX, READ, OR WRITE clause expected but ';' found

Possible Cause of Error

You may be attempting to declare a property but have omitted the read and write methods (or the optional *index* reserved word).

Quick Fix

Make sure you provide read and write methods for your properties.

The correct syntax when declaring a variable without an *index* specifier is:

```
property Zeitgeist: Longint read GetWithIt
                       write SetEmUpJoe;
```

The correct syntax when using the *index* specifier is:

```
property Zeitgeist: Longint index 0
    read GetWithIt write SetEmUpJoe;
```

Additional Information

See "Index Specifiers" in Delphi help for information on when you may want to use these.

Index does not exist

Possible Cause of Error

1. You may have attempted to change to an index (either at design time by editing a TTable's IndexName property or at run time in code) which has not been created for the table. For example, the following code:

    ```
    Table1.IndexName := 'CustomerCredit';
    ```

    would generate the error message under discussion if you have not defined an index named CustomerCredit for Table1.

2. You may have changed the TableName property of a TTable component, and the IndexName property still refers to the previous table.

3. You may be using Oracle tables and neglected to prepend the table name to the TQuery component's IndexName property. For example, you may have provided the following as the value:

    ```
    Molehill
    ```

Quick Fix

1. Create the index before attempting to change to it. You can accomplish this using Database Desktop or Data Definition Language (a subset of SQL used for SQL databases such as Interbase, Oracle, and MS SQL Server), or in code.

2. Delete the value in the IndexName property or change it to the appropriate value for the current table.

3. You may need to specify a fully qualified name for the index in a TQuery component's IndexName property. For example, if you have a table named Mountain and an index named Molehill, set the property as:

```
Mountain.Molehill
```

Additional Information

The code that causes this error will still compile, because as far as the compiler "knows," you are going to create the index in code before calling it.

To create an index in code (as opposed to at table design time), use the Add-Index procedure. See "AddIndex" in Delphi help for more information.

> 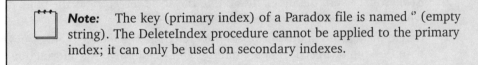 **Note:** The key (primary index) of a Paradox file is named '' (empty string). The DeleteIndex procedure cannot be applied to the primary index; it can only be used on secondary indexes.

Index is out of date

Possible Cause of Error

You probably have an inconsistency between a Paradox table (.DB) and one of its index files. One or more index files is probably corrupt or out of sync with its corresponding table. A user may have closed the application improperly or experienced a crash with the program active.

The Paradox table's primary index file is the name of the file with a PX extension. The secondary index files are the name of the table followed by extensions of .XG*n* and .YG*n* (where *n* is a hexadecimal number).

This may have occurred due to one of the following reasons:

1. You modified the table (added or edited records) while the table itself (*.DB) was in a different directory than the index files.

2. You modified the contents of the table using another application.

3. Your system crashed while you were adding or editing a record.

4. You may be accessing Paradox tables on a network from a client machine running Windows 95 and have a version between 4.00.1111 and 4.00.1114 of Microsoft's Virtual Network Redirector file VREDIR.VXD.

5. You may be attempting to edit a record in a table or insert a record into a table whose index is not maintained.

6. You may be experiencing network problems.

7. You may be using Windows NT and opportunistic locking.

> **Note:** Another potential cause of this problem is faulty hardware, such as a bad hard drive.

Quick Fix

I. Delete the existing index files, and then re-create the indexes (in either Database Desktop or in code). See "AddIndex" in Delphi help for information on creating indexes in code.

Always make sure the index files are in the same directory as the table itself when you add records to or edit the table.

2. Delete the existing index files, and then re-create the indexes (either in Database Desktop or in code). See "AddIndex" in Delphi help for information on creating indexes in code.

To reduce the likelihood of the same thing happening again, follow these steps:

Delphi I

a. Select **Tools | BDE Config**.

b. Select **Paradox** in the Driver Name list box.

c. Ensure that the Strict Integrity setting is True.

d. Select **File | Exit**.

e. Select **Yes** to save changes.

32-bit Delphi

a. Select **Tools | BDE Administrator**.

b. Select the Configuration tab.

c. Expand the Drivers node in the tree-view list.

d. Expand the Native node in the tree-view list.

e. Select **PARADOX**.

f. Set Strict Integrity to True.

g. Select **Object | Exit**.

h. Select **Yes** to save the change.

3. Delete the existing index files, and then re-create the indexes (in either Database Desktop or in code). See "AddIndex" in Delphi help for information on creating indexes in code.

4. Replace the "bad" version of VREDIR.VXD. The original release (4.00.955) and 4.00.1116 are apparently fine. VREDIR.VXD should be located in C:\Windows\System. You can download an updated file from Microsoft's web site.

5. If you want to edit records in or insert records into a table, do not use non-maintained indexes. Set the index(es) to "maintained." To specify indexes as defined on Paradox tables, follow these steps:

   a. Open Database Desktop.

   b. Open the table you want to work with (**File | Open | Table**).

   c. Select **Tools | Utilities | Restructure** (or click the Restructure icon).

   d. Select **Secondary Indexes** from the Table Properties drop-down list.

   e. Select the **Define** button. The Define Secondary Index dialog will display.

   f. Highlight the index you want to set as "maintained."

   g. Select the Maintained check box in the Index Options section of the dialog.

   h. Select **OK** to save your modifications.

6. Consult your network administrator.

7. You need to edit (or create, if necessary) two system registry settings by following these steps:

   a. Select **Start | Run** from the Windows 95 desktop.

   b. Enter **regedit** in the Open combo box and select the **OK** button.

   c. Navigate to HKEY_LOCAL_MACHINE\System\CurrentControlSet\Services\LanmanServer\Parameters.

   d. Edit or add the key (Name) **EnableOplock** and set its value (Data) to 0.

   e. Edit or add the key (Name) **UseOpportunisticLocking** and set its value (Data) to 0.

   f. Reboot for the setting to take effect.

Additional Information

The index files (.PX, .XG*n*, and .YG*n*) must be present with the table as records are added, so that the index files can be updated. If not, the table's timestamp (when it was last updated) and the index files' timestamps will not match, indicating their data is not synchronized.

A discussion of the auxiliary index files Paradox uses follows:

<Tablename>.PX

The .PX file contains the table's primary key information. If you designate a field or group of fields as the primary key, this file is created.

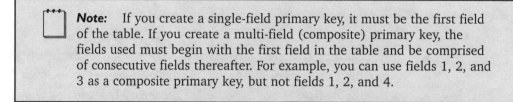

Note: If you create a single-field primary key, it must be the first field of the table. If you create a multi-field (composite) primary key, the fields used must begin with the first field in the table and be comprised of consecutive fields thereafter. For example, you can use fields 1, 2, and 3 as a composite primary key, but not fields 1, 2, and 4.

Note: The following data types cannot be included in a primary key: Binary, Byte, Formatted Memo, Graphic, Logical, Memo, and OLE.

The Logical/TBooleanField type contains too few possible values (two) to be a valid primary key. A primary key's value must be unique within the table, and so your table would be limited to a maximum of two records. You <u>can</u>, however, create a secondary (non-unique) index on a Logical/TBooleanField, in order to sort the table by the N and Y values contained therein. See "Secondary Indexes" and "Creating Secondary Indexes" in Database Desktop help for more information.

The Memo/TMemoField type is potentially very large, which could have a severe negative impact on performance, as the primary key values would have to be compared with one another and sorted accordingly.

The other data types listed above are comprised of data which cannot be compared for indexing/sorting purposes (for example, how would you determine the relational positions of two bitmaps, one of Bullwinkle the Moose and the other of Michael Jordan?).

<Tablename>.X*nn*

Files with the .X*nn* extension (where *nn* is a hexadecimal number) contain secondary index information.

<Tablename>.Y*nn*

Files with the .Y*nn* extension (where *nn* is a hexadecimal number) contain secondary index information.

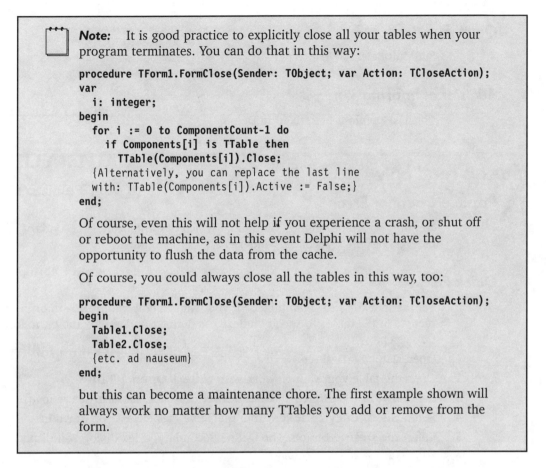

Note: It is good practice to explicitly close all your tables when your program terminates. You can do that in this way:

```
procedure TForm1.FormClose(Sender: TObject; var Action: TCloseAction);
var
  i: integer;
begin
  for i := 0 to ComponentCount-1 do
    if Components[i] is TTable then
      TTable(Components[i]).Close;
  {Alternatively, you can replace the last line
  with: TTable(Components[i]).Active := False;}
end;
```

Of course, even this will not help if you experience a crash, or shut off or reboot the machine, as in this event Delphi will not have the opportunity to flush the data from the cache.

Of course, you could always close all the tables in this way, too:

```
procedure TForm1.FormClose(Sender: TObject; var Action: TCloseAction);
begin
  Table1.Close;
  Table2.Close;
  {etc. ad nauseum}
end;
```

but this can become a maintenance chore. The first example shown will always work no matter how many TTables you add or remove from the form.

5. Non-maintained indexes are obsolete—they are a holdover from Paradox 1.0 for DOS.

Index is out of range

Possible Cause of Error

You may have selected an item in a list box with the MultiSelect property set to False. For example, the following will generate this error message:

```
ListBox1.Items.Add('Peter, Bugs, and Roger');
ListBox1.Selected[0] := True;
```

Quick Fix

Set MultiSelect to True.

Additional Information

This is a Delphi 2 bug, fixed in Delphi 3.

Index is read only

Possible Cause of Error

You may be attempting to edit a table which has one or more secondary indexes, but these secondary indexes are not maintained.

Quick Fix

Set the index(es) to "maintained" if you want to edit the records in or insert records into a table. To specify indexes as defined on Paradox tables, follow these steps:

1. Open Database Desktop.
2. Open the table you want to work with (**File | Open | Table**).
3. Select **Tools | Utilities | Restructure** (or click the Restructure icon).
4. Select **Secondary Indexes** from the Table Properties drop-down list.
5. Select the **Define** button. The Define Secondary Index dialog will display.
6. Highlight the index you want to set as "maintained."
7. Select the Maintained check box in the Index Options section of the dialog.
8. Select **OK** to save your modifications.

Additional Information

If you do not need to ever edit or add to the data in a table (in other words, you are working with a read-only table), you can improve performance by creating indexes that are <u>not</u> maintained.

Index not found

Possible Cause of Error

You may be attempting to open a dBASE table without its production index (.MDX) file.

Quick Fix

Move the production index (.MDX) file into the same directory as the table or remove the table's dependency on the file. To do the latter, see TI #2711 on the Delphi CD-ROM or on Inprise's web site.

Additional Information

TI stands for Technical Information. If you do not have access to the CD-ROM, you can find them on Inprise's web site (**www.inprise.com**).

INSERT and UPDATE operations are not supported on autoincrement field type

Possible Cause of Error

You may be attempting to assign a value to an Autoincrement field using the SQL Insert or Update operations. For example, you may have tried something like this:

```
update "MACABRE.DB"
set
  OttoIncrease = :SomeNum,
  DrOctopus = :Villain,
  EightHead = :DistinguishingFeature
where
  Name = :OLD_Name
```

or this:

```
insert into "MACABRE.DB"
  (OttoIncrease, DrOctopus, EightHead)
values
  (:SomeNum, :Villain, :DistinguishingFeature)
```

Quick Fix

Do not attempt to edit (via Update) or assign (via Insert) values in Autoincrement fields.

Additional Information

Autoincrement fields are read-only and thus cannot be edited. The Autoincrement field by its very nature should not be manually edited. By being automatically incremented, each value should be unique. If you were able to manually change the value, you could end up with multiple identical values, which would result in a key violation. For that reason, Autoincrement fields are read-only.

You can specify the starting value for Autoincrement fields using the Minimum value property in Database Desktop. Otherwise, the value will always start with 1 and increase by 1 with each record. In this way, Autoincrement fields are somewhat akin to checks you order from your financial institution.

Insufficient memory for this operation

Possible Cause of Error

You may have run several query operations, especially with the RequestLive property set to True, but have neglected to release the memory these require by calling the Unprepare method.

Quick Fix

Call Prepare before opening the query, and Unprepare upon finishing it. For example, you might do something like this:

```
with Query1 do
  begin
    SQL.Add('Select * from Bakery');
    Prepare;
    try
      Open;
      {do whatever}
    finally
      Unprepare;
    end;
  end;
```

Additional Information

 Note: Make sure you are through with the results of the query or stored proc and have closed it before you call Unprepare. If you call Unprepare on an open query, you will get the error message "Cannot perform this operation on an open dataset."

If you get this error during database operations, you might find it advantageous to double the SHAREDMEMSIZE setting in the BDE Configuration utility from its default of 2048 to 4096, or even quadruple it, if necessary, to 8192.

See "BDE Initialization Error $2501."

Insufficient SQL rights for operation

Possible Cause of Error

You may be attempting to perform an action on a table that resides on a SQL server for which you have not been granted the corresponding rights. For example, you may be attempting to edit a record in a table for which you only have read (not write) privileges.

Quick Fix

Consult your SQL server administrator to obtain the necessary rights. If you <u>are</u> the (perhaps "de facto") administrator, consult the documentation for the particular server (Interbase, MS SQL Server, Oracle, etc.) that you are using.

Additional Information

If you are going to administer security yourself, consider setting up several groups, assigning rights to those groups, and then assigning individuals to the groups. You might also consider limiting users' access to views and stored procedures (preventing full access to the tables themselves).

Insufficient table rights for operation

Possible Cause of Error

You may be attempting to set a password-protected table's Active property to True without having first provided a password.

Quick Fix

Provide the password before attempting to set the Active property to True.

Additional Information

If you need to password-protect a Paradox table to prevent access to it, you can achieve this using Database Desktop, or you can do it in code. To password-protect a Paradox table in Database Desktop, follow these steps:

1. Select **Tools | Utilities | Restructure** (or click the Structure icon).
2. Select **Password Security** from the Table Properties drop-down list.

3. Select the **Define** button.

4. Enter the password twice for verification.

5. Select **OK**.

Your table will now be encrypted. The table can be opened, but the information will not be readable. For example, before password-protecting/encrypting a table, you can open it and see information in this format:

```
DE          White          QB               Favre
```

However, after encryption, the same information appears this way:

```
þ__å(cö_ÿ‡āî⬚ð.jā½y*+8f⬚÷£_"³VG|_Løā:āø:ūé5!ô'Y›
a_R†2ÙÆØ^M_9¢=Ñ,"]¯ï⬚x_ä"&Õk*-§Ì'_
$āA⬚_ôÂ_í«S<cT«Ô@`c~»
```

To bypass the password dialog box from appearing at run time, you can provide the password in code (of course, anyone with access to your source code can then see the password, but you may want to do this during development to save time, and then remove it before deployment). You can supply the password in code this way:

```
Session.AddPassword('Kennwort58');
Table1.Active := True;
```

Integer constant too large

Possible Cause of Error

1. You may have specified an integer constant that requires more than 32 bits to represent (in other words, a number greater than 2,147,483,647) in Delphi 1, 2, or 3. For example, the following will generate this error:

```
procedure OnKeyPress(var Key: Smallint); dispid
                              2147483648;
```

Similarly, the following will also cause this error in a .DLL (library unit):

```
procedure JerryJeffWalker;
begin
  { Whatever }
end;
exports
  JerryJeffWalker index 2800000000;
```

2. You may have assigned an integer value to a real, or floating-point, data type (double, Extended, Comp, etc.) For example, the following will generate this error:

```
var
  r: double;
. . .
r := 2222222222;
```

Quick Fix

1. Stay between the range of -2,147,483,648 and 2,147,483,647 (inclusive) in integer assignments prior to Delphi 4. The following works fine:

```
procedure OnKeyPress(var Key: Smallint); dispid
                              2147483647;
```

2. This will compile with a smile:

```
var
  r: double;
. . .
r := 2222222222.22;
```

Additional Information

> **Note:** Delphi 4 has a larger integer type, namely Int64. Using Int64, stay between the range of -9,223,372,036,854,775,807 and 9,223,372,036,854,775,807. The following works fine:
>
> ```
> var
>   i: Int64;
> begin
>   i := 9223372036854775807;
> ```
>
> The maximum value that can be stored in the Int64 type is over 9.2 quintillion. Even Bill Gates' "net worth" could be represented using this integer type!

See "Integers | Integer Types" in Delphi help for more information.

Interface mismatch. Engine version different

Possible Cause of Error

You may be attempting to execute a database program created with a version of Delphi (and thus, the BDE) which is newer than the version that is installed on the system generating this error message.

Quick Fix

When deploying a Delphi database application, include the version of the BDE with which the application was developed if it is possible that the user does not already have it installed.

In fact, it is always a good idea to keep the most current version of the BDE on your system, as it will maintain backward compatibility and also include new features and functionality as well as any patches for previous bugs that have been fixed.

Additional Information

Installing the most current version of the BDE will work with programs created with the most current as well as older 32-bit versions of Delphi*. For example, the BDE version which shipped with Delphi 2 (3.5) is not compatible with programs created in Delphi 3. The BDE version which shipped with Delphi 3, though, <u>is</u> compatible with both Delphi 2 and 3 (it is backward-compatible).

If you need to install the newer version of the BDE on users' machines, you can use InstallShield Express, which ships with 32-bit Delphi, to create installation diskettes to serve this purpose.

 *Note:　32-bit versions of the BDE are incompatible with Delphi 1.

Interface type required

Possible Cause of Error

You may have used two class types in the declaration of an ActiveForm class type, like this:

```
TActiveFormX = class(TActiveForm, TActiveForm)
```

Quick Fix

You need to use a class type followed by an interface type in the declaration of an ActiveForm class type, like this:

```
TActiveFormX = class(TActiveForm, IActiveFormX)
```

Additional Information

See "Class type required" for this error message's "opposite number" (this is an example of how to keep a programmer busy).

Internal error: < >

Possible Cause of Error

These types of errors are extremely rare in Delphi. They are caused by a programming error in the compiler itself.

1. If the error code is L1317, it is Delphi 3 specific. The error may be related to Delphi 3's Code Insight features.

2. If the error code is URW337 with Delphi 2 or L1086 with Delphi 3, you may get it while attempting to compile. If you then attempt to compile again, you may receive the error message "Fatal Error: Unit SysUtils was compiled with a different version of System."

3. If the error code is C3254, it is apparently Delphi 2 specific. You may have made an assignment to the implicit "Result" variable in asm code.

Quick Fix

1. Do a "Build All" (**Project | Build All**) as opposed to a simple compile (Project | Compile).

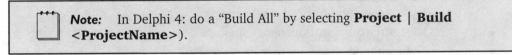

> **Note:** In Delphi 4: do a "Build All" by selecting **Project | Build <ProjectName>**).

2. Try a "Build All" as noted for #1 above, or first delete all of the project compiled unit (.DCU) and package (.DCP) files and then recompile. If that still doesn't solve the problem, shut down Delphi and then restart it to "reset it" so that it no longer "thinks" it is dealing with a modified version of the System unit.

3. Upgrade to Delphi 3 or higher (wherein this problem is fixed).

Additional Information

2. This error is usually raised when the compiler cannot determine if a compiled unit (.DCU) or package (.DCP) file needs to be recompiled. If you are using packages (run time or design time), you may find it advantageous to create a directory expressly for package (.DCP) files. You can do this by selecting **Tools | Environment** and the Library tab, and then making the appropriate

entry in the DCP Output Directory combo box. This will help ensure that the compiler always uses the newest package (.DCP) file. If you are using packages, you might find it advantageous to verify that all packages have the {$IMPLICITBUILD ON} compiler switch enabled.

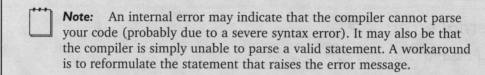

Note: An internal error may indicate that the compiler cannot parse your code (probably due to a severe syntax error). It may also be that the compiler is simply unable to parse a valid statement. A workaround is to reformulate the statement that raises the error message.

Internal Error; Near: query shellmgr

Possible Cause of Error

You may be using the Local Interbase server and have a Dell Pentium Pro with Windows NT 4 pre-installed.

Quick Fix

Follow these steps to modify the system registry setting:

1. Select **Start | Run** from the Windows 95 desktop.
2. Enter **regedit** in the Open combo box and select the **OK** button.
3. Navigate to HKEY_LOCAL_MACHINE\Software\Microsoft\Windows NT\CurrentVersion\WinLogon\Shell.
4. Change the Shell setting from Explorer.EXE userhook to Explorer.EXE.
5. Reboot for the setting to take effect.

Additional Information

The machine in question makes a system registry setting in order to load an extension to Explorer. Aren't those alternative shells a pain? They are just another opportunity to confuse Joe Sixpack (and cause software incompatibilities).

Invalid argument to date encode

Possible Cause of Error

You may have provided a value to the EncodeDate function which is not a valid date. For example, the following will generate this error message, as February 29, 2000, is not a valid date (there is no leap year if the year is divisible by 400):

```
var
  MyDate: TDateTime;
begin
  MyDate := EncodeDate(2000, 2, 29);
  Label1.Caption := DateToStr(MyDate);
```

Quick Fix

Verify that all values being passed through the Year, Month, and Day parameters are valid (taken as a whole) before making the assignment. For example, test the user's entry by attempting to typecast the entered value inside a *try...except* statement like this:

```
procedure EncodeThisDate(YearValue, MonthValue, DayValue: Word);
var
  CoddAndDate: TDateTime;
begin
try
  CoddAndDate:= EncodeDate(YearValue,MonthValue,DayValue);
except
  on EConvertError do {handle exception}
```

Additional Information

The EncodeDate function accepts three variables: Year, Month, and Day. The range of valid values for the Year parameter are 1 through 9999. The range of valid values for the Month parameter are 1 through 12. The range of valid values for the Day parameter are from 1 to either 28, 29, 30, or 31, dependent on the values set for month <u>and</u> year.

Invalid argument to time encode

Possible Cause of Error

You may have passed a value to the EncodeTime function which is out of the valid range of values for at least one of its four parameters.

Quick Fix

Verify that all values being passed through the Hour, Min, Sec, and MSec parameters are valid before making the assignment. For example, test the user's entry by attempting to typecast the entered value inside a *try...except* statement like this:

```
procedure EncodeThisTime(HourVal, MinuteVal,
         SecondVal, MillisecondVal: Word);
var
  EncodedTime: TDateTime;
begin
try
  EncodedTime := EncodeTime(HourVal,MinuteVal,SecondVal,MillisecondVal);
except
  on EConvertError do {handle exception}
```

Additional Information

The EncodeTime function accepts four variables: Hour, Min, Sec, and MSec. The range of valid values for the Hour parameter are 0 through 23. The range of valid values for the Min and Sec parameters are 0 through 59. The range of valid values for the MSec parameter are from 0 to 999.

Invalid Batch Move Parameters

Possible Cause of Error

You may have selected the same table as both the Source and the Destination property in a TBatchMove component and then attempted to call the execute method either at design time (by right-clicking the TBatchMove component and selecting Execute from the context menu) or in code. For example, assuming the BatchMove component is named BatchMove1, the following code would generate this error message:

```
BatchMove1.Execute;
```

Quick Fix

Select different tables for the Destination and Source properties.

Additional Information

See "TBatchMove" in Delphi help for more information.

Invalid Bind Type

See "Unknown SQL Error."

Invalid BLOb handle [in record buffer]

Possible Cause of Error

You may be accessing large BLObs and your BDE BLOB SIZE setting is too small.

Quick Fix

Increase the BLOB SIZE setting in the BDE Configuration utility. To do so, open the BDE Configuration/Administrator utility and navigate to Configuration | Drivers | <Your DBMS>. For example, if you are using Interbase, navigate to Configuration | Drivers | Native | INTRBASE | BLOB SIZE.

If you are using a TQuery, decrease the amount of records that are being returned in the result set.

Additional Information

> **Note:**   If you are using a live result set, the BLOBS TO CACHE and BLOB SIZE settings in the BDE will have no effect.

Invalid BLOb Size

Possible Cause of Error

Despite the error message, the problem may be that your table does not have a unique clustered index.

Quick Fix

Create a unique, clustered index for the table.

Additional Information

A clustered index is one that is actually physically stored on disk in the order of the index. For that reason, you can only have one clustered index on a table.

Invalid class string

Possible Cause of Error

1. You may have entered a value in the ServerGUID property of a TDCOMConnection, TMIDASConnection, TOLEEnterpriseConnection, or TRemoteServer component that does not conform to the expected format.
2. You may have entered a value for the ServerName property of a TRemoteServer component, but neglected to specify the ServerGUID.

Quick Fix

1. Use the format:

    {00000002-0000-0000-C000-000000000046}
2. Supply a valid ServerGUID (see #1 above).

Additional Information

1. You must supply the beginning and ending braces as shown above. See "GUIDs," "ServerGUID," and "GUIDToString function" in Delphi help for more information.
2. The ServerName property of TRemoteServer is optional; the ServerGUID is not.

Invalid class typecast

Possible Cause of Error

You may be attempting to typecast a variable as an object with which it is not compatible.

Quick Fix

Typecast the variable as an object of the same type as the variable or an ancestor of that type.

Additional Information

Here is an example of code that produces the error message under discussion:

```
procedure BrandoAsToughGuy(Sender: Tobject);
var
  b: TObject;
begin
  b := TButton.Create(nil); {This works, as
            TButton is a descendent of TObject}
  with B as TMemo do {this produces error message, as TMemo is not a
            descendent of TButton}
end;
```

Invalid compiler directive: < >

Possible Cause of Error

1. You may have an $ELSE or $ENDIF compiler directive that is not preceded by an $IFDEF, $IFNDEF, or $IFOPT directive. For example, the following will generate this error message:

```
uses
  Windows, Messages, SysUtils, Classes,
  Graphics, Registry, {$ELSE} IniFiles,
  {$ENDIF} Controls;
```

The following will also cause the same error, as there is a space between the brace ({) and the dollar sign ($), which makes it a comment rather than a compiler directive:

```
uses
  Windows, Messages, SysUtils, Classes,
  Graphics, { $IFDEF WIN32} Registry,
  {$ELSE} IniFiles, {$ENDIF} Controls;
```

2. You may have specified an $IFOPT compiler directive without a subsequent compiler option; or without a subsequent plus (+) or minus (–) sign to designate whether you are testing for the compiler option being on or off; or you used the long form of the compiler directive. For example, the following will generate this error message:

```
{$IFOPT} //compiler option missing
```

as will the following:

```
{$IFOPT I} //+ or - missing
```

as will the following:

```
{$IFOPT IOCHECKSON} //cannot use long form of compiler options with the
IFOPT compiler directive
```

Quick Fix

1. The correct way to use the compiler directives shown above is:

```
uses
  Windows, Messages, SysUtils, Classes,
  Graphics, {$IFDEF WIN32} Registry,
  {$ELSE} IniFiles, {$ENDIF} Controls;
```

2. The correct way to use the compiler directive shown above is:

```
{$IFOPT I+}
. . .
{$ENDIF}
```

Additional Information

See "Compiler directives" in Delphi help for more information.

Invalid field name

Possible Cause of Error

1. You may have specified a field name in the SQL property of a TQuery that does not exist in the table. For example, the following will generate this error if there is no such field as Films in the Documentaries table:

```
SELECT Films
FROM Documentaries
WHERE Director = 'Sayles' OR 'Morris'
```

2. You may not have specified the SQL statement in the precise way (syntactically) in which Delphi expects to see it. For example, the following SQL statement may generate this error message:

```
SELECT *
FROM Customers
WHERE State = 'CA'
```

Quick Fix

1. Verify that you only attempt to access fields that actually exist in the database.

2. You may need to capitalize the table name and enclose the field name in double quotes. Given the SQL statement above, you may have to do it this way:

```
SELECT *
FROM CUSTOMERS
WHERE CUSTOMERS."State" = 'CA'
```

Additional Information

If you are connecting to a SQL server database, familiarize yourself with the SQL syntax for the particular DBMS you are using, as well as the exact features it supports (which vary from vendor to vendor).

Invalid field size

Possible Cause of Error

You may have attempted to create a string field in code but neglected to assign it a size. For example, the following line will generate this error message:

```
Add('DIVISIONNAME', ftString, 0, False);
```

Quick Fix

Always assign a size to fields of type ftString, ftBCD, ftBytes, ftVarBytes, ftBlob, ftMemo or ftGraphic.

Additional Information

Not only is size not applicable to certain field types, even among those to which it <u>does</u> apply, it can mean different things. For string and byte fields, Size refers to the number of bytes the field will allocate for each instance. When applied to a BCD field, Size is the number of digits after the decimal point. For a BLOb, memo, or graphic field, the Size parameter determines the number of bytes that are stored in the actual database table (the remainder being stored in an .MB file).

Invalid field type

Possible Cause of Error

You may be attempting to select an autoincrement field from a table using a TQuery component's SQL property while using Cached Updates.

Quick Fix

Although it is true you cannot edit an autoincrement field, you can select them even under the above circumstances by upgrading to version 4.01 or higher of the BDE.

Additional Information

It would not be good to allow autoincrement fields to be updated, as they are typically used as automatically generated primary fields.

Invalid file name

Possible Cause of Error

1. You may be using version 3.5 of the BDE and Windows 95B (4.00.950b, also known as Win95 OSR2) while accessing tables whose path contains long filenames and/or spaces in the directory or file names.

2. You may be exceeding the maximum path length, if your NOS is Novell.

3. You may have an apostrophe in a directory name to which you have assigned an alias. For example, if you create a directory named What'sUpDoc, and then create an alias named BugsBunny that points to it, you will get this error message.

Quick Fix

I   If you are using version 3.5 of the BDE (which shipped with Delphi 2) and Windows 95B with long filenames enabled (FAT32), you need to install version 3.5f of the BDE in order to access tables whose paths include long filenames or spaces.

An alternative is placing the tables in a path which does not include long path names or spaces.

2.   Consult your Novell documentation to see what the maximum path length is for your version of Netware.

3.   Rename the directory, removing the apostrophe.

Additional Information

1.   Download the newest version of the BDE from Borland's web site. You can download version 3.5f of the BDE from Borland's web site at **www.inprise.com/techsupport/bde/utilities.html**.

The name of the patch is "BDE v3.5 32-Bit core DLLs including FAT32 enhancement."

2.   If you subsequently get a "Path too long" error message, update your Paradox tables to level 7. See "Higher table level required" for instructions on how to do this.

You can check your version of Windows by right-clicking the My Computer icon on the desktop and selecting Properties from the context menu. The OS version number is contained on the General page.

3.   It is not good practice to use "special" symbols (such as single quotes) in directory or file names.

Invalid floating point operation

Possible Cause of Error

1.   You may have attempted to assign a number to a floating-point data type that was too large. For example, the following will generate this error:

```
var
  Gates, Turner, McCartney: currency;
begin
  Turner := 922337203685477.5807;
  McCartney := 922337203685477.5807;
  Gates := Turner+McCartney; {error occurs here}
```

> **Note:** In Delphi 4, the Real type has changed to a 64-bit implementation and is equivalent to Double. Real can now be used as the data type of a published property. The former implementation of Real is now called Real48.

2. You may have tried to convert a real number to an integer using the Round or Trunc functions, and the number was too large to fit into an integer. For example, either of the following examples will generate this error:

Example 1

```
var
  RolyPoly: Integer;
  hyper: extended;
begin
  hyper := 2222222222.22;
  RolyPoly := Round(hyper);
```

Example 2

```
var
  Line: Integer;
  Workmans: Comp;
begin
  Workmans := 2222222222.22;
  Line := Trunc(Workmans);
```

3. Your machine may lack a math coprocessor.

Quick Fix

1. Ensure that you do not assign numbers that are too large, either by explicitly preventing such in code or by enclosing the assignment statements in a *try...except* block.

2. Enclose the call to Round or Trunc in a *try...except* block:

```
const
  crlf = #13#10;
. . .
var
  WhatGoesAroundComesA: Integer;
  bent: double;
try
  WhatGoesAroundComesA:= Round(bent);
except
  on EInvalidOp do
```

```
        MessageDlg('The real number was too long'+crlf+
                  'to fit into an Integer type',
                  mtError, [mbOK], 0);
end;
```

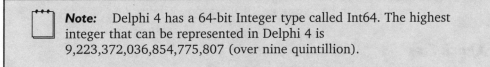

Note: Delphi 4 has a 64-bit Integer type called Int64. The highest integer that can be represented in Delphi 4 is 9,223,372,036,854,775,807 (over nine quintillion).

3. You can either upgrade to a machine that does have a math coprocessor (which performs floating-point operations in hardware), or set the {$N-} compiler directive at the top of your unit.

Additional Information

1. See "Real Types" in Delphi help for more information.

2. In the examples given above, the more specific error message accompanying "EInvalidOp" is "Invalid floating point operation."

See "Integer constant too large."

Invalid function result type

Possible Cause of Error

You may have declared a function with a result or return type of File. For example, the following generates this error message:

```
function GetFromCabinet: file;
```

Quick Fix

Do not use File as the return or result type of a function.

Additional Information

See "Function declarations" and "Function Calls" in Delphi help for more information.

Invalid GUID format

Possible Cause of Error

You may have manually altered a GUID. For example, you may have removed one of the numbers from a GUID in a Type Library.

Quick Fix

Do not modify GUIDs. They are automatically generated for you, a sort of "autorandom" number.

Additional Information

GUID stands for Globally Unique IDentifier. See "GUIDs" in Delphi help for more information.

Invalid index/tag name

Possible Cause of Error

1. You may be attempting to add an index name that is already being used. For example, the following will generate this error message, as the same name is used for both indexes:

```
AddIndex('Verzeichnis','Stadt',[]);
AddIndex('Verzeichnis','Land',[]);
```

2. You may be attempting to assign a single-field index a name other than that of the field it references and have not supplied the ixCaseInsensitive index option parameter. For example, the following will generate this error message, as the name provided for the index is not the same as the field's name:

```
AddIndex('ndxStadt','Stadt',[]);
```

3. You may be attempting to pass a value to the AddIndex method's TIndexOptions variable that is not appropriate for the table type. For example, you may be supplying the ixExpression value to a Paradox table, which can only be used with dBASE tables.

4. You may be attempting to create more than one primary index. For example, if you already have a primary index on a field, the following will generate this error message:

```
AddIndex('Stadt','Stadt',[ixPrimary]);
```

Quick Fix

I. Verify that you do not assign an index of the same name more than once. You can check to see if an index already exists in this way:

```
if not Table1Stadt.IsIndexField then
  AddIndex('ndxStadt','Stadt',[]);
```

2. Either assign the same name to the index as the field name, like this:

```
AddIndex('Stadt','Stadt',[]);
```

or add the ixCaseInsensitive index option parameter, like this:

```
AddIndex('ndxStadt','Stadt',[ixCaseInsensitive]);
```

3. Assign index options that are appropriate for the table with which you are working.

4. Do not assign more than one primary index (ixPrimary) per table.

Additional Information

2. Indexes comprised of multiple columns can be given names besides those of the columns without supplying the ixCaseInsensitive index option parameter.

If you assign the index the same name as the field, do not include the ixCaseInsensitive index option parameter. For example, a composite index on columns City and State could be defined this way:

```
AddIndex('CityState','Stadt;Land',[]);
```

3. See "TTable.AddIndex" in Delphi help for more information.

4. If you have a primary index on your table (recommended) on a single column, it must be on the first column in the table. If you have a composite primary key, it must begin with the first column and be comprised of consecutive columns thereafter. In other words, a composite primary key can be placed on columns 1, 2, and 3, but not on 1 and 3 (or 1, 2, and 4, etc.).

Invalid index descriptor

Possible Cause of Error

You may have attempted to create an index on a dBASE table using the Add-Index method and passed an invalid index option. For example, the ixCaseInsensitive option is not valid for dBASE tables, so the following will generate this error message:

```
Table1.AddIndex('Area','Area',[ixCaseInSensitive]);
```

Quick Fix

Use only index types appropriate for the table with which you are working.

Additional Information

See "AddIndex" in Delphi help for more information.

Invalid index expression

Possible Cause of Error

You may be attempting to create a composite index on a dBASE table, but have not passed the ixExpression index option constant to the AddIndex method. For example, the following will generate this error message:

```
Table1.AddIndex('ndxCityState','City+State', []);
```

Quick Fix

Pass the ixExpression to the IndexOptions parameter of the AddIndex method:

```
Table1.AddIndex('ndxCityState','City+State', [ixExpression]);
```

Additional Information

See "AddIndex" in Delphi help for more information.

Invalid message parameter list

Possible Cause of Error

1. You may have declared a message handling method and provided more than one parameter. For example, the following will generate this error message:

```
procedure WMChar(var Message: TWMChar; s: string); message WM_CHAR;
```

2. You may have removed, or failed to add, the *var* reserved word in the message handler's declaration:

```
procedure WMChar(Message: TWMChar); message WM_CHAR;
```

Quick Fix

1. Remove additional parameters from the declaration.
2. Add the *var* reserved word to the declaration.

Additional Information

A message procedure accepts one (and only one) parameter. It must be a var parameter.

The above message handling method should be:

```
procedure WMChar(var Message: TWMChar); message WM_CHAR;
```

See "Message handlers" in Delphi help for more information.

Invalid package file < >

Possible Cause of Error

1. You are probably attempting to load a file which has an extension other than .DPL or .DPC on the Packages page of the Project Options dialog box after selecting Install Packages from the Component menu, selecting the Add button, and then specifying a file from the Add Design Package dialog box.
2. If the file does have one of the appropriate extensions, it is either not in actuality a package file, or it has become corrupt.

Quick Fix

1. Select a file with either a .DPL extension (Delphi package library) or .DPK extension (Delphi package).
2. Re-create the package file, if necessary.

Additional Information

You may get this error if you installed a package, then moved or deleted some of its constituent files. Selecting the check box to attempt to "add back" the package (and its page on your component palette) can cause this error. Remove the package (click the **Remove** button), return the required files to one of the directories in Delphi's search path, and then add the package back using the **Add** button.

Invalid Parameter

Possible Cause of Error

You may have neglected to specify a TableName in the Destination TTable while attempting to execute a batch move operation using the TBatchMove component.

Quick Fix

You must designate both the Source and the Destination tables when using the TBatchMove component.

Additional Information

See "TBatchMove" in Delphi help for more information.

Invalid path

See "Invalid file name."

Invalid pointer operation

Possible Cause of Error

You may be attempting to free memory that has already been freed. For example, passing Dispose or FreeMem a nil pointer generates this error message. The following code can potentially produce the error message under discussion. The reason for this is that the memory is always freed in the Finally part, but in the case of an exception, it is first freed in the Except part. This causes subsequent execution of the Finally part (which always executes, with or without an exception) which attempts to free the memory again, producing the error:

```
procedure FinallyFree;
var
   Homework: Pointer;
begin
   GetMem(Homework,32);
   try
```

```
      try
        {Try this...}
        {Try that...}
      except
        FreeMem(Homework,32);
      end; //except
    finally
      {The following works fine unless there is an exception, in which
       case an attempt is made to free the memory a second time}
      FreeMem(Homework,32);
    end; //finally
  end;
```

Quick Fix

Ensure that you do not try to free memory that has already been freed. For example, to ensure that you do not attempt to free memory that has already been freed under the scenario above, do this:

```
procedure FinallyFree;
var
  Homework: Pointer;
begin
  GetMem(Homework,32);
  try
    try
      {Try this...}
      {Try that...}
    except
      FreeMem(Homework,32);
    end; //except
  finally
    {The following works fine unless there is an exception, in which
     case an attempt is made to free the memory a second time}
    if not Assigned(Homework) then
      FreeMem(Homework,32);
  end; //finally
end;
```

Additional Information

See "New," "Dispose," "FreeMem," and "GetMem" in Delphi help for more information.

Invalid property value

Possible Cause of Error

1. You may have assigned a value to a property that is not valid for that property. For example, entering the name of a nonexistent component into a form's ActiveControl property or entering Maybe into a component's Enabled property (a Boolean property which accepts only True or False) will generate this message.

2. A form (.DFM) file may contain a reference to a method to which no event handler is currently assigned.

Quick Fix

1. Enter a value that is valid for the property in question. If a combo box is provided, choose a value from its list.

2. Remove the line from the .DFM file or remove the reference to the method from the events page of the Object Inspector.

Additional Information

1. All the controls on the form will display in the drop-down list for the Active-Control properties (such as TButtons, TEdits, etc.), but graphical components (such as TLabel, TImage) as well as dialog boxes, system timers, etc., will not, as they cannot receive focus and therefore cannot be the "active" control.

2. To receive this message, you may have responded to the message "The < > [method,property] referenced by < > does not exist. Remove the reference?" by selecting the No button. If you select Yes, the reference will be removed from the form (.DFM) file, and the error message under discussion would not be generated.

Invalid property value on line < >

Possible Cause of Error

You may have a syntax error in a .DFM file.

Quick Fix

View the .DFM at the line number indicated in the error message to see what is causing the problem (**Search | Go to Line Number...**).

Additional Information

.DFM files are the textual representations of forms. They describe what objects are on the form, where on the form they are displayed, and their property settings.

You can edit the .DFM file by right-clicking a form and selecting View As Text from the context menu. Changes you make in the .DFM are reflected on the form itself, just as changes you make on the form, such as placing components on it and setting their properties, are reflected in the .DFM file (right-click inside the .DFM file's code window and select View As Form to see the form). This is called "two-way" editing.

In the following snippet from a .DFM file, a comma which does not belong appears. This would elicit the error message above, designating line 5 as the location of the problem.

```
object Form1: Tform1
  Left = 200
  Top = 106
  Width = 544
  Height = ,375 {here's the problem}
  Caption = 'Form1'
  Font.Charset = DEFAULT_CHARSET
  Font.Color = clWindowText
  Font.Height = -11
  Font.Name = 'MS Sans Serif'
  Font.Style = []
  PixelsPerInch = 96
  TextHeight = 13
end
```

Invalid resource format

Possible Cause of Error

You may be attempting to load a 16-bit resource in 32-bit Delphi.

Quick Fix

Load the resource in a 32-bit resource editor, such as the Image Editor (in 32-bit Delphi), and then save it.

Additional Information

Opening and then saving the resource in the 32-bit editor will save it as a 32-bit resource.

Invalid type

See "Unknown SQL Error."

Invalid Type Conversion

See "Unknown SQL Error."

Invalid typecast

Possible Cause of Error

1. You may be attempting to typecast one object or type to an object or type with which it is not compatible.
2. You may be attempting to compare types across module boundaries (.EXE to .DLL or .DLL to .DLL).

Quick Fix

1. Typecast types to compatible types only (and don't twist your tongue doing it). You can test for compatibility using the *is* and/or *as* operators. For example, to perform an operation on a component only if it is a TTable, you can do something like this:

```
for i := 0 to ComponentCount-1 do
  if Components[i] is TTable then
    TTable(Components[i]).Close;
```

2. Avoid typecasting between module boundaries. As a workaround, you can make use of callback functions, so that all type checking/casting occurs within the same module.

Additional Information

These are the types of conversions which are allowed:

➤ An ordinal or pointer type to an ordinal or pointer type

➤ A character, string, array of char, or pchar to a string

➤ An ordinal, real, string, or variant to a variant

> ➤ A variant to ordinal, real, string, or variant
> ➤ A variable reference to any type of the same size

> **Note:** You can cast Real (floating-point) data types to integers using the Trunc and Round functions.

This (ordinal to ordinal) works:

```
Chicago := Boolean(0);
```

but this (ordinal to string) does not:

```
Memphis := Boolean('False');
```

> **Note:** The *is* and *as* operators do not work when passing objects across module boundaries, that is, between .EXE and .DLL or between .DLLs.

Invalid use of keyword

Possible Cause of Error

1. There may be a syntax error in a TQuery component's SQL statement. For example, you may be attempting to use a parameter in the FROM clause, or you may have left out the FROM clause altogether. For example, this will generate the error message under discussion:

```
SELECT *
FROM :Rebel
```

as will this:

```
SELECT *
WHERE Rebel = 'Without a clause'
```

2. You may not have any column names following the SELECT clause and/or any table names following the FROM clause.

3. You may have used the GROUP BY keyword (keyclause) without having used any aggregates in the SELECT clause (such as COUNT, SUM, MIN, MAX, AVG, etc.).

4. You may be using Oracle and have not used all caps in the SQL statement.

5. You may have a field name with spaces in the SELECT part of your SQL statement and have not prepended it with the table or alias name to the field.

Quick Fix

1. Insert the FROM clause along with the name of the table(s) from which you want to retrieve records. You cannot use parameters (with the ":parameter-name" syntax) in the SELECT or FROM part of a SQL statement. See "Additional Information" below for information on how to allow the user to select the table and/or fields at run time using the Format function.

2. Provide at least one column name following SELECT and at least one table name following FROM.

3. If you use a GROUP BY statement, provide at least one aggregate function in the SELECT clause, and group by all non-aggregate columns you specify in the SELECT clause. For example:

```
SELECT Fruit, Vegetable, Spice, Count(Dessert)
FROM Speisekarte
WHERE Calories > 1000
GROUP BY Fruit, Vegetable, Spice
```

4. Use all caps in Oracle SQL. For example:

```
SELECT
  SOMEFIELD
FROM
  'SOMEALIAS.SOMETABLE'
WHERE
  SOMEFIELD < 0
```

5. If you reference a field name that contains spaces, you must not only enclose it in quotes (" "), but also prepend the table or alias name. For example, if the name of the field is:

   One Flew Over The Coders Desk

you must reference it like this:

```
SELECT
  TABLENAME."One Flew Over The Coders Desk"
  . . .
```

Additional Information

SQL statements that return result sets require a SELECT clause (which specifies the columns to return in the result set; you can either name them individually or use "*" to represent all columns). Additionally, such SQL statements need a FROM clause (which specifies the table or tables from which to retrieve the columns).

Note: TQuery parameters are only allowed in the WHERE clause of a SQL statement, so replace any parameters you may have elsewhere with either a hard-coded value or use the Format function to provide a variable.

If you want to provide the name of the fields and/or tables to retrieve at run time, you can use the Format function to do this. For example, you can allow the user to dynamically select the table from which to retrieve all records in this way:

```
with Query1.SQL do
  begin
    Add('SELECT *');
    Add('FROM ' + Format('%s, [Edit1.Text]));
    . . .
```

You could similarly programmatically and dynamically supply the columns in the SELECT clause.

An alternative way of accomplishing the same thing would be to assign values to variables and then reference them in the SQL property:

```
var
   tablename: string;
begin
  tablename := Edit1.Text;
  with Query1.SQL do begin
    Add('SELECT * FROM ' + tablename');
  . . .
```

The SQL ORDER BY statement is used to sort the result set. For example, you may sort by last name ascending (from A to Z).

To illustrate, if you had a table with several entries in its City and State columns, sorting them by City and then concatenating them (City +', '+ State) might produce something like this:

```
Anchorage, Alaska
Angels Camp, California
Bethany, Oklahoma
Brookfield, Wisconsin
Brooklyn, New York
Eureka, California
Fort Bragg, California
Helena, Montana
Jenny Lind, California
Mokelumne Hill, California
```

San Andreas, California
Zenia, California

The GROUP BY statement is used to perform aggregate operations (such as SUM, COUNT, AVG, MIN, MAX) on groups of records with a column value in common. For example, in a table containing names of NBA players, their team affiliation, and their salary, you could group by team with a SUM on the salary column, which would break the table into a single row representing each team, displaying the total salary of all players on the team.

Invalid variant type conversion

Possible Cause of Error

1. You may have attempted to convert one data type to another in an operation that does not seem logical (at least, not to the compiler). For example, the following two snippets will generate this error message:

```
procedure DivideVariants;
var
  v1,v2: variant;
begin
  v1 := 100;
  v2 := 'Ciao, baby';
  v1 := v1 div v2; {error generated here}
end;
. . .
{Table1Area is a TFloatField}
StringGrid1.Cells[1,1] := Table1Area.AsVariant + 'great oogly moogly';
```

2. You may have attempted to assign the name "null" to an index using the Add-Index method. For example, the following will generate this error message:

```
begin
  with Table1 do begin
    Close;
    Exclusive := True;
    AddIndex(null,'ModemAdapter',[]);
```

Quick Fix

1. Use variant type conversions only in a way that is logical and can be understood by the compiler. For example, here is an example of a variant type conversion that is allowed:

```
procedure DivideVariants;
var
```

```
   v1,v2: variant;
begin
  v1 := 100;
  v2 := '3';
  v1 := v1 div v2; //produces Result 33
end;
```

2. Indexes based on a single column of the underlying table should have the same name as the column. Indexes based on multiple columns (composite indexes) should have names that are descriptive of the fields they contain. Do not name an index "null."

Additional Information

See "Variants: assigning values" in Delphi help for more information.

Key Violation

Possible Cause of Error

1. You may be attempting to add a primary value which already exists in the table.
2. You may have attempted to append records from a table with a primary key to a table without a primary key using the TBatchMove component in batAppendUpdate mode.

Quick Fix

1. Prevent the entering of duplicate primary values. You can prepare for this possibility by enclosing your code in a *try...except* block if you want to present the users with a customized message, and perhaps move the cursor back to the field which holds the primary key. For example, in the code that responds to the key violation, you could do something like this:

```
const
  crlf = #13#10;
. . .
try
  Table1.Post;
except
  on E: Exception do
    if E.Message = 'Key violation' then
      begin
        MessageDlg('That value already exists'+crlf+ 'in the table.
                Please try again.', mtError,[mbOK], 0);
```

```
        Edit1.Color := clRed;
        Edit1.SetFocus;
     end;
  end;
  . . .
```

> **Note:** The duplicated value causing the problem may be a "null"—in other words, the column was left blank. The first time a null value is added, it is accepted, as it is a unique value (unless other constraints exist requiring the value to be within a certain range). One record can contain a null value in the primary column. If this is done, though, it was probably not intentional. Any subsequent attempts to add "null" as the value will generate the error message under discussion.

2. Try again after creating the same primary key in the Destination table, or use TBatchMove's batAppend mode to move the records.

Additional Information

Getting a key violation is better than the alternative—having multiple records with the same value in a primary column. This is definitely one of those areas where "error messages are your friends."

Label < > is not declared in current procedure

Possible Cause of Error

You may be attempting to use a *goto* statement with a label that is not declared in the same procedure as the call to *goto*.

Quick Fix

If you use labels and *goto* statements, they must appear within the same procedure.

Additional Information

Borland Pascal does not allow label/*goto* statements to cross procedure boundaries, although standard Pascal does. Labels and their corresponding *goto* statements are usually used in dealing with errors, and Delphi provides a better way: exception handlers. See "Exceptions" in Delphi help for more information.

Real programmers don't use *goto* statements anyway. ;-)

Label already defined: < >

Possible Cause of Error

You may have defined a label more than once. For example, the following will generate this error message:

```
procedure Etikett;
label 1;
begin
1:
  if (Jordache or Nike) then goto 1;
1:
end;
```

Quick Fix

Define labels once and only once.

Additional Information

Labels and their corresponding *goto* statements are usually used in dealing with errors, and Delphi provides a better way: exception handlers. See "Exceptions" in Delphi help for more information.

Real programmers don't use *goto* statements anyway. ;-)

Label declaration not allowed in interface part

Possible Cause of Error

You may have attempted to declare a label in the Interface part of a unit. For example, the following will generate this error message:

```
var
  Form1: Tform1;
  label GypsiesTrampsAndThieves;
implementation
```

Quick Fix

Do not declare labels in the Interface part of a unit (prior to the *implementation* reserved word).

Additional Information

Labels and their corresponding *goto* statements are usually used in dealing with errors, and Delphi provides a better way: exception handlers. See "Exceptions" in Delphi help for more information.

Real programmers don't use *goto* statements anyway. ;-)

Label declared and referenced, but not set

Possible Cause of Error

You may have declared and called a label (with a *goto* statement), but the label is not defined. For example, the following will generate this error message:

```
procedure Alamo;
label SpursThatJingleJangleJingle;
  begin
    goto SpursThatJingleJangleJingle;
  end;
```

Quick Fix

You must include a place for the *goto* statement to go to:

```
procedure Alamo;
label SpursThatJingleJangleJingle;
  begin
    if { some condition } then
      goto SpursThatJingleJangleJingle;
    . . .
    SpursThatJingleJangleJingle:
    . . .
  end;
```

Additional Information

Labels and their corresponding *goto* statements are usually used in dealing with errors, and Delphi provides a better way: exception handlers. See "Exceptions" in Delphi help for more information.

Real programmers don't use *goto* statements anyway. ;-)

Label expected

Possible Cause of Error

You may have referenced a label in a *goto* statement and defined it, but have not declared it. For example, the following will generate this error message:

```
function Junction: variant;
begin
  if TankIsEmpty then
    goto Shell;
  { ... }
Shell: { ... }
end;
```

Quick Fix

Declare the label before referencing and defining it:

```
function Junction: variant;
Label Shell
begin
  if TankIsEmpty then
    goto Shell;
  { ... }
Shell: { ... }
end;
```

Additional Information

Labels and their corresponding *goto* statements are usually used in dealing with errors, and Delphi provides a better way: exception handlers. See "Exceptions" in Delphi help for more information.

Real programmers don't use *goto* statements anyway. ;-)

Left side cannot be assigned to

Possible Cause of Error

1. You may be attempting to assign a value to a constant. For example, this produces the error message under discussion:

```
const
  crlf = #13#10;
. . .
crlf := #8#8#8#8#8#8#8#8;
```

2. You may be attempting to assign a value to a constant parameter (a formal parameter that is prepended with the *const* reserved word). For example, the following produces the error message under discussion:

```
procedure Popeye(const IYamWhatIYam: string);
var
  s: string;
begin
  s := IYamWhatIYam; {no problem here}
  IYamWhatIYam := 'et 2, Brutus?'; {not allowed}
end;
```

as it attempts to assign a value to the constant parameter IYamWhatIYam.

3. You may be attempting to assign a value to a function's return value outside of the function. For example, the following produces the error message under discussion:

```
function GiveMeAnH: char;
begin
  Result := 'H'
  { assigning to 'Result' same }
  { as assigning to GiveMeAnH }
end;
begin
  GiveMeAnH := 'H'; { this is a no-no }
end.
```

4. You may be attempting to increment or decrement a non-ordinal value using the Inc or Dec functions. For example, the following will generate this error message:

```
inc('orporated');
dec('10.0');
```

5. You may have attempted to assign a value to a pointer to a pointer. For example, both assignment statements in this procedure generate this error message:

```
procedure DysfunctionalPoynters;
type
  iptr = ^Integer;
var
  i,j:integer; p: pointer; q:iptr;
begin
  ^p := q;
  ^q := p;
end;
```

Quick Fix

1. Do not make assignments to constants. Either remove the assignment statement or change the constant to an initialized variable/typed constant.

2. Do not make assignments to const parameters. Either remove the assignment statement or change the variable from a const parameter to var or value parameter.

3. Do not make assignments to the result of a function outside of the function itself.

4. Increment and decrement ordinal values only:

    ```
    inc(i); { where i is an Integer variable }
    dec(10);
    ```

5. Do not attempt to assign a value to a pointer to a (typed or untyped) pointer.

Additional Information

4. Inc and Dec take an optional second parameter, which specifies how much to increment or decrement the variable being manipulated.

See "Assignment Statements" in Delphi help for more information.

Line number must be between 1 and < >

Possible Cause of Error

You are attempting to go to a line number in the Delphi editor that does not exist in the current unit.

Quick Fix

Enter a number that is no greater than the number of lines the current unit contains.

Additional Information

You can go directly to a line number in the active unit by selecting Search | Go To Line Number... and then entering a number in the Go To Line Number dialog box and pressing OK.

Line too long [more than 255 characters]

See "String [literal]s may have at most 255 elements."

List capacity out of bounds (<>)

Possible Cause of Error

You may have assigned a value to a list's Capacity property greater than the value of MaxListSize. In Delphi 1, MaxListSize is 16,380. In 32-bit Delphi 2, it is 134,217,727. For example, the following will generate this error message (Liszt is a TList variable):

```
Liszt.Capacity := 2222222222;
```

Quick Fix

Assign a value less than or equal to 16,380 in Delphi 1 and less than or equal to 134,217,727 in 32-bit Delphi to the Capacity property.

Additional Information

See "Capacity" in Delphi help for more information.

List index out of bounds (<>)

Possible Cause of Error

1. (A) You may have attempted to reference an element of a list that does not exist. For example, the following will produce the error message under discussion, as no element 1 has been assigned (as the list is zero-based):

```
procedure
var
  sl: TStringList;
  s: String;
begin
  sl := TStringList.Create;
  sl.Add('Samuel Langhorne Clemens');
  s := sl.Strings[1];   {cannot access anything beyond Strings[0],
                          as nothing else exists}
end;
```

1. (B) One of many other ways to generate this error message is to call TStrings' Move method, supplying an invalid parameter for one or both of the arguments:

```
var
  NoneAttached: TStrings;
begin
```

```
NoneAttached := TStringList.Create;
NoneAttached.Move(0,1);
```

2. You can also get this error by deleting items from a list in a *for...to* loop which uses the original count of items in the list as the final value, as the count of items will then dynamically decrease (but the *for* loop will attempt to continue as far as the original value of Count–1). For example, the following may cause this error:

```
var
  i: integer;
begin
  with ListBox1 do
  begin
    Items := ListBox2.Items;
    for i := 0 to Items.Count-1 do
      if Items[i]='' then Items.Delete(i);
  end;
end;
```

3. You may have removed one or more fields from a database table's index and have not as yet updated any FindKey statements which referenced the index in its old format (where the index was comprised of more fields). For example, if you changed the fields in an index called DudeOrDudette from FirstName;Nickname;LastName to just FirstName;LastName and then called FindKey with the following while that index was active, you would get the error message under discussion:

```
FindKey('Clarence','Gatemouth','Brown');
```

4. You may be connecting to a database using an ODBC connection, and one or more ODBC .DLLs are missing.

5. You may be attempting to access an element in a list before that element has been inserted.

Quick Fix

1. (A) Ensure that you have made an assignment to the element of the list that you want to access before referencing it. Using the above example, you could either reference element 0:

```
. . .
s := sl.Strings[0];
. . .
```

or add element 1 to the TStringList before referencing it:

```
sl.Add('Samuel Langhorne Clemens'); {element 0}
sl.Add('John Griffith London'); {element 1}
s := sl.Strings[1]; {s = 'John Griffith London'}
```

I. (B) Assign values to the elements you want to swap before calling the Move method:

```
var
  NoneAttached: TStrings;
begin
  NoneAttached := TStringList.Create;
  try
    NoneAttached.Add('move me');
    NoneAttached.Add('me too');
    NoneAttached.Move(0,1);
  . . .
```

2. Exchange the *for* loop control variable (0 in the example above) and the final value (Items.Count–1 in the example above), and use a *for...downto* construct:

```
var
  i: integer;
begin
  with ListBox1 do
  begin
    Items:=ListBox2.Items;
    for i := Items.Count-1 downto 0 do
      if Items[i]='' then Items.Delete(i);
  end;
end;
```

3. Verify that the current index (at the time you call FindKey) does not contain fewer fields than you are passing to FindKey. In the example given above, you would have to alter your FindKey statement to read:

```
FindKey('Clarence','Brown');
```

4. Ensure that all necessary ODBC files are present and accounted for.

5. Wait until the element has been populated before attempting to access its value.

Additional Information

The number in parentheses (in the error message) indicates the index that does not exist which you attempted to access.

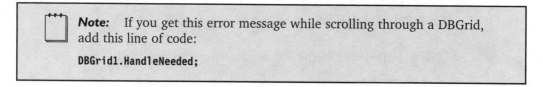

Note: If you get this error message while scrolling through a DBGrid, add this line of code:

```
DBGrid1.HandleNeeded;
```

Local class, interface or object types not allowed

Possible Cause of Error

You may have attempted to declare a local class. For example, the following will generate this error message:

```
procedure TForm1.Button8Click(Sender: Tobject);
type
  ELOCALError = class(Exception);
. . .
```

Quick Fix

Declare all class types as global, not local (within a procedure or function).

Additional Information

See "Class Types" in Delphi help for more information.

Local class or object types not allowed

See "Local class, interface or object types not allowed" above.

Local procedure/function < > assigned to procedure variable

Possible Cause of Error

1. You may have attempted to assign a local procedure or function to a procedure variable.
2. You may have attempted to pass a local procedure or function as a variable.

Quick Fix

1, 2. Do not assign local procedures or functions to procedure variables or pass them as variables.

Additional Information

The reason this is not allowed is that the local procedure or function could be called when the procedure or function to which it belongs is not active, potentially leading to access violations.

Lock file [has grown] too large

Possible Cause of Error

You may be using Paradox tables and one or more of the following scenarios applies:

1. Multiple users are accessing the same Private Directory.
2. The executable and the tables are in the same directory.
3. The BDE Local Share setting is True.
4. You are executing multiple simultaneous query operations against a TTable.
5. You may be using Cached Updates and are calling a TDataset's ApplyUpdates method but are neglecting to call CommitUpdates afterwards. If this is the case, you may not have even been aware you were using Paradox tables—you may be using Oracle or MS SQL Server or some other "big iron" database back end (in this scenario, Paradox tables are created for you "behind the scenes").

Quick Fix

1. Set the Private Directory to a directory on each user's hard disk (such as C:\Temp\{ Executable Name }). You could do that programmatically in this way:

```
var
  Extension, ExecName, PrivDir : String;
  ExtensionPos: Integer;
. . .
ExecName := ExtractFileName(Application.ExeName);
Extension := ExtractFileExt(Application.ExeName);
ExtensionPos := Pos(Extension, ExecName);
Delete(ExecName,ExtensionPos,4);
PrivDir := 'C:\Temp\' + ExecName;
if not DirectoryExists(PrivDir) then
  CreateDir(PrivDir);
if DirectoryExists(PrivDir) then
  Session.PrivateDir := PrivDir
else
  raise Exception.Create('Private Directory ' + ' was not created!');
end;
```

2, 4. Place the executable and the tables in separate directories.

3. If you do not have multiple executables simultaneously accessing the same tables, set Local Share (in the System page of the BDE Configuration/Administration utility) to False. Leave it (or set it to) True if machines on a peer-to-peer network are accessing the table(s) via their own copy of the executable.

5. Always call CommitUpdates after ApplyUpdates.

Additional Information

5. ApplyUpdates sends the updates to the database. CommitUpdates flushes the local cache.

It is preferable to use a TDatabase component and call its ApplyUpdates method (as opposed to calling TDataset's ApplyUpdates method). TDatabase's ApplyUpdates method accepts an array of TDatasets as arguments (ApplyUpdates for TDatasets takes no argument). TDatabase's ApplyUpdates method automatically calls CommitUpdates for each Dataset argument that you supply it with.

> **Note:** Do not set the PrivateDir setting to a root directory on a drive; always specify a subdirectory.

If your executable and tables share the same directory, the lock (.LCK) file will increase in size every time a query is run.

You need to set Local Share to True if your tables are also being accessed by non-BDE database engines, such as JET or ODBC.

If Local Share is set to False, no lock (.LCK) files at all are created.

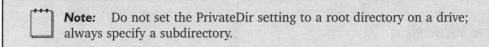

Lock time out

Possible Cause of Error

It may be that an application that is attempting to access a table has placed a write lock on the lock (.LCK) file while it searches it to make sure there is not an exclusive lock on the table (which would prevent it from accessing the table). At the same time, another application that already has a lock on the table is attempting to access the lock file to release its lock, but cannot because of the write lock the other application has applied. The application that placed the write lock (which wants access to the table) locates the lock the other application set, and continues checking the lock file. This does not allow the other application an opportunity to access the lock file so as to release the lock it placed. After a specified interval of time (the lock timeout period) with this deadlock prevailing, the above error message displays.

Quick Fix

Close both "dueling" applications and delete all *.LCK files.

Additional Information

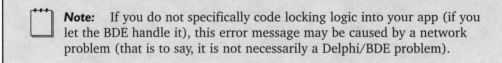

Note: If you do not specifically code locking logic into your app (if you let the BDE handle it), this error message may be caused by a network problem (that is to say, it is not necessarily a Delphi/BDE problem).

Lock Violation

Possible Cause of Error

1. You may be executing a database program created in Delphi 1 on a machine running Windows 95 which also contains the database tables.

2. You may be using the 16-bit BDE on "mixed networks" (having combinations of Windows 3.x/Windows 95/Windows NT machines).

Quick Fix

1. There are two ways to rectify the problem if it is due to the above scenario:

   ➤ Recompile the application in Delphi 2.

   -OR-

   ➤ Move the tables to a machine running Windows 3.x.

2. Follow these steps on each Windows 95 machine:

   a. Select **Start | Control Panel**.

   b. Double-click the System icon.

   c. Select the Performance Page.

   d. Select the **File System** button.

   e. Select the Troubleshooting page.

   f. Select **Disable New File Sharing & Locking Semantics**.

   g. Reboot.

Additional Information

If you want to leave the setup as it is, it may be worthwhile to try one or both of these series of steps:

Disable New Locking Semantics

1. On the Windows 95 machine, select **Start | Settings Control Panel**.
2. Double-click the System icon.
3. Select the Performance page.
4. Select the **File System** button.
5. Select the Troubleshooting page.
6. Select **Disable New File Sharing and Locking Semantics**.

Disable Write-behind Caching

1. Follow steps 1-6 above.
2. Select **Disable Write-behind Caching for all drives**.

Lookup information for field '< >' is incomplete

Possible Cause of Error

You may be attempting to reference a lookup field whose table has been removed from the form or project. For example, you may have created a calculated field based on a field in a related table and subsequently removed the table (thereby removing the reference to it). If you then reference that field, you will get the error message under discussion.

Quick Fix

Do not remove any components or elements that are relied on by other members of your form or project.

Additional Information

Lookup fields can be useful in displaying information that can be deduced from other columns. This saves space in the tables and is a flexible way of displaying pertinent data. A common example is to create a calculated field that multiplies the quantity sold by the price per item.

Low bound exceeds High bound

Possible Cause of Error

You may have declared a subrange whose lower bound is greater than the higher bound. For example, both of the following produce this error message:

```
type
  YellowSubmarange = 12..1;
  HomeHomeOnTheRange = 'w'..'c';
```

You may have declared a case label range where the larger element appears first. For example, the following will generate the error message under discussion:

```
case Vehicles of
  0:    ShowMessage('Hoofin'' it');
  2..1: ShowMessage('Motorin'');{should be 1..2}
  . . .
```

Quick Fix

Declare subrange types and case label ranges linearly (from lower to higher).

Additional Information

See "Subrange Types" and "Case Statements" in Delphi help for more information.

Master has detail records. Cannot delete or modify

Possible Cause of Error

Detail records may exist that reference the Master record you are attempting to delete.

Quick Fix

If you want to delete a Master record that has associated child records in a Detail table, you must first delete the child records from the Detail table.

You can do this programmatically by using a SQL DELETE statement in the Master table's BeforeDelete event. For example, if you wanted to delete all references to a particular athlete from a database, you might first delete the Detail records like this:

```
procedure TForm1.Table1BeforeDelete(DataSet: TDataSet);
begin
  with Query1 do
  begin
    SQL.Clear;
    SQL.Add('DELETE FROM STATS');
    SQL.Add('WHERE STATS."NO" = 32');
    Prepare;
    try
      ExecSQL;
    finally
      Unprepare;
    end;
  end;
end;
```

Placing this type of code in the BeforeDelete event allows the Master record (which no longer has any children in the Detail table, once the above SQL statement is executed) to be deleted.

Additional Information

Detail records are ones that are related to the master via a "foreign key" field (which is normally the primary key field of the master table).

With Paradox tables, you can set the Update rule to Cascade or Prohibit when setting up referential integrity. (Referential integrity is at work in displaying the error message under discussion—it is preventing you from deleting records which would create "orphaned" records in the Detail table.) The Cascade setting will change the related value in the Detail table also when you change the primary key value in the Master table. The Prohibit setting will prevent you from changing or deleting the primary values in the Master table if it has "children" in the Detail table.

Note: To set the Update mode for Paradox tables, follow these steps:

1. With the table you want to work with open in Database Desktop, select the Restructure icon (the table with a wrench in front of it).

2. Select **Referential Integrity** from the Table Properties drop-down list box (you must first have a Master-Detail relationship defined between two related tables).

3. Select either the Cascade or the Prohibit check box from the Update Rule section.

Master has detail records. Cannot empty it

Possible Cause of Error

You may be attempting to empty a Master table to which the following two conditions apply:

➤ Update is set to Prohibit.

➤ The table contains records which have child records in a Detail table.

Quick Fix

Delete the child records in the Detail table first, and then empty the Master table.

Additional Information

See "Master has detail records. Cannot delete or modify."

Master record missing

Possible Cause of Error

You may have attempted to enter a value in the foreign key field of a Detail table which does not have a matching primary key value in the Master table.

Quick Fix

If you are entering records into the Detail table (and not the master), you can be certain to select a value that exists in the Master table's primary key by using a TDBLookupComboBox and hooking it to the Master table's primary key field.

If you are entering both Master and Detail records simultaneously, you can be sure you are posting the Master records first by using the BeforeInsert event of the TTable component that represents the Detail table, something like this:

```
procedure TOrderForm.TblDetailBeforeInsert(DataSet: Tdataset);
begin
   if TblMaster.State = dsInsert then
   begin
     TblMaster.Post;
     TblMaster.Edit;
   end;
end;
```

Additional Information

See "Master Tables" in Delphi help for more information.

Maximum Validity Check Failed

Possible Cause of Error

You may have tried to assign a value to a TBCDField, TCurrencyField, TFloat-Field, or TIntegerField that is larger than the MaxValue setting you gave the field in Database Desktop. For example, you may have set a MaxValue of 100000 for the TCurrencyField Salary and then attempted to assign a value greater than that to the field:

```
TblEmployeesSalary.Value := 112000;
```

Quick Fix

Increase the MaxValue setting in Database Desktop or assign a value less than or equal to the setting to the field. Alternatively, you can set the TField property's MaxVal setting in the Delphi IDE.

Additional Information

Setting the MaxValue property in the Delphi IDE will result in a more informative error message if you subsequently assign a value that is too large, namely "<> is not a valid value for field <>. The allowed range is <> to <>."

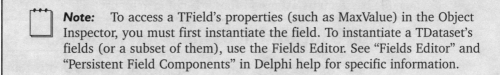

> **Note:** To access a TField's properties (such as MaxValue) in the Object Inspector, you must first instantiate the field. To instantiate a TDataset's fields (or a subset of them), use the Fields Editor. See "Fields Editor" and "Persistent Field Components" in Delphi help for specific information.

See "MaxValue" in Delphi help for more information.

Memo too large

Possible Cause of Error

You may be running Delphi 2/BDE 3.5/MS SQL Server 6.5 on NT4, using a table with a unique index.

Quick Fix

Download the latest patch/update for MS SQL Server.

Additional Information

A fix that has been suggested is setting the Drivers Flag in the BDE Configuration utility to 1 (Drivers | MS SQL | Drivers Flag).

Metafile is not valid

Possible Cause of Error

You may be loading a file into a TImage's Picture property that, although it has a .WMF or .EMF extension, is not in actuality a metafile.

Quick Fix

Ensure that any file you attempt to load into a TImage component's Picture property is indeed a valid graphics file.

Additional Information

Delphi provides native support for four graphic file formats, namely .BMP (bitmap), .ICO (icon), .WMF (Windows MetaFile), and .EMF (Enhanced MetaFile).

It may be that the file's extension was changed so that it appears to be a metafile based on its extension (but it is not in actuality).

See "Unknown picture file extension:<>."

> **Note:** This error message occurs both with invalid .WMF and .EMF files.

Method <> hides virtual method of base class <>

Possible Cause of Error

1. You may have attempted to redeclare an inherited virtual method with the *virtual* directive. For example, the ancestor class may look like this:

```
type
  TBass = class
    procedure WalkAndRock; virtual;
  end;
```

and the descendent like this:

```
type
  TGuitar = class
    procedure WalkAndRock; virtual;
  end;
```

2. You may have declared a method which has the same name as a virtual
    method in the base class, but forgot to (or deliberately did not) use the *over-
    ride* directive. For example, the following produces the error message under
    discussion:

```
type
  TAndCrumpets(TComponent)
  . . .
  public
    constructor Create(AOwner: TComponent);
```

Quick Fix

1, 2. Add the *override* directive to a virtual method from an ancestor class, like this:

```
type
  . . .
  public
    constructor Create(AOwner: TComponent); override;
```

Then, use the *inherited* reserved word to implement the functionality from the
ancestor class before adding the new functionality.

```
Constructor TForTwo.Create(AOwner: TComponent);
begin
  inherited Create(AOwner);
  FGuest := 'Tillerman';
  . . .
```

Additional Information

You can promote an inherited method or property by redeclaring it in the section wherein you want it to appear in the descendent class. When promoting
a property from an ancestor class, you do not need to specify the property
type or read and write methods—simply provide the name of the property in
the Public or Published section, like this:

```
published
  property OfAlcatraz;
```

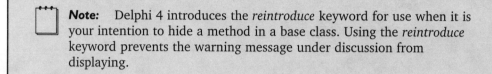

> **Note:** Delphi 4 introduces the *reintroduce* keyword for use when it is
> your intention to hide a method in a base class. Using the *reintroduce*
> keyword prevents the warning message under discussion from
> displaying.

Method < > not found in base class

Possible Cause of Error

You may have appended the *override* directive to a method, but the method
does not exist in an ancestor class.

Quick Fix

Ensure that any methods you attempt to override exist in an ancestor class. If
they do not, remove the *override* directive.

Additional Information

See "Virtual methods" in Delphi help for more information.

Method < > with identical parameters exists already

Possible Cause of Error

You may have declared two methods with the same signature (name, number,
argument types, and order of parameters). For example, the following will
generate this error message:

```
constructor Create(AOwner: TComponent);
                overload; override;
constructor Create(AOwner: Tcomponent);
                overload;
```

Quick Fix

Ensure that any methods you attempt to overload differ in their signature from other methods that you have also given the *overload* directive. For example, in the above case you may do something like:

```
constructor Create(AOwner: TComponent);
                    overload; override;
constructor Create(AOwner: TComponent;
                i:integer); overload;
```

Additional Information

Notice that it would not be valid to append the *override* directive to more than one of the overloaded methods, as the overridden method can only share an identical parameter list with at most one of the uniquely overloaded methods you declare. If you appended the *override* directive to both methods, you would get a "Declaration of <> differs from previous declaration" error message.

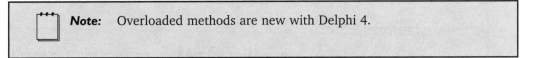

Note: Overloaded methods are new with Delphi 4.

Method identifier expected

Possible Cause of Error

1. You may have first received the "Undeclared Identifier:<>" error inside a procedure or function that is not a member of the unit's type declaration, and then attempted to rectify this by prepending the class name (such as TForm1) to the identifier. For example, if you have a procedure that looks like this:

```
procedure loopdeloop;
begin
  Label1.Caption := IntToStr(SizeOf(Byte));
end;
```

you will get the "Undeclared Identifier:<>" error. If you then prepend the name of the class type like this:

```
procedure loopdeloop;
begin
  TForm1.Label1.Caption := IntToStr(SizeOf(Byte));
end;
```

you will receive the error message under discussion.

2. You may have declared a private field in a property's Read or Write clause within the Automated section of a type.

Quick Fix

1. Remove the T from the type name. For example, this will compile fine (assuming your form variable is Form1):

```
procedure loopdeloop;
begin
  Form1.Label1.Caption := IntToStr(SizeOf(Byte));
end;
```

2. Properties in Automated sections must reference methods, rather than fields, in their Read and Write clauses.

Additional Information

See "Object-oriented programming | Programming with Delphi Objects" in Delphi help for more information.

Microsoft Transaction Server is not installed

Possible Cause of Error

You may have selected Run | Install MTS Objects... but do not have MTS installed.

Quick Fix

To install MTS Objects, you must first install MTS (Microsoft Transaction Server).

Additional Information

This menu item is available in Delphi 4 only. It is grayed out unless you have added an MTS Data Module to your project. Presumably, you will not select the Run | Install MTS Objects... menu item unless you have MTS installed. In other words, you will probably only get this error message if you are experimenting (playing around/hacking).

Minimum Validity Check failed

Possible Cause of Error

You may have tried to assign a value to a TBCDField, TCurrencyField, TFloat-Field, or TIntegerField that is smaller than the MinValue setting you gave the field in Database Desktop. For example, you may have set a MinValue of 20000 for the TCurrencyField Salary and then attempted to assign a value smaller than that to the field:

```
TblEmployeesSalary.Value := 19000;
```

Quick Fix

Decrease the MinValue setting in Database Desktop or assign a value greater than or equal to the MinValue setting to the field. Alternatively, you can set the TField property's MinVal setting in the Delphi IDE.

Additional Information

Setting the MinValue property in the Delphi IDE will result in a more informative error message if you subsequently assign a value that is too small, namely "<> is not a valid value for field <>. The allowed range is <> to <>."

 Note: To access a TField's properties (such as MinValue) in the Object Inspector, you must first instantiate the field. To instantiate a TDataset's fields (or a subset of them), use the Fields Editor. See "Fields Editor" and "Persistent Field Components" in Delphi help for more information.

See "MinValue" in Delphi help for more information.

Mismatch in datapacket

Possible Cause of Error

You may be attempting to read from a stream without setting its position to the beginning before reading from it. For example, the following will generate this error message:

```
var
  Consciousness: TMemoryStream;
begin
  Consciousness:= TMemoryStream.Create;
  try
```

```
      ClientDataSet1.SaveToStream(Consciousness);
  ClientDataSet1.LoadFromStream(Consciousness);
    finally
      Consciousness.Free;
    end;
  end;
```

Possible Cause of Error

Set the position of the stream to 0 before attempting to read from it:

```
var
  Consciousness: TMemoryStream;
begin
  Consciousness:= TMemoryStream.Create;
  try
    ClientDataSet1.SaveToStream(Consciousness);
    Consciousness.Position := 0; {add this line}
    ClientDataSet1.LoadFromStream(Consciousness);
  finally
    Consciousness.Free;
  end;
end;
```

Additional Information

See "TClientDataset" in Delphi help for related information on storing data in memory.

Missing comma

Possible Cause of Error

You may be using Delphi 1.0 and supplying several parameters to a TQuery's SQL property.

Quick Fix

Get the 1.02 patch from the Inprise web site.

Additional Information

Always keep up with the latest Delphi and BDE (as well as SQL Server database, if applicable) patches for best performance.

See "Queries" in Delphi help for more information.

Missing Data Provider or Data Packet

Possible Cause of Error

1. You may have attempted to set the Active property of a TClientDataSet component to True without having specified a TProvider component in the ProviderName property (the Data Provider is missing).

2. The Provider may have returned no records (the Data Packet is missing).

Quick Fix

1. Supply the name of a TProvider component to the TClientDataSet's Provider-Name property.

2. Provide code that tests for and responds to the possibility of retrieving no data from the application server. For example, you might try one of the following:

```
if ClientDataSet1.RecordCount = 0 then
  { ... }
if ClientDataSet1.IsEmpty then
  { ... }
if (cds.BOF) and (cds.BOF) then
  { ... }
```

Additional Information

2. See "RecordCount," "BOF," "EOF," and "IsEmpty" in Delphi help for more information.

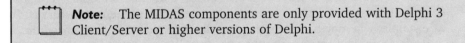

Note: The MIDAS components are only provided with Delphi 3 Client/Server or higher versions of Delphi.

Missing ENDIF directive

Possible Cause of Error

You may have an $IFDEF, $IFNDEF, or $IFOPT compiler directive that is not paired with an $ENDIF directive. For example, the following will generate this error message:

```
uses
  Windows, Messages, SysUtils, Classes, Graphics,
```

```
Registry, {$IFDEF Leppard} IniFiles,
{$IFNDEF DumbAndBlindKid} Controls;
```

Quick Fix

Make sure each {$IFDEF} statement has a matching {$ENDIF} statement.

Additional Information

See "Invalid compiler directive:< >."

Missing operator or semicolon

Possible Cause of Error

1. You may have left out a semicolon at the end of a line.
2. You may have omitted an operator between operands. For example, in a *with...do* statement, you may have forgotten the *do*:

   ```
   with Table1
   begin
   ```
3. You may have omitted the concatenation operator (+) between strings defined one after the other.
4. You may have had the single quote (') on its own line and then attempted to compile. You may have then gotten the error message "Unterminated string" followed by the error message under discussion.
5. You may be calling a procedure or function that is not in scope, yet another procedure or function with the same name but a different signature is. For example, you may be attempting to call the standard Delete procedure declared in the System unit, but are instead (inadvertently) calling the Delete method which is introduced in TStringList.

Quick Fix

1. Always add the statement terminator to the end of each line, unless you are simply breaking up an *if* statement over several lines.
2. Add the missing operator (*do* in this case):

   ```
   with Table1 do
   begin
   ```
3. If you have a string spread out over multiple lines, concatenate them using the string concatenation operator (+).
4. Remove the stray single quote.

5. Qualify the call by prepending the name of the unit in which the procedure or function you want to use is declared. For example, to rectify the above scenario, use System.Delete. Alternatively, move the unit which contains the identifier you want to access beyond the one which contains the same-named unit in your Uses clause. For example, if you are attempting to use the DeleteFile procedure in the SysUtils unit, move that unit past the Windows unit in your Uses clause, as the Windows unit in 32-bit Delphi also contains a DeleteFile procedure.

Additional Information

1. Note that you need to append a semicolon to the end of each <u>statement</u>. Normally, this is the same as appending a semicolon to the end of each line; however, that is not always the case. An *if* statement, for example, may be spread over several lines. You must wait until the end of the statement to add the semicolon.

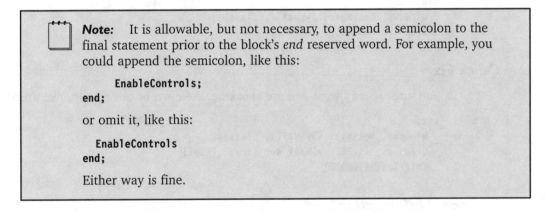

Note: It is allowable, but not necessary, to append a semicolon to the final statement prior to the block's *end* reserved word. For example, you could append the semicolon, like this:

```
    EnableControls;
end;
```

or omit it, like this:

```
  EnableControls
end;
```

Either way is fine.

3. Here is how to concatenate a string on multiple lines (leaving out the string concatenation operator (+) would generate the error message under discussion):

```
s := 'What would you rather eat: the fat from '
   + 'behind a caribou''s eyeball or a frosted'
   + 'poptart? (McFee) ';
```

You can also concatenate strings on the same line and display them on multiple lines, or concatenate property values with string literals. For example, to display a message to the user spread out over several lines in a dialog box (on one line of code), you can do this:

```
ShowMessage('It was the'+#13#10+'best of times');
```

You can also incorporate and concatenate variables, property values, and string literals in a single line of text, like this:

```
ShowMessage('Listen: ' + Edit1.Text + ' ' + s +'!')
```

5. See "Constant or type identifier expected" and "Undeclared Identifier:<>." If identical identifiers appear in multiple units, the unit that appears last in the Uses clause is the one that will be "seen" by the compiler.

Missing or invalid conditional symbol in <$> directive

Possible Cause of Error

You may have added the $IFDEF, $IFNDEF, $DEFINE, or $UNDEF directives without specifying which conditional symbol you intended to check, define, or undefine. For example, the following will generate this error message:

```
uses
  Windows, Messages, SysUtils, Classes,
  Graphics, {$IFDEF} Registry, { . . . }
```

Quick Fix

You must specify what you are checking, defining, or undefining, like this:

```
uses
  Windows, Messages, SysUtils, Classes,
  Graphics, {$IFDEF WIN32} Registry, {$ELSE}
  IniFiles, {$ENDIF}
```

Additional Information

See "Conditional Directives" in Delphi help for more information.

Missing parameter type

Possible Cause of Error

You may have declared a procedure or function which takes one or more value parameters whose types are not specified. For example, the following will generate this error message:

```
procedure fudgsicle(a);
```

Quick Fix

You must specify the data type when declaring procedures or functions that accept value parameters. For example, to fix the declaration above, you could do this:

```
procedure fudgsicle(a: byte);
```

Additional Information

You can declare procedures and functions which accept variable (var) or constant (const) parameters without specifying the data types. The following two declarations are legal:

```
procedure fudgsicle(var a);
procedure fudgsicle(const a);
```

Missing right quote

Possible Cause of Error

You may have a single (unmatched) quote in a SQL statement.

Quick Fix

Remove the solitary quote or add the missing/matching quote.

Additional Information

See "QuotedStr" in Delphi help.

Missing TableName property

Possible Cause of Error

1. You may have attempted to perform an action on a table for which you have not supplied a DatabaseName property value.

2. You may have tried to instantiate the fields of a table at design time by double-clicking a TTable component and then selecting Add Fields from the context menu (without setting the TTable's TableName property to a valid table).

3. You may have attempted to set a TTable component's Active property to True without having set the TableName property to a valid table.

Quick Fix

1. Select one of the BDE aliases that have been created on your system from the drop-down list of the DatabaseName property.

   Alternatively, supply the fully qualified path to the directory wherein the tables reside. For example, in a default installation of Delphi, you could attach to the DBDEMOS alias by selecting it from the drop-down list or by directly entering a path, such as:

   ```
   C:\Program Files\Borland\Delphi X\Demos\Data
   ```

2, 3. Select a table from the TTable component's TableName property combo box and then retry the operation. If there are no tables listed, you will first have to set the DatabaseName property. To do this, select an alias from the DatabaseName property's combo box or enter the path (if using local tables as opposed to SQL tables). There will now be a list of tables that belong to the alias (or are located in the directory/path supplied). Select one of them.

Additional Information

You can set the DatabaseName property to look for the tables in the same directory where the executable resides by entering "/." (a forward slash followed by a period) as the DatabaseName property. This is a compromise between an alias and a hard-coded path. It is not as rigid as a hard-coded path, but not as flexible as an alias.

> **Note:** Placing the tables in the same directory as the executable can lead to problems. See "Directory Is Busy."

Module <>s time/date changed. Reload?

Possible Cause of Error

1. You may have (inadvertently?) started several instances of Delphi.
2. You may have checked out a version of a file from a version control system (such as PVCS) that either predates or postdates one that is already loaded in your project (it is a different version of the file, in other words).

Quick Fix

1. Close all unnecessary instances of Delphi.

2. If it was your intention to do so (check out a different version of the file), select the **Yes** button to dismiss the dialog and replace the existing file with the one you are checking out.

Additional Information

You might see this error message if you highlight multiple Delphi files in Explorer and then accidentally click one of the files twice in quick succession. This performs a double-click on all the files highlighted, and an instance of Delphi is started for each individual file. If this happens, you may also get the error message "One or more lines were too long and have been truncated."

> **Note:**   Delphi 4 allows you to have multiple projects open simultaneously. See "Project Manager" in Delphi (4) help for more information.

Module header is missing or incorrect

Possible Cause of Error

1. You may have changed the name of the source file outside of the IDE (for example, in Windows Explorer).
2. You may have omitted the Uses clause from a unit's Interface section.

Quick Fix

1. Change the file's name back to its original name.
2. Reinstate the Uses clause and include at least one unit in it.

Additional Information

1. If you change a unit's name outside Delphi, this change is not automatically relayed to the rest of the project which "knows" it by its former name. Therefore, do not do this.
2. You can include a "thin" unit to satisfy the necessity of "using" at least one unit. You could create a "dummy" unit which just contains the bare necessities for a unit to be syntactically correct but which provides no functionality to serve this purpose. For example, if you simply add a unit to your project, it will look like this:

```
unit Unit2;
interface
implementation
end.
```

You can then change its name to "Whatever" (or whatever) and use it in the other unit.

Note: This error message is to Delphi source and form files what the "Index is out of date" error message is to Paradox tables. In the case of Paradox tables, the table and its corresponding index files should always travel together. Similarly, Delphi source (.PAS) and form (.DFM) files need to be kept in synchronization with one another. For this reason, they must both be available when a form file is being loaded as well as when it is being saved. The .DFM file is the "blueprint" from which the form file is dynamically created when loading, and similarly needs to be present when saving so that changes in the form can be written to it in order for the two files to stay in sync.

The source file (.PAS, .DPR, or .DLL) needs to have a valid module header. The module header is comprised of the reserved word unit (.PAS), program (.DPR), or library (.DLL), followed by an identifier such as Unit1 or Project1, and finally a semicolon. For example, an unmodified form will have a module header similar to this:

`unit EyeSeaux;`

The identifier (EyeSeaux above) must be the same as the unit name. In other words, the unit name in this case would be EyeSeaux.PAS.

When you subsequently open the file EyeSeaux.PAS, Delphi will expect to find the identifier EyeSeaux in the module header. The same principle holds true for .DPRs (project files) and .DLLs (library files).

Multiple Net Files found

Possible Cause of Error

1. Two or more users may be attempting to access the same database table, but they do not share the same NET DIR setting.
2. If all users have the same NET DIR setting, it may be that there is an old .LCK file that points to a different path for the NetDir directory.
3. You may have a corrupted PDOXUSRS.NET or PDOXUSRS.LCK file.

Quick Fix

I. Configure each user's machine so that they all use the same NetDir (PDOXUSRS.NET) file. You can do so by following the steps appropriate for your version of Delphi:

Delphi I

If each user has their own copy of the BDE on their machine, you can use the BDE Configuration utility to assign the net file directory. To do so, follow these steps:

a. Open the BDE configuration utility.

b. With the Paradox entry highlighted in the Driver Name list box, enter the complete path to the shared network directory wherein to store and reference the network control file (PDOXUSRS.NET) in the NET DIR setting.

c. Select **File | Exit** and save your changes.

If any users do not have a copy of the BDE Configuration utility, ensure that the actual location of your IDAPI.CFG FILE (C:\IDAPI by default) matches that shown in the [IDAPI] section of WIN.INI for the CONFIGFILE01 entry.

If necessary, move the file to match the entry in WIN.INI or change the entry in WIN.INI to match the location of the file.

Delphi 2

If each user has their own copy of the BDE, you can use the BDE Configuration utility to assign their Paradox net file directory. To do so, follow these steps:

a. Open the BDE Configuration utility (BDECFG32.EXE) by selecting **Start | Programs | Delphi | BDE Config**.

b. With the Paradox entry highlighted in the Driver Name list box, enter the complete path to the shared network directory wherein to store and reference the network control file (PDOXUSRS.NET) in the NET DIR setting.

c. Select **File | Exit** and save your changes.

See "32-bit Delphi" below.

Delphi 3 and 4

If each user has their own copy of the BDE, you can use the BDE Administrator utility to assign their Paradox net file directory. To do so, follow these steps:

a. Open the BDE Configuration utility (**Start | Programs | Borland Delphi X | BDE [Configuration, Administration]**).

b. Select **Object | Open Configuration....**

c. Open IDAPI32.CFG.

d. Navigate to Configuration\Drivers\Native\Paradox in the tree-view in the Configuration pane at the left of the BDE Administrator.

e. Enter the complete path for the directory wherein you want the network control file to reside. Select a shared network directory to which all users of the Paradox tables in question have read, write, create, and delete rights.

f. Select **Object | Exit** and then **Yes** to save the changes you made.

32-Bit Delphi

If any users do not have a copy of the BDE Configuration/Administration utility, you can consult their system registry settings to ensure that the actual physical location of IDAPI32.CFG (C:\Program Files\Borland\Common Files\BDE by default) matches that shown in the system registry.

If necessary, move the file to match the entry in the system registry or change the entry in the system registry to match the location of the file.

> **Note:** Another way to set the network file directory in 32-bit Delphi—but doing so dynamically as the program runs rather than creating a persistent system registry setting—is to assign the shared network directory you are going to use for the network control file to the Session's NetFileDir property. For example, you could do something like this:
>
> ```
> const
>   SharedNetDir := 'K:\LanCon\';
> . . .
> implementation
> . . .
> procedure TForm1.OnCreate(Sender: Tobject);
> begin
>   if DirectoryExists(SharedNetDir) then
>     Session.NetFileDir := ' '
>   else
>     ShowMessage('Couldn't connect to shared
>       Paradox network net file directory');
> end;
> ```
>
> Make sure that you set the NetFileDir property prior to any attempt to access the tables, either directly or indirectly. It is a good idea to close all tables before the program closes, and then open them soon after startup or as necessary.

2. Make sure that no users are connected to the tables wherein the .LCK file is located, and delete it.

3. Verify that no BDE users on the network are using the tables, and then delete the corrupted PDOXUSRS.NET and/or PDOXUSRS.LCK file(s). The files will be automatically regenerated as needed.

Additional Information

1. This may happen when you make a database available to multiple users on a network who previously only accessed BDE tables locally (on their own hard drive). In this case, each user's NET DIR setting might be their own root drive (C:\). This would result in the following:

   a. The first user accesses the tables, and supplies his own hard drive as the NetDir directory. No problem.

   b. The second user attempts to access the tables, and also supplies his own hard drive as the NetDir directory. There are now two different PDOXUSRS.NET files attempting to control access to the tables, and the error message under discussion is generated.

3. The PDOXUSR.NET and PDOXUSRS.LCK files can become corrupted if a BDE program is abnormally terminated (such as in the event of a crash).

   The BDE can detect whether the tables are on a network drive, but it cannot detect whether the tables are on a machine that serves as a dedicated server or if the machine is a client as well as a server (in other words, it is a peer in a peer-to-peer network).

   Dedicated servers notify client applications if a file is locked or has been modified. Peer-to-peer networks do not normally provide this functionality, though (even a "server" machine in a peer-to-peer network is not a true dedicated server). To achieve this type of functionality with peer-to-peer networks, set Local Share to True in the BDE Configuration utility (System page/node) on all client machines which access the tables.

> **Note:** Setting Local Share to True is unnecessary for Novell File Server networks.

See "Directory is controlled by other .NET file" for more information.

Multiple Paradox Net files found/in use

See "Directory is controlled by other .NET file" and "Multiple Net Files found" for more information.

Name conflicting

Possible Cause of Error

You may be attaching to a multiple instance DCOM Server and are using a TDatabase component whose HandleShared property is set to False.

Quick Fix

Set the TDatabase component's HandleShared property to True.

Additional Information

See "COM" in Delphi help for more information.

Name not unique in this context

Possible Cause of Error

You may be using a TDatabase component whose HandleShared property is set to False.

Quick Fix

Set the TDatabase component's HandleShared property to True.

Additional Information

HandleShared is a Boolean property that indicates whether a TDatabase component can share its BDE handle in a session.

By setting HandleShared to True, you avoid namespace conflicts. There are two situations where this is potentially a problem:

➤ TDatabase components in a remote data module
➤ TDatabase components in data modules that you inherit from the Object Repository

Never-build package <> must be recompiled

Possible Cause of Error

You may have made modifications to another package which is required by the package referenced in the error message.

Quick Fix

Manually recompile the package referenced in the error.

Additional Information

See "Packages" in Delphi help for more information.

No address specified

Possible Cause of Error

You may have attempted to set the Connected property of a TSocketConnection to True without having provided a value for the Address property.

Quick Fix

Specify the appropriate address in standard Internet dot notation (four byte values). You can supply the value either in the Object Inspector or in code; for example, to provide the address in code:

```
SocketConnection1.Address := 131.228.6.1;
```

Additional Information

The Address property of the TSocketConnection refers to the IP address of the server on which the DCOM object resides. If you do not know the address, you can supply the hostname in the Host property. This, however, is slower than setting the Address property, as the address must then be looked up for the host.

> **Note:** Do not attempt to modify the Address after the connection has been established, as this will raise an ESocketError exception.

> **Note:** A server may expose multiple addresses.

No argument for format '<>'

Possible Cause of Error

You may not have supplied the same number of arguments as format specifiers while using the Format function. For example, the following will generate this error message because there are three format specifiers, but only two arguments have been provided:

```
Label1.Caption := Format('The %s of %s will win the %s,['Baltimore',
                          'World Series']);
```

Quick Fix

Supply an argument for each format specifier you use. For example, to fix the example shown above, do it this way:

```
Label1.Caption := Format('The %s of %s will win the %s,['Birds',
                          'Baltimore','World Series']);
```

Additional Information

See "Format function," "Format specifier," and "Format Strings" in Delphi help for more information.

No code was generated for the current line

Possible Cause of Error

1. You may be attempting to run to the cursor location, but you selected Run | Run To Cursor or pressed F4 while on a line that did not generate code. For example, it may be a procedure header (as opposed to an assignment statement).

2. The line in question may have not generated code because it was not linked into the project. If the code is not called, Delphi's smart linker will leave it out to reduce code size. For example, if you include the following procedure in your unit:

```
procedure TForm1.DontCallUs;
. . .
```

but it is never called by another procedure or function, it will not be linked in, and so no code will be generated for it.

3. You may be on a line that did indeed generate code, but the unit is not part of the current project. It may be that the unit in question is not found in the Uses clause of any of the units which <u>are</u> a part of the project.

4. It may be that you have a copy of a unit open that is stored in a different location than the copy of the unit which <u>is</u> part of the project. For example, you may have a unit named Usee that is stored in the project's directory (for instance, C:\User), but you have opened a copy of the Usee unit that is stored in a different directory (for instance, C:\UserBkup).

Quick Fix

1, 2. Remove the breakpoint. If desired, place the cursor on a line of code in the current project which did generate code, such as an assignment statement within a procedure or function which is called from within the project.

3. Add the unit to the Uses clause of at least one of the units that is a part of the project. To add a unit that exists in another location/directory to your project, select **Project | Add to Project...**, navigate to the unit, highlight it, and select the **Open** button.

4. Close the unit which is stored in a location other than that you have designated for it in the Project Manager, and open the copy of the unit that resides in the correct location/directory. Select **View | Project Manager** to see the units included in the project and their location.

Additional Information

2. Delphi's smart linker will remove procedures that are not used by your program (that is, unless they are virtual methods of an object that is linked in).

3, 4. See "Project Manager" in Delphi help for more information.

No definition for abstract method < > allowed

Possible Cause of Error

You have defined a method which was declared abstract earlier in the same unit. For example, the following will generate this error message:

```
procedure VAndA; virtual; abstract;
. . .
procedure TForm1.VAndA;
var
  FrozenCustardLovers: string;
begin
  FrozenCustardLovers := 'Gillespie, Goetzke,
          Pomranky, Prado, Sardina, Taylor';
end;
```

Quick Fix

Remove either the definition of the function or the *abstract* directive from the method's declaration.

Additional Information

You cannot define an abstract method within the same class where it was defined. Abstract signifies that it must be overridden. Since it <u>must</u> be overridden, there is no "base class" implementation of an abstract method for a descendent to inherit.

No MDI forms are currently active

See "Cannot create form. No MDI forms are currently active."

No MDI Parent Active

Possible Cause of Error

1. You may have neglected to designate the main form of your MDI application as the MDI parent form.
2. You may be dynamically creating the main MDI form.

Quick Fix

1. Set the main form's FormStyle property to fsMDIForm.
2. Allow Delphi to automatically create your main form. It must be created before child forms.

Additional Information

Multiple Document Interface programs are considered passé in 32-bit Windows. Of course, there's no law against being old-fashioned.

No Provider Available

Possible Cause of Error

You may have assigned the Data property of a TDataSet's Provider property to the Data property of a TClientDataSet without adding BDEProv to your Uses section. For example, the following will generate this error message (if BDE-Prov is not in your Uses section):

```
procedure TForm1.FormCreate(Sender: Tobject);
begin
  ClientDataSet1.Data := Table1.Provider.Data;
end;
```

Quick Fix

Add BDEProv to your Uses section.

Additional Information

Providers are normally associated with MIDAS and debuted with Delphi 3. If you are using Delphi 3, be sure you have the latest upgrade and/or patch for full functionality and best performance. In particular and among other things, the DBClient.DLL file was updated and enhanced following release 3.0.

No SQL statement available

Possible Cause of Error

1. You may have called TQuery's Prepare method, but the SQL property has no statement associated with it.
2. You may have attempted to add fields to a TQuery component using the Field Editor without first assigning a SQL statement to the TQuery component's SQL property.
3. You may have called a TQuery object's Open or ExecSQL methods when the SQL property was empty.
4. You may have attempted to set a DecisionQuery component's Active property to True without specifying a SQL statement for its SQL property.

Quick Fix

1. Remove the call to Prepare or assign a SQL statement to the TQuery component either at design time or in code before calling Prepare.
2. Assign a valid SQL statement to the TQuery component's SQL property before attempting to instantiate design-time fields for it.
3. Ensure that you only call a TQuery's ExecSQL method when the SQL property is not empty. For example, you could check for this condition with the following code:

```
procedure TForm1.ExecuteAndClearClick(Sender: Tobject);
begin
  with Query1 do begin
    if SQL.Count <> 0 then begin
      ExecSQL;
      SQL.Clear;
    end;
  end;
end;
```

> **Note:** Of course, this does not guarantee that the SQL property contains a valid and syntactically correct SQL statement, only that the SQL property is not empty.

4. Supply a SQL statement, either in the IDE or in code, for the DecisionQuery's SQL property.

Additional Information

1. To add a SQL statement to a TQuery component in code, follow this example:

```
with Query1 do
  begin
    SQL.Add('Select * from RoundTablePizza');
    SQL.Add('Where Kind = 'ItalianGarlic'');
    Prepare; {optional}
    Open;
  end;
```

You can spread the SQL statement over as many lines as you like. This helps to break the statement down into its logical constituent parts.

2. The advantages of instantiating fields for a TQuery component is (a) you have access to the fields' properties (including event handlers, such as OnValidate) at design time, and (b) you can create calculated fields using the Fields Editor. For more information about creating calculated fields using the Fields Editor, see "New Field dialog box" in Delphi help.

No user transaction is currently in progress

Possible Cause of Error

You may have called a TDatabase component's Commit method without first starting a transaction with a call to StartTransaction.

Quick Fix

Call StartTransaction before attempting to commit the operations carried out during a transaction.

Additional Information

By using a TDatabase component, you can group a set of operations on a database in a transaction, and then save these or reject these as a group. You begin a transaction with a call to StartTransaction and then call either Commit or Rollback based on whether you want to save or discard the changes or additions made during the transaction.

Here is a simple example of using database transactions:

```
begin
  with Database1 do begin
    StartTransaction;
    try
      { do your thing here }
      if { a condition is met } then
        Commit;
      else
        Rollback;
    except
      Rollback;
    end; {except block}
  end;    {with block}
end;
```

For more information on database transactions, see "Handling Transactions" in Delphi help.

No Web browser could be located

Possible Cause of Error

You have attempted to log on to a web site or view an .HTML document, but Delphi cannot locate a web browser on your system.

For example, you may have selected Inprise Home Page, Delphi Home Page, or Inprise Programs and Services from the Help menu.

Quick Fix

Install a web browser. Do not move it or remove it from the directory to which it is installed.

Additional Information

In some versions of Delphi, Microsoft Internet Explorer is provided on the Delphi CD. If you do not have a browser and want one, this is an option. Netscape's browser products are another attractive option. Additionally, there are other browsers available commercially and as freeware. And then again, you could create your own web browser using Delphi.

NODEFAULT clause not allowed in OLE automation section

Possible Cause of Error

The *nodefault* clause is not allowed in an Automated section.

Quick Fix

Remove the *nodefault* clause from the Automated section.

Additional Information

Delphi 2 and above has five visibility specifiers: *Private*, *Protected*, *Public*, *Published*, and *Automated* (the *Automated* specifier was not available in Delphi 1). A class's properties can specify a storage specifier of *stored*, *default*, or *nodefault*. These storage specifiers are not allowed in the Automated section, though.

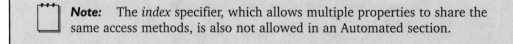

> **Note:** The *index* specifier, which allows multiple properties to share the same access methods, is also not allowed in an Automated section.

Not enough actual parameters

Possible Cause of Error

1. You may have called a procedure or function without supplying all the parameters needed. For example, you may have tried something like this:

```
MessageDlg('Eat at Joe''s, mtCustom,[mbOK]);
{ You forgot to add the Help Context (HelpCtx) variable }
```

2. You may be attempting to override an ancestor's method, but have not supplied all the parameters declared in the ancestor. For example, the following will generate this error message, as the constructor being overridden declares a parameter of type TComponent:

```
type
  TYoopdl = class(TComponent)
    private
      FOutstanding: string;
    public
      constructor Create; override;
  end;
. . .
constructor TYoopdl.Create;
begin
  inherited Create; {this line causes the error}
  FOutstanding := 'yowza-bop';
end;
```

3. You may have been attempting to inspect whether an event handler is in effect for an event property by testing whether its value is nil, like this:

```
if TrueIdentity.OnValidate = nil then
```

Quick Fix

1. Supply the missing parameter(s). For instance, to fix the example above, add the final parameter, like this:

```
{You must provide the parameter, even if there is no help topic created for
the message}
MessageDlg('Eat at Joe''s,mtCustom,[mbOK],0);
{If there actually was a help context id, for example #11, you would do it
like this:}
MessageDlg('Eat at Joe''s,mtCustom,[mbOK,mbHelp],11);
```

2. Remove the inherited part of the constructor's definition to create a new constructor, rather than inheriting from TComponent's constructor. To inherit TComponent's constructor, add the parameter to the declaration, definition, and call, like this:

```
constructor Create(AOwner: TComponent);
. . .
constructor TCmpntDescendent.Create(AOwner: TComponent);
begin
  inherited Create(AOwner);
. . .
```

> **Note:**   Doing this causes the warning message "Method <Create> hides virtual method of base type <TComponent>," though. To simply "silence" the warning in Delphi 4, add the *reintroduce* keyword to the declaration, and remove the inherited call, like this:
>
> ```
> type
>   TYoopdl = class(TComponent)
>     private
>       FOutstanding: string;
>     public
>       constructor Create; reintroduce;
>   end;
> . . .
> constructor TYoopdl.Create;
> begin
>   FOutstanding := 'yowza-bop';
> end;
> ```

3. Use the Assigned function to make the test, like this:

```
if not Assigned(TrueIdentity.OnValidate) then
```

Additional Information

1. Highlight the name of the function in your code and press **<F1>** to view the help (from which you can ascertain the number, type, and order of parameters expected).

2. TObject's constructor contains no parameter. TComponent's constructor does. See TObject's declaration in the System unit and TComponent's declaration in the Classes unit for the specifics.

Not enough file handles

Possible Cause of Error

You may have too many applications/files open for your system to handle.

Quick Fix

Increase the Files setting in your CONFIG.SYS file. Increase it to a number between its current setting and 255.

Increase the MaxFileHandles setting in the BDE Configuration utility's System page/node to a number a little less than the number to which the CONFIG.SYS Files= line is set.

Additional Information

Paradox tables consist of a number of related files, such as .DB, .MB, .PX, .XG*n*, .YG*n*, etc. Several of these files could be simultaneously open, each needing its own handle.

Not in cached update mode

Possible Cause of Error

You may be attempting to access a record's OldValue property, but the Data-Set's CachedUpdates property is set to False.

Quick Fix

Set the DataSet's CachedUpdates property to True before attempting to access the OldValue of a record.

Additional Information

You can programmatically check to make sure if CachedUpdates is true in this way:

```
if Table1.CachedUpdates = True then
  ClassicVal := OldValue;
```

You might also want to verify that the record is not a new one, in which case it will not have an old value:

```
if (Table1.CachedUpdates = True) and
   (Table1.State <> dsInserting) then
     LegacyVal := OldValue;
```

See "At End of Table" for related information.

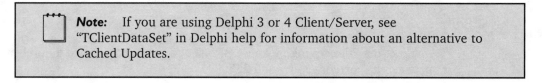

Note: If you are using Delphi 3 or 4 Client/Server, see "TClientDataSet" in Delphi help for information about an alternative to Cached Updates.

Not initialized for accessing network files

Possible Cause of Error

1. You may have an invalid setting in the IDAPI.CFG file regarding the location of the network file directory.

2. You may have an invalid setting in WIN.INI or the system registry as to the location of the BDE Configuration file (IDAPI.CFG).

Quick Fix

1. Set the NetDir setting in the Drivers | Paradox section of the BDE Configuration utility to a shared network directory to which all users who will access the tables have read, write, and create rights.

2. Follow the instructions specific to your version of Delphi:

Delphi I

Verify that the setting in WIN.INI in the [IDAPI] section points to the correct location in the CONFIGFILE01= line. For example, if the BDE configuration file IDAPI.CFG is located in C:\IDAPI (the default), the section should read:

```
[IDAPI]
ConfigFile01=C:\IDAPI
```

If necessary, move the file to match the entry in WIN.INI or change the entry in WIN.INI to match the location of the file.

32-bit Delphi

Verify that the location of IDAPI32.CFG (C:\Program Files\Borland\Common Files\BDE by default) matches that shown in the system registry.

If necessary, move the file to match the entry in the system registry or change the entry in the system registry to match the location of the file.

Additional Information

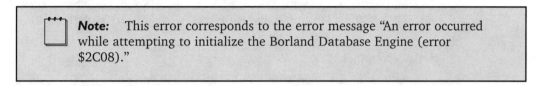

> **Note:** This error corresponds to the error message "An error occurred while attempting to initialize the Borland Database Engine (error $2C08)."

The network file directory will contain the PDOXUSRS.NET file, which controls access to the tables and manages locks.

To set the BDE Configuration/Administration utility's NET DIR setting, follow these steps:

1. Create a directory on a shared network directory to which all users who must access the database tables have read, write, and create rights.

2. Set NetDir in each user's BDE Configuration file (IDAPI.CFG, modified via the BDE Configuration utility or the system registry) to the directory created in step 1.

> **Note:** Delphi/Paradox is not the only product that uses the BDE. At least some versions of the following do also: C++ Builder, JBuilder, dBASE, IntraBuilder, Quattro Pro, and WordPerfect.

How to Create an Alias using the BDE Config Tool

In Delphi 1, the BDE Config Tool is BDECFG.EXE. In Delphi 2, it is BDECFG32.EXE. In Delphi 3 and 4 it is BDEADMIN.EXE. In Windows 95, it is available by selecting Start | Programs | Borland Delphi X | BDE Administrator.

To create an alias with the BDE Configuration/Administration Tool, follow these steps:

1. Select **Start | Programs | Borland Delphi X | BDE [Configuration, Administration]**.

2. With the Databases tab active, select **Object | New...**, and then select the type of alias you want to create (for example, Standard for a Paradox database).

3. Verify that the Type setting corresponds to the type of database you have created or will create (Standard for Paradox, dBASE, and ASCII, Access for MS Access, etc.).

4. If you selected a Standard driver (to create a Paradox database, for instance), set the Path to the location of the database (ServerName for Interbase and Oracle; Database Name for MS SQL Server and MS Access, Sybase, and Informix; DB2 DS2 for DB2). If using Path, you can enter a DOS path, as in:

```
Append:
I:\LessTaken\Diff
```

5. Set the Path to the location of the database. You can enter a DOS path, as in:

```
K:\HallOfFame\Baseball
```

or, in 32-bit Delphi, you can use UNC (Universal Naming Convention), which is of the format:

```
\\ServerName\ShareName\ShareDir.
```

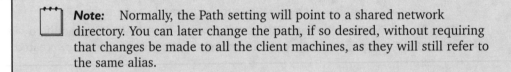

> **Note:** Normally, the Path setting will point to a shared network directory. You can later change the path, if so desired, without requiring that changes be made to all the client machines, as they will still refer to the same alias.

Number is out of range

Possible Cause of Error

1. You may have attempted to add a primary index to a table that already has a primary key defined.

2. You may be attempting to create a primary index on a field other than the first field of the table.

Quick Fix

1. You can only have one primary index per table. You can add secondary indexes in code to dBASE and Paradox 7 tables, but not Paradox 3.5, 4, or 5 tables.

2. Set the primary index to the first field of the table only. In the case of a composite primary key/index, the fields must be the first ones in the table (consecutive, beginning with the first field).

Additional Information

This is an EDatabaseEngine error. If a table already has a primary key (required for a Paradox table), the following will produce the error message under discussion:

```
Table1.AddIndex('P2','RedGreenBlue',[ixPrimary]);
```

If you are using a Paradox 7 table, you can, however, create additional unique indexes, like this:

```
Table1.AddIndex('U2','IrishRockers',[ixUnique]);
```

If you are not using a Paradox 7 table and attempt the above, you will get a "Higher table level required" error message. See that entry for more information.

The index options you can set in the final parameter are ixPrimary, ixUnique, ixDescending, ixCaseInsensitive, and ixExpression.

You cannot use ixPrimary or ixCaseInsensitive with a dBASE table. You cannot use ixExpression with a Paradox table.

Number of elements differs from declaration

Possible Cause of Error

You may have declared a typed constant array, but have supplied a different number of elements than declared. For example, both of the following will generate this error message:

```
{ not enough elements provided }
const
   LeadingLeadingMen: array[0..4] of string =
        ('Brando','Bogart','DeNiro','Duvall');
{ too many elements provided }
const
   LeadingLeadingMen: array[0..4] of string =
                ('Brando', 'Bogart', 'DeNiro', 'Duvall', 'Peck', 'Sinise');
```

Quick Fix

Change the size of the array you are declaring, or add or subtract the necessary number of elements.

Additional Information

See "Arrays" in Delphi help for more information.

One or more lines were too long and have been truncated

Possible Cause of Error

1. You may have, perhaps inadvertently, started up several instances of Delphi.
2. You may have attempted to open a non-Delphi file in the IDE. For example, you may have selected File | Open..., selected Any File (*.*) from the Files of Type combo box, and then attempted to open a .DOC (Microsoft Word) file.

Quick Fix

1. Close all unnecessary instances of Delphi.
2. Open the non-Delphi file in the appropriate program or from Windows Explorer.

Additional Information

You might see this error message if you highlight multiple Delphi files in Explorer and then accidentally click one of the files twice in quick succession. This, in effect, performs a double-click on all the files highlighted, and an instance of Delphi is started for each individual file.

You may also get the error message "Module < >s time/date changed. Reload?" in conjunction with this error message.

Only register calling convention allowed in OLE automation section

Possible Cause of Error

You may have specified a calling convention other than Register in a class's Automated section. For example, the following will generate this error message:

```
automated
  procedure blip; stdcall;
```

Quick Fix

Do not specify any calling convention other than Register (the default) in an Automated section.

Additional Information

The Automated section made its debut with Delphi 2 and fell largely into disfavor subsequent to Delphi 2. It is retained primarily for backward compatibility.

Operation not allowed on sorted string list

Possible Cause of Error

You may be attempting an invalid filter operation on a string field. For example, you may have set a TDataset's Filter property to something like:

```
common_name > graphic
```

Quick Fix

Only use logical (as in reasonable) filter expressions. In the above example, a string value is compared with a graphic. This is illogical (does not make sense).

Additional Information

If your sorted string list really needs an operation, take it to Bitbucket General Hospital.

Operation not applicable

Possible Cause of Error

1. You may be developing a multi-tier application and are using an outdated copy of DBClient.DLL

2. You may be attempting to access the RecordCount property without first calling TQuery's Last procedure.

3. You may have included a memo field in a query, for example:

```
SELECT
  STRINGFIELD, INTEGERFIELD, AMEMOFIELD
FROM
  SIMTABLE
```

Quick Fix

1. Upgrade to the latest version of the BDE for your version of Delphi.

2. Call Query.Last before accessing the RecordCount property. For example:

```
. . .
var
  Retrieved: Integer;
begin
  with qryQuarry do
  begin
    Open;
    Last;
    Retrieved := RecordCount;
    . . .
    Close;
  end;
end;
```

3. Remove the memo from the SQL SELECT statement.

Additional Information

Multi-tier ("thin") client applications require DBClient.DLL to be deployed on all machines running the client app.

Operation not supported

Possible Cause of Error

1. If you get this error in connection with a query, it usually indicates that there is something wrong with the syntax of the SQL statement.

2. You may be using parentheses instead of brackets while indexing into an array. For example, the following will generate this error if you have declared an array called Synergy:

```
i := Synergy(0);
```

Quick Fix

1. Examine your SQL statement closely. Consult the documentation for the database you are using. Syntax differs among various implementations.

2. Remember to enclose indexes into arrays in brackets, like this:

```
i := Synergy[0];
```

Additional Information

1. Common SQL syntax errors are:
   ➤ Using single quotes where double quotes are needed (and vice versa).
   ➤ Forgetting to uppercase table names (where this is required by the particular brand of SQL you are using).

Operator not applicable to this operand type

Possible Cause of Error

1. You may have attempted to use an operator applicable to integers on floating-point operands, or vice versa. For example, the following will generate this error message:

```
procedure TForm1.Table1CalcFields(DataSet: TDataSet);
{ all 3 fields are Tfloat fields; "Percentage" is a calculated field }
begin
  Table1Percentage := Table1MySalary div Table1AllTheMoneyInTheWorld;
end;
```

2. You may have gotten the test of a set element backward. For example, you would get this error message if you coded the following:

```
if [dsEdit, dsInsert] in State then
  . . .
```

3. You may have inadvertently used two plus (+) signs to concatenate a string. For example, the following will generate this error message:

```
var
  s:string;
. . .
s := 's'++'t';
```

4. You may have attempted to assign to a dereferenced untyped pointer, like this:

```
. . .
var
  p: pointer;
begin
  p^ := 5;
```

or this:

```
type
  TParty = (Boston, DelFuegos, JGeils);
var
  JustAnotherBand: TParty;
  BradleyDelp: pointer;
begin
  JustAnotherBand:=Boston;
  BradleyDelp^ := JustAnotherBand;
```

5. You may be calling a procedure as if it is a function that returns a Boolean value. For example, you may be calling a procedure named ValidateState like this:

```
if not ValidateState then
```

6. You may have attempted to use the *is* or *as* operators on one or more operands of type Variant. For example, if GoodEnough and WellAndGood are both Variant variables, any of the following will generate this error message:

```
if GoodEnough is WellAndGood then . . .
if GoodEnough is Integer then...
with GoodEnough as WellAndGood do...
with WellAndGood as Boolean do...
```

7. You may have been attempting to assign the result of a Boolean expression that uses the *not* operator to a Boolean variable or property, and neglected to enclose the expression to be tested in parentheses. For example, the following will generate this error message:

```
btnNew.Enabled := not CurrentMode = Restrict;
```

Quick Fix

1. Do not use *div* with float fields; use "/" instead:

```
. . .
Table1Percentage.Value := Table1MySalary.Value /
            Table1AllTheMoneyInTheWorld.Value;
. . .
```

2. Do it this way:

```
if State in [dsEdit, dsInsert] then
    . . .
```

3. Remove the extra plus sign (+) from your code.

4. Use a typed pointer type, like this:

```
procedure ThatWasAGood;
type
  iptr = ^Integer;
var
  i,j: integer;
  p:   pointer;
  q:   iptr;
begin
  p := @I;
  q := p;
  q^ := j;
  i := q^;
end;
```

or this:

```
type
  TParty = (Boston, DelFuegos, JGeils);
var
  JustAnotherBand: TParty;
  TomScholz: ^TParty;
begin
  JustAnotherBand:=Boston;
  TomScholz^ := JustAnotherBand;
```

5. Call the procedure directly or change the procedure to a function which returns a Boolean value.

6. Do not use the *is* or *as* operators on Variant operands.

7. Enclose the Boolean expression test in parentheses, like this:

```
btnNew.Enabled := not (CurrentMode = Restrict);
```

Additional Information

3. Two plus signs (++) are used in the C programming language as an increment operator. Perhaps C++ should be spoken "C incremented" (as opposed to "C plus plus").

6. It is also illegal to use the ^ operator on Variant operands.

   See "Operators" in Delphi help for more information.

Order of fields in record constant differs from declaration

Possible Cause of Error

You may have declared a typed constant (initialized variable) which initializes the members of a record in an order other than that in the record's declaration. For example, the following will generate this error message.

```
Type
  TTresHombres = record
    Z: String;
    Zee: String;
    Top: String;
  end;
var
  TresHombres : TTresHombres = (Zee: 'Billy'; Z: 'Dusty'; Top: 'Frank');
```

Quick Fix

Initialize the values in the same order they appear in the Type (record) declaration:

```
Type
  TTresHombres = record
    Z: String;
    Zee: String;
    Top: String;
  end;
var
  TresHombres : TTresHombres = (Z: 'Dusty'; Zee: 'Billy'; Top: 'Frank');
```

Additional Information

As implied above, typed constants are really initialized variables, although they are sometimes declared in Const sections.

Ordinal type required

Possible Cause of Error

You may have used a non-ordinal type in a location or situation where an ordinal type is required. Any and all of the following will generate this error message:

```
{ a }
type
  GilligansIsland = 'Ginger'..'MaryAnne';
{ b }
var
  i: Integer;
  s: String;
begin
  for i := 0 to ColCount-1 do
    strgrd.Cells[i,s];
{ c }
Type
  GoodViewing = set of string;
{ d }
var
  SixPack: string;
begin
  case SixPack of
  'Pilsner Urquell':    'Czech Republic';
  'Lambic':             'Belgium';
  'Becks':              'Germany';
  'Guinness Stout':     'Ireland';
  'Sprechers':          'USA';
```

Quick Fix

Only use ordinal types in the above situations. For example, all of the following are legal:

```
{ a }
type
  TGilligansIsland = (Ginger, MaryAnne, Professor, Gilligan, Skip,
                      MrHowell, MrsHowell);
{ b }
var
  i,j: Integer;
begin
  for i := 0 to ColCount-1 do
    strgrd.Cells[i,j];
{ c }
Type
  TChoppers = set of byte;
{ d }
procedure GetLabel(WineChoice: TDryRedWine);
var
  Etikett: String;
```

```
begin
  case WineChoice of
  Zinfandel:         Etikett := 'Stevenot';
  CabernetSauvignon:Etikett := 'Sutter Home';
  Burgundy:          Etikett := 'Almaden';
end;
```

Additional Information

There are four ordinal types which are predefined in Object Pascal: Integer, Char, WideChar, and Boolean. Object Pascal also allows the user (programmer) to create/declare user-defined enumerated types, which are another ordinal type.

Out of memory

Possible Cause of Error

1. You may have run out of memory. Verify that your swap file is large enough and that there is still plenty of space on the hard disk.
2. You may have supplied the Format function with too many arguments for it to handle.

Quick Fix

1. Verify that you have enough RAM, your Windows swap file is large enough, and that you have at least 10 percent of the hard drive space free.
2. Break the string you want to format into several strings, and then concatenate the results when you are finished.

Additional Information

See "Memory" and "Format Strings" in Delphi help for more information.

Out of system resources

Possible Cause of Error

You may have too many windows open.

Quick Fix

Where possible, dynamically create forms to minimize the amount of resources used at any given time. For example, to create an About box only when it is needed, attach code like this to the event which you want to use to create the About Box:

```
Form1 := TForm1.Create(Self);
try
  Form1.ShowModal;
finally
  Form1.Free;
end;
```

Additional Information

Remember that all Windows controls that have a handle are considered windows by Windows. You could get this error message from having a slew of buttons, etc., active at the same time.

Overflow in conversion or arithmetic operation

Possible Cause of Error

You may have a corrupt .DCU file.

Quick Fix

Follow these steps to determine which .DCU file is corrupt and then rebuild it:

1. Make backup copies of your .DCU files.
2. Delete a .DCU in the project directory.
3. Recompile the project.
4. Continue steps 2 and 3 (deleting a different .DCU each time, of course) until you no longer get the error message.

Additional Information

The .DCU that you deleted immediately prior to the project compiling without the error is the one that caused the error.

Overloaded procedures must be marked with the 'overload' directive

Possible Cause of Error

You may have attempted to overload a method, but neglected to supply the *overload* directive to one or both of the methods. For example, the following will generate this error message:

```
constructor Create(AOwner: TComponent);
                   overload; override;
constructor Create(AOwner: TComponent;
                   i:integer);
```

Quick Fix

Append the *overload* directive to both methods, like this:

```
constructor Create(AOwner: TComponent);
                   overload; override;
constructor Create(AOwner: Tcomponent;
                   i:integer); overload;
```

Additional Information

> **Note:** Overloaded methods are new with Delphi 4.

See "overload" in Delphi help for more information.

Overriding automated virtual method < > cannot specify a dispid

Possible Cause of Error

You may be attempting to declare a new dispid for an automated procedure you are overriding.

Quick Fix

Use the originally assigned dispid in all descendents.

Additional Information

See "Automated Components" in Delphi help for more information.

Package < > already contains unit < >

Possible Cause of Error

You may be attempting to compile a package which requires (either through the Requires clause or the package list) another package, and both packages (the one you are attempting to compile and the one that it requires and is mentioned in the error message) contain the unit specified in the message.

Quick Fix

Remove the unit mentioned in the error message from one of the packages, or remove the package mentioned in the error message from the Requires clause of the package you are attempting to compile.

Additional Information

Packages which use or are used by one another cannot contain the same unit.

Package < > can't be installed because another package with the same base name is already loaded (< >)

Possible Cause of Error

1. You may have attempted to reinstall a package that has already been installed on your system.
2. You may have attempted to install a component into a package by following these steps:
   a. You selected Component | Install Component.
   b. You selected the Into New Package page.
   c. In the Package File Name combo box, you supplied the name of an existing package into which to install the component.

Quick Fix

1. Refrain from installing the same package multiple times.
2. To install a component into an existing package, select the Into Existing Package page in the Install Component dialog box.

Additional Information

See "Packages | About Packages" in Delphi help for more information.

PACKED not allowed here

Possible Cause of Error

You may be attempting to use the *packed* keyword on a type other than set, array, record, object, class or file. For example, the following will generate this error message:

```
type
  House = Extended;
  CamdenYards = packed House;
```

Quick Fix

Only use the *packed* keyword on set, array, record, object, class or file types.

Additional Information

See "Packed keyword" in Delphi help for more information.

Page Fault in module < > at < >

Possible Cause of Error

You may be attempting to display a form which has been freed. For example, either of the following will generate this error message if the form has been created and then freed:

```
Form1.Show;
Form1.ShowModal;
```

Quick Fix

Search for an open form of the type you want to create with code like the following:

```
var
  i, Chihuahua: Integer;
begin
  Chihuahua := -1;
  for i := 0 to Screen.FormCount-1 do
```

```
      if Screen.Forms[i] is TForm1 then
         Chihuahua := I;
   if Chihuahua >= 0 then
     Screen.Forms[Chihuahua].Show
   else
     begin
       Form1 := TForm1.Create(Self);
       Form1.Show;
   end;
end;
```

Additional Information

See "Access Violation."

Page name cannot be blank

Possible Cause of Error

You may be attempting to use the Component Wizard to create a new component but deleted the entry from the Palette Page drop-down list.

Quick Fix

Enter a new name for the Palette Page entry, or select one from the drop-down list.

Additional Information

The Palette Page is the page on which the component will be installed.

Param < > not found

Possible Cause of Error

You may have removed a parameter from a list, but neglected to update the code that references the parameter. For example, you may have had a SQL statement such as:

```
INSERT INTO ABC.Alphabet
(SQU_ID, LetterCode, ReportedOn, EffectiveDate)
VALUES(:squid, :ltrcode, :sysDate, :effDate')
```

and then taken out the ReportedOn field and the :sysDate parameter, so that it is now:

```
INSERT INTO ABC.Alphabet
(SQU_ID, LetterCode, EffectiveDate)
VALUES(:squid, :ltrcode, :effDate')
```

while the :sysDate parameter is still referenced elsewhere in code, such as:

```
Params.ParamByName('sysDate').AsDateTime := Now;
```

Quick Fix

Remove (or comment out) the reference to the parameter.

Additional Information

Alternatively, you may want to retain the parameter, but supply it a Null value. Given the example above, you could do that this way:

```
INSERT INTO ABC.Alphabet
(SQU_ID, LetterCode, ReportedOn, EffectiveDate)
VALUES(:squid, :ltrcode, NULL, :effDate')
```

> 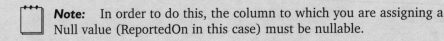 **Note:** In order to do this, the column to which you are assigning a Null value (ReportedOn in this case) must be nullable.

Parameter < > not allowed here due to default value

Possible Cause of Error

You may have attempted to combine two variables in a method declaration with the same default value, like this:

```
procedure PTBoat(i: Integer; j, k: Integer = 0);
```

Quick Fix

Place the second variable (k, in the case above) in its own delimited section, like this:

```
procedure PTBoat(i: Integer; j: Integer = 0;
                            k: Integer = 0);
```

Additional Information

Default parameters are new with Delphi 4.

Passthrough SQL connection must be shared

Possible Cause of Error

You may be using Microsoft Access and attempting to update the results of a query.

Quick Fix

Set the SQLPASSTHRU MODE setting in the BDE Configuration utility for the Access driver to SHARED AUTOCOMMIT (Drivers | Access | SHARED AUTOCOMMIT).

Additional Information

See "Using Passthru SQL" in Delphi help for more information.

Path not found. File < >

Possible Cause of Error

You may be attempting to open or activate a TTable component whose DatabaseName property points to a location for the table in the TableName property that differs from the actual location of the table. The table may have been moved or deleted, or the alias was not set up properly.

Quick Fix

Move the table to the location specified in the error message (that is where Delphi is searching for it).

Alternatively, if the table is in the location where you want it, but the alias is pointing elsewhere (as demonstrated by the error message and the path given), edit the Alias in the BDE Configuration/Administration tool to point the path to the location of the table.

Additional Information

See "TTable" in Delphi help for more information.

Path too long

Possible Cause of Error

You may be using Paradox tables below level 7.

Quick Fix

Promote your table level to 7 using the BDE configuration utility. See "Higher table level required" for instructions on how to do this.

Additional Information

See "Higher table level required" and "Invalid file name."

Pointer type required

Possible Cause of Error

You may be attempting to apply the pointer dereferencing operator (a caret ^) to an identifier that is not a pointer. For example, both of the following will generate the error message under discussion:

```
{ Exhibit A }
procedure ItsNotPoliteTo;
var
  i, j: Integer;
  p: Pointer;
begin
  p := @i;
  i^ := j; //this raises the error, as i is not
           a pointer and cannot be dereferenced
{ Exhibit B }
procedure ItsNotPoliteTo;
var
  i, j: Integer;
  p, q: Pointer;
begin
  p := @i;
  q := i^; //this raises the error, as i is not
           a pointer and cannot be dereferenced
```

Quick Fix

Only use the dereferencing operator (^) with pointers. Here is an example of error-free use of the dereferencing operator:

```
procedure ThanksForThe;
type
  iptr = ^Integer;
var
  i, j: Integer;
  p: Pointer;
  q: iptr;
begin
  p := @I;
  q := p;
  q^ := j;
  i := q^;
end;
```

Additional Information

See "Pointer Types" in Delphi help for some pointers about pointers.

Printing in Progress

Possible Cause of Error

You may be attempting to print a text file, but neglected to close the file. For example, you may be doing something like this:

```
procedure TfmRSXL.btnPrintClick(Sender: Tobject);
var
  Palindrome: System.Text;
begin
  AssignPrn(Palindrome);
  Rewrite(Palindrome);
  Writeln(Palindrome,'SIT ON A POTATO PAN OTIS');
  . . .
```

Quick Fix

Close the text file when you are through with it, like this:

```
procedure TfmRSXL.btnPrintClick(Sender: Tobject);
var
  Palindrome: System.Text;
begin
```

```
AssignPrn(Palindrome);
try
  Rewrite(Palindrome);
  Writeln(Palindrome,'SIT ON A POTATO PAN OTIS');
  . . .
finally
  CloseFile(Palindrome);
end;
end;
```

Additional Information

Besides the Writeln standard procedure, you can also use the Printer's Canvas' TextOut method to print text. See "TextOut method" and "Printers Unit" in Delphi help for more information.

Procedure cannot have a result type

Possible Cause of Error

You may have declared a procedure, but given it a result type. For example, the following will generate this error message:

```
procedure FetchMySlippersFido: TSlippers;
```

Quick Fix

Either replace the *procedure* keyword with the *function* keyword, or delete the result type.

Additional Information

If you need or prefer to use a procedure, but you also want the procedure to modify a value, you can pass a var parameter to the procedure:

```
procedure HotEnoughForYa(var globalWarming: Boolean);
var
  Centigrade: integer;
begin
  Centigrade := StrToInt(Edit1.Text);
  if Centigrade > 77 then
    globalWarming := True;
end;
```

Procedure FAIL only allowed in constructor

Possible Cause of Error

You may have called Fail somewhere other than in a constructor. For example, the following will generate this error message:

```
if Grade in ['D','F'] then Fail;
```

Quick Fix

Only call Fail from within a constructor.

Additional Information

Even within a constructor, do not call Fail as a matter of course.

Procedure or Function name expected

Possible Cause of Error

You may have specified an identifier other than that of a procedure or function in an Exports clause. For example, if Yoopdl is the name of an integer variable, the following in a library (.DLL) file will generate this error message:

```
exports
  yoopdl;
```

Quick Fix

Only procedures and functions from the current unit can be exported. For example, if DutyFree is the name of a procedure or function declared in the .DLL, the following is a valid use of the *exports* keyword:

```
exports
  DutyFree;
```

Additional Information

See ".DLLs" in Delphi help for more information.

Program or unit < > recursively uses itself

Possible Cause of Error

You may have added the name of the current unit to its own Uses clause (in either the Interface or Implementation section). For example, the following will generate this error message:

```
unit TheGooch;
interface
uses
  Windows, Messages, SysUtils, Classes,
  Graphics, Controls, Forms, Dialogs,
  StdCtrls, TheGooch;
```

Quick Fix

Remove the self-referencing declaration.

Additional Information

See "Circular Unit Reference to [< >]."

Project < > raised exception class < > with message < >. Process stopped. Use Step or Run to continue.

Possible Cause of Error

This error message is quite generic. It simply tells you the name of the project that was active when the error message occurred (which should be pretty obvious anyway), the exception class involved (which will be fairly general, such as ERangeError, EInvalidCast, EInvalidPointer, EStringListError) and the exact message the exception class provides for this specific error.

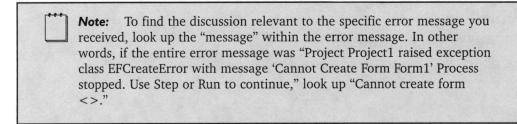

Note: To find the discussion relevant to the specific error message you received, look up the "message" within the error message. In other words, if the entire error message was "Project Project1 raised exception class EFCreateError with message 'Cannot Create Form Form1' Process stopped. Use Step or Run to continue," look up "Cannot create form < >."

Quick Fix

The error message within the error message should give you a good clue about what the actual problem is. For example, the full text of the error message may be something like "Project Manhattan raised exception class ERangeError with message Range Check Error. Process stopped. Use Step or Run to continue." Also, since the integrated bugger will normally stop on the line following the one that caused the error (if you have the Break on Exception option enabled), you can see exactly which statement is currently unacceptable to the compiler.

Additional Information

In order to "continue" by "stepping" or "running," as the message invites you to do, press **F8** to step or **F9** to run. Either one will carry you past the line on which the error occurs and display the error the end user would see in this situation in a message box (the error under discussion is not seen by the end user, only by the developer, and in fact the developer himself will not see it if the Break on Exception toggle is not checked)*.

To return to the design-time environment in order to work on the problem:

Press **Ctrl+F2**.

-OR-

Press **Alt+R**, **E**.

-OR-

Select **Run | Program Reset**.

*To select Break on Exception, follow these steps:

1. Select **Tools | Environment Options**.
2. Select the Preferences page.
3. In the Debugging section, check the Break on Exception check box.

Property < > does not exist in base class

Possible Cause of Error

You may have declared a property without declaring its type. For example, you may have done something like:

```
published
  property ValuesKeepSkyrocketing;
```

Quick Fix

If the property is meant to be new to this class, add the property's data type, as well as read and write fields or methods. For example, the above declaration should be something like:

```
published
    property ValuesKeepSkyrocketing read FOrbes
                write SetSkyrocketingValues;
```

Additional Information

To redeclare an ancestor's property and promote it to a more visible section (from Protected to Public to Published or from Public to Published), all you need to do is enter its name in the section to which you want to promote it—it is not necessary to add the full declaration when you promote an inherited property through redeclaration. (That is why the compiler is expecting to find this property in the base class when you have not provided a full declaration.)

Declaring a property by name only (omitting the property's data type and read and write methods) is the correct way to redeclare a property from an ancestor class. That is why the error message indicates the compiler tried to locate the property in a base (ancestor) class. You would do this if you wanted to promote the property to a more visible specification (such as from Private to Published). For example, if in a descendent of TNotebook you wanted to promote the inherited Brush property from Public to Published, you could simply do this:

```
published
  Brush;
```

If you are declaring a new property, however, you need to specify its data type and read and write methods as shown below if you are using "direct access" to get and set the value in the data field:

```
private
  FRealEstate: Currency;
protected
  { }
public
  { }
published
    property RealEstate: Currency read FRealEstate write FRealEstate;
```

If you are using "direct access" to read the value, but using a mutator (method) to set the value (which you will oftentimes want to do), use the following methodology:

```
private
  FRealEstate: Currency;
  procedure SetRealEstate(Value: Currency);
protected
  { }
public
  { }
published
    property RealEstate: Currency read FRealEstate
                                write SetRealEstate;
```

Provider name was not recognized by the server

Possible Cause of Error

You may have made changes to the server application without rebuilding the entire project.

Quick Fix

Select **Project |Build All**.

Additional Information

See "Multi-tiered Applications" in Delphi help for more information.

Published field < > not a class nor interface type

Possible Cause of Error

You may have attempted to declare a field which is not of a class type in a class's Published section. For example, the following will generate this error message:

```
type
  TScantyClass = class
    published
      eye : Integer;
    end;
```

Quick Fix

Declare properties of class types only. For example, the following will compile, as the class now has an Integer member (Feye):

```
type
  TScantyClass = class
  public
    Feye: Integer;
  published
    property eye: Integer read i;
```

Additional Information

See "Class types" and "Class type compatibility rules" in Delphi help for more information.

Published property <> cannot be of type <>

Possible Cause of Error

You may have attempted to declare a property of a type other than Ordinal, Single, Double, Extended, Comp, String, Set (of up to 16 elements in Delphi 1; up to 32 elements in 32-bit Delphi), or Method Pointer.

Quick Fix

Declare properties of the following types only: Ordinal, Single, Double, Extended, Comp, String, Set (of up to 16 elements in Delphi 1; up to 32 elements in 32-bit Delphi), or Method Pointer.

Additional Information

Among the more popular types which are disallowed are Arrays and Real.

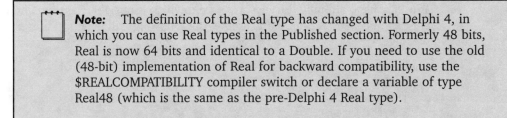

Note: The definition of the Real type has changed with Delphi 4, in which you can use Real types in the Published section. Formerly 48 bits, Real is now 64 bits and identical to a Double. If you need to use the old (48-bit) implementation of Real for backward compatibility, use the $REALCOMPATIBILITY compiler switch or declare a variable of type Real48 (which is the same as the pre-Delphi 4 Real type).

See "Class types" and "Class type compatibility rules" in Delphi help for more information.

Published real property < > must be Single, Double, or Extended

Possible Cause of Error

You may have attempted to publish a property of type Real in Delphi 1, 2, or 3. For example, the following will generate this error message:

```
. . .
private
  FElCamino: Real;
public
  { Public declarations }
published
  property ElCamino: real read FElCamino
                         write SetElCamino;
```

Quick Fix

Change the declaration from Real to Single, Double, or Extended. For example, change the above to:

```
. . .
private
  FElCamino: Single;
public
  { Public declarations }
published
  property ElCamino: Single read FElCamino
                          write SetElCamino;
```

Additional Information

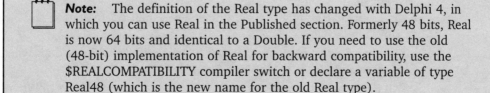

Note: The definition of the Real type has changed with Delphi 4, in which you can use Real in the Published section. Formerly 48 bits, Real is now 64 bits and identical to a Double. If you need to use the old (48-bit) implementation of Real for backward compatibility, use the $REALCOMPATIBILITY compiler switch or declare a variable of type Real48 (which is the new name for the old Real type).

See "Class types" and "Class type compatibility rules" in Delphi help for more information.

PutObject to undefined item

Possible Cause of Error

You may be attempting to assign an object to a string list which does not have a corresponding string.

Quick Fix

Assign a string before attempting to assign a corresponding object. You can assign an empty string at first, if you like.

Additional Information

If you don't need a corresponding string, use a TList instead of a TStringList to store the objects.

Query Is Too Complex

Possible Cause of Error

You may have the TQuery's UpdateMode set to UpWhereAll.

Quick Fix

Change the TQuery's UpdateMode to UpWhereKeyOnly or UpWhereChanged.

Additional Information

The UpdateMode locates the record you have changed, to verify it has not been changed between the time you first read the record and when you attempt to post the changes to the record. It can locate the record based on checking any of the following:

➤ The key field(s) only (which it does when the UpdateMode is UpWhereKeyOnly).

➤ The key field(s) plus any that you have modified (which it does when the UpdateMode is set to UpWhereChanged).

➤ All fields (which it attempts to do if you set UpdateMode to UpWhereAll). Checking all the fields can result in a severe performance hit; thus, the error message.

Query makes no sense

Possible Cause of Error

You may be attempting an insert, but have specified column names rather than values to be inserted. For example, the following will generate this error message:

```
INSERT INTO TEAM VALUES (Catcher, Pitcher, Shortstop, Centerfield)
```

Quick Fix

Specify parameters or literal values in the SQL INSERT statement. For example, to use parameters, do it this way:

```
with qryUpTheMiddle do
begin
  if Active then
    Close;
  SQL.Clear;
  SQL.Add('INSERT INTO TEAM VALUES (:Catcher, Pitcher, :Shortstop,
                                :Centerfield)');
  ParamByName('Catcher').AsString :=
                  edtCatcher.Text;
  ParamByName('Pitcher').AsString :=
                  edtPitcher.Text;
  ParamByName('Shortstop').AsString :=
                  edtShortstop.Text;
  ParamByName('Centerfield').AsString :=
                  edtCenterfield.Text;
  ExecSQL;
end;
```

To specify literal values, replace the SQL.Add line with:

```
SQL.Add('INSERT INTO TEAM VALUES ('Hoiles', 'Mussina', 'Bordick',
                            'Anderson')');
```

Additional Information

Consult the documentation for your database for specifics on its flavor of SQL and its syntax.

Range check error

Possible Cause of Error

1. You may have attempted to index into an array providing a number that is larger than the size of the array. For example, the following would produce the error under discussion:

```
procedure TForm1.Button2Click(Sender: Tobject);
var
  i: integer;
  a: array[1..16] of integer;
begin
  i := 17;
  a[i] := 1; {attempt to assign to element 17 of array a, whose highest
             element is 16}
end;
```

2. You may have attempted to assign a value to a variable that was too large for the data type of the variable. For example, an attempt to assign a negative number or a positive number above 255 to a Byte variable would generate the error message under discussion.

Quick Fix

1. When assigning to an array, verify that the element of the array to which you are attempting to make an assignment is within the array's declared dimensions.

2. Declare variables with data types that contain the entire range of values that the variable may need to hold.

Additional Information

See "Range Checking" in Delphi help for more information.

Read failure. File: < >.val

Possible Cause of Error

You may have attempted to set the Active property of a TTable component which represents a Paradox table to True when the table contains a corrupt .VAL file.

Quick Fix

Delete the table's corresponding .VAL file. For example, if the table is named AGNES, the file you will want to delete and then re-create would be named AGNES.VAL.

Additional Information

.VAL files are created when you specify minimum, maximum, and default values for a Paradox table using Database Desktop.

Instead of specifying these settings in Database Desktop, you can do it directly in Delphi by instantiating the fields in the table* and then setting their DefaultValue, MaxValue, and MinValue properties.

 * To instantiate your table's fields at design time, use the Fields Editor. See "Fields Editor" and "Persistent Field Components" in Delphi help for more information.

Read or Write clause expected but identifier < > found

Possible Cause of Error

You may have neglected to supply a *read* or *write* specifier to the declaration of a property which requires such. For example, since properties which are used to implement interfaces by delegation require a *read* specifier, the following will generate this error message:

```
property SomeInterface: ISomeInterface
        implements ISomeInterface;
```

Quick Fix

Add a *read* specifier along with a corresponding field or function to the declaration, like this:

```
FSomeInterface: ISomeInterface;
property SomeInterface: ISomeInterface read
  FSomeInterface implements ISomeInterface;
```

Additional Information

See the "Implements getter must be register calling convention" error message entry and "Implementing Interfaces by delegation" in Delphi 4 help for more information.

 Note: The *implements* directive is new with Delphi 4.

Record/Key Deleted

Possible Cause of Error

1. You may have set a bookmark, changed the index, and then attempted to return to the location specified by the bookmark.

2. You may have placed a filter on a result set and then altered the definition of the filter by adding or removing a field or fields from the filter.

Quick Fix

1. Do not change indexes while a bookmark is active.

2. Disable the filter, make the edit, and then reenable the filter.

Additional Information

See "bookmarks," "indexes," and "filters" in Delphi help for more information.

Record, object or class type required

Possible Cause of Error

You may have attempted to use the *with* reserved word on a variable. For example, the following will generate this error message:

```
var
  JAndJWentUpTheVerticallyChallengedMountain: Boolean;
. . .
with
  JAndJWentUpTheVerticallyChallengedMountain do
    if True then False;
```

Quick Fix

Specify the variable explicitly, like this:

```
if JAndJWentUpTheVerticallyChallengedMountain = True then
  JAndJWentUpTheVerticallyChallengedMountain := False;
```

Additional Information

Use the *with* reserved word with the types mentioned in the error message, such as TQuery components, etc.

Record Locked by another User

Possible Cause of Error

You may be attempting to edit a record while another user has it locked.

Quick Fix

Try again later to edit the record, first verifying whether the change you intend making has not already been made by the other user.

Additional Information

Only one user can place a write lock on a record. Several users can simultaneously view the same record (each of them placing a read lock in the process), but only one can edit it (for which a write lock is obtained).

Redeclaration of < > hides a member in the base class

Possible Cause of Error

1. You may have created a descendent of a class and declared a property or method that has the same name as one in the class from which you inherited, but you have not used the *override* directive.
2. A new version of a base class may have been installed which has added new properties and/or methods bearing the same name as properties and/or methods in descendent classes.

Quick Fix

1. If you want to inherit the functionality of the original property or method, use the *override* keyword when you declare it. If you want to declare a new property or method, select a name other than one that has already been used in a base class.

2. Rename the property or method in the descendent.

Additional Information

1. If you want to hide a property or method declared in a base class, you can deliberately "screen it out" by declaring a property or method of the same name. See "Method < > hides virtual method of base class < >."

> **Note:** You can prevent this warning message from displaying in Delphi 4 by using the new *reintroduce* keyword. For example, if you want to obscure a method that appears in an ancestor (you do not want to inherit its functionality and do not want to use it at all, but rather code your own routine of the same name), do something like this:
>
> ```
> type
>   first = class
>     public
>       function Petticoat(b,w,h: byte): string;
>                                         virtual;
>   end;
>   second = class(first)
>     public
>       function Petticoat(color: TColor): string;
>                                     reintroduce;
>   end;
> ```

Redeclaration of property not allowed in OLE automation section

Possible Cause of Error

You may have attempted to promote an inherited property to a descendent's Automated section.

Quick Fix

Remove the property from the Automated section. Promote it to another section (such as Public or Published), if desired.

Additional Information

The *automated* visibility specifier made its debut with Delphi 2. It is retained in Delphi 3 and 4 mostly for backward compatibility.

Required package < > not found

Possible Cause of Error

You may be attempting to compile a package which contains a unit (either explicitly by name or implicitly via a unit used by the named unit) in its Requires clause which does not exist or is not in Delphi's search path.

Quick Fix

Ensure that you spelled the name of the required package file correctly, and that any units it references reside in a directory that is in Delphi's search path.

Additional Information

To inspect and/or modify Delphi's search path, select **Tools | Environment Options**, then the Library tab and Library Path combo box. Packages should normally be installed to the \Windows\System directory.

REQUIRES clause is incorrect

Possible Cause of Error

You may have omitted the terminating semicolon to a package source file's Requires clause or added the file extension to the declaration.

Quick Fix

Ensure that the package files listed do not contain file extensions and that the list is terminated with a semicolon.

Additional Information

Any of the following will produce the error message under discussion:

```
requires
  vcl30    { terminating semicolon is missing }
requires
  vcl30,   { spurious comma; semicolon missing }
requires
  vcl30.dpk; { extension not allowed }
```

Ensure that the Requires clause looks like this (it may list multiple packages):

```
requires
  vcl30;
```

Selection contains a component introduced in an ancestor form which cannot be deleted

Possible Cause of Error

You may be attempting to delete an inherited component from a descendent form.

Quick Fix

Do not attempt to remove any components that were inherited from the ancestor.

Additional Information

The error message under discussion points out the necessity to avoid inheriting from classes which contain more than what you want in your descendent. At the same time, if you are creating an ancestor class to be inherited from, such as a form that can be inherited using visual form inheritance (available in 32-bit Delphi), keep it as generic as necessary to allow it to be used in its entirety in descendent forms.

When you inherit from a class or component, you can only add to, but not subtract from, the ancestor. A look at the source code behind a simple ancestor form and its descendent (created using visual form inheritance) shows how this works behinds the scenes.

Here is the source code for a simple ancestor form:

```
unit Unit1;
interface
```

```
uses
  Windows, Messages, SysUtils, Classes,
  Graphics, Controls, Forms, Dialogs;
type
  TForm1 = class(TForm)
    Button1: TButton;
  private
    { Private declarations }
  public
    { Public declarations }
  end;
var
  Form1: Tform1;
implementation
{$R *.DFM}
end.
```

As you can see, the only object that has been added to the form is a TButton, declared as Button1: TButton;.

When you inherit from this form (by selecting File | New, and then selecting the form from the page with the same name as that of the current project), the source code is:

```
unit Unit2;
interface
uses
  Windows, Messages, SysUtils, Classes,
  Graphics, Controls, Forms, Dialogs;
type
  TForm2 = class(TForm1)
  private
    { Private declarations }
  public
    { Public declarations }
  end;
var
  Form2: Tform2;
implementation
{$R *.DFM}
end.
```

As you can see, there is no explicit declaration for a TButton in the descendent class. However, it is implicit in the TForm2 = class(TForm1) declaration, as this is saying, in effect, that TForm2 is inheriting everything from TForm1 (including the button). If you were allowed to remove anything from TForm2 that was inherited from TForm1, the above declaration would no longer be valid, and the link of inheritance would be broken.

Server Execution Failed

Possible Cause of Error

You may have attempted to set the Connect property of a TDCOMConnection, TOLEEnterprise, or TRemoteServer component to True without having specified a valid ServerName or ServerGUID property.

Quick Fix

Supply a valid ServerName or ServerGUID property for a server that has been registered on your machine.

Additional Information

> **Note:** The MIDAS components are only provided with Delphi 3 Client/Server or higher versions of Delphi.

Session name missing

Possible Cause of Error

You may be attempting to set a TSession component's Active property to True without first providing a value for its SessionName property.

Quick Fix

Either provide a value for the TSession component's SessionName property or set its AutoSessionName property to True.

Additional Information

Do not confuse the TSession component's Name and SessionName properties. The Name property, as with all components, refers to the name of the component itself. A TSession component's SessionName property is the name of the session that TDatabase and TDataset (TTable, TQuery, and TStoredProc in all versions of Delphi; TClientDataSet in Delphi Client/Server versions 3 and 4; TNestedTable in Delphi 4) components refer to via their own SessionName properties to show which session they are linked to (useful in multi-threaded applications, which may contain multiple sessions).

So the TSession component provides a SessionName either directly (when you enter the name at design time or provide one in code) or indirectly (when you set the AutoSessionName property to True), and TDatabase and TDataset components select an available SessionName from a combo box.

Share not loaded. It is required to share local files

Possible Cause of Error

Your SYSTEM.INI or AUTOEXEC.BAT file may be missing a line that is required by the BDE (Share is not loaded).

Quick Fix

Add **DEVICE=*vshare** to the [386Enh] section of your SYSTEM.INI file or add **SHARE.EXE** to your AUTOEXEC.BAT file, and then reboot.

Additional Information

 Note: This error message corresponds to "An error occurred while attempting to initialize the Borland Database Engine (error $2C09)."

To edit the SYSTEM.INI file from Windows Explorer, follow these steps:

1. Locate SYSTEM.INI. It should be in the Windows directory (C:\Windows).
2. Double-click it to open it.
3. Locate the [386Enh] section.
4. Add **DEVICE=*vshare** if it is missing below the [386Enh] section.
5. Close SYSTEM.INI, saving your changes.
6. Reboot.

To edit the AUTOEXEC.BAT file from Windows Explorer, follow these steps:

1. Locate and then right-click on **AUTOEXEC.BAT**. It should be in the root directory (C:\).
2. Select **Edit** from the context menu.
3. At the bottom of your AUTOEXEC.BAT file, enter **SET SHARE=C:\dos\share /F:4096 /L:40**.
4. Reboot.

To edit AUTOEXEC.BAT from a DOS window, follow these steps:

1. Enter **Edit autoexec.bat** and press the **Enter** key.

2. Enter **SET SHARE=C:\dos\share /F:4096 /L:40** at the bottom of the file.

3. Save the file by selecting **File | Exit** and then **Yes** to save changes.

4. Type **autoexec** and press the **Enter** key.

Slice standard function is only allowed as open array argument

Possible Cause of Error

You may have called the Slice function but are not sending the result to a procedure or function which expects an open-array argument. For example, the following will generate this error message:

```
procedure Chop;
begin
  Slice(Dice,2);
```

Quick Fix

Slice can only be used to send a subset of an open array to a procedure or an array expecting an open-array argument. Here is an example of how Slice can be used:

```
var
  Form1: TForm1;
  pare: array[0..11] of integer;
. . .
function Dice(EightWillSuffice: array of integer): integer;
var
  i,sum: Integer;
begin
  sum := 0;
  for i := low(EightWillSuffice) to
          high(EightWillSuffice) do
    sum := sum + EightWillSuffice[i];
  Result := sum;
end;
procedure Peel;
begin
  Dice(Slice(pare,3));
end;
```

Additional Information

See "Slice" in Delphi help for more information.

> **Note:** Slice made its debut with Delphi 2.

SQL is too complex

Possible Cause of Error

You may be attempting to post records with the UpdateMode property of the corresponding TTable or TQuery set to UpWhereAll.

Quick Fix

Use the UpWhereChanged or UpWhereKeyOnly UpdateMode setting instead of UpWhereAll.

Additional Information

The UpWhereAll UpdateMode setting can (internally) create a long, complex SQL statement. Although it is, of course, not <u>wrong</u> to use the UpWhereAll UpdateMode setting, some database drivers are not robust enough to handle it. See "UpdateMode" in Delphi help for more information.

Stack overflow

Possible Cause of Error

1. You may have declared too many variables (or a few very large variables, such as arrays) in a local procedure or function in a unit compiled with the {$S+} (stack checking on) compiler directive.
2. You may have declared too many global variables (or a few very large global variables).
3. You may be using deep recursion (intentional) or have an infinite loop (unintentional) in your program.
4. You may be passing an entire (large) record as an argument.

5. You may be using too many large procedures and/or functions that call each other.

6. You may be passing large parameters by value.

Quick Fix

1. Reduce the number of variables you are using or increase the size of the stack. You can increase stack size using the {$M} compiler directive. The syntax for using it is:

   ```
   {$M minstacksize,maxstacksize}
   ```

   The default values are 16384 and 1048576. The first figure is the initial committed size of the stack; the second is the total reserved size of the stack. To double the initial committed size and leave the total reserved size as is, add the following to the top of your unit:

   ```
   {$M 32768, 1048576}
   ```

2. Pare down the size and number of your global variables.

3. If you are not deliberately using recursion, check for code in event handlers such as OnChange where you may causing a change, thus tripping the event again, which causes the change again, which trips the event again, etc., ad nauseum.

4. Pass pointers to records rather than passing the records themselves.

5. Break up large procedures and/or functions into smaller ones.

6. Pass large variables as variable or constant parameters.

Additional Information

3. Getting this error while deliberately using recursion is more of a problem in Delphi 1 than 32-bit Delphi, although infinite recursion (such as described above in an OnChange event) will be a problem in 32-bit Delphi/Windows also.

5. If a procedure or function takes up more than one screen, it would be good to separate it out to multiple smaller procedures.

6. Parameters passed as var or const take up only four bytes each, as they are pointers.

   See "Stack Overflow" in Delphi help for more information.

Statement expected, but expression of type < > found

Possible Cause of Error

You may be attempting to call the Abort method from the SysUtils unit, but also have the dbiProcs or BDE unit in your Uses section.

Quick Fix

Qualify your call to Abort by prepending the name of the unit:

```
SysUtils.Abort;
```

Additional Information

Both the SysUtils and the dbiProcs (Delphi 1)/BDE (32-bit Delphi) contain an Abort method. In these types of situations, be specific/explicit about which one you intend to use by prepending the name of the unit in which the procedure or function you want to use resides to the name of the procedure or function.

STORED clause not allowed in OLE automation section

Possible Cause of Error

You may be attempting to use the Stored clause in the Automated section.

Quick Fix

Remove the Stored clause from the Automated section.

Additional Information

Delphi 2 and above has five visibility specifiers: *Private, Protected, Public, Published,* and *Automated* (Delphi 1 does not contain the *Automated* specifier). A class's properties can specify a storage specifier of *stored, default,* or *nodefault.* These storage specifiers are not allowed in the Automated section, though.

> **Note:** The *index* specifier, which allows multiple properties to share the same access methods, is also not allowed in an Automated section.

Stream Read Error

Possible Cause of Error

You may be attempting to load a form created in 32-bit Delphi in Delphi 1.

Quick Fix

If it is feasible, upgrade to a 32-bit version of Delphi, preferably the newest version (Delphi 4 at the time of writing). If you must persist in using Delphi 1 with the form created with 32-bit Delphi, remove all features specific to 32-bit Delphi from the form (.DFM) file. Load it into a text editor (such as Notepad) to do so.

Additional Information

Some of the things that make 32-bit Delphi form (.DFM) files "foreign" to Delphi 1 is long strings, the TCollection type, and form inheritance.

String constant truncated to fit STRING[ ]

Possible Cause of Error

You may have assigned a string to a variable which is smaller than the size of the string you are attempting to assign. For example, the following will give you this error message:

```
var
  s: String[3];
begin
  s := 'string';
```

Quick Fix

Redeclare the size of the string, or assign a string that will fit into the variable. For example, either of the following solutions will work:

```
var
  s: String[6];
begin
  s := 'string';
```

-OR-

```
var
  s: String[3];
```

```
begin
  s := 'str';
```

Additional Information

See "Strings" in Delphi help for more information.

String [literal]s may have at most 255 elements

Possible Cause of Error

1. You may have declared a short string with more than 255 elements. For example, the following declaration will generate this error message:

```
var
  s: string[256];
```

2. You may have assigned a string of more than 255 elements to a short string. For example, if you declare a ShortString variable:

```
var
  s: ShortString;
```

and then assign to it a string that is longer than 255 elements, this error message will be the result.

3. You may have assigned a string longer than 255 elements on a single line in the code editor (even with long strings this error will occur in this situation).

4. You may have declared a string constant with more than 255 characters. For example, if you assigned the text of the Gettysburg address in its entirety to a string constant, you would get this error message.

Quick Fix

1. Make sure that the size you declare when using a ShortString is less than 256.

2. Do not assign a string longer than 255 elements to a ShortString variable.

3. Break up the string over several lines using the + string concatenation operator.

4. Reduce the size of the string constant or declare several constants and concatenate them, like this:

```
const
  SomewhatLong = '{A string constant < 256}';
  KindOfLong   = '{A string constant < 256}';
  SortOfLong   = '{A string constant < 256}';
  WorkAroundVeryLongString = SomewhatLong + KindOfLong + SortOfLong;
```

Additional Information

See "String Types" in Delphi help for more information.

Syntax error in query. Incomplete query clause

Possible Cause of Error

You may be attempting to "access" an Access table which has spaces in its name, but have neglected to encase the table name in brackets. For example, you may have done something like:

```
SELECT *
FROM
  "ROUND TABLE"
```

Quick Fix

Enclose the table name in brackets, like this:

```
SELECT *
FROM
  [ROUND TABLE]
```

Additional Information

See Delphi's "Localsql.hlp" as well as SQL documentation for your particular database for vendor-specific SQL syntax.

Table cannot be opened for exclusive use

Possible Cause of Error

You may be attempting to carry out an action on an open table which requires that the table be closed before the action can be carried out. For example, you cannot empty a table (by calling TTable's EmptyTable method) or add indexes to an open table.

Quick Fix

First close the table by calling TTable's Close method, or set its Active property to False. Then you can carry out the action, after which you can call TTable's Open method or set the Active property to True.

Additional Information

Open is a method of TTable, which you call like this:

```
Table1.Open;
```

Active is a property of TTable, which you set like this:

```
Table1.Active := True;
```

If you try to add a second index on the same field in code, this error message is produced. For example, the second line in the following code snippet produces this error:

```
Table1.AddIndex('LastNameAsc', 'LastName', []);
Table1.AddIndex('LastNameDesc', 'LastName', [ixDescending]);
```

Table corrupt—other than header

Possible Cause of Error

You may be using Paradox tables on an NT network and have not set Local-Share to True on each of the clients and/or have opportunistic locking enabled.

Quick Fix

Set Local Share to True (on the System page of the BDE Configuration utility) on all the clients and/or disable opportunistic locking.

Additional Information

To disable opportunistic locking, you need to edit (or create, if necessary) two system registry settings by following these steps:

1. Select **Start | Run** from the Windows 95 desktop.
2. Enter **regedit** in the Open combo box and select the **OK** button.
3. Navigate to HKEY_LOCAL_MACHINE\System\CurrentControlSet \Services\LanmanServer\Parameters.
4. Edit or add the key (Name) **EnableOplock** and set its value (Data) to 0.
5. Edit or add the key (Name) **UseOpportunisticLocking** and set its value (Data) to 0.
6. Reboot for the setting to take effect.

Table does not exist

Possible Cause of Error

1. You may have an error in your SQL statement. Check the spelling in TQuery's SQL property, as you may have misspelled the name of the table.

2. You may have attempted to set a TTable's Active property to True without providing a valid DatabaseName property.

3. You may be attempting to use the TBatchMove component with its Update-Mode property set to anything other than Copy, and the Destination TTable does not correspond to an existing table in the location specified by the DatabaseName property.

4. You may be attempting to access Oracle tables via a SQL statement (using TQuery) with the RequestLive property set to True, but have neglected to uppercase the table names.

5. You may be attempting to access MS SQL Server tables, and have neglected to prepend dbo. to the table name. For example, you may be using the following type of SQL statement:

```
SELECT *
FROM
    Cooper
```

6. You may be attempting to access a table that is active in another thread or connection.

Quick Fix

1. If you have misspelled the table name, edit the SQL statement.

2. Provide the name of a valid Alias as the TTable component's DatabaseName property.

3. Verify that the Dataset you have specified as the Source (TQuery, TStoredProc, or TTable) exists and that the TTable you have specified as the Destination exists.

4. Uppercase table names when accessing Oracle.

5. Prepend dbo. to the table name. For example:

```
SELECT *
FROM
    dbo.Cooper
```

6. Verify that the table you are attempting to access is open in the current thread (if your application is a multi-threaded app). Check the SQLPASSTHRU MODE for your database driver in the BDE Configuration utility. If it is set to NOT SHARED, you may be attempting to read a temporary table from one connection which is available through another connection.

Additional Information

    5.   dbo stands for "database owner."

Table does not support this operation

Possible Cause of Error

    1.   You may be using SQL Anywhere and TTable's RecordCount method on a table which contains memo fields.

    2.   You may be accessing MS SQL Server tables and neglected to prepend dbo. to the table name. For example, you may have a SQL statement like:

```
SELECT *
FROM UHF
```

    3.   You may be attempting to call Refresh on a TQuery against a SQL Server (Oracle, MS SQL Server, Interbase, etc) database with a complex query or one that involves joins.

Quick Fix

    1.   If you are calling RecordCount to determine whether its count is 0, you could check instead if the table is simultaneously at the beginning and end of the file, like this:

```
if (tblHollow.bof) and (tblHollow.eof) then
```

If you want to know how many records are in the table, you can use a SQL statement such as:

```
SELECT COUNT(*)
FROM MONTECRISTO
```

    2.   Prepend dbo. to the table name; for example:

```
SELECT *
FROM dbo.UHF
```

    3.   Call the TDataset's Close and then Open methods instead of Refresh if you get this problem with Refresh.

Additional Information

See your database-specific documentation for the particular peculiarities regarding the flavor of SQL it supports.

Table is busy

Possible Cause of Error

1. You may have attempted to add an index in code (using TTable's AddIndex method) without having exclusive access to the table.

2. You may have attempted to copy records from one table to another using the TBatchMove component in batCopy mode while the destination table was open.

3. You may have attempted to open a table in Exclusive mode when another user had the table open.

4. You may have a table open in the IDE (or in Database Desktop), and are subsequently attempting to open it at run time in your project.

5. You may be calling TTable's EmptyTable method and the table is active/open.

Quick Fix

1. First close the TTable and set its Exclusive property to True.

2. Close the destination table before copying records to it. You can do this by calling TTable's Close method or by setting the TTable component's Active property to False.

3. Enclose the call setting the Exclusive property to True in a *try...except* block so you can provide the user a message informing him of the problem if it is impossible to use the table exclusively due to another user already having the table open.

4. Set the Active property of the TTable in the IDE to False.

5. Call a TTable's Close method or set its Active property to False before attempting to call EmptyTable.

Additional Information

Multiple users can view the same information simultaneously, but multiple users cannot edit the same information simultaneously.

5. You must have exclusive use of the table before calling EmptyTable.

Attempting to set the table's Exclusive property to True while the Active property is True produces the error message "Cannot perform this operation on an open dataset." See that entry for more information.

> **Note:** It is a good practice to open tables as they are needed (at run time), and close them when they are no longer needed. At the latest, close them when your application terminates. You can do this by cycling through the components, and setting each table's Active property to False, like this:
>
> ```
> procedure TForm1.FormClose(Sender: TObject; var
>                            Action: TCloseAction);
> var
>   i: integer;
> begin
>   for i := 0 to ComponentCount-1 do
>     if Components[i] is TTable then
>       TTable(Components[i]).Close;
>   {Alternatively, you can replace the last line
>   with: TTable(Components[i]).Active := False;}
> end;
> ```
>
> Of course, you could always do it this way, too:
>
> ```
> procedure TForm1.FormClose(Sender: TObject; var
>                            Action: TCloseAction);
> begin
>   Table1.Close;
>   Table2.Close;
>   {etc. ad nauseum}
> end;
> ```
>
> but this can become a maintenance chore. The first example shown will always work no matter how many TTables you add or remove from the form.

If another user has a table open in Exclusive mode and you attempt to open it, you will receive the "File is Locked" error message. See "File is Locked. Table: <> User: <>" for specific information.

Table is full

Possible Cause of Error

You may be exceeding the maximum capacity of a Paradox table.

Quick Fix

You will have to either increase the block size in the BDE Configuration/Administration utility or upsize your database to a SQL server database such as Interbase (or Oracle, MS SQL Server, etc).

To increase the block size in the BDE Configuration utility, change the Block Size parameter in the Drivers | Paradox page/node of the BDE Configuration utility. All future Paradox tables will reflect the new setting. To apply the settings to an existing table, create a new table, borrowing the structure of the existing table, and then copy the tables from the original table to the new one.

> **Note:** If you only need to increase the block size of the table you are currently working with (the one for which you received this error message), you can download a utility from Borland's web site to do so. Point your browser at:
>
> www.inprise.com/devsupport/bde/utilities.html
>
> and look under 32 Bit Utilities | Paradox Table Alter.

Additional Information

> **Note:** This is BDE error $2507.

Paradox tables can be a maximum of 65,536 (64 K) blocks. The default block size is 2048 (2 K), so the default maximum size of a Paradox table is 128 MB.

Increasing the block size to 32,768 (32 KB) will allow you to create 2 GB tables.

The following table shows the maximum table size based on the BDE Configuration utility/administrator Block Size setting:

Block size	Maximum table size
2 K	128 MB
4 K	256 MB
8 K	512 MB
16 K	1024 MB
32 K	2048 MB

> **Note:** If you are using Level 3 or 4 Paradox tables, the largest block size you can use is 4096/4 KB. 16 KB and 32 KB are available in Level 5 and 7 (there is no level 6).

Table is read only

Possible Cause of Error

1. You may have attempted to call a TTable's Edit or Delete method with the TTable's ReadOnly property set to True.

2. You may be attempting to edit the results of a query that joins tables.

3. You may be attempting to edit the results of a query on one table with RequestLive set to False.

Quick Fix

1. First set the ReadOnly property to False, then call the Edit or Delete method. Ensure that the TTable's Active property is set to False before attempting to set the ReadOnly property.

2. Use Cached Updates to edit the result set of a joined query.

3. Set RequestLive to True.

Additional Information

TTable's Delete method deletes the current record only. To delete all the records from a table, use the EmptyTable method. To delete not only all the records, but also the table itself (the structure), use the DeleteTable method. The TTable must be closed first before calling DeleteTable.

To selectively delete records that match a certain criteria, use a TQuery component and set its SQL property based on the following:

```
DELETE FROM Expendable {to delete all records}
DELETE FROM OutstandingDebts
WHERE Amount > 10 { to delete all records with a value greater
                    than 10 in the amount column }
```

Table is not indexed

Possible Cause of Error

You may be attempting to create a secondary index on a Paradox table which does not have a primary index.

Quick Fix

Create a primary index on a table before you create a secondary index. You can do this either using Database Desktop or in code. To create the primary index using Database Desktop, click in the Key column (or press the space bar) of the first 1..*n* columns of the table.

To create a primary index in code, use the following as an example:

```
AddIndex('Stadt','Stadt',[ixPrimary]);
```

Additional Information

If the primary key is on one column only, it must be on the first column. If it is a composite key, it must begin with the first column and include every column between the first and last columns you want to use (for example, if you want to use the first and third columns as a composite key, you must also use the second column). If you are adding the index in code, separate the columns that comprise the composite primary key with semicolons, like this:

```
AddIndex('DogfaceInterface','Name; Rank;
         SerialNumber',[ixPrimary]);
```

See "Secondary Indexes" in Delphi help for more information.

Table or View does not exist

Possible Cause of Error

1. You may not have rights to view the table or view you are attempting to access.

2. You may be using a query with its RequestLive property set to True and have not used uppercase in specifying the table name. For example, the following may generate this error message:

```
SELECT * FROM Round
```

Quick Fix

1. If you have the rights to assign rights, give yourself rights to view the table or view—whew! If you do not have rights to assign rights, see your database administrator.

2. If the TQuery component's RequestLive property is set to True, use uppercase when specifying the table name. For example:

```
SELECT * FROM ROUND
```

Additional Information

Consult the documentation specific to the database type you are using regarding accepted syntax for the flavor of SQL used with the particular database. For example, Oracle uses PL/SQL, Microsoft MS SQL Server uses Transact SQL, etc.

TActiveFormX declaration missing or incorrect

Possible Cause of Error

You may have changed the name of a CoClass prior to changing the name of the form.

Quick Fix

Edit the form (.DFM) file by right-clicking on the form and selecting View As Text from the context menu. Find the line:

```
object ActiveFormX: TActiveFormX
```

and change it to the name of your instance variable and its class type, for example:

```
object Whatever: TWhatever
```

Then right-click on the .DFM and select **View As Form** from the context menu.

Additional Information

See "ActiveX Applications" in Delphi help for more information.

Text after final END

Possible Cause of Error

You may have some text below the final *end*. (The final end has a terminating period rather than a terminating semicolon.)

Quick Fix

Remove the offending lines.

Additional Information

This error sometimes continues even after deleting text below the final *end*, but does not prevent compilation. In this case, "ignored by compiler" is appended to the error message.

The <> method referenced by <>.<> does not exist. Remove the reference?

Possible Cause of Error

You may have removed a method from your code, but the form retains a reference to it on its events page.

Alternatively, you may be attempting to assign an event handler to an event which may indeed exist (despite the error message), but the event handler is not declared in the Published part of the type declaration.

Quick Fix

Select **Yes** to remove the reference to the code that no longer exists.

Additional Information

If you select Yes, the reference to the method will be removed from the form's events page (it will no longer be "hooked" to any particular event).

If you remove a method from the Implementation part without removing its declaration in the Interface part, you get an "unsatisfied forward" error message. If you remove the declaration from the Interface part without removing the method from the Implementation part, you get an "undeclared identifier" error message. If you remove both (but have attached the method to an event in the Object Inspector), the above message displays when you attempt to compile.

In a regular form or unit .PAS file, there is no explicit "published" declaration. All of the components and methods you add are automatically added to the Published section, but it is not designated as being such. Everything that is not explicitly designated otherwise (i.e., *private* or *public*) is published. The methods you use as event handlers must be declared in the Published section for them to produce RTTI (run-time type information) and thus be available as appropriate methods to which an event can be assigned. The skeleton of this type of file as produced by Delphi when you add your first form to a project looks like this:

```
unit Unit1;
interface
uses
  Windows, Messages, SysUtils, Classes,
  Graphics, Controls, Forms, Dialogs;
type
  TForm1 = class(TForm) {This is the published section}
  private
    { Private declarations }
  public
    { Public declarations }
  end;
var
  Form1: TForm1;
implementation
{$R *.DFM}
end.
```

After you add a button and an event handler for it, your .PAS file looks like this:

```
unit Unit1;
interface
uses
  Windows, Messages, SysUtils, Classes,
  Graphics, Controls, Forms, Dialogs;
type
  TForm1 = class(TForm) {This is the published section}
    Button1: Tbutton;     {Components you place on the form are placed
                            in the published section}
    procedure Button1Click(Sender: Tobject);
  {Event handlers you create are also placed in the published section}
  private
    { Private declarations }
  public
    { Public declarations }
  end;
var
  Form1: TForm1;
implementation
{$R *.DFM}
end.
```

This is in contrast to a component .PAS file, which contains explicit Private, Protected, Public, and Published sections. The following code is what you will start with if you use the Component Wizard to create a new component based on the TStringGrid component:

```
unit StringGrid1;
interface
uses
  Windows, Messages, SysUtils, Classes,
  Graphics, Controls, Forms, Dialogs, Grids;
type
  TStringGrid1 = class(TStringGrid)
  private
    { Private declarations }
  protected
    { Protected declarations }
  public
    { Public declarations }
  published
    { Published declarations }
  end;
procedure Register;
implementation
procedure Register;
begin
  RegisterComponents('Samples', [TStringGrid1]);
end;
end.
```

The < > method referenced by < >.< > has an incompatible parameter list. Remove the reference?

Possible Cause of Error

You may have changed the method's original parameter list (the one in the Interface part).

Quick Fix

Modify the method's parameter list in the Interface part so that it matches the one in the Implementation part.

Additional Information

If you select Yes, the reference to the method will be removed from the form's events page (it will no longer be "hooked" to any particular event).

The Edit Buffer of < > is marked read-only

Possible Cause of Error

You may be attempting to edit a locked file. For example, you may be attempting to make changes to a file which you checked out of a file control system such as PVCS as "read only."

Quick Fix

Check the file out as writeable, and then make your changes.

Additional Information

You may be indirectly attempting to edit the file. For example, you may have attempted to place a component on a form, which then attempts to write to both the unit (.PAS) and underlying form (.DFM) file.

The Master Source property of < > must be linked to a DataSource

Possible Cause of Error

You may have attempted to set the MasterFields property of a TTable component without first having set the MasterSource property.

Quick Fix

Select a TDataSource component as the TTable's MasterSource property, and then set the MasterFields property.

Additional Information

See "Master/Detail forms" in Delphi help for more information.

The OLE control may possibly require support libraries that are not on the current search path or are not present on your system

Possible Cause of Error

You may be attempting to install a 16-bit VBX (Visual Basic Control) in 32-bit Delphi.

Quick Fix

Install 16-bit VBXs in Delphi 1 only (not in 32-bit Delphi).

Additional Information

For 32-bit Delphi (and Windows in general, for that matter), you will need 32-bit OCXs (as opposed to VBXs).

The package already contains unit named < >

Possible Cause of Error

You are attempting to install a component into a package which already contains a component with the same name.

Quick Fix

Check whether the unit you are trying to install is the same as the one which already exists in the package (as opposed to a component with different functionality but the same name).

If the unit is indeed the very same, simply desist from trying to install it a second time. If it is different in functionality but not name, rename the unit you are attempting to install and then try again.

Additional Information

Like most things, packages have advantages and disadvantages. First the bad news: Packages add complexity to the development and deployment process and introduce more potential problems. One of Delphi 1's selling points (over Visual Basic, in particular) was that you could create a "one file" solution: All you needed to deploy was a single .EXE. (Of course, this does not take into account database applications, where other files need to be distributed.) Packages force you to deliver multiple files to a user.

The good news about packages is they can save RAM and hard disk space if the target machine has multiple applications written in Delphi installed on it. Rather than having Delphi's core functionality built into each executable, packages allow you to deploy a "thin executable" which calls packages (Delphi-specific .DLLs) as needed to implement its functionality.

The package already requires a package named < >

Possible Cause of Error

You may have attempted to add a package to another package's Required section which has already been specified in that package's Required section.

Quick Fix

Select **OK**. The package is not added a second time.

Additional Information

See "Packages" in Delphi help for more information.

The path entered does not exist

Possible Cause of Error

You may have selected the Finish button in the Application Wizard without specifying a valid path in the Enter the path in which to store this application edit box.

Quick Fix

Enter or navigate to (using the **Browse** button) a valid path wherein you want to save the application.

Additional Information

The path must not only be on a valid drive and be a valid name, but it also must exist—Delphi will not create the directory for you if it does not already exist.

The project already contains a form or module named < >

Possible Cause of Error

You may be attempting to give a form or unit the same name as one that is already part of the project. It may be that you are trying to give a form the same filename as the component name you assigned it (or the name Delphi assigned it by default) in the Object Inspector (for example, Form1).

Quick Fix

Specify a unique name for the form or unit.

Additional Information

The name you assign a form in the Object Inspector is the name of the class (Form1 by default). The class becomes an object at run time, when it is instantiated.

The name under which you save the unit is the filename (Unit1 by default). This is the name you will see in Open and Save dialog boxes, Windows Explorer, etc.

In code, refer to the form by its class/object name, except in the Uses section. For example, here is a simple form's declaration:

```
unit Unit1; {default file name of first form or unit in project}
interface
uses
  Windows, Messages, SysUtils, Classes, Graphics,
     Controls, Forms, Dialogs;
type
  TForm1 = class(TForm) {default class name of first form in project}
  private
  { Private declarations }
  public
  { Public declarations }
  end;
var
  Form1: Tform1; {default object variable and class name of first form
                  in project}
implementation
uses    {optional auxiliary uses section; useful for avoiding "Circular
          Unit Reference" errors}
```

```
Unit2;  {refer to other forms in uses sections by their file names
        (not component names)}
{$R *.DFM}
end.
```

The search string cannot be blank

Possible Cause of Error

You may have attempted to search for a string in the Delphi IDE using Search | Find, but neglected to enter a string for which to search in the Text to Find combo box.

Quick Fix

Enter a string for which to search.

Additional Information

To have the text at the cursor automatically entered in the Find Text dialog's Text to Find combo box on activating the dialog, follow these steps:

1. Select **Tools | Environment Options**.
2. Select the Editor page.
3. Check the Find Text at Cursor check box.

The Find Text dialog allows many parameters to be set. Select its Help button to learn the nuances of these.

The selected bitmap is larger than 24x24

Possible Cause of Error

While creating a component template, you may have attempted to save a palette icon bitmap that is too large to be displayed properly in the space allotted for bitmaps on the component palette page.

Quick Fix

Select a bitmap that is no larger than 24 pixels square as the palette icon bitmap to represent the component template.

Additional Information

The default icon for a component template is that of a) the first component selected if you selected the components using the mouse and the Shift key, or b) the left or topmost component if you selected the components by dragging over them with the mouse.

If you do not want to use the default icon, you can create one (remember to make it no larger than 24 x 24 pixels) in the Image Editor or another bitmap-manipulating program such as Microsoft Paint.

To create an icon with the Image Editor, follow these steps:

1. Select **Tools | Image Editor**.
2. Select **File | New... | Bitmap file** (not Icon file, although the Component Template Information dialog box calls it a Palette Icon).
3. Set both Width and Height to 24.
4. Select **View | Zoom In** up to four times (depending on your preference).
5. Create the bitmap you want to use as your palette "icon."
6. Save the bitmap file.

The transaction isolation level must be dirty read for local databases

Possible Cause of Error

You may have set a TDatabase component's TransIsolation property to either tiReadCommitted or tiRepeatableRead while using a "local," or desktop, database such as Paradox or dBASE.

Quick Fix

Change the TDataBase's TransIsolation property to tiDirtyRead while using local tables (such as Paradox and dBASE).

Additional Information

Dirty Read displays all changes as they occur (even if another user is making changes that may or may not be later committed). Most SQL server databases, such as Interbase, Oracle, MS SQL Server, etc., do not support Dirty Read. If you set the TransIsolation property to Dirty Read while using these databases, they will promote this setting to the next available one (the least restrictive one available on the particular platform).

Repeatable Read guarantees that the user's view of a record will not change while he views it. Even if another user edits (and even commits) the record, the original snapshot of the record continues to be displayed.

Read Committed only displays changes made to records after the transaction of which the change is a part has committed.

See "TransIsolation" in Delphi help for more information.

The type library has syntax errors

Possible Cause of Error

You have probably omitted something necessary from the Type Library, such as an interface for a CoClass.

Quick Fix

Based on the more specific error displayed in the status bar at the bottom of the Type Library editor, correct the syntax error.

Additional Information

An error which may be displayed in the Type Library's status bar following the error message under discussion (which displays in a message box) is "A CoClass must implement at least one interface." Refer to the discussion of that error message for specific information.

This form of method call only allowed for class methods

Possible Cause of Error

1. You may have been attempting to call a normal method using the class type rather than an instance (variable) of the type. This is only allowed for class methods—not normal methods.
2. You may have forgotten to prepend the class type to the name of a method.
3. You may be attempting to call an abstract method from within the unit in which it was declared.

Quick Fix

1. Where necessary, ensure that you use an instance, or variable, of the type, rather than the type name itself.

2. Verify that you are prepending the class type to the method name. For example, if you have declared a method ToMyMadness as part of a form's type declaration, the following definition in the Implementation part will produce the error message under discussion:

```
procedure ToMyMadness(var Dogweight: Byte);
begin
  if dogweight < 100 then Kick(hard) else Run;
end;
```

This works fine (prepending the class name to the method name):

```
procedure TForm1.ToMyMadness(var Dogweight: Byte);
begin
  if dogweight < 100 then Kick(hard) else Run;
end;
```

This may be as simple a fix as deleting the T from the beginning of the class type's name. For example, if you try this (attempting to dynamically create an About box):

```
TAboutBox := TAboutBox.Create(Application);
try
  TAboutBox.ShowModal;
finally
  TAboutBox.Free;
end;
```

you will receive the error message under discussion. You must do it this way (remove the T from the variable name):

```
AboutBox := TAboutBox.Create(Application);
try
  AboutBox.ShowModal;
finally
  AboutBox.Free;
end;
```

3. Do not call abstract methods from within the unit in which they were declared.

Additional Information

3. To override an abstract method, you must create a class that descends from the class wherein the abstract method was declared and then use the *override* directive. For example, if the base class's type declaration looks like this:

```
type
  TBassist = class
    procedure Walk; virtual; abstract;
```

```
      procedure Rock; virtual; abstract;
      procedure Thump; dynamic; abstract;
   end;
```

its methods can be overridden in a descendent class like this:

```
type
  TGarryTallent = class(TBassist)
    procedure Walk; override;
    procedure Rock; override;
    procedure Thump; override;
  end;
```

This package already contains unit named < >

Possible Cause of Error

You are attempting to install a unit into a package that already contains a unit of that name.

Quick Fix

If the unit is indeed the same unit, simply refrain from installing it a second time. If the units are different but are named the same, rename the second unit and then add the component.

Additional Information

When you install a component in Delphi 3 or 4, it is placed into a package. You can place the component in an existing package or a new package. The default is to place any components you add into DCLUSR[30,40].DPK (Delphi User's Components).

This type cannot be initialized

Possible Cause of Error

You may be attempting to declare a typed constant (initialized variable) of file, text, textfile, or variant. For example, the following will generate this error message:

```
argyle: array[0..1] of variant = ('zig','zag');
```

The error message will also be generated if you replace "variant" with "text," "file," or "textfile."

Quick Fix

Replace the invalid type with one that is allowed, such as:

```
argyle: array[0..1] of string = ('zig','zag');
```

Additional Information

See "Initialized variables" in Delphi help for more information.

Token not found

Possible Cause of Error

You may have omitted a necessary part of a SQL statement. For example, you may have entered:

```
FROM
  Customer
WHERE
  AmountOwed > 0
```

Quick Fix

Enter the missing necessary element. In the above case, this is the SELECT [Field list] part.

Additional Information

A basic SQL SELECT statement has the format:

```
SELECT *    { Field list }
FROM
  Customer { Table list }
WHERE        { optional where clause }
  AmountOwed > 0
```

Token not found. Token :dbo. line number: I

Possible Cause of Error

You may be using a TQuery component with its RequestLive property set to True and have not enclosed the owner/table name in double quotes. For example, your SQL statement may look something like:

```
SELECT *
FROM dbo.COOPER
```

Quick Fix

Enclose the owner name (dbo) and table name in double quotes:

```
SELECT *
FROM "dbo.COOPER"
```

Additional Information

See "RequestLive" in Delphi help for more information.

Too many actual parameters

Possible Cause of Error

1. You may have supplied more parameters to a procedure or function than the number with which it was declared.

2. You may be attempting to pass more than 255 individual parameters to an OLE automation procedure or function.

3. You may be calling a procedure or function of which there are at least two manifestations, and the compiler "thinks" you are attempting to call a different one than you have in mind.

Quick Fix

1. Consult the declaration of the procedure or function to see the amount, type, and order of arguments it expects.

2. Do not pass more than 255 arguments to an OLE automation procedure or function.

3. Prepend the name of the unit wherein the procedure or function you intend to call is defined to the procedure or method.

Additional Information

3. A couple of examples where this somewhat commonly occurs is with the Append and Abort procedures. The Append procedure is declared in the System unit; TDataset's Append method is in the DB unit (dbiProcs in Delphi 1). The TStrings class also has an Append method, in the Classes unit. Abort is both a procedure defined in SysUtils and a method of the TPrinter class, defined in the Printers unit.

See "Open-array parameters" in Delphi help for more information.

Too many connections

Possible Cause of Error

You may be using too many database connections by directly referring each TTable, TQuery, and TStoredProc component to a BDE alias via their DatabaseName property.

Quick Fix

Use a TDatabase component. Set the Alias property of the TDatabase component to the BDE alias (or path name). Set the DatabaseName property of all the TTable, TQuery, and TStoredProc components to the Name property of the TDatabase component.

Additional Information

By using a TDatabase component, you reduce the number of connections your application uses to one (they all share the connection the TDatabase component establishes). The TTable, TQuery, and TStoredProc components use a "local alias" by referring to the TDatabase component in their DatabaseName property.

Too many files open

Possible Cause of Error

1. You may be attempting to write to a CD-ROM.
2. You may be neglecting to close files after you open them.
3. You may have the Files setting in CONFIG.SYS set too low.
4. You may have your project in a directory with a long path name, such as:

```
C:\ToShiningSea\Breeze\Benson\Bull\Jordan\Almond\Mark\Aurelius
```

Quick Fix

1. CD-ROM stands for "Compact Disc-Read Only Memory"; as it is indeed a read-only device, you cannot write to a CD-ROM.
2. Always be sure to call CloseFile when you are through with a file. For example:

```
var
  texan: TextFile;
begin
  AssignFile(texans, 'LoneDove.txt');
  Rewrite(texans);
  Writeln(texans, 'Larry McMurtry wrote about
              the cattle drive to Montana.');
  CloseFile(texan);
end;
```

3. Set the Files= line in CONFIG.SYS to a number higher than its current setting, for example to 100 or even 255, if necessary.

4. Move your project to a location with a shorter path, such as:

```
C:\MeFeelMe
```

Additional Information

2. Failing to call CloseFile on a file could cause you to lose some or all data written to the file (some or all of the data may not get flushed to the disk).

3. When moving projects from one directory to another, do not move the project's .DSM file, as it contains directory information (and will therefore point back to the previous directory).

Too many locks on table

Possible Cause of Error

You may have modified more than 255 records during a transaction with a Paradox table.

Quick Fix

Limit the number of edits made in a single transaction.

Additional Information

If you use a TDatabase component, you can use its StartTransaction method (terminated by either Commit or Rollback) to treat a group of operations as a single transaction—either they will all fail as a group (Rollback) or all succeed as a group (Commit).

Each record that is modified consumes a lock. The maximum number of locks is 255, so the maximum number of records you can modify in one transaction is the same number.

Note: If you need to modify more than 255 records at one time, place an exclusive lock on the table, perform the modifications, post, and release the exclusive lock. To set or release an exclusive lock on a table, simply set this Boolean property like so:

```
Table1.Exclusive := True; { or False }
```

Too many open cursors

Possible Cause of Error

You may have too many tables open.

Quick Fix

Close tables when you are finished using them. If you use a relatively small amount of tables (up to several dozen), you can probably wait until program shutdown to close the tables. If you use upwards of a hundred tables, you should close the tables as soon as you are through using them.

Additional Information

You cannot increase the number of cursors available to you from the BDE. The number of tables you can have open at any one time is 127. If you receive this error while less than 127 tables are open, you may have run into a limitation of your particular back-end database server rather than the BDE. For example, in Oracle the number of simultaneously open cursors can be set (a separate and distinct limit from that set by the BDE). Consult your DBMS documentation for details.

> **Note:** To close all tables at once, for example as the program is closed, you can do this:
>
> ```
> procedure TForm1.FormClose(Sender: TObject; var
>                            Action: TCloseAction);
> var
>   i: integer;
> begin
>   for i := 0 to ComponentCount-1 do
>     if Components[i] is TTable then
>       TTable(Components[i]).Close;
>   {Alternatively, you can replace the last line
>   with: TTable(Components[i]).Active := False;}
> end;
> ```
>
> Of course, you could always do it this way, too:
>
> ```
>         procedure TForm1.FormClose(Sender: TObject; var
>                                    Action: TCloseAction);
> begin
>   Table1.Close;
>   Table2.Close;
>   {etc., ad nauseum}
> end;
> ```
>
> but this can become a maintenance chore. The first example shown will always work no matter how many TTables you add or remove from the form.

Too many open files

Possible Cause of Error

1. You may have more files open than Windows can "handle."
2. You may have more files open than the MAXFILEHANDLES limit in the BDE Configuration utility.

Quick Fix

1. Increase the Files= line in CONFIG.SYS to a number higher than that to which it is currently set, for example to 100 or even 255, if necessary.
2. Increase the MAXFILEHANDLES setting on the BDE Configuration/Administration utility's System page or System | Init node.

Additional Information

See "Too many files open."

Too many parameters

Possible Cause of Error

1. You may be supplying more parameters to a procedure or function than the number given in its declaration. For example, if you call the standard procedure Release (which does not take a parameter) and pass it a parameter, you will receive the error message under discussion:

```
Release(MeLetMeGo);
```

2. You may be attempting to call a static method in a descendent class which has the same name as a static method in an ancestor class, but the variable type is of the ancestor type (although the descendent type is instantiated). For example, the following will generate this error message, as static methods are resolved by variable (TGramps in this case), not instance (TYoungWhipperSnapper in this case), type:

```
type
  TGramps = class
    procedure NoteOrTriad(note: string);
  TYoungWhipperSnapper = class(TGramps)
    procedure NoteOrTriad(note1, note2, note3: string);
. . .
var
  Gitfiddle: TGramps;
begin
  Gitfiddle:= TYoungWhipperSnapper.Create;
  Gitfiddle.NoteOrTriad(1,2,3)
```

Quick Fix

1. Consult the definition of the procedure or method you are calling to ascertain the signature (number, type, and sequence of parameters) it needs.

2. To call TYoungWhipperSnapper's NoteOrTriad method, declare Gitfiddle as a TYoungWhipperSnapper or declare NoteOrTriad virtual in TGramps and override it in TYoungWhipperSnapper.

Additional Information

See "Not enough actual parameters."

Translate error, value out of bounds

Possible Cause of Error

1. You may be copying data from one machine to another (such as a client to a server) where the date formats do not match.

2. You may be copying data from one database type to another, and the date formats do not match.

3. You may be working with a dBASE table and are using a different language driver than the one originally used (the one with which the table was created and/or data was subsequently added).

Quick Fix

1. Use the same date format on both machines.

2. Convert the date format to that of the destination database before or during copying.

3. In the BDE Configuration utility (Drivers | dBASE | LangDriver), change the Language Driver setting to the one originally used.

Additional Information

Empty or null dates in 32-bit Delphi are not really blank, but rather 12/31/1899. In Delphi 1, the starting date is 1/1/1. The starting point was changed to provide OLE automation compatibility.

Tried to search marked block but it is invalid

Possible Cause of Error

You may have the IDE set up to search the marked block (rather than perform a global search), but there is no marked block.

Quick Fix

Mark a block to search, or change the option to search globally (select the Global check box in the Scope section of the Find dialog).

Additional Information

Take note of the other search options that are available in the Find dialog.

Type < > has no type info

Possible Cause of Error

You may be attempting to retrieve a pointer to type information for a type which cannot be used in a published property and therefore does not have any run-time type information associated with it. For example, the following generates this error message:

```
var
  BirdDog: Pointer;
begin
  BirdDog := TypeInfo(file);
```

Quick Fix

You can use TypeInfo only on types which can be used in published properties, namely Integer, Extended, String, TMethod, and Variant.

Additional Information

See "TypeInfo" in Delphi help for more information.

Type < > is not yet completely defined

Possible Cause of Error

You may have set the ancestor class the same as the descendent class in a Type section. For example, the following will generate this error message:

```
type
  TForm3 = class(TForm3)
```

Quick Fix

Change the class from which the descendent is inheriting (the ancestor class) to a valid one. For example, in the case above, the following would prevent the error from reoccurring:

```
type
  TForm3 = class(TForm)
```

Additional Information

See "Forms" in Delphi help for more information.

Type < > must be a class to have a PUBLISHED section

Possible Cause of Error

You may have declared a classic/legacy/old-style object and attempted to furnish it with a Published section. For example, the following will generate this error message:

```
type
  TStendahl = Object
    RedAndBlack: TMemo;
  published
    Languages: Integer;
```

Quick Fix

Change the type to a class or remove the Published section.

```
type
  TStendahl = class { TObject if not specified }
. . .
```

Additional Information

See "Class declarations" in Delphi help for more information.

Type < > must be a class to have OLE automation

Possible Cause of Error

You may have declared a classic/legacy/old-style object and attempted to furnish it with an Automated section. For example, the following will generate this error message:

```
type
  TModel = object
    Black: TColor;
  automated
    AssemblyLines: Integer;
```

Quick Fix

Change the type to a class or remove the Automated section.

```
type
  TModel = class { TObject if not specified }
. . .
```

Additional Information

See "Automation" in Delphi help for more information.

Type < > needs finalization—not allowed in file type

Possible Cause of Error

You may be declaring long strings in a File of Record type. For example, the following will generate this error message:

```
type
  TDateRec = File of record
    FlowSnakes, Snirt: Integer;
    Bouldershades: String;
  end;
```

Quick Fix

Remove the string from the record or declare it as a short string either explicitly (by declaring it as type ShortString) or implicitly (by providing it with a length, such as String[20]). For example, to fix the above, do this:

```
type
  TDateRec = File of record
    FlowSnakes, Snirt: Integer;
    Bouldershades: string[20];
  end;
```

Additional Information

You cannot use long strings in a File of Record because the strings themselves are stored in records (not pointers to the strings), and thus the size of the record cannot be ascertained in advance. In a File of Record, long strings need to be allocated, initialized, and finalized.

Type expected but < > found

Possible Cause of Error

You may have entered an illegal character as a type identifier. For example, the following will generate this error message:

```
type
  ShesNotMy = @
```

Quick Fix

Use valid type identifiers. Here are examples of valid declarations of a class type, an enumerated type, and a subrange type:

```
{class}
type
  TForm1 = class(TForm)
  . . .
{enumerated}
type
  Cartwrights = (Dunn, Nelson, Owen, ShannonC, ShannonJ, StSure, Szajki);
{subrange}
type
  Ratings = 1..4
```

Additional Information

This error message is usually the result of a typo or an omission.

> **Note:** If you entered:
>
> ```
> type
>   Proto = &
> ```
>
> you would get the error message "Illegal character in input file:< >."

Type expected but real constant found

Possible Cause of Error

You may have left out one of the required two periods in an array type declaration. For example, the following will produce the error message under discussion:

```
type
  gross = array[0.143] of integer;
```

To avoid the error, you must supply the second period between the low and high bounds of the array (0 and 143 in the example):

```
type
  gross = array[0..143] of integer;
```

Quick Fix

Supply the second period in the array type declaration between the low and high bounds of the array.

Additional Information

This is how to declare and use an array:

```
type
  gross = array[0..143] of integer;
...
var
  grody: gross;
...
  grody[0] := StrToInt(Edit1.Text);
  grody[1] := StrToInt(Edit2.Text);
...
```

You can initialize all the values in the array in the OnCreate event of the form like so:

```
procedure TForm1.FormCreate(Sender: Tobject);
var
  w: word;
begin
  for w:=0 to sizeof(gross)-1 do grody[w]:=0;
end;
```

Type of expression must be BOOLEAN

Possible Cause of Error

1. You may have used a conditional statement in an *if, while,* or *loop* statement which is not a Boolean (cannot be evaluated as being either True or False). For example, the following will generate this error message:

```
if Form1.Name then
```

2. Sometimes this error message is caused by a syntax error when you are attempting to typecast the Sender parameter. For example, the following line will produce the error message under discussion:

```
if (Sender as TDBEdit)Tag = 8 then
```

Quick Fix

1. Be sure to evaluate Boolean conditions where the compiler rightly expects a True/False answer. For example, this will compile:

```
if Form1.Name = 'Sake' then
```

2. In this event, you need to add the "dot scoping operator" between the Sender typecast as a TDBEdit and its Tag property:

```
if (Sender as TDBEdit).Tag = 8 then
```

Additional Information

Some languages and environments refer to Boolean as Logical (including Paradox).

Type of expression must be INTEGER

Possible Cause of Error

You may have specified the length of a string as something other than an integer value. For example, the following will generate this error message:

```
Wisconsin: String['cheese'];
```

as will this:

```
Boysenberry: String[3.14];
```

Quick Fix

If you are going to implicitly declare a short string, provide it with an integer value between 1 and 255 (if you want a string of length 1, though, you may want to declare a char instead).

Additional Information

See "Integers" in Delphi help for more information.

Type mismatch [in expression]

Possible Cause of Error

You may have attempted to perform an aggregate operation in a SQL statement on a non-numeric field. For example, the following will give you this error message if the field State is non-numeric:

```
SELECT AVG(State)
FROM CUSTOMER
```

Quick Fix

Perform mathematical operations on numeric fields only, for example:

```
SELECT AVG(Salary)
FROM NFLQBacks
```

Additional Information

See "Types" in Delphi help for more information.

TYPEINFO standard function expects a type identifier

Possible Cause of Error

You may have attempted to call the TypeInfo function, but provided an argument that was not a type. For example, the following will generate this error message:

```
var
  BirdDog: pointer;
. . .
BirdDog := TypeInfo('yowza-bop');
```

Quick Fix

Supply the TypeInfo function only with types that can be used in published properties, namely Integer, Extended, String, TMethod, and Variant.

Additional Information

See "TypeInfo" in Delphi help for more information.

Types of actual and formal var parameters must be identical

Possible Cause of Error

You may be attempting to pass an actual parameter that differs in type from the var formal parameter defined for the procedure or function. For example, the following will generate this error message:

```
procedure TForm1.Button1Click(Sender: TObject);
  procedure Snowblind(var nish: Variant);
  begin
    nish := 'nash, I was takin'' a bash';
  end;
begin
  Snowblind(Query1);
end;
```

Quick Fix

Verify that all parameters you pass share the same data type with the formal parameter of the procedure or function to which you pass it.

Additional Information

If the formal parameter is not a variable parameter, the error message is "Incompatible Types: < > and < >." In the case above, the exact error message would be: "Incompatible Types: 'Variant' and 'TQuery.' "

Unable to load GDS[32].DLL

Possible Cause of Error

You may have attempted to drop an IBEventAlerter component on a form, but the corresponding Interbase .DLL is not installed on your system. You may have elected not to install Interbase when you loaded Delphi.

Quick Fix

If you did not install Interbase when you installed Delphi, install Interbase from the CD-ROM to use the local version of Interbase which comes with Delphi.

Additional Information

See the Interbase documentation that you received with Delphi for more information.

Unable to load RPTSMITH.EXE

Possible Cause of Error

The [ReportSmith] section of DELPHI.INI may have been removed, or does not reflect the current location of ReportSmith.

Quick Fix

Open DELPHI.INI (in the Windows directory by default) and add or modify the ReportSmith entry so that it reflects the location of ReportSmith. By default, the entry will be:

```
[ReportSmith]
ExePath=C:\RPTSMITH
```

Additional Information

Delphi 1 contained ReportSmith. Delphi 2 contained both ReportSmith and QuickReports (although ReportSmith was somewhat hidden). Delphi 3 and 4 contain QuickReports only. Of course, you are not limited to using either of these two reporting tools. You can use other report generating tools, such as ReportPrinter Pro, Crystal Reports, etc., or even "roll your own" custom coded reports without using a report engine.

Undeclared Identifier: < >

Possible Cause of Error

There are several possible causes of this error message.

1. You may have assigned a value to a variable that was not declared at all or is not in scope (in which case the left side of the assignment statement generated the error).

2. You may have assigned a value to a property that is not appropriate for that property (in which case the right side of the assignment statement generated the error).

3. You may have prepended the class name to a method in the Interface part of a unit (which is necessary in the Implementation part, but is unnecessary and not allowed in the Interface part).

4. You may have misspelled the identifier either at the point of declaration or implementation.

5. It may be that you are referencing an object, procedure, or function that resides in a unit that is not included in your Uses section. For example, you may be calling the ShowMessage or MessageDlg function without having the Dialogs unit in your Uses section, or you may be referencing the Clipboard object without having the Clipbrd unit in your Uses section.

6. You may have altered the ancestor in the form's type declaration. For example, if you changed the ancestor from Form1 to Application, like this:

```
{ Should be TForm1 = class(TForm) }
TForm1 = class(TApplication)
```

you would get the error message under discussion.

7. You may be attempting to access an identifier that is declared in another unit's Private section.

8. You may be attempting to free an instance of an interface with a call to Free. For example, the following will generate this error message:

```
type
  ILittleDog = interface(IUnknown)
  ['{51DDE8C0-CBE2-11D1-9BDB-444553540000}']
  function FetchedPaper: Boolean;
  function getBarkType: string;
  procedure setBarkType(Value: string);
  property BarkType: string read getBarkType
                           write setBarkType;
  end;
TPoodle = class(TInterfacedObject, ILittleDog)
    FBarkType: string;
    function FetchedPaper: Boolean;
    function getBarkType: string;
    procedure setBarkType(Value: string);
. . .
procedure TForm1.Button1Click(Sender: TObject);
var
  Fifi: ILittleDog;
begin
  Fifi := TPoodle.Create;
```

```
    try
      . . .
    finally
      Fifi.Free;
    end;
  end;
```

Quick Fix

1. Verify that any variable you are assigning to is declared and in scope. If it is intended to be a global variable, declare it either in the Interface part of the unit or in a separate Globals unit created expressly for variables that you want to reference from multiple units. If the variable is intended to be a local variable, verify that you have declared it. If the identifier is a procedure or function, verify that the unit which contains it is included in one of your Uses sections (Interface or Implementation).

2. Assign values to variables or properties that are appropriate for such.

3. Remove the class name from the method in the Interface section. It is already implicitly assigned.

4. Verify that you have spelled the identifier the same in both its declaration and definition, as well as any assignments relative to it.

5. Add the necessary unit to your Uses section. To determine which unit you need to add when calling an Object Pascal procedure or function, look up the procedure or function in Delphi help and note the unit wherein the procedure or function is defined (and then add it to your Uses section).

6. Revert the type declaration to its prior state.

7. Do not attempt to call a method declared in another class's Private section. Do not attempt to directly access a field declared in another class's Private section either. Access the value, if possible, through the public or published property that accesses the private field. For example, the TSpeedButton class, declared in Buttons.PAS, contains the following:

```
private
  . . .
  FFlat: Boolean;
published
  . . .
  property Flat: Boolean read FFlat write SetFlat default False;
```

You can indirectly access the FFlat private field by assigning to or reading from the Flat property, but you cannot directly write to or read from the FFlat field. Depending on your point of view, you may consider this either minor or major.

8. Do not call Free for interface instances.

Additional Information

7. You can access another class's public and published methods and properties as long as you are "using" the unit wherein the class is declared. You also have access to the Protected section if you are creating a descendent class of the class in question. You never have access to a Private section in another unit, though.

8. Interface instances are freed, or released, automatically on the following occasions:

   ➤ The interface variable goes out of scope

   ➤ You assign a different interfaced object to the interface variable

   ➤ You assign nil to the interface variable

   See "< > is not a valid component name."

Unexpected end of command

Possible Cause of Error

You may have left out part of a statement, for example a SQL statement such as the following which fails to specify the column that is being used as the primary key:

```
ALTER Table Placemats
ADD CONSTRAINT pkSlogan primary key
```

Quick Fix

Provide the missing element of the statement, for example the name of the primary column:

```
ALTER Table Placemats
ADD CONSTRAINT pkSlogan primary key (Slogan)
```

Additional Information

Do not place a primary key constraint on a column that is nullable. A primary key must contain unique values, and thus can only contain at most one null value.

Unit < > was compiled with a different version of < >

Possible Cause of Error

1. You may have assigned a unit the same name as a unit that is already on Delphi's library search path.

2. You (or the author of the unit in question) may have changed the declaration of a symbol in the Interface part of a unit, and another unit which references this (modified) unit in its Uses clause cannot be recompiled because the source (.PAS) file is not available.

Quick Fix

1. Rename your unit.

2. Choose one of the following solutions:

   a. If possible, locate the first unit mentioned in the error message, move it into the same directory where the corresponding compiled unit file (.DCU) currently resides, and recompile.

   b. Use an older version of the second unit mentioned in the error message (one that predates the modification).

Additional Information

1. Adopt a naming convention that will make name collisions highly unlikely. For example, if your name is Rupert Pupkin, you could prepend rp to your unit names, such as rpMain, rpGlobal, etc.

Unit version mismatch: < >

Possible Cause of Error

1. You may have given a unit a name which already exists in the VCL or RTL, such as Buttons, SysUtils, etc.

2. You may have altered the VCL source code.

Quick Fix

1. Use unique names for your units; try to establish a naming convention which will guarantee uniqueness, such as prepending or appending your initials, your company's initials, etc.

2. Do not alter the VCL source code unless you have a <u>very</u> good reason for doing so, and are willing to provide your own technical support from that point on.

Additional Information

1. The compiler will not stop you from naming your unit the same thing as an existing unit, for example, Buttons.
2. The VCL source code is intended primarily for reference; altering it is not recommended.

Unknown Column

See "Unknown SQL Error."

Unknown database

Possible Cause of Error

1. You may have specified a database alias or path for the DatabaseName property of a TDatabase or of a TDataset (TTable, TQuery, or TStoredProc in all versions of Delphi; TClientDataset in Delphi Client/Server versions 3 and 4; TNestedTable in Delphi 4) component that is not recognized.
2. You may have attempted to set a TDatabase component's Connected property to True without providing a value for the AliasName property.
3. The database engine configuration file (IDAPI32.CFG in 32-bit Delphi, IDAPI.CFG in Delphi 1) may have been moved or deleted.

Quick Fix

1. If you provided a path for this property, the path should be "fully qualified"* and the database used must be either Paradox or dBASE. If the DatabaseName property is an alias, ensure that the alias has been properly set up.
2. Provide a value for the AliasName property before setting the Connected property to True.
3. Ensure that the system registry setting pointing to the location of IDAPI32.CFG corresponds with the file's actual location.

Additional Information

1. * "Fully qualified" means that an explicit, or absolute, path name is given (as opposed to a relative path name). **\Borland\delphi 3** is an example of a relative path name. **C:\No\Evel\Hear\No\Knevel** is an example of an absolute path.

To create a BDE alias, follow these steps:

a. Select **Database | Explore**.

b. In SQL Explorer/Database Explorer, select **Object | New**.

c. Select the driver type you want from the combo box (select **Standard** if you are working with Paradox or dBASE tables) and select the **OK** button.

d. The new alias will display in the Database page in the left pane with a default name such as Standard1.

e. Right-click the new alias, select **Rename** from the context menu, and enter the name you want to give the alias.

f. In the Definition page in the right pane, select the appropriate driver from the Default Driver combo box.

g. Enter the path to the database in the Path edit box.

h. Select **Object | Exit**, and then **Yes** to save the changes you just made.

3. The default location for the database engine configuration file (IDAPI32.CFG) is:

```
C:\Program Files\Borland\Common Files\BDE
```

To inspect the system registry setting for the location of IDAPI32.CFG, follow these steps:

a. Select **Start | Run**.

b. Enter **regedit** in the Open combo box and select the **OK** button (or press the **Enter** key).

c. Navigate to HKEY_LOCAL_MACHINE\Software\Borland\Database Engine.

The data for CONFIGFILE01 will display the path where the configuration file is located. If it differs from the location of your copy of IDAPI32.CFG, either move the file to the location pointed to by the system registry setting (recommended), or change the system registry setting to match the current location of the file.

If you have no IDAPI32.CFG file on your system, copy it from the Delphi CD into the appropriate location.

If you are going to deploy a database application on other machines, you must ensure that the target machines set up the database alias if one is used for database access. You can do this with InstallShield or in code. See "AddAlias" in Delphi help for an example of how to create an alias in code. See the InstallShield documentation for instructions on supplying an alias with their installation utility.

If you are using a path (instead of an alias), one method you can use to ensure that the database is always found is by following one of these steps:

➤ Instruct users to keep all database files in the same directory as the application.

-OR-

➤ Set the DatabaseName property to */.*

> **Note:** Placing the tables in the same directory as the executable can lead to problems. See "Directory Is Busy."

Unknown directive: < >

Possible Cause of Error

1. You may be using incorrect syntax in a procedure or function declaration. The problem may be simply a misspelling or a missing semicolon.

2. You may be attempting to declare a method as virtual, dynamic, abstract, or overloaded outside of a class declaration.

3. You may be attempting to intercept a Windows message but have neglected to place a semicolon before the *message* directive. It is not expected and therefore "unknown" by the compiler without a preceding semicolon.

   For example, this will cause the error:

   ```
   procedure wmcommand(var Message: Tmessage) message WM_COMMAND;
   ```

4. You may have added the *stored* directive to a procedure in a class's Private, Protected, or Public section(s). For example, the following will generate the error message under discussion:

   ```
   procedure Setuuuu(b: string) stored;
   ```

Quick Fix

1. Ensure that the syntax you are using is correct and that what you are trying to do is "legal" according to the Delphi compiler.

2. Declare all virtual, dynamic, abstract, and overloaded methods within a class type declaration.

3. When intercepting Windows message, remember the semicolon prior to the *message* directive.

```
procedure wmcommand(var Message: Tmessage);
                    message WM_COMMAND;
```

4. Do not use the *stored* directive in a class's Private, Protected, or Public section.

Additional Information

2. To be of value as virtual, dynamic, or abstract methods, these methods must be members of a class so that the class can be inherited from (and the methods overridden). Virtual methods contain the *virtual* directive; dynamic virtual methods contain the *dynamic* directive; and abstract methods contain either the *virtual* or the *dynamic* directive followed by the *abstract* directive. Overloaded methods have the *overload* keyword appended to their declaration.

3. You can take advantage of the Windows messages as a debugging or educational tool. For example, to ascertain how often and when your program is sent the WM_ACTIVATE message from Windows, declare this procedure:

```
procedure wmactivate(var Message: TMessage);
                     message WM_ACTIVATE;
```

and then write a message to a text file every time Windows sends this message to your application:

```
var {This is in the interface section}
  TForm1: TForm;
  tf: TextFile;
  ...
procedure TForm1.FormCreate(Sender: Tobject);
begin
  AssignFile(tF,'trakmsgs.txt');
  if FileExists('trakmsgs.txt') then
    Append(tF)
  else
    Rewrite(tF);
  WriteLn(tF,DateTimeToStr(Now));
end;
...
procedure TForm1.wmactivate(var Message: TMessage);
begin
  {inherit Delphi's response to the message}
  inherited;
  Writeln(tf,'The activate message was sent');
end;
...
```

```
procedure TForm1.FormDestroy(Sender: Tobject);
begin
  CloseFile(tF);
end;
```

Of course, you could do this for as many Windows messages as you like (search for "WM_" in Delphi help for a list of Windows messages), and it is even easier to create such a "message trail" for your application's event handlers. Simply double-click the events you are interested in on the events page for any and all forms and components and enter the Writeln statement similar to the one shown above. For example, you could track a form's OnPaint event like so:

```
procedure TForm1.FormPaint(Sender: TObject);
begin
  Writeln(tf,'Paint event was called');
end;
```

Unknown Identifier

Possible Cause of Error

You may be referencing something that is declared in a unit that you have not added to your unit's Uses clause.

Quick Fix

Determine the missing unit based on the identifier which the compiler is stumbling over. If it is a Delphi identifier, you can do this by placing the cursor in the identifier and hitting the F1 key. The help screen dealing with the identifier will identify in which unit the identifier is declared. If the identifier is not a Delphi identifier, it is either from a third party or one of your own. In either case, once you determine the unit in which the identifier is declared, add this unit to your Uses clause.

Additional Information

You can "use" another unit either by adding it to the Uses clauses in the Interface part (automatically created for you by Delphi and initially populated with several standard units), or by adding your own Uses clause directly beneath the *implementation* reserved word.

Unknown picture file extension: < >

Possible Cause of Error

1. You may be attempting to load a file with an extension other than .BMP, .ICO, .EMF, or .WMF into an Image's Picture property. For example, the following line will produce the error message under discussion:

```
Image1.Picture.LoadFromFile('Sunflowers.txt');
```

2. You may have omitted the file extension when referencing the file.

Quick Fix

1. Only load the appropriate file types into TImage's Picture property.
2. Always explicitly include the graphic file extension (.BMP, .ICO, .WMF, or .EMF).

Additional Information

You must specify image files with one of the graphics formats recognized by Delphi. For example, any of the following are valid:

```
Image1.Picture.LoadFromFile('C:\VG\WheatFieldWithCrows.BMP');
Image2.Picture.LoadFromFile('C:\VG\TheStarryNight.ICO');
Image3.Picture.LoadFromFile('C:\VG\SelfPortraitWithHat.WMF');
Image4.Picture.LoadFromFile('C:\VG\ThePotatoEaters.EMF');
```

> **Note:** You can work with other grapic formats via third-party components or by writing your own code to do so.

Unknown SQL Error

Possible Cause of Error

You may be accessing a SQL Server database and have added or dropped a column or index, or toggled a null/not null designation while Enable Schema Cache was set to True in the BDE Configuration utility.

> **Note:** The latter part of the error message may be "Unknown Column," "Invalid Bind Type," "Invalid Type," "Invalid Type Conversion," or "Column not a BLOb."

Quick Fix

Set Enable Schema Cache to False in the BDE Configuration utility before making any such changes.

Select the Help button in the BDE Configuration utility for specific information about these settings for the driver you are configuring.

Additional Information

If the schema is cached (Enable Schema Cache is set to True), changes made to the (database) schema during run time will not be recognized by the BDE. The schema must remain static if you are going to have schema caching set to True. Besides the Enable Schema Cache setting, SQL Server databases (such as Interbase, MS SQL Server, Sybase, Oracle, etc.) also have the Schema Cache Dir, Schema Cache Size, and Schema Cache Time settings in the Driver page/node of the BDE Configuration utility.

Unknown user name or password

Possible Cause of Error

You may have entered an invalid password in the Database Login dialog box after one of the following:

a. You attempted to set a TDatabase component's Connected property to True, either at design time or at run time (in code).

b. You called a TDatabase or TTable component's Open method.

c. You attempted to set a TTable's Active property to True, either at design time or at run time (in code).

Quick Fix

Supply the correct password to the Database Login dialog box and then select the **OK** button.

Additional Information

>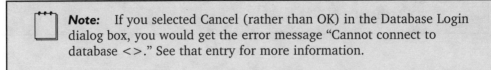
> **Note:** If you selected Cancel (rather than OK) in the Database Login dialog box, you would get the error message "Cannot connect to database < >." See that entry for more information.

You can avoid having to continually enter a password while you're developing your application by either setting the password in code or via the TDatabase component's Parameter Overrides section.

To set the password in code, add a line like the following to a point in the code prior to any attempt to access the database (for example, in the form's OnCreate event):

```
Session.AddPassword('Kennwort');
```

To set the password using the TDatabase component's Parameter Overrides, follow these steps:

1. Double-click the TDatabase component.
2. Verify that the correct Name and Alias are displayed.
3. Deselect the Login Prompt check box.
4. Select the **Defaults** button.
5. Add the password to the Password= line in the Parameter Overrides list box.

Alternatively, you can supply an event handler for the OnLogin event.

> **Note:** If the database requires access protection, remember to remove these passwords before deployment. Otherwise, anybody with access to the source code could discover the password.

Unsatisfied forward or external declaration: < >

Possible Cause of Error

This error message appears when you have a forward or external declaration of a procedure or function, or a declaration of a method in a class or object type, and you don't define the procedure, function, or method anywhere. It may be that the definition has, in fact, been omitted, or perhaps its name is just misspelled. Note that a declaration of a procedure or function in the Interface part of a unit is equivalent to a forward declaration—you have to supply the implementation (the body of the procedure or function) in the Implementation part. Similarly, the declaration of a method in a class or object type is equivalent to a forward declaration. You may need to prepend the class name to the procedure. For example, if you have declared a method called PlayBaseball, the definition in the Implementation part must be the following (assuming the class is TForm1):

```
TForm1.PlayBaseball;
```

Quick Fix

Define the procedure or function declared in the Interface part of the unit in the Implementation part of the unit.

Additional Information

Declaring a method in the Interface section is like promising that you will provide the rest of the information later (below, in the Implementation section). You must "keep your promise" by doing so.

Unsupported 16bit resource

Possible Cause of Error

You may be attempting to install a component in 32-bit Delphi which has an affiliated .DCR (icon bitmap resource) file that was created with a 16-bit tool (such as the Image Editor in Delphi 1).

Quick Fix

Load the .DCR file into the Image Editor of any 32-bit version of Delphi and save it (it will be saved in 32-bit format). Try again to install the component.

Additional Information

You may need to edit the .DCR file in the Image Editor for the change to 32 bit to "take." For instance, you can change a pixel, revert the change (**Ctrl+Z**), and then save it (or make some other change and subsequently undo it).

Unterminated string

Possible Cause of Error

1. You may have forgotten the closing apostrophe (single quote) at the end of a string.
2. You may have spread a string over several lines in the Delphi code editor, but neglected to terminate each line with an apostrophe.

Quick Fix

1. Include an apostrophe at the end of each string.
2. Include an apostrophe at the end of each line of a multi-line string.

Additional Information

To spread a string over multiple lines, use the "+" operator to concatenate the lines. Here is an example:

```
s := 'Das fesche Umherstolzieren des Hahns '
      + 'ist ein bekannter Anblick.'
      + 'Was fehlt dir, mein Junge?';
```

USES clause is missing or incorrect

Possible Cause of Error

You may have a syntax error within the Interface part's Uses clause.

Quick Fix

Verify that there is one comma between all units referenced in the Uses clause and a semicolon at the end.

Additional Information

In Delphi 1, you can also get this error message if you do not have a Uses clause in a library (.DLL) file.

Variable < > inaccessible here due to optimization

Possible Cause of Error

The variable or property value you are attempting to "watch" or inspect has been "optimized out" at this point of the program's life.

Quick Fix

Turn off the optimization compiler switch by adding one of the following directives:

```
{$O-}
{$OPTIMIZATION OFF}
```

Additional Information

See "Optimization" in Delphi help for more information.

Variable required

Possible Cause of Error

You may be attempting to pass an array to a procedure or function, but have neglected to enclose the array in brackets. For example, the following will generate this error message:

```
procedure MeinVaterWarEinWandersmann(Sender: TObject);
  procedure LiliMarlene(fournums: array of integer);
  begin
    . . .
  end;
begin
  LiliMarlene(StrToInt(Edit1.Text),
              StrToInt(Edit2.Text),
              StrToInt(Edit3.Text));
end;
```

Quick Fix

Enclose the array in brackets:

```
. . .
LiliMarlene([StrToInt(Edit1.Text),
            StrToInt(Edit2.Text),
            StrToInt(Edit3.Text)]);
```

Additional Information

Delphi 4 introduces dynamic arrays.

Variant does not reference an OLE object

Possible Cause of Error

You may be attempting to access an OLE object assigned to a Variant variable that has not been registered on your system.

Quick Fix

Register the OLE object on all machines that will reference it. See "Class not registered" for specific information.

Additional Information

See "Variant Types" in Delphi help for more information.

Variant is not an array

Possible Cause of Error

You may have attempted to access an element of a Variant data type variable, such as a string. For example, you may have attempted something like this:

```
var
  CoderCandy: Variant;
begin
  CoderCandy := 'Melts In Your Mug, Not In Your Mitt';
  { the following line generates the error }
  Label1.Caption := CoderCandy[1]+'&'+CoderCandy[1];
  { so does this one }
  CoderCandy[4] := 'u';
end;
```

Quick Fix

Do not attempt to index into a Variant to which you have assigned a string value.

Additional Information

See "VarArrayCreate" and "VarIsArray" in Delphi help for more information.

Vendor initialization failure: ORA[NT]7[1,2,3].DLL

Possible Cause of Error

The BDE could not find the Oracle .DLL you have specified in the BDE Configuration/Administration utility's Vendor Init parameter.

Quick Fix

Determine which version of ora*.DLL is on your machine. Using the BDE Configuration/Administration utility, enter the name of this file in the Vendor Init setting. This file should be located in the \BIN subdirectory of your Oracle directory, for example C:\ORAWIN95\BIN.

Additional Information

See your Oracle documentation for more information on the .DLLs required by your version of Oracle.

Windows Socket Error: (10060), on API 'connect'

Possible Cause of Error

You may have attempted to set a TRemoteServer's Connected property to True while the ConnectType property is set to ctSockets, but the application server has not been configured.

Quick Fix

Run the Scktsrvr program (SCKTSRVR.EXE) on the application server machine. It is located by default in C:\Program Files\Borland\Delphi X\Bin.

Additional Information

See "MIDAS" in Delphi help for more information.

Write error on <>

Possible Cause of Error

The disk to which the compiler is attempting to write a file may be full.

Quick Fix

Remove the dross from the drive and try again. For example, large documents and graphics files that you do not need can be deleted or backed up to a separate device.

Additional Information

Use the Windows defrag utility to rearrange (defragment) your hard disk. This will improve performance, as files can be written to fewer areas (preferably one contiguous area) instead of being spread out over several areas on the hard disk.

> **Note:** If your machine is connected to a network, consult your network administrator before defragging.

You cannot add a <> to the current project because it is not an ActiveX library. Click OK to start a new ActiveX library project

Possible Cause of Error

You may have selected File | New... | ActiveX | ActiveForm or ActiveX Control while a "conventional" (non-ActiveX) project was open.

If you are using Delphi 4, you may have selected File | New... | ActiveX | MTS Automation object with a non-ActiveX project open in the IDE.

Quick Fix

Select **OK** to close the current project, start a new ActiveX Library project, and add the item you selected.

Additional Information

See "ActiveX Applications" in Delphi help for more information.

You cannot specify a size for a field of this type

Possible Cause of Error

You may be attempting to change the data type of a field in Desktop Database, for example from A (Alpha) to N (Number), but the previous Size value is still specified, which does not apply to the data type to which you are changing the field.

Quick Fix

First delete the value from the Size column, then change the data type in the Type column.

Additional Information

Some data types require a size value, others allow a size value but it is not required, and others do not allow a size value. See "Paradox Field Types and Sizes" in Database Desktop online help for more information.

You must open a project before you can add an Automation Object

Possible Cause of Error

You may have attempted to create an Automation object with no project open. For example, you may have selected File | New..., and then selected Remote Data Module from the New page.

Quick Fix

Open an existing project or create a new project before attempting to add an Automation object.

Additional Information

Once a project is open, you can create a new Automation object by selecting File | New..., selecting the ActiveX tab, and then double-clicking the Automation Object icon.

You must select a VCL class

Possible Cause of Error

You may be attempting to create an ActiveX control using the ActiveX Control Wizard, but failed to provide a VCL class on which to base your ActiveX control in the VCL Class Name combo box.

Quick Fix

Select a component from the VCL Class Name combo box or type one in.

Additional Information

To create an ActiveX control using the ActiveX Control Wizard, use an existing Delphi component and then convert it into an ActiveX control.

In this way, you can use "Delphi" components in other environments that support ActiveX controls, such as C++ Builder, Visual Basic, PowerBuilder, etc.

Your application is not enabled for use with this driver

Possible Cause of Error

1. You may be attempting to use SQL Links with a version of Delphi below Client/Server.
2. You may be attempting to use an ODBC driver with Delphi Standard or Trial.
3. You may have originally had a "lesser" version of Delphi on your system, and installed Delphi Client/Server without uninstalling the previous version.

Quick Fix

1. Upgrade to Client/Server or use Paradox tables. Or use dBASE or ODBC.
2. Upgrade to Delphi Professional or use Paradox or dBASE tables.
3. Uninstall the previous version of Delphi, and then install Delphi Client/Server.

Additional Information

Of course, you could always buy Delphi Enterprise, which had an original price of about $45,000. Chickenfeed! Cheap (at twice the price)! A mere pittance! etc. Contact Inprise for details on deals.

See "Application is not licensed to use this feature."

Index

If you are looking for a specific error message, refer to the table of contents. The error messages are listed there alphabetically, and are thus not reproduced here.

$2108, 48, 101
$2109, 48, 98
$2501, 47, 58
$2507, 436
$2C08, 48, 383
$2C09, 48
$3E06, 100
$IFOPT, 314
$LINK, 56
$REALCOMPATIBILITY, 45
$RUNONLY, 2
.BMP, 60
.BPL, 72
.DCP, 307
.DCR, 188, 196, 481
.DCU, 57, 58, 153, 395
.DFM, 9, 107, 124, 199, 212-214, 220, 228, 232, 239, 326-327, 366, 428
.DLL, 86, 105, 128, 173, 366, 405
.DLLs, 68
.DOF, 292
.DPC, 323
.DPK, 3, 255, 257, 323
.DPL, 72, 73, 323
.DPR, 18, 22, 68, 117, 153, 232, 366
.DSK, 230, 231, 292
.DSM, 230, 292, 455
.EMF, 60, 352
.ICO, 60
.INI, 238
.LCK, 183, 345
.MAP, 153
.MB, 153
.MDX, 300
.NET, 183
.OPT, 292
.PAS, 212-214, 232, 366
.RES, 22, 195, 231, 292
.VAL, 414
.WMF, 60, 352

/ operator, 191
16-bit resource, 481
Abort procedure, 427, 453
abstract classes, 145-146
Abstract method, 373, 449
abstract methods, 41, 144
abstract virtual methods, 40
Access, see Microsoft Access
access specifier, 252
accessor, 197
ActiveControl property, 326
ActiveForm, 85-86, 130, 214, 231, 306
ActiveX, 24-25, 32, 86, 128-129, 214, 231, 487
    control, 488
        Control Wizard, 11, 160, 488
        Library, 85, 486
actual parameters, 453, 467
adding an entry to the system registry, 95
ADD CONSTRAINT, 471
AddFieldDefs, 245
AddIndex method, 7, 35, 244, 251, 332
AddPassword, 480
aggregate functions, 120, 329
aliases, local (standard), 264
AliasName property, 473
Alpha fields, 252
ALTER TABLE, 471
Append, 202, 255, 453
Application Wizard, 445
Application.CreateForm, 68
ApplyRange, 241
ApplyUpdates, 344
array, 138
array properties, 126, 178
as operator, 329
ASCII table, 180
asm, 307
Assigned, 380
AssignFile, 202, 254-256, 258
AssignPrn, 403

AsVariant, 287, 332
Auto-Create Forms, 46
AUTOEXEC.BAT, 423
Autoincrement, 35
Automated section, 146-147, see also OLE
    automation section
automated virtual method, 396
automation, 427
Automation Object, 5, 24-25, 487
Automation server, 214, 231
AutoSessionName property, 74, 86, 105, 111,
    197, 229
Available Forms, 46
AVG, 329

Batch Move parameters, 310
BDE, 165, 183, 248, 367, 423
        Administrator, 184
        alias, 454
        Config Tool, 102
        configuration, 187
        Configuration utility, 184, 352, 381
        .DLLs, 157
        Error 8453, 119
        Initialization Error $2501, 47
        unit, 427
BDEProv, 374
BeforeDelete event, 348
BeforeInsert event, 350
BeforePost event, 37, 243
blank Name property, 218
block size, 435-436
Boolean, 7
Break on Exception, 45, 407
Break procedure, 63, 65

C++, 391
C0000008, 236
C3254, 307
Cached Updates, 344, 437
CachedUpdates mode, 55
CachedUpdates property, 381
caHide, 91
calculated field, 110, 238, 245, 250, 347
calling convention, 146, 175
caMinimize, 92
CanModify, 115
Capacity property, 340
Cascade, 349
Case label, 192, 348
CD, xxix
character-level validation, 34, 39
Chr, 267
class methods, 449
class type, 240, 450, 463

class typecast, 313
CloseFile, 189, 203, 256, 258, 404
CMPLIB32.DCL, 70
CoClass, 24-25, 439, 449
Code Completion, 132
Code Insight, 132, 307
code templates, 209
Column not a BLOb, 479
COM, 133
Commit, 167, 271, 377
CommitUpdates, 344
compile-time errors, xxiii
compiler directive, 313
compiler directives, 56
        settings, 52
Compiler page, 52
compiler switch, 2
COMPLIB.DCL, 70
component template, 447-448
Component Wizard, 200, 399, 442
ComponentState, 116
composite index, 322
composite key, 35
conditional symbol, 362
CONFIG.SYS, 381, 454, 457
CONFIGFILE01, 88, 97, 99, 101-102, 157, 184,
        229, 367, 474
Configure Palette, 49
Connect property, 422
Connected property, 108-109, 112, 128, 167,
        171, 371, 479
ConnectType property, 171, 485
constant parameter, 140, 338
ConstraintErrorMessage, 38
Contains page, 147
Continue procedure, 63, 76
conversion functions, 201
CoUninitialize, 133
COUNT, 329
CPU window, 67
CreateDir procedure, 187
CreateOLEObject, 210
creating an alias with the BDE Config Tool, 102
creating forms dynamically, 68
creating tables and fields in code, 244
creation order, 110
csReading, 116
cursor handle, 82
CustomConstraint, 38

DAO, 95-96
Data Packet, 359
Data Provider, 359
data segment, 165
database alias, 473

database driver, 432
Database Form Wizard, 85
DatabaseName property, 112-113, 117, 120,
    167, 193, 263, 363, 401, 432
DateToStr, 309
dBASE, 249, 251, 320-322, 459, 473
DBCLIENT.DLL, 95, 169-170, 387
dbiProcs, 427, 453
DCOM, 171
deadlock, 345
dedicated servers, 369
default directive, 127, 246
default
    icon, 448
    parameters, 127, 401
    property, 126, 177
    storage specifier, 127, 178-179
    value, 152, 179, 400
Default clause, 176
DefaultExpression property, 37, 152
DefaultValue, 415
Delete method, 112, 344, 437
DeleteFile procedure, 361
DeleteIndex procedure, 295
DeleteTable method, 112, 437
Delphi's search path, 28
Delphi 4, xxxi, 11, 15, 23, 33, 42, 45, 47, 50,
    67-68, 70-72, 97, 102, 110, 127, 129, 135,
    154, 156, 160-161, 172, 195, 222, 281, 285,
    292, 305, 307, 318, 319, 354-356, 365, 401,
    410, 411, 416, 418, 422, 473, 484, 486
Delphi Connection, 135
DELPHI.INI, 468
Deploy.TXT, 97, 101
dereferencing, 164
dereferencing operator, 402
design-time errors, xxiii
Detail records, 348
Detail table, 350
direct access, 409
DirectoryExists function, 182
Dirty Read, 448
dispid, 189-190, 304, 396
dispinterface, 28-29
Dispose, 324
div operator, 191
DLLPATH, 99
Drivers Flag, 352
duplicate database name, 229
duplicate resource, 221
duplicate session name, 229
dynamic
    arrays, 484
    linking of .DLLs, 106
    methods, 197
dynamic directive, 476
dynamically creating forms, 212

EAssertionFailed, 53
EClassNotFound, 202
EConvertError, 15
Edit buffer, 443
edit mode, 169
EditMask property, 39, 152, 243
EDivByZero, 191
EInOutError, 203
EInvalidImage, 202
EMethodNotFound, 202
EmptyTable method, 434, 437
Enable Schema Cache, 478
EncodeDate, 309
EncodeTime, 310
encryption, 304
Engine Configuration File, 118
enumerated type, 179, 463
EOLESys, 133
Erase, 255
EReadError, 202
ERegistryError, 238
ERegistryException, 238
error code, 173
Error in Module, xxvi
ESocketError, 371
EStreamError, 201
Exception.Create, 38
exclusive lock, 345, 456
Exclusive mode, 255
Exclusive property, 112-114, 434
ExecSQL method, 217
Exit procedure, 63, 65, 164
explicitly closing tables, 299
expression indexes, 249, 251
external declaration, 480
ExtractFileExt, 344
ExtractFileName, 186, 344

F, 75
FAIL, 405
Fatal Error, xxvi
field types, 290
field-level validation, 34, 37-38
FieldDefs, 35, 194
FieldKind property, 249
FieldByName, 241
fields used in properties, 252
File of Record, 462
FileExists, 202, 258
FileMode property, 254
FileNew, 210

FileOpen, 210
Filter property, 244-245, 387
Finalization section, 43, 174
FindKey, 249, 341
FindNearest method, 249
FixedCols property, 265-266
FixedRows property, 266
fkInternalCalc, 245
floating-point types, 17
Flush procedure, 189
for loop control variable, 267
foreign key, 250, 349
form inheritance, 27, 218
Formal var parameter, 467
Format function 331, 394
FormStyle property, 77, 374
forward declaration, 480
FreeMem, 324
fsMDIChild, 84
fsMDIForm, 84

gds*.DLL, 467
General Protection Fault, 41
GetActiveOLEObject, 210
GetMem, 324
GetProcAddress, 106
global variables, 162
goto statements, 334-337
GoToNearest method, 249
graphical controls, 211
GROUP BY, 247, 329-330, 332
GUID, 29, 79, 128, 320
GUIDToString function, 312

Halt procedure, 63, 66
handle, 395
HandleNeeded, 273
HandleShared property, 229, 370
host application, 85

I/O checking compiler directive, 203
I/O Error, xxvi
I/O Error 102, 256
I/O Error 103, 261
I/O Error 104, 262
I/O Error 105, 263
IBEventAlerter, 367
icon default size, 205
IDAPI, 95, 101-102, 156, 367
IDAPI configuration file, 157
IDAPI.CFG, 88, 102, 118, 157, 367, 382, 473
IDAPI01.DLL, 100-102
DAPI32.CFG, 88, 118, 157, 228, 473
IDAPI32.DLL, 98, 101
IDataBroker, 129, 154, 158
IDPROV32.DLL, 95

Implementation section, 481
Implementation Uses section, 123
implements directive, 195, 284-285, 415
ImportedConstraint property, 38
incompatible parameter list, 442
index directive, 177, 246, 378, 427
index options, 385
IndexFieldCount, 249
IndexFieldNames property, 7, 150, 241
IndexName property, 7, 150, 241, 249
IndexOptions, 322
initialization, 164, 174
Initialization section, 43
initialized variables, 93, 165 392, 451
INSERT INTO, 399
insert mode, 169
InsertRecord, 143, 253
Instance variable, 439
insufficient memory for this operation, 59
Int64, 305, 319
integer types, 19
Interface, 24-25, 29, 195, 231, 469
    property, 284
    section, 469, 481
    Uses section, 122
Invalid Bind Type, 479
Invalid Type, 479
Invalid Type Conversion, 479
IP address, 371
is operator, 329
IsEmpty, 359
IUnknown, 469

joined query, 437

KeepConnection property, 109, 167

L1086, 307
L1317, 307
LangDriver, 459
Length function, 206
linking two tables, 252
LoadFromFile, 83, 106, 204
LoadFromStream, 358
LoadLibrary, 106
Local Share, 344, 369, 431
local variables, 162
locating a file using Windows Explorer, 87
Lock file, 345
logic errors, xxiii
LongInt, 51
lookup field, 347
loops, 63

Master table, 350
MasterFields, 443
MasterSource property, 121, 443

math coprocessor, 318
MAX, 329
MaxFileHandles, 381, 457
maximum table size, 436
MaxListSize, 340
MaxValue property, 20, 152, 351
MDI, 84
MDI child form, 91
message handlers, 198
message handling method, 197-198, 259, 322
message parameter list, 322
metafiles, 131
methods used in properties, 252
Microsoft Access, 95, 401
MIDAS, 375, 422
MIN, 329
MinValue property, 20, 152, 357
mod operator, 191
module boundaries, 328
MS Access, see Microsoft Access
MTS, 356
multi-threaded, 105, 111, 133
multi-tier, 387
multiple-instance DCOM Server, 370
mutator, 197, 409

Net files, 366
NetDir, 168, 186, 366, 382
NetFileDir property, 168, 185, 368
network files, 382
nodefault directive, 246
nodefault, 378
NOT SHARED, 432
Notification method, 42
NT network, 431

Object Pascal directives, 10
Object Pascal reserved words, 9
object types, 343
ODBC, 341, 488
ODBC32.DLL, 156
OldValue property, 55, 381
OLE, 159
    automation, 15, 176, 293, 453, 461
    automation section, 190, 198, 378, 386, 418
    Automation server, 210
    control, 444
    DLLs, 214, 231
    object, 484
OnActivate event, 77
OnCalcFields event, 110
OnChange event, 426
OnExit event, 38
OnLogin event, 480

OnShow event, 77
OnValidate event, 37, 39, 243
open-array argument, 424
OpenKey, 237
opportunistic locking, 431
optimizer, 66
Ord, 267
ORDER BY, 248, 331
ordinal, 410
ordinal types, 266, 394
orphaned records, 349
Overflow checking, 51
overload directive, 281, 355, 396, 476
overloading, 47
override directive, 355

package, 3-4, 6, 28, 31, 57, 71, 73, 100, 154, 307, 323, 370, 397, 419, 444-445, 451
Package Editor, 87, 147
packed keyword, 398
PageIndex property, 12
palette bitmaps, 188
Palette Page, 399
Paradox, 62, 87, 105, 119, 151, 181, 183-184, 197, 241, 243, 248, 297, 344, 349, 381-382, 415, 431, 435, 473
Paradox data types and their corresponding Delphi TField descendents, 289
Paradox limitations, 166
Paradox Net Files, 369
Parameter Overrides section, 480
parent, 148
Password-protecting a table, 303
Path setting, 103
PDOXUSRS.LCK, 366, 369
PDOXUSRS.NET, 168, 183, 185, 366, 369
peer-to-peer networks, 369
picture validation, 152
plain unit, 214
pointer, 138, 162, 164, 324, 338, 403, 460
Pos function, 187, 344
primary index, 36, 437
primary key, 35, 151, 242
    constraint, 471
primary value, 333
Private Directory, 182, 344
private field, 75
PrivateDir, 168, 181-182, 187
Prohibit, 349-350
Project < > raised exception class, xxv
Project Manager, 46
Provider property, 374
published properties, 46
Published section, 461
PVCS, 187, 364, 443

Query Builder, 161
Read Committed, 449
read lock, 417
read specifier, 75
Read statement, 262
Readln statement, 262
ReadOnly property, 437
ReadOnly property (TTable), 104, 113
ReadString, 237
Real constant, 464
Real type, 411
record-level validation, 34, 36
RecordCount property, 359, 387
recursion, 425
referential integrity, 8
regedit, 95
Register procedure, 257
RegisterClass procedure, 69, 201
RegisterComponents procedure, 69, 199
Registration unit, 257
reintroduce directive, 354, 418
Release procedure, 458
Remote Data Module, 487
Rename, 255
Repeatable Read, 449
ReportSmith, 135, 468
Repository, 8, 10, 218
RequestLive property, 119, 302, 432, 437
Required section, 445
Required property, 152, 243
Requires clause, 420
Reset procedure, 255, 261
Resource .DLLs, 23
resource file, 23, 188
resource format, 327
result set, 217, 247-248
result type, 269, 404
Rewrite, 202, 255-256, 258, 403
RLINK32.DLL, 159
Rollback, 167, 271
RootKey, 237
Round, 318
RowCount, 266
RTTI, 440
Run To Cursor, 372
run-time errors, xxiii-xxiv
Runtime Error 215, 51

SAVECONFIG, 99
SaveToFile method, 82-83
SaveToStream, 358
Schema Cache Dir, 479
Schema Cache Size, 479
Schema Cache Time, 479

SCKTSRVR.EXE, 485
scope, 470
SDI, 84
search using Windows Explorer, 221
secondary index, 152, 437
secondary key, 241
ServerGUID property, 79, 312, 422
ServerName property, 79, 103, 312, 422
SessionName property, 105, 113
SetLength, 206
SetRangeEnd, 241
SetRangeStart, 241
SHARE.EXE, 423
SHARED AUTOCOMMIT, 401
SHAREDMEMLOCATION, 42, 44, 58-59
SHAREDMEMSIZE, 44, 58, 302
ShortString, 165, 429
ShowModal, 46, 103
Smart Linker, 372
socket, 70
SQL, 120
    Links, 488
    Rights, 303
SQLPASSTHRU MODE, 401, 432
standard driver, 103
StartTransaction method, 108, 167, 271
static method, 41, 107
StdOLE, 159
STDOLE.TLB, 159
STDOLE2.TLB, 159
STDVCL*.DLL, 95, 154, 226
STDVCL.TLB, 155
STDVCL32.DLL, 129, 156, 158
STDVCL32.TLB, 160
STDVCL40.DLL, 129, 156, 160
storage specifier, 177, 291
stored directive, 246, 475
stored procedure, 136
StoredProcName property, 120, 218
streaming, 221
string resources, 162
string tables, 162
StrToDate, 15
StrToDateTime, 16
StrToFloat, 17
StrToTime, 19
subrange, 348
subrange type, 142, 463
SUM, 329
symbol file, 230
Synchronize method, 232
System unit, 280
System.Append, 203
SYSTEM.INI, 423

System.Text, 202
SysUtils, 307

table level, 275
table-level validation, 34-36
TableName property, 7, 112-113, 244
TableType property, 113
TBatchMove component, 180
TBits, 61
TChart, 125
TDatabase component, 167
TDataset modes/states, 169
TDateTimePicker, 15
TDBLookupComboBox, 39
TDBLookupListBox, 39
Terminate procedure, 63, 65
Text type, 142
TextFile, 202, 256, 258, 261
TextOut method, 404
TField, 20
thin executable, 445
thread, 232
time out, 345
TInterfacedObject, 469
TMonthCalendar, 15
Tool-Tip Expression Evaluation, 67
TOptions, 251
TPageControl, 220
Transaction Isolation level, 448
TransIsolation property, 448
TRegistry, 237
TRegSvr, 156
TReport, 257
Trunc, 318
TSession component's Name and SessionName
    properties, 422
TStoredProc, 136, 217
TStrings, 83, 145
TTabbedNotebook, 220
type identifier, 12
Type Library, 5, 24-25, 155, 158-160, 449
Type Library/DLL, 226
Type section, 123, 236
typecasting, 328
typed constants, 93, 95, 162-165, 392, 451
TypeInfo, 460, 466

UNC, 186

unique clustered index, 312
Unknown Column, 479
Unprepare method, 113, 302
untyped pointer, 389
UPDATE, 301
UpdateMode property, 412, 425
UpWhereAll, 412, 425
UpWhereChanged, 412, 425
UpWhereKeyOnly, 412, 425
URW337, 307
UseBroker property, 171
user-defined data type, 166
Uses clause, 213

valid component names, 13
validity checks, 152
var parameter, 404
variable parameter, 140
Variant type conversion, 332
varOLEStr, 223
varString, 223
VarToStr, 233
VCL, 26
VCL30.DPL, 70
VCL40.DPL, 70
virtual directive, 352, 476
virtual methods, 40, 145
Virtual Network Redirector file, 295
visibility specifiers, 147
visual form inheritance, 218-219
VREDIR.VXD, 61-62, 295

WaitFor method, 232
Web Deploy, 59
Web sites, Delphi-centric, xxvii
WIN.INI, 97, 101, 118, 157, 184, 367, 382
WinCRT, 262
windowed controls, 91, 211, 223
Windows, 395
    messages, 259, 475-476
    resources, 172
Windows.PAS unit, 237
write lock, 417
Write procedure, 189
write specifier, 75
write-only property, 115
Writeln, 256, 258, 403
Writeln procedure, 189

About the CD

The CD-ROM accompanying this book contains the text of the book in Microsoft Word and TXT formats, freeware components, freeware programs written in Delphi, Windows help files, and a Delphi database FAQ. For descriptions of these components and how to use them, please see "What's on the CD" in the Introduction.

 Note: Opening the CD package makes this book nonreturnable.